King William and the Scottish Politicians

To Claire and Stephen

King William and the Scottish Politicians

P.W.J. RILEY

JOHN DONALD PUBLISHERS LTD
EDINBURGH

© P.W.J. RILEY 1979

All rights reserved. No part of this publication may be reproduced in any form or by any means without the prior permission of the publishers, John Donald Publishers Ltd., 138 St Stephen Street, Edinburgh

ISBN 0 85976 040 5

Printed in Great Britain by Bell & Bain Ltd., Glasgow

Acknowledgements

IT is a pleasure to acknowledge the co-operation of those who have been good enough to allow access to their manuscripts, permitting reference to be made to them for publication. For these reasons I am grateful to the duke of Buccleuch and Queensberry, the duke of Marlborough, the duke of Portland and the duke of Roxburghe. My thanks are also due to the Committee on General Administration of the Church of Scotland, by whose kind permission quotations are made from the records of the General Assembly. I have received a great deal of courtesy and assistance from the staffs of the Scottish Record Office and the National Library of Scotland for which I take this further opportunity of thanking them. Mr John Simpson of the University of Edinburgh kindly checked some references, thus saving me from what, at the time, would have been an inconvenient journey.

Note on Dates, etc.

All dates have been printed in old style unless otherwise indicated. The beginning of the year has been taken as 1 January which was, of course, the practice in Scotland, unlike England where the official year began on 25 March.

In all quotations spelling, punctuation and capitalisation have been modernised unless there seemed to be special reasons for retaining the original form.

P.W.J.R.
University of Manchester, 1979

Contents

	page
Acknowledgements	v
Note on Dates, etc	v
Abbreviations	ix
Introduction	1
1 The Magnates and the Revolution	11
2 Hamilton, Melville and the Club	22
3 Melville and the Dalrymples	47
4 Johnston, Tweeddale and the Magnates	81
5 The Magnate Resurgence	107
6 The Establishment of the Queensberry Interest	117
7 Queensberry and the Rise of the Country Party	125
8 Queensberry *versus* the Rest	141
Appendix A: Members of the Convention Parliament, 1689-1702	165
Appendix B: The Opposition of 1700-1702	179
Bibliographical Note	187
Index	188

Abbreviations

APS	*Acts of the Parliament of Scotland,* ix, x, ed., T. Thomson (Edinburgh, 1822 and 1823).
Balcarres	Colin, Earl of Balcarres, Memoirs touching the revolution in Scotland, 1688-90 (Bannatyne Club, 1841).
BL, Add. MSS	British Library, Additional Manuscripts.
Browning, *Danby*	A. Browning, *Thomas Osborne, Earl of Danby and Duke of Leeds, 1632-1712,* 3 vols. (Glasgow, 1944-51).
Buccleuch (Drum.)	Muniments of the duke of Buccleuch at Drumlanrig Castle. These papers are unnumbered and uncalendared. Particular categories are referred to in abbreviated form:
Carstares	'Letters from Mr Carstares, 1700'
Church and State	'Queensberry Papers on Church and State'
Col.	'Colnaghi MSS.'
Pringle	'Letters from Robert Pringle, 1701 and 1702'
Queensberry Letters	'Letters to the Duke of Queensberry'
Seafield	'Letters from the Earl of Seafield, 1700-1702'
Seven Letters	'Bundle of Seven Unsigned Letters [from Murray of Philiphaugh], 1707' [*sic* for 1701]
Stair	'Letters from the Earl of Stair and the Officers of State, 1700-1706'
Union	'Letters on the Treaty of Union'.
Burnet	G. Burnet, *History of His Own Time*, 6 vols. (Oxford, 1833).
Caldwell Papers	*Selections from the family papers preserved at Caldwell* (Maitland Club, 1854).
Carstares S.P.	*State Papers and Letters addressed to William Carstares,* ed. J. McCormick (Edinburgh, 1774).
CSP (Dom.)	*Calendar of State Papers (Domestic).*
Culloden Papers	*Culloden Papers,* ed. H.R. Duff (London, 1815).
Drummond and Bulloch, *The Scottish Church*	A.L. Drummond and J. Bulloch, *The Scottish Church, 1688-1843* (Edinburgh, 1973).

Dunlop, *Carstares*	A. Ian Dunlop, *William Carstares and the Kirk by Law Established* (Edinburgh, 1967).
Ferguson, *Scotland*	W. Ferguson, *Scotland: 1689 to the Present* (Edinburgh, 1968).
Foxcroft, *Halifax*	H.C. Foxcroft, *The Life and Letters of Sir George Savile, bart., first Marquis of Halifax*, 2 vols. (London, 1898).
Foxcroft, *Supplement*	H.C. Foxcroft, ed., *A Supplement to Burnet's History of My Own Time* (Oxford, 1902).
Fraser, *Annandale Book*	Sir W. Fraser, *The Annandale Family Book*, 2 vols. (Edinburgh, 1894).
Fraser, *Cromartie*	Sir W. Fraser, *The Earls of Cromartie — their Kindred, Country and Correspondence*, 2 vols. (Edinburgh, 1879).
Fraser, *Melvilles*	Sir W. Fraser, *The Melvilles, Earls of Melville, and the Leslies, Earls of Leven*, 3 vols. (Edinburgh, 1890).
Halliday, 'The club . . . '	James Halliday, 'The Club and the Revolution in Scotland, 1689-90', *Scottish Historical Review* xlv (1966).
HLRO	House of Lords Record Office.
HMCR	Reports of the Historical Manuscripts Commission. These are cited in the form: *HMCR Johnstone MSS.*, for example.
Hume, *Diary*	Sir David Hume of Crossrig, *A Diary of the Proceedings in the Parliament and Privy Council of Scotland* (Bannatyne Club, 1828).
Japikse	*Correspondentie van Willem III en van Hans Willem Bentinck*, ed. N. Japikse (The Hague, 1927-37).
Leven and Melville Papers	*Letters and State Papers Chiefly Addressed To George, Earl of Melville . . . 1689-1691* (Bannatyne Club, 1843).
Macpherson	J. Macpherson, *Original Papers containing the Secret History of Great Britain . . .* (London, 1775).

Marchmont Papers	*A Selection from the Papers of the Earls of Marchmont in the possession of the Right Honourable Sir George Henry Rose*, 3 vols. (London, 1831).
NLS	National Library of Scotland. MSS referred to are from the Yester papers and are cited by their call numbers.
NUL, Portland	Nottingham University Library, Portland collection.
Proceedings	*An Account of the Proceedings of the Estates of Scotland, 1689-1690*, 2 vols. (Scottish History Society, 1954-5).
RSCHS	*Records of the Scottish Church History Society.*
Seafield Correspondence	*Seafield Correspondence from 1685 to 1708*, ed. J. Grant (Scottish History Society, 1912).
SHR	*Scottish Historical Review.*
SRO	Scottish Record Office. The main collections used are listed below and are cited by their call numbers: Cullen House Papers (GD248) Leven and Melville Muniments (GD26) Mar and Kellie Muniments (GD124) Ogilvy of Inverquarity Muniments (GD205) Records of the Commission of the General Assembly (CH1) Secretary Johnston's Letter Book (SP3/1)
Vernon	*Letters illustrative of the Reign of William III 1696 to 1708 . . . by James Vernon*, ed. G.P.R. James, 3 vols. (London, 1841).
Wodrow, *Analecta*	R. Wodrow, *Analecta, or Materials for a History of Remarkable Providences* (Maitland Club, 1842-3).

Introduction

CASUAL acquaintance has led many to dismiss Scottish history as little more than a catalogue of bloody calamities. Even the more persevering have occasionally been tempted to accept this as a fair description. Scotsmen themselves, naturally enough, know that most occurrences, bloody or not, were at bottom quite well-intentioned, unless there is reason to suspect English involvement. No interpretation of events can then be too sinister. The reign of William II and III is notorious for calamity and English influence alike and, on the strength of Killiecrankie, Glencoe, the 'lean years' of famine and the Darien tragedy, perhaps deservedly so. Civil war, massacre and disaster — natural and self-inflicted — made the period from 1688 to 1702 years of affliction. But less spectacularly, for indecision, misgovernment and sheer administrative inertia the reign has rarely, if ever, been equalled.

Neglect was partly to blame. To a king involved with the United Provinces and the political fortunes of the three British kingdoms, Scotland was of marginal interest. And for much of the time William was either fighting a war, or preparing for the conduct of the next, against the then greatest power in Europe — Louis XIV's France. So Scotland was almost always on the periphery of his attention. It was the letter he never managed to write, the visit he never found time to make.

William's objectives in Scotland can easily be stated. The problems of security and the highlands, largely conterminous, needed to be dealt with. A durable settlement of Scottish government and religion was essential after the tremors of the revolution. Ideally such arrangements needed to be of a kind which aroused minimal dissent and, preferably, were hardly noticed. The new king himself would have liked as little interference as possible with the pre-revolutionary system both in church and state, relying on a change of monarch and attitude to reconcile the disaffected. Without question he was predisposed to the maintenance of the royal prerogative and strong executive power. And, in the long run, he sought to tap his northern kingdom as a source of manpower for his armies and of money to defray a fraction of their cost, though even that fraction, for a poor country, could be burdensome. Previous seventeenth-century sovereigns would not have considered such aims extravagant. Only when one appraises the obstacles to their achievement in William's reign do most of his objectives appear to have been unattainable.

The king was perhaps temperamentally unfitted for dealing with Scotland. He preferred political questions to be simple and capable of straight answers. For long enough he resisted the appointment of two Scottish secretaries of state on the ground that he would rather have one version of affairs — presumably even the wrong one — than two conflicting versions.[1] But after the revolution Scottish affairs were complicated and their problems intractable. Some of the difficulties were inherent in the structure of Scottish society and politics. Others were due to the circumstances of the revolution, although the ground had been well prepared. During the months following the departure of James VII and II, what were to be the main problems of Scottish government until the union had all, in some form, appeared: the difficulty of organising an adequate court party, the ambition and intransigence of the greater nobles, the exploitation of religion for political ends, systematic opposition springing mainly from personal, if sometimes justifiable, resentment and, not least, the impact on Scotland of English internal politics. Such influences combined to produce in Scotland a revolution settlement that left the power of the crown severely impaired and gave rise to a religious establishment more divisive than any previous one. The consequent tensions were to render the government of Scotland ineffective. As his reign progressed with ever-increasing complications, William became inclined to exasperation and a reluctance even to think of Scotland, much less take action there. His major disillusionment seems to have resulted from his experience of Scottish politicians, their capacity for incessant intrigue and their tendency to proffer self-interested advice without regard for the wider consequences. An incident of 1696 epitomised the king's attitude. Importunate Scots were infesting the court, whispering and insinuating in the interest of whatever faction they happened, however briefly, to be associated with. On the discovery, in February 1696, of the plot to assassinate him, William convened a meeting of the Scottish privy councillors then in London and, it was reported, '... standing with his back to the fire he told them that he understood there were great differences amongst them which tended more to the hindrance of his service and the good of their country ... ' His proposed remedy was simple. They were to lay aside private animosities, return to Scotland and get on with their respective jobs.[2] Manifestly his earnest desire was that, sufficiently encouraged, the Scots would compose their differences, problems would disappear and henceforth he would be left in peace. Nothing, of course, was more unlikely.

It took William a long time to achieve even a little appreciation of the nature of Scottish politics. Whether he ever reached a full understanding is doubtful. At the revolution his ignorance of Scotland and its affairs was comprehensive. He also suffered greatly from advice. There was not only an embarrassing quantity of it, but much was inspired by self-interest and the greater part of it was bad. His closest advisers were *émigrés* with little or no first-hand experience of politics in the higher levels. One tion was the former president of session, Sir James Dalrymple of Stair, who had gone abroad after refusing to take the test oath of 1681. With him in exile were others who lacked his experience. Lord Melville and Sir Patrick Hume of Polwarth were two who had made dramatic escapes for the sake of their liberty and, very probably, their lives. Gilbert Burnet, a learned though garrulous episcopalian minister, had gone less spectacularly into exile but had acquired some influence. Erstwhile members of the British section of William's intelligence service, which had relied extensively on expatriate Scots, retained access to the king: William Carstares, a presbyterian minister accused of complicity in the Ryehouse plot, James Johnston, son of Archibald Johnston of Wariston, and Robert Ferguson, the 'Plotter', who seemed not to care which side he was on as long as it involved drama and conspiracy.[3] And, above all, William trusted Bentinck, his friend from childhood, soon to be created earl of Portland. Bentinck's information was derived from conversation with Scotsmen and an evaluation of the intelligence reports. What all this kept hidden from William was the fact that Scottish politics were not ordinarily concerned with public aims and interests. During the years of resistance and conspiracy before the revolution it might have seemed that they were, but times were then extraordinary. Fugitives from the government of King Charles or James had made a choice, or had had a choice made for them, on which they could not easily renege. But usually in day-to-day affairs most Scottish politicians acted as if control of the processes and profits of government were for them ends in themselves. As subjects of what had become a subordinate kingdom they were almost entirely divorced from decision and responsibility. In consequence, any policy tended to be no more than an affectation and to many a matter of almost complete indifference.

The major problem, insoluble in post-revolutionary Scotland, was that of satisfying the interests of the greater nobles. It proved impossible to satisfy, however briefly, a bare majority of them. Each made use of all the influence he could muster from status, land, family and the ramifications of patronage in attempts to secure a monopoly of the apparatus of government. The object of attaining such control was the rewarding of friends and the harassment of enemies for the purely selfish reason of extending personal power. Faced with this situation, those severally employed to manage William's Scottish business, hampered by the king's inertia and frequently by the demands of their own ambition, were helpless. Combinations of Atholl, Argyll, Hamilton and Queensberry, the four major interests which flourished from the revolution to the union of 1707, were too much for the crown and its advisers to handle. To these magnates the events of 1688 and 1689 were little more than a heaven-sent opportunity for each to improve his position in relation to the others. All, at one time or another, had forfeited some of James's favour, though equally all had either served him or compromised. As magnates, with the preservation of their families and estates as a first priority, they could hardly have avoided bowing their heads in whatever temple they happened to be, but some were looked upon, seemingly to their own astonishment, as having been more deeply committed to James than others. Atholl and Queensberry had both held high office since the restoration. Their rivals were quick to brand them as collaborators and oppressors. Argyll, younger than the others, had a past reeking of shiftiness, prevarication and betrayal but at the revolution this unsavouriness was obscured by the family habit of dying as presbyterian martyrs. Hamilton was regarded as uncompromised with the pre-revolutionary governments, though with little justification, since any freedom from taint on his part was really the measure of his failure to achieve recognition from either Charles or James. He had tried hard enough. At one point, and a crucial point at that, he had been in grievous danger of backing a loser by offering James a refuge in Scotland.[4] None of this deterred him, in the circumstances of 1689 and 1690, from exploiting to the utmost his spurious reputation. In so doing he gave William his first surfeit of the higher Scottish nobility.

Religion was another major source of trouble. At the revolution Scotland was an ecclesiastical minefield in which any step was an invitation to disaster. This had been a recent development. Until the post-restoration reigns the differences between presbyterians and episcopalians within the Scottish church had not been unduly significant except to the ideologically committed or the obsessively precise. Alternation between a presbyterian and an episcopalian ascendancy, it has been suggested, did no more violence to the Church of Scotland and allegiance to it than party electoral swings inflict on the constitutional fabric of the United Kingdom.[5] But the period between 1660 and 1688 had seen the firm identification of Scottish bishops with the unedifying representatives of the executive power. One consequence had been the birth of a strong presbyterian mythology. In this, presbyterians figured as the sole object of persecution after the restoration and hence the backbone of resistance to an arbitrary government. Subsequently the revolution of 1688-9 injected into the situation the dangerous issue of loyalty, presbyterianism being equated with Williamite allegiance and episcopalians identified with jacobitism. It became unlikely that the extremes, at any rate, of the two religious outlooks could coexist within the same church. Either one or the other would be maintained by coercion, whether exerted by the crown or anyone else. The existence of both within the same establishment, or of two churches within the same small kingdom, was not considered, except by a few deluded episcopalians, to be a possibility. The two previous reigns made it probable that there would be demands for the imposition of a presbyterian establishment, enforced conformity and even calls for retribution in one form or another. A number of Scots, both ministers and laymen, remained open-minded on the subject of church government but in 1689 this was not a stance advisable to take up openly. Ten years previously a parliamentary list had described some surprising persons as 'indifferent' on the subject of church government. They were men who, after the revolution, were to be found posing as the backbone of hard-line presbyterianism.[6] Their new-found allegiance was most probably a political choice. Some presbyterians, ragged and matted, were coming in from the wilderness, but others were mingling with them in disguise to dissociate themselves from the previous regime and to claim the revolution as their own.

The religious issue in Scotland, then, was more formidable even than in England. Whatever his private beliefs as a Dutch calvinist, William favoured for Scotland an episcopalian settlement. His reasons were political. Episcopacy was generally held to be more compatible with monarchy than was presbytery and, anyway, excessive religious differences between the two kingdoms were better avoided. English politicians shared William's view that a Scottish religious settlement could not be made without any reference to the situation in England. Both whigs and tories were of the same mind in this. But the majority of William's *émigré* advisers — Burnet excepted — favoured a moderate presbyterian establishment. Their views, the refusal of the Scottish bishops to respond to William's overtures[7] and, above all, events in the convention in 1689 and 1690, combined to defeat William's aims and disappoint the hopes of many Scots. The Scottish church establishment was to become, almost violently, presbyterian.

This outcome was merely one of the legacies of the revolution, of 1688-90, which ensured that Scotland would remain chronically impossible to govern. It added to Anglo-Scottish relations a religious tension consistently and blatantly exploited for political ends, providing the disaffected with an excuse for 'loyal' and 'reasonable' opposition in the name of toleration for episcopalians. There was more. By a constitutional change opposition was given far wider scope than previously. A crucial aspect of the revolution settlement was the abolition, despite all William's efforts, of the steering committee of the Scottish parliament — the 'articles', one of the court's chief instruments for managing the legislature. For a vital period during the making of the settlement this issue caused the initiative in the Scottish parliament to be surrendered to the opposition.

That two key parts of the revolution settlement were so uncongenial to William and destructive of stability in Scotland is the measure of the collapse of royal power at the flight of James II and VII. This setback for the crown was due primarily to a breakdown in the patronage network as a direct result of the revolution crisis. Its re-establishment should have been a first priority. William's — and Scotland's — only hope of stable government had lain in a swift revolution settlement which retained for the crown as much as possible of its former power. Whatever one's ultimate opinion of either the royal prerogative and its exercise in Scotland or the eventual outcome of its breakdown, this remains true. To that extent the stress laid by Sir John Dalrymple in 1689-90 on the maintenance of royal power in Scotland was not misplaced. Unfortunately Dalrymple's apparent aim was defeated by his own determination to frustrate any possible rivals to his family's advancement. William's acceptance of advice from servants of such devouring ambition as Dalrymple led to a ruinous delay in the settlement. After this first crucial period, whatever was attempted came too late. The way had been opened for the disruption of parliament by the generally resentful rank and file, organised usually by one or more of the magnates who had been able to add even more powerful weapons to their already formidable armoury. The Scottish estates had been transformed almost overnight from an assembly which merely endorsed the will of the executive into an institution with considerable power. What it lacked was a sense of corporate responsibility and any concept of Scottish interest. Such a parliament, more open to obstruction than ever before, could hardly fail to become an arena for deciding the personal rivalries of the higher nobility. And, of course, the revolution had presented them with the possibility of an alternative sovereign which they were not slow to exploit. The result was a dislocation of Scottish government which the court proved quite unable to deal with.

In such circumstances, the *sine qua non* of managing Scotland was the creation of a court interest broadly enough based to provide stability. Under the union of the crowns one solution, perhaps the only one, would have been to create a Scottish court party round the nucleus of a single magnate interest, or magnate alliance, well supported by clients and fully backed by the sovereign and the English court. The various elements of this court party would need to be able and willing to collaborate. Excluded interests would have to be rendered too weak to challenge the court with any hope of success. Of course, continual surveillance of the controlling group would be called for to ensure that it did not cause gratuitous offence, or subject personal rivals to uncalled-for indignities and deprivation. Only under such conditions could the will of the monarch be made effective in Scotland. For the greater part of William's reign they cried out in vain for fulfilment, perhaps unavoidably so because under the circumstances they proved virtually impossible to meet. The intractability of the problem can hardly be laid at William's door, but that during the reign only one unwitting approach to a solution was made which both began and ended in misapprehension, perhaps a whole series of misapprehensions, must be the king's responsibility.

William's ministers and advisers importuned him and jostled in rivalry, stumbling in the process from one unsuccessful device to the next. Some schemes of government were cobbled together in haste; others were based on inaccurate appraisals or even no more than a desire to outmanoeuvre rivals. The king himself remained above the battle, as far as possible insulating himself from it by his reliance on Portland and Carstares to whom he delegated Scottish business and who constituted his main channel of communication.

To the Scottish political struggle itself William gave only cursory attention, interfering rarely, to little purpose and then doing more harm than good. By the end of his reign William had abandoned hope of governing Scotland within its existing relationship with England though very probably he had come to the right conclusion for the wrong reasons. The king and others had been misled into identifying the Scottish problem with that of reconciling the presbyterian and episcopalian interests which seemed to form the basis of the political division, whereas the real trouble was magnate ambition pursued to extremes.

Superficially this religious interpretation seemed justified. After the presbyterian settlement, all ministries faced the problem of the relationship between the church establishment and those it chose to regard as dissenters. Far more serious, politically, was the apparent expression of this conflict at parliamentary level. There were those who paraded their staunch presbyterian allegiance just as there were those who made no secret of preferring episcopacy. Of the inability of the more powerful members of each group to co-operate there was no doubt. But the nature of the division was in reality more complex.

Just before the revolution and during its progress significant groups emerged. There were, naturally, convinced presbyterians and equally committed episcopalians. However, the majority, although they might have been averse from the political bishops of the last reigns or the prospect of over-zealous presbyterianism, did not greatly care. Some, for a variety of reasons, had moved by 1688 into a revolutionary position which they advertised by expressing presbyterian views, it being difficult to indicate revolutionary sympathies publicly in any other way. Subsequently they found it difficult not to be carried in the wake of zealots from whom they could not dissociate themselves even when they came to feel presbytery was being driven too far. Others, finding themselves irrevocably compromised by more or less close association with the previous administrations, chose to formalise their position either by remaining episcopalian or by conforming only minimally with the church establishment. A man's religious allegiance, therefore, tended to be decided by his relationship to those who comprised the central administration rather than the other way round. But the foundations had been laid of the myth that Scottish political divisions were fundamentally religious.

There certainly seemed to be in Scotland two compartments, one labelled 'presbyterian' and the other 'episcopalian'. Inside each could always be found a few of the same people, like building bricks in a play box. Some were wedged in corners, not to be dislodged; others were left tumbling about in the bottom, too hard to reach. But the rest were moved from one box to the other according to circumstances without much regard for the labels. 'Presbyterian' was a name applied to an assortment of people: committed Williamites, courtiers identified with the revolution settlement and adopted, especially, by those afraid of being squeezed out and who, in self-defence, branded their rivals 'episcopalian' as a euphemism for crypto-jacobite. There was indeed a group of men who, however willing to accept the revolution once it had taken place, were stamped by their earlier attitudes as no more than reluctant revolutionaries if not actually disaffected. A few of them were both reluctant and disaffected but by no means all. However, those who had taken up presbyterianism as the mark of revolutionary zeal and wanted their reward were over-anxious to label all others as counter-revolutionary. In that they acted from insecurity they might have been sincere but they were nonetheless wrong. Seafield was afterwards to comment: ' . . . the late king [William], being induced upon mistakes and misinformation, did choose to settle his government in Scotland on a party and an angry party. Several were put in whose former practices had not been very conformable to the revolution principles and many were put out who were firm in these principles . . . '[8] He was oversimplifying of course, since William had seldom been prepared to plump for one party, but he was obviously thinking in political and personal, not religious, terms. In so far as anything, apart from personal ambition, decided political alignment, it was each man's attitude, real or suspected, to the revolution and the bitterness left by scars received, in the main, before 1688. Even when they were all in office there was little basis for collaboration between Dalrymple and Cockburn of Ormiston, Tarbat and Marchmont, Murray of Philiphaugh and Baillie of Jerviswood. For some of these men there were limits to what political action they could even consider, but there was enough scope for others to change sides. Their professed religious affiliation could be modified, or at least the company they kept, if that seemed necessary, though what religious views they had underwent no real change. Most succeeded in remaining fairly detached on the subject of religion, which was quite obviously not the decisive consideration. As Philiphaugh was to write in Anne's reign: 'I think her majesty has other affairs ado than either to make the rest of Scotland episcopal or the north presbyterian . . .'[9]

However, the problem was almost always referred to, even at the highest levels, in religious terms, but for the most part no more than a form of jargon was involved, in Scotland at least. People on occasion showed a grasp of the impious truth whilst being reluctant to abandon the religious terminology. As one put it in 1691, ' . . . religion serves here sometimes as a pretext . . . One may say that the middle course which his majesty has chosen, in leaving the government to the presbyterians on one side, and favouring the episcopalians with his royal protection on the other, is the surest and only way of preserving the peace in Scotland . . . '[10] Yet the various steps taken demonstrate that the king and some of his advisers had not wholly recognised the problem. They concentrated their efforts on the reconciliation of two religious groups without realising they were merely pushing men from one group to the other since most were motivated by little but private interest.

This constant miscalculation meant that, failing a union of the two kingdoms, the task of governing Scotland became an impossible one. By 1701 this was recognisably so, since the catalogue of unsuccessful prescriptions was impressive. Consequently William had come to recognise the need for union. The intransigence to be found in Scottish politics, whether religious in origin as William and those close to him seemed to think, or springing from personal ambition and obstinacy as it did in fact, had to be broken down by immersion in a larger unit. In fact the revolution settlement and William's misunderstanding of the situation it created had made union necessary. William fell into many errors in relation to Scotland, but none so fundamentally serious as those committed at his and Mary's first acceptance of the throne. This accumulation of mistakes impelled the two kingdoms, albeit by a circuitous route, to the union of 1707. But before that consummation was reached, the Scots had been subjected to maladministration and misgovernment and had, at times, been deprived of almost any government at all whilst they and the English bore with each other in an increasingly strained and bitter relationship.

The importance of the revolution settlement makes it for Scotland the focal point of William's reign. Its external aspect can be summarised with fair brevity, though the reasons for its emergence demand examination in detail. Ostensibly, when it became clear that a revolution had taken place in England, a commendably brisk approach was made towards securing a Scottish settlement. Such Scottish nobles and gentry as were in London in January 1689 met as a council to establish formal relations with William. The duke of Hamilton took the chair. With virtual unanimity they agreed to ask William to accept responsibility for Scotland's interim administration and to give orders for electing a convention of estates.[11] William saw no reason to object and elections were held, not uncommonly in an atmosphere of excitement and violence. Extreme presbyterian crowds in the south-west 'rabbled' ministers of whom they disapproved, turning them out of their manses. The mere fact that Sir Francis Scott of Thirlestane was rumoured to favour a regency ruled out any possibility of his being elected in East Lothian.[12] Not surprisingly those who thought James should be ejected and those willing, with however much conviction, to espouse presbyterianism as the 'popular' cause, were well represented in the estates. They were for the most part the same people.

The convention which met on 14 March 1689 had, before it was transformed into a parliament, its hour of glory. It falls into that distinguished group of assemblies which, in the face of unprecedented emergency, have taken on great responsibilites and magnificently discharged them. Its reign was shorter and its tribulations fewer than those of the English long parliament or the national assembly of France, but the convention did well. The tasks of trying to keep the country under control and provide for its future constitution were attempted in a city humming with plots and rumours of plots, under the shadow of Edinburgh castle held by the jacobite duke of Gordon. There were overt threats from a large force of south-western presbyterians and from the rather flamboyant behaviour of a small group gathered round the viscount of Dundee before he rode off to the north to raise the highlands for King James. The earl of Tweeddale had forecast 'metalled doings' on the part of the convention should there be any jacobite threat.[13] He was proved right. To the limits of its capacity the convention provided for the security of the kingdom. Numerous Scottish peers and lairds, exhilarated by the atmosphere of alarms and excursions, raised troops of horse and companies of foot and rode off briskly to wherever the action was thought likely to be.[14]

From the start of proceedings the majority of the convention showed itself to be Williamite and anti-episcopalian. Active presbyterians were aggressive and vocal. Others found it advisable to be discreet. Any lingering affection for episcopacy or respect for pre-revolutionary law was interpreted as support for the old government and so better kept quiet. The claims of the departed king and episcopal authority were alike treated with scant respect. James had written to the convention in a hectoring tone demanding nothing short of full submission so that even his supporters felt he had done his cause no good.[15] The business of the convention proceeded as if James had never uttered.

With only five dissenting votes the throne was declared 'forfaulted'.[16] At the opening of the convention the bishop of Edinburgh had prayed that God should have compassion on King James and restore him,[17] but, as this supplication went unheeded, the bishops were increasingly absent.[18] When they put in an appearance they were continually needled. At the end of one day's business ' . . . one of the bishops offered to say prayers, as the custom is, upon which it was moved that King James being no more our king, he must pray for him at his peril. The bishop discreetly said only the Lord's Prayer'.[19] Episcopacy was subsequently voted a grievance by one hundred and six or seven votes to thirty-two.[20]

The throne was offered to William and Mary jointly, though a contract was implied. The offer of the throne was intended to be conditional on the acceptance by William and Mary of two documents drafted in the convention: the 'grievances' against the post-restoration governments and what came to be called the claim of right. On their formal acceptance the two sovereigns were to be asked to turn the convention into a parliament. The offer and requests were carried to England by a representative from each of the three estates: Argyll for the nobles, Sir James Montgomerie of Skelmorlie for the barons and Sir John Dalrymple for the burghs.[21] William and Mary accepted the throne and complied with the convention's wish to be styled a parliament.

The session of 1689 was a disaster for the court. Parliament met in June with Hamilton as lord high commissioner, William entertaining hopes of the emergence of a stable constitutional and religious settlement. In the face of concerted and determined resistance from an opposition known as the 'club', the failure of the court was complete. All its proposals for the reform, rather than the abolition, of the articles were blocked.[22] The 'club' extended its attack more directly to the royal prerogative by objecting strongly to the process by which the civil court, the court of session, was to be re-established in the new reign. In addition an act[23] was voted to incapacitate from holding office persons who in parliament's view were undesirable. William was not inclined to make such concessions and the 'club' refused to modify its demands. So an *impasse* was reached and parliament was adjourned.

In an attempt to rectify the damage done in the 1689 parliament a further session was held early in 1690 with Melville, one of the former *émigrés*, as commissioner. He succeeded in reaching a settlement, but only by a complete surrender to opposition demands, an extremity which William had hoped to avoid. The Scottish church was established on presbyterian lines. Control of the church's discipline was effectively handed over to the sixty or so high presbyterian ministers still surviving from those deprived in 1661 for refusal to accept episcopacy. Ministers who had at any time subscribed to episcopacy — the 'conform clergy' — even if subsequently deprived, were to be discriminated against. Lay patronages were abolished as an unwarrantable secular interference in ecclesiastical affairs, which they perhaps were, but to the lay patrons and the king the measure looked very much like disappropriation. And, in addition, the standing committee of the articles was abolished. From the court's point of view the settlement was very unsatisfactory. It was accepted, though, as better than no settlement at all, an outcome which at one time had seemed not unlikely.

Melville's subsequent success, during the session of 1690, in breaking up the opposition was due, not to astute management, but to the opportune discovery that some of the club leaders had been involved in jacobite conspiracy. As the jacobite connection became known, the bulk of the opposition in alarm hastened to dissociate themselves from the men they had hitherto unanimously supported.

It is important to question how and why the convention parliament had become, from the point of view of the crown, so much out of hand. The answer illustrates the problems which fell to William on his assumption of responsibility for Scotland. Almost entirely they were rather sordid problems arising from the clash of personal ambition and the needs of political management. The idea that he was facing a struggle between opposing religious principles was one of William's major delusions. Principles that did flourish—and they were few—sprang directly from the revolution itself and were indicative of little more than insecurity and a dread of further violence. And such was the nature of Scotland's social and political structure that the aspirations and prejudices of humbler folk made little impact on the central government. They could be signalled only by outbreaks of disorder which could either be suppressed or ignored but which, save in very exceptional circumstances, made little difference either way. What follows has therefore to be exclusively a study of political chicanery at the highest levels. It is not calculated to lighten anyone's spirit whether he be Scot or Englishman.

NOTES

1. Foxcroft, *Halifax*, ii, 218.
2. *HMCR Hastings MSS*, ii, 256, [Dr N. Johnston] to Huntingdon, 18 Feb. [16]95[/6].
3. For their pre-revolutionary activities see John Carswell, *The Descent on England* (London, 1969), 25-30 et passim.
4. J. R. Western, *Monarchy and Revolution* (London, 1972), 228.
5. G. Donaldson, *Scotland: Church and Nation through 16 Centuries* (London, 1960), 75 et seq. See also Drummond and Bulloch, *The Scottish Church*, chap. 1.
6. J. R. Jones, 'The Scottish constitutional opposition in 1679', *SHR* (1958), 37-41.
7. W. L. Mathieson, *Politics and Religion in Scotland, 1550-1695* (Glasgow, 1902), 348-9; D. H. Whiteford, 'Jacobitism as a factor in Presbyterian-Episcopalian relationships in Scotland, 1689-90', *RSCHS*, xvi, 140-2.
8. *HMCR Laing MSS*, ii, 42-5, Seafield's 'memorial', c. 1703.
9. BL, Add. MSS 6420, 8, to [Queensberry], 16 Mar. 1703.
10. *CSP (Dom.), 1691-2*, 62-3, 'Memorial concerning affairs in Scotland' [1691].
11. For this Scottish 'council' see *Proceedings*, ii, App., 293-7, 7-10 Jan. 1689.
12. NLS, MS 7026, 141, Tweeddale to Yester, 21 Feb. [16]89.
13. *Ib.*, 160, same to same, 16 Mar. [16]89.
14. For examples of the measures taken see *Proceedings*, i, 1 et seq., 9, 16, 22, 66, et passim, and *APS*, ix, 11, 13.
15. Balcarres, *Memoirs*, 26-8.
16. *Ib.*, 35.
17. *Proceedings*, i, 1.
18. *Ib.*, 16.
19. *Ib.*, 26; NLS, MS 7026, 184, Tweeddale to Yester, 4 Apr. [16]89.
20. *Ib.*, 195, Tweeddale's unofficial minutes, 8-10 Apr. 1689.
21. Sir W. Fraser, *Memorials of the Montgomeries, Earls of Eglinton*, 2 vols (Edinburgh, 1859) prints the text of the instructions to the commissioners: ii, 342. The order in which the commissioners were to proceed is perhaps implied but not precisely directed.
22. See above, p. 4.
23. The term 'act' was used in Scotland for measures at all stages of the legislative process and not reserved for those which had received the royal assent.

1

The Magnates and the Revolution

EVENTS in England towards the end of 1688 were not immediately recognised by many Scots as the beginning of a revolution. The Scottish privy council had known of the possibility of invasion since September but a landing by William of Orange seemed likely to do no more than modify the conduct of King James. Those with ambition glimpsed new opportunities in whatever developments were imminent. Estranged Scottish nobles thought James might be driven at last into coming to terms with them. Officers of state thought not only of keeping their posts but of changing them for the better. Within the administration the accepted view was that intervention by William would merely turn the kaleidoscope, letting the distribution of places fall into another pattern. In all probability the only sufferers would be James's chief ministers, recent converts to catholicism, the upstart Drummond brothers: Perth, lord chancellor, and Melfort, secretary of state. The rest would depend on individual astuteness. It was to be every man for himself. At a very early stage two of the magnates, recently eclipsed, were found leading a move to prise out the Drummonds. George Stirling, an Edinburgh apothecary, stirred up anti-catholic riots in the capital. Atholl and Queensberry at once took the opportunity of asking Perth to leave the city, in his own interest and that of everybody else, so they told him.[1] Dalrymple, as lord justice clerk, and Tarbat, as lord clerk register, were hoping to be appointed joint secretaries of state. They were not alone in entertaining expectations of that kind. Sir George Mackenzie, the 'Bloody Mackenzie' of presbyterian mythology, saw no reason why he should not continue in office.[2]

James's flight from England did not in the least affect the attitude of Scottish politicians. Whether they improved their prospects by coming to terms with James or William seemed immaterial. Officers of state were soon absolving themselves from the obligations of the test oath, times having changed. They argued that since James had never taken the coronation oath the test did not bind them.[3] Of infinitely more importance to individuals than the identity of the sovereign was having the good fortune or foresight to be in the right place when the decisions were taken. Most people favoured London. A mass exodus to England took place of officers of state and privy councillors. Government was left almost entirely unprovided for, which worried no one but the very few left behind. Thirteen privy councillors went in December, leaving a bare quorum to cope with the maintenance of order.[4] By the following month it was impossible to raise even a quorum.[5] Revenue collection had broken down and troops were having to be put out at free quarter.[6] There was no centralised machinery of justice and the administration of law in the kingdom was being left to private enterprise with some areas under mob rule.[7]

One Scottish magnate saw in this state of affairs what he at first thought was an opportunity for personal advancement. John Murray, first marquess of Atholl, seems to have looked on William's arrival as intended for the especial benefit of himself and his family. Before the revolution was even embarked upon he and his eldest son, lord John Murray, had been in touch with William.[8] A personal following in the council was prepared to gamble on Atholl's becoming lord chancellor if the government were reshuffled.[9] He himself thought his appointment highly probable and his influence at least assured. In this belief he was prepared to take the lead in the Williamite cause. Amongst other moves he procured from the privy council an address of gratitude to William.[10] To ensure, as he imagined, *de facto* control of the administration he agreed to stay in Scotland with a very few councillors whilst the rest went to London,[11] but before long Atholl discovered that he had very seriously miscalculated. Shrewder operators such as Tarbat and Sir John Dalrymple were using him as a front man. As long as there was any risk of William's failing, their object was to ensure that Atholl should take the blame.[12] Three weeks' self-denial in Edinburgh convinced Atholl that he was in the wrong place, being outmanoeuvred by those who had gone to London. So, swallowing his earlier talk of its being his duty to stay in Scotland he, too, left for the English court where he was able to appraise the situation more realistically.[13] It seemed that by far the loudest, if not the most rational, voice at court was that of Hamilton, which boded no good for Atholl. Another discovery, which seems to have surprised him, was that in quarters increasingly regarded as influential, he was *persona non grata*. Leaders of the presbyterian interest, joined by their recently arrived *émigré* brethren, were meeting regularly at the Ship Tavern in St James's Street where 'they consulted what was to be done to have the government secured to themselves and to have all others debarred . . .'[14] Amongst those they especially wished to see excluded was Atholl. Tarbat and Dalrymple had quickly read the signs and dropped Atholl to find other means of advancement. Realising the lack of substance in his earlier illusions, Atholl continued to assure William of his support in the forthcoming convention but resumed his more usual connections with those whose inclinations were jacobite.[15]

At the beginning of the convention he found himself to be the episcopalian and jacobite candidate for the presidency of the estates. Election would have been a disadvantage to him. To gain the leadership of the Williamite party was worth taking some small risk; to support either side for the benefit of someone else was ludicrous. As a means of escape Atholl was reduced to mustering his own interest in support of his rival, Hamilton.[16] Subsequently he took refuge in petty evasion, becoming a notorious absentee from the convention though always falling just short of having himself blacklisted. He took no part in approving the convention's letter to William, nor did he attend to sign it. Instead he made excuses and asked that the letter be sent to him for signature.[17] On the rare occasions he attended, it was only to differ from the majority on innocuous points or such questions as could be represented as matters of conscience, particularly those with which William himself was known to have sympathy: opposition to declaring episcopacy a grievance, for example, or to proposed limitations on royal power. Such issues apart, he claimed to have supported William.[18] The points on which he opposed had been carefully chosen and there was even a possibility that his sincerity might not be questioned.

Before the 1689 parliament Atholl had withdrawn. He went to Bath, for his health he said, leaving his son, lord John, in charge of the estates.[19] There was rather more to explain away when fifty of the Atholl men joined Dundee's jacobite resistance and fought at Killiecrankie. Lord John claimed to have been away from home at the time. Atholl blamed some of the servants for disloyalty.[20] It is interesting that some twenty-five years later, in the 'Fifteen rising, the family's behaviour and its justification were not dissimilar. Perhaps they were merely unfortunate.

Queensberry's conduct fell into almost the same pattern. William Douglas, first duke of Queensberry, had served under Charles II and James. Early in James's reign he had first of all been demoted from the office of lord treasurer and then dismissed. When it seemed that William's arrival would force James to terms with the neglected magnates, Queensberry thought he saw an opportunity of regaining influence. He envisaged his preparatory task as twofold: to see off the Drummonds and to forestall any attempt by Atholl to seize advantage from the crisis. With the former object in mind he joined Atholl in requesting Perth to leave Edinburgh for the sake of public order,[21] but he also had plans for blocking any possibility of Atholl's advancement to the chancellorship. Before Queensberry left for London the two magnates had quarrelled violently.[22]

In London the duke set out to rival Hamilton's claims on William's favour. He seemed inclined to pose as a protestant martyr and somewhat overplayed his hand. His story was that he had forfeited his post under James through his steadfast refusal to turn catholic. In fact James's flight was Queensberry's undoing. He was admirably placed for coming to terms with a chastened James since his wealth and administrative experience made him useful in high office. But with most of the men who came to England with William he had no reputation at all, having been compromised by his association with the two previous sovereigns. Till his death zealous presbyterians were suspicious of him and bore malice.

But he, like other magnates, had too much at stake to deter him from anything rash. His reputation for avarice was widespread and it is true that when he brooded on his 'sacrifices' in the cause of religion what hurt him most was the loss of £20,000 he claimed to have been offered if he became catholic.[23] Once he realised that a monopoly of the administration was beyond his reach, particularly in competition with Hamilton, he modified his immediate aims. His new object was to retain what money and influence he had and to tout for lesser but still significant posts such as the governorship of Edinburgh castle.[24] But he, too, kept a foot in each camp. Drumlanrig, his eldest son, had been the first Scotsman of considerable rank openly to join William after his landing. Afterwards his personal fidelity to the revolution, whatever his motives, was so well known that jacobites abandoned all hope of converting him. However, his father's behaviour was more equivocal. He preserved a lifeline to James by stickling over details in the convention and showing vigour in acts of petty self-assertion.[25] The jacobites were convinced he was one of them[26] and on his return to Edinburgh in 1689 he was widely looked upon as one of the leaders of the jacobite interest.[27] Like Atholl and other high wire performers, he appeared in the estates only for formal votes over the grievances and the claim of right. Together with Marischal, Cassillis and Kintore, these two magnates helped to muster the only five votes against both these compilations.[28]

After the convention Queensberry wrote to William: 'I doubt not but my son has informed your majesty of the hard things done to me by some great men here, and how concerned they have been to discourage me from attending the convention and though these methods obliged me to desert the house for several days, yet when I heard your majesty's business was to be done, I went there, and owned your service in all points with such concern that I presume my greatest enemies will not have the impudence to charge me with the least remissness . . .' These enemies, according to Queensberry, were more concerned to indulge their private resentments than to serve the crown.[29] And all this was a quite dishonest account of the duke's behaviour during the convention. He and his kind were playing the game that came naturally to them. The revolution had seemed not only to provide an opportunity of improving their own interests but also the possibility of an alternative government. As a means of insurance and of securing increased bargaining power, a flirtation could be carried on with both. Those who branded Atholl and Queensberry as jacobites flattered them since neither had anything in mind but his own interest. And what both were finding hard to digest in 1689 was the fact that they had been overreached by Hamilton.

Without having done much to earn it, William Douglas, third duke of Hamilton, was suddenly in the position of the most influential magnate in Scotland. He was a choleric, blustering man who used his temper and a capacity for contradicting everyone, even himself, as a means of self-assertion. William had many reservations about Hamilton and was to acquire more. Yet, as the only Scottish magnate of any political experience who was for some reason looked upon as being uncompromised during the previous reigns, he was strongly placed. Men in his position could not be ignored and he intended to exploit this state of affairs to the full. Through the winter of 1688-9 he was in London making a great stir, acting as the Scots' self-appointed leader. His importunity and general officiousness made co-existence with him all but impossible. Would-be rivals, and even mere spectators, tended to wait in trepidation to see what Hamilton thought of this, that or the other proposal.[30] Speculation about his aims was a conversational topic that winter. Tweeddale's not improbable conjecture was that he wanted to be lord treasurer. But, like Cézanne, Hamilton believed in advancing all of the canvas all of the time. It seemed that he also had an urge to be chancellor, governor of one or other of the royal castles, and to have jobs for all his sons. He would not be satisfied until the Scottish revolution had been turned into a Hamilton family concern.[31]

Yet even here there remained a suspicion that the family's bets were being hedged. At a meeting of the Scottish 'council' in London, with Hamilton in the chair, unanimity was disturbed by the solitary voice of the duke's eldest son, the earl of Arran. He moved that James should be asked to return and call a free parliament, a proposal which 'seemed to dissatisfy the whole meeting, and the duke of Hamilton, their president, father to the earl . . .'[32] The motion was not seconded but was doubtless noted in the quarters for which it was intended, whether or not the duke was in full connivance. To be fair, both the duke and duchess found their son something of an enigma. The Duchess Anne later remarked in a quite different connection that James was 'the strangest man that ever I knew or heard of in my life'.[33]

So, of the Scottish magnates who had direct dealings with William, each wanted only to be in a dominant position. Given the opportunity, none would settle for anything short of a monopoly of influence. Queensberry and Atholl, disappointed but, as they hoped, only temporarily, faced both ways and bided their time. Family circumstances prevented Argyll from challenging the others although quite soon he was to show signs of asserting himself. One handicap was his eldest son's being too young to be put to political use. Argyll had to make up for it by occasionally being on both sides at once, which provided some insurance but reduced his political effectiveness. Hamilton had come out firmly as a Williamite, a position qualified only slightly by Arran's public stance. His attitude to the revolution enabled him to maintain his pre-eminence, and his election as president of the convention strengthened it. Although proceedings in the estates were occasionally disrupted by his bad-tempered outbursts and some oddities of behaviour, conduct of business remained on the whole brisk and efficient. The convention's decision to settle the throne on William and Mary confirmed the duke's public standing in both Edinburgh and London. One of the court's major problems was to be the inescapability of employing him.

William himself had still not spoken on questions of policy and to that fact was due much of the relative freedom from trouble enjoyed during the first meeting of the estates. Until the convention had done its work William's responsibility for Scotland's administration was temporary. As soon as William and Mary accepted the offer of the throne and took the oath, Scottish policies would necessarily be planned in London. Court attitudes to persons and measures would then have to be made plain and would almost certainly lead to conflict. The old tentacles of management and patronage had been severed by the revolution. No established network existed to act as the basis of a disciplined court organisation. The rowdy election atmosphere of 1689 was one result of this. Later developments weeded out of the estates a minority disinclined for revolution so that, although those who remained were all to some degree Williamite they were not yet courtiers, merely aspiring to be such. Furthermore the fact of revolution and the proceedings of the convention had generated a heightening of ambition. James Stewart noted the effect on the convention's rank and file membership: '... the late omnipotence of our estates hath raised men's spirits beyond the ordinary pitch'.[34] William and his advisers, whoever he chose, faced the task of recreating a court interest in a babble of expectancy. Unless the old influences were quickly replaced by a suitable disposal of offices and the establishment of a new patronage network, parliament would be unmanageable. Already too many people were hoping for far more than they could or would be given. For such reasons some opposition to the court was bound to have developed in the parliament of 1689. Any appointment at all could not be other than unwelcome to some who would not hesitate to express their resentment. And this was the point at which William made the biggest mistake, in relation to Scotland, of his entire reign. It was to prove irrevocable. That so many people in 1689 were not only disappointed but enraged is a serious reflection on the advice William had chosen to take. The arrangements which emerged from consultation in London were inept. The court went into the parliament of 1689 with an interest so negligible as to be ridiculous.

A court, in the sense of an official administrative interest, began to come into existence with the first appointments. Melville was made secretary of state, Sir John Dalrymple became lord advocate, whilst nominations were made to a new privy council and court of session. Some of these appointments were more significant than others. Initially Melville's appointment signified no political weight on his part. His reputation was that of a doleful, complaining man, a slow correspondent and an inefficient administrator, singularly unfitted for the job he had been given.[35] The earl of Crawford was similarly unsuited for his function as president of the parliament. It is possible that both were appointed on account of their impeccable revolutionary antecedents and their wide circle of presbyterian acquaintance. More probably both were preferred as unexceptionable nonentities to camouflage the advance of the Dalrymples to whom they could hardly have been considered a threat. Everything points to a steady and concerted attempt by the Dalrymples to expand their own power as rapidly as possible. But they were a family with few well-wishers in 1689, and after the revolution their ambitions very probably did as much damage to royal policy as did those of the magnates.

During James's reign the family had been unusual in managing to straddle the fence. Sir James Dalrymple of Stair had given up his post as president of session and gone into exile rather than take the test oath of 1681 which bound subscribers to attempt no alteration in either church or state. This had given him the advantage of a place at the centre of revolutionary planning, since to leave unused his political and legal talents would have seemed folly to William. Stair's son, Sir John, remained in Scotland later to serve King James as lord advocate for long enough to be popularly associated with some of the administration's more dubious measures. This had not endeared him to the new men of the revolution. Nor did his blatant appetite for power increase his popularity. But he, too, had something to offer William. An able lawyer and administrator, he was prepared to serve the new court as he had done the previous one as long as the rewards were forthcoming. His concentration on practicalities and his avoidance of abstract principles appealed to William, who consequently looked upon Sir John with unusual favour.

From the beginning of the revolution, if not before, Sir James Dalrymple and his eldest son were planning the re-establishment and expansion of the family's interest. In London, in the winter of 1688-9, Sir James was very active, associating himself with the *émigré* interest and making a big show of being 'high' presbyterian — one of the 'violent party' as lord Yester had it. In Edinburgh, in the convention, Sir John was with equal ostentation embracing moderate principles and cultivating alliances with those of similar views. In Tweeddale's opinion all this indicated some 'hedging'.[36] Sir James was not a member of the convention and throughout its sitting remained in London acting as a channel of communication between William and Portland at court and Melville in Edinburgh.[37] He told Melville that Portland would invite him ' . . . to come up hither, your advice being so necessary at this time, when places are to be settled, in which I forbear to move till you come . . .'[38], a statement which sheds more light on Dalrymple's influence than Melville's, however low Sir James pitched his voice in public.[39] Both father and son had been put on the new privy council. A further opportunity arose through the murder of Sir George Lockhart, Sir James's successor as president of session. Sir James wrote to Melville: ' . . . that shameful murder of Sir George Lockhart touched the king much, and made him say to me he saw it now necessary that I should resume my place again, which I was willing, though it was my right, that he should enjoy it, being younger and abler to endure the toil than I . . . '[40] He was appointed president. The nomination of his proposed colleagues in the court of session provoked wrath, smelling as some thought too much of past hardships. James Murray of Philiphaugh, later one of the second duke of Queensberry's foremost advisers, was singled out as ' . . . a person under bad characters, having had a chief hand in ruining many families, and taking the life of a very honest gentleman . . . ,'[41] There was a general assumption that the nominations were inspired by Sir James Dalrymple and for many the interest of the family was beginning to seem too large.[42]

If it is accepted that these appointments were intended primarily as part of a scheme for managing the 1689 parliament, it is just possible to discern a faint rationale behind them. The preferment of Melville and Crawford can be taken as a necessary attempt to pacify the presbyterians, but at low cost, by the appointment of sympathetic nonentities. A fair spectrum of interests, reputedly presbyterian and episcopalian of varying shades, appeared in the commission for the new privy council. All the magnates were either personally included or their interest represented.[43] This could be looked upon as an attempt to broaden the base of the court, but as a scheme for recruiting support for the ministry it was utterly inadequate, attempting too much with no possibility of success. In fact it deserved to fail. No one outside their respective families was likely to be gratified by the appointment of Melville and Crawford. Many were annoyed by the inclusion in the privy council of men associated with the previous administration.[44] Hamilton objected violently to the appointment of anybody at all not of his own interest.[45] And no one was satisfied by mere inclusion in such a portmanteau privy council. So, if the dispositions of 1689 were intended as a means of managing the parliamentary session, they were the product of an extraordinary miscalculation. But they can be seen in a very different light. As a way of subduing Hamilton and keeping out rivals to the Dalrymples the arrangements proved no more successful but they made considerably more sense. The activities of Sir John Dalrymple taken in conjunction with the court's treatment of Hamilton make it seem likely that to some of William's advisers the management of parliament was almost a secondary consideration.

There is no doubt that after the revolution the newly emerging court group had to look on Hamilton as one of its main problems. He had become increasingly possessed by the conviction that the mantle of Lauderdale had fallen upon him and that his destiny was to be William's viceroy in Scotland. His behaviour made the scale of his delusions apparent. William, thinking him far too importunate, had taken a firm dislike to him.[46] Yet he was the obvious man to be commissioner to the 1689 parliament. After his presidency of the convention he could not be ignored, but William felt unable to pay the price of his co-operation. The virtual monopoly of patronage which he was likely to demand would have alienated too many other interests. Certainly, Queensberry, Atholl and Argyll would have taken umbrage, and if there had been any chance of gaining their collaboration it would have been folly to invite obstruction. The fact was, however, that there was no such possibility, but William was to find this out the hard way. At the time he seems to have been persuaded that the best way of handling Hamilton was to use him as a figurehead whilst denying him the satisfaction of parading as the great disposer of places. When decisions were taken the duke was to be by-passed. Patronage was to be kept out of his hands, in the hope that he would serve in expectation of future rewards. This severe limitation on his powers was, incredibly, supposed to be noted by everyone save Hamilton himself. To keep others from jealousy he was expected to be satisfied with nothing. If such was the court's calculation — and it seems to have been — it was far removed from reality. With a precision amounting almost to genius, the king's advisers were planning a monumental court failure. Hamilton having been first, as he judged, slighted, was then to be put in a position from which he could inflict incalculable damage. The result was very likely worse than almost any other scheme that could have been envisaged. So, whilst it could have emerged from a very inept handling of the problem of Hamilton and his competitors, and although William and Portland might well have been persuaded to accept it as a possible solution, it seems more probable that the scheme had been originally inspired by the Dalrymples' concern for their own ambitions.

Hamilton had suspected that major decisions were to be made in London without his being consulted. Once the estates had asked to be turned into a parliament, its management would largely depend on whoever's advice William chose to take. As president of the convention Hamilton had been debarred from conveying the offer of the throne to William and Mary, a task which was obviously an opportunity for the advancement of those chosen. He gained no reassurance from the estates' choice of commissioners.[47] Argyll was too powerful for the duke's liking. Montgomerie of Skelmorlie was blatantly consumed by ambition. Nor was there much charity between Hamilton and any of the Dalrymple family. So vital consultations concerning the meeting of parliament were going to take place in London whilst Hamilton remained in Edinburgh, excluded from influence and deprived of any voice in appointments or measures. He began to feel that, whatever the estates might officially have decided, he was against a meeting of parliament until he himself had spoken fully to William. He wrote in these terms to the king, angling for an invitation to London[48] which no one at court intended he should be given. He began to make a noise about appointments.[49] He secured an official representation from the committee of estates — the caretaker administration between the convention and parliament — asking specifically that before any parliament met, Hamilton and others should be summoned to court to provide information.[50] Nevertheless it was decided in London that parliament was to meet in June 1689 and that Hamilton, without consultation, was to be lord high commissioner.[51] Hamilton could conclude only that all his fears had been justified.

The duke had shown a considerable and not unreasonable reluctance about accepting the post of commissioner without first having seen the king and exerted some influence on the drafting of his own instructions. He had written personally to William and at last openly asked permission to go to London.[52] Melville did what he could to pacify him[53] but Sir John Dalrymple's reaction was less placatory: '... The letter from the committee [of the estates],'[54] he wrote, 'gives no satisfaction here. It is understood that your grace did moderate the forwardness of some in the convention; but the very proposals insinuate diffidence in the king's management. The consequences of mistakes at this time, when our deliverance is not perfected, may be fatal. These sent here, seeing the king is determined, have looked about for a balance in our government, and to take their own shares. I do not believe it in the power of your grace's enemies, or malice itself, to prevail with the king to neglect the services you have done, and are capable to render him. I confess it's hard to receive instructions at second hand, but I should be heartily sorry, both upon the account of the public, and your grace's interest, if anything should induce you to mar so fair a work; it might justify the surmises your grace points at, and gratify those who insinuate your grace had more regard to yourself than the public, should you stop upon the resentment that you have not been advised in the disposal of the public offices or trusts . . . the king and the world must be sensible that none besides your grace can bring this session to a happy and peaceable conclusion, upon which very much depends . . . '[55]

Dalrymple was being much less than honest. Of the three delegates from the convention only he had received anything material, having outsmarted Argyll and Skelmorlie, who had been fobbed off with places on the privy council. The lord advocate had warned Hamilton against 'mistakes at this time' but Hamilton himself could not have done much worse than anger and disappoint both Argyll and Skelmorlie, which is what the court had managed to do. About the position of his family Dalrymple told Hamilton: ' . . . for my father, he lives in the country very abstract, and I see some still retain their humour against him. For myself I have taken occasion to signify very little . . . '[56] Anyone capable of believing that ought not to have been in politics, or possibly anything else, and Hamilton expected the worst. His enemies for the time being seemed to have identified themselves. Friction between the duke and Sir John Dalrymple became the normal state of affairs.

Quite soon Dalrymple provided an opportunity for open dispute. The cause was a piece of administrative sharp practice designed to give him control of the great seal, a manoeuvre which gave Hamilton the excuse for blowing off a great head of steam. It probably did him a power of good although hindering the conduct of business. Dalrymple had foisted on an unsuspecting or complaisant Melville a warrant for one Alexander Inglis, related to Dalrymple's wife, to be keeper of the great seal. On the strength of this warrant Inglis appended the seal to two commissions: Dalrymple's own as lord advocate and one for Sir William Lockhart as solicitor-general. This was not only improper but a gratuitous rebuff to Hamilton, nominal head of the administration whose wide-ranging ambitions embraced the post of lord chancellor. With the full support of the privy councillors in Edinburgh Hamilton exploded the force of his accumulated resentment in a letter to Melville who seemed to have no idea how he had become involved. He blamed Inglis[57] but Lockhart knew better. Inglis's commission had been drafted in haste and rushed through by Dalrymple himself. In Lockhart's opinion the commission was bad and ought to be revoked ' . . . Sir John Dalrymple will certainly give you a full account of this matter,' he wrote to Melville, ' and to tell the truth, being both father and mother to it, he is obliged to defend it . . .'[58]

Dalrymple tried to brazen it out. The intent of the commission, he said, was to ensure that the king's will prevailed over Hamilton and the council who could otherwise take it upon themselves to block warrants.[59] This was plausible, up to a point. It is the exercise of the 'king's will' for Dalrymple's benefit which excites suspicion. The new lord advocate was exposing one of his most serious flaws as a royal servant — a proneness to administrative and political short cuts. To envisage the opposition they were likely to generate seemed beyond the reach of his imagination and even when protest materialised he almost always underestimated it. There was to be a whole series of such incidents up to Glencoe and beyond.

Meanwhile, before, during and after the parliament, Hamilton fought for what he considered to be his due. He made use of threats, direct and indirect, exhibitions of rage unnerving to experience, erratic and arbitrary behaviour, petty criticism and sheer obstinacy. As a result he placed himself in quite preposterous situations. He gave the lie to Crawford in full parliament, not at all troubled that Crawford was in the right and that some of those present knew it.[60] As long as Hamilton was in business such episodes abounded: the issue of who was to sign privy council acts, a quorum or the president only, over which Hamilton's choler reached such heights that the question had to be allowed to lapse;[61] the duke's devising a long and complicated oath which privy councillors were to take on one knee, bible in hand, a procedure to which some councillors took very strong exception. Such obstruction afflicted Hamilton with the spleen to the extent that no business could be done.[62] At no time was he an easy man to live with and, when embarked on personal conflict, he was unbearable. The reason was simple enough. A powerful and haughty magnate, feeling himself slighted, was determined to make himself a nuisance in the only ways he knew. In the process he showed an utter disregard of any concept of duty or service beyond the needs of his own ambition. The pinnacle of his campaign was reached in the parliament of 1689 when the court, with bitterness and frustration, had to witness the spectacle of the king's high commissioner collaborating with the opposition and scarcely bothering to conceal it. But others besides Hamilton were to blame.

NOTES

1. Balcarres, *Memoirs*, 13-15; NLS, MS 7026, 81, Tweeddale to Yester, 11 Dec. 1688.
2. *Ib.*, 98, same to same, 1 Jan. 1689.
3. *Ib.*
4. *Ib.*, 81, same to same, 15 Dec. 1688.
5. *Ib.*, 119, same to same, 31 Jan. [16]89.
6. *Ib.*, 90, same to same, 23 Dec. 1688; *ib.*, 105, same to same, 17 Jan. 89; *ib.*, 112, same to same, 29 Jan. 1689.
7. *Ib.*, 119, same to same, 31 Jan. [16]89; *ib.*, 122, same to same, 2 Feb. [16]89.
8. Balcarres, *Memoirs*, 7-8.
9. NLS, MS 7026, 106, Tweeddale to Yester, 19 Jan. 1689.
10. Balcarres, *Memoirs*, 13-15, 17-18.
11. NLS, MS 7026, 81, Tweeddale to Yester, 15 Dec. 1688; *ib.*, 85, same to same, 16 Dec. 1688.
12. Balcarres, *Memoirs*, 14.
13. NLS, MS 7026, 79, Tweeddale to Yester, 8 Jan. 1688[/9].
14. Balcarres, *Memoirs*, 18-19.
15. *Ib.*, 22-4; *Leven and Melville Papers*, 12, Atholl to William, 13 Apr. 1689.
16. APS, ix, 3; Balcarres, *Memoirs*, 25.
17. NLS, MS 7026, 167, Tweeddale to Yester, 25 Mar. [16]89.
18. *Ib.*, 170, same to same, 26 Mar. [16]89; *Leven and Melville Papers*, 12, Atholl to William, 13 Apr. 1689.
19. *Ib.*, 21, Atholl to Melville, 21 May 1689; *ib.*, 52, same to same, 8 Jun. 1689.
20. *Ib.*, 54, lord J. Murray to Melville, 11 Jun. [1689]; *ib.*, 173, same to same, 17 Jun. 1689; *ib.*, 445, Atholl to same, 19 Jun. 1690; *ib.*, 498, same to same, 22 Aug. 1690.
21. See above, p. 11.
22. NLS, MS 7026, 81, Tweeddale to Yester, 11 Dec. 1688; *ib.*, 85, same to same, 16 Dec. 1688.
23. Japikse, ii, 15-21, Polwarth's report on Queensberry, 12 Feb. 1687; NLS, MS 7026, 92, Tweeddale to Yester, 28 Dec. 1688.
24. *Ib.*, 75, same to same, 4 Jan. 1688[/9]; *ib.*, 100, same to same, 3 Jan. 1689.
25. See, e.g., *ib.*, 108, same to same, 22 Jan. 1689.
26. Balcarres, *Memoirs*, 22-4.
27. NLS, MS 7026, 145, Tweeddale to Yester, 26 Feb. [16]89.
28. *Ib.*, 167, same to same, 25 Mar. [16]89; *ib.*, 170, same to same, 26 Mar. [16]89; *ib.*, 195, Tweeddale's unofficial minutes, 8-10 Apr. 1689.
29. *Leven and Melville Papers*, 11, Queensberry to William, 13 Apr. 1689.
30. NLS, MS 7026, 147, Tweeddale to Yester, 28 Feb. [16]89. For Polwarth's opinion of him: Japikse, ii, 15-21, 12 Feb. 1687.

31. NLS, MS 7026, 111, Tweeddale to Yester, 26 Jan. 1689; *ib.*, 127, same to same, 7 Feb. [16]89; *ib.*, 145, same to same, 26 Feb. [16]89.
32. *Proceedings*, ii, App., 294; D. H. Whiteford, 'Jacobitism as a factor in Presbyterian-Episcopalian relations in Scotland 1689-90', *RSCHS*, xvi, 140.
33. R. K. Marshall, *The Days of Duchess Anne* (London, 1973), 214.
34. *Leven and Melville Papers*, 162-5, to William Denham [sic for Denholm?], 11 Jul. 1689.
35. Foxcroft, *Halifax*, ii, 217. On his dismissal Melville's records as secretary were found to be in disorder: SRO, GD26, xiii, 35/1, Johnston to Melville, 2 Mar. 1693. For the peculiarities of his administration see pp. 58-9, 61-2, 71-2 below.
36. NLS, MS 7026, 102, Tweeddale to Yester, 10 Jan. 1689; *ib.*, 119, same to same, 31 Jan. [16]89; *ib.*, 137, same to same, 16 Feb. [16]89.
37. *Leven and Melville Papers*, 3-8, 10 *et seq.*
38. *Ib.*, 13, 21 Apr. [1689].
39. For Sir James's views on the use of office for raising a family's status see *HMCR Johnstone MSS*, 138-9, to Crawford, 9 Jul. 1689.
40. *Leven and Melville Papers*, 8, 9 Apr. 1689. See also *HMCR Johnstone MSS*, 137-8, same to Crawford, 30 May 1689.
41. *Leven and Melville Papers*, 77, J. Hay to Melville, 24 Jun. 1689. Philiphaugh had been a crucial witness at the trial of Robert Baillie of Jerviswood. For the other nominations see *Proceedings*, i, 148. Not all those nominated at this time were finally appointed. This episode, as well as subsequent events, indicates that Foxcroft (*Supplement*, 540-44) overestimated the solidarity of her 'Scoto-Dutch alliance'.
42. Stair was said to have opposed a council in London in the hope of himself being commissioned to go to Scotland to hold a meeting of heritors: HLRO, Willcocks MSS, 18, 1 Jan. [16]89, [Yester] to Tweeddale.
43. For the list: *CSP (Dom.)*, 1689-90, 109-10, 18 May 1689.
44. *Leven and Melville Papers*, 79, Crawford to Melville, 25 Jun. 1689; *ib.*, 23, James Stewart to [   ], 24 May 1689.
45. *Ib.*, 20-22, to Melville, 21 May 1689.
46. Foxcroft, *Halifax*, ii, 205, 217.
47. See above, p. 9.
48. *Leven and Melville Papers*, 16, 30 Apr. 1689.
49. *Ib.*, 20-22, to Melville, 21 May 1689.
50. *APS*, ix, 94-5.
51. Fraser, *Melvilles*, ii, 126-7, Melville to Hamilton, 31 May [1689].
52. *Leven and Melville Papers*, 20-21, Hamilton to Melville, 21 May 1689; *ib.*, 25-7, 25 May 1689.
53. *Ib.*, 149, Jun. 1689; Fraser, *Melvilles*, ii, 126-7, 31 May [1689].
54. See above.
55. Macpherson, App., 189-90, 30 May 1689.
56. *Ib.*
57. *Leven and Melville Papers*, 58, Hamilton to Melville, 18 Jun. 1689; *ib.*, 50, Melville to Hamilton, Jun. 1689 (clearly in reply to Hamilton's letter but dated 8 Jun. by the editor).
58. *Ib.*, 70, to Melville, 20 Jun. 1689; *ib.*, 62, to same, 18 Jun. 1689.
59. *Ib.*, 63, Dalrymple to Melville, 18 Jun. 1689.
60. *Ib.*, 75-6, Hamilton to Melville, 23 Jun. 1689; *ib.*, 79-81, Crawford to same, 25 Jun. 1689; *ib.*, 198-201, same to same, 27 Jul. 1689. The king's letter to the privy council seems to have been an attempt to remedy the situation: *CSP (Dom.)*, 1689-90, 183.
61. Fraser, *Melvilles*, ii, 145, Hamilton to the king, 16 Jan. [1690]; *ib.*, 146, Melville to Hamilton, 21 Jan. [1690].
62. *Carstares S.P.*, 125-7, Crawford to Carstares, 19 Dec. 1689; Fraser, *Melvilles*, ii, 145, Melville to Crawford, 16 Jan. [1690].

2
Hamilton, Melville and the Club

IT was in June 1689 that the task of persuading parliament to accept a settlement which would satisfy the king was embarked upon. The court interest available for the job was negligible and even the little there was proved to be split with jealousy and acrimony. Hamilton's heart was not in his work and he was at loggerheads with most of his nominal colleagues.

William's letter to the parliament was couched in general terms: ' . . . We have authorised our commissioner to pass such things into laws as have been lately under your consideration, in relation to the grievances . . . and likewise for establishing the church government, according to your desires and inclinations, and for redressing the laws and securing you against all the articles of your grievances, whereby we have done all upon our part to render you happy and contented . . . '[1] All of which seemed to promise fair. Hamilton's instructions corresponded to the royal letter.[2] Yet there were hidden obstacles and reservations. The duke, having had no say in the policy for which he was now responsible, did not feel at all committed to it. William, advised that some steering committee was necessary in the interests of court business, had decided that the articles should not be abolished as requested in the grievances but modified instead. And although both letter and instructions were seemingly quite open on the subject of church government, Hamilton knew very well that some settlements would be more acceptable to William than others. Not only William's inclinations but English opinion had to be constantly borne in mind.[3] Later, as the printing of Hamilton's instructions was ordered after the court's defeat in 1689, Balcarres was as near the truth as anybody when he said it 'laid all the blame at his[4] door, although it was well known the duke had made his court ill if he had granted what was in them . . . '[5] Melville's later capitulation as lord commissioner to the demands of parliament in 1690, though within the limits of his instructions, certainly left the court somewhat soured towards him.

When the estates met on 5 June 1689, Hamilton at once went out of his way to indicate that he was not necessarily to be regarded as being at one with his colleagues.[6] His subsequent actions made plain what he had in mind. The only moment of harmony between the court and the estates sprang from a near-unanimity over the act transforming the convention into a parliament.[7] After this, throughout the rest of the session, the court was under violent and incessant attack from the opposition groups known collectively as the 'club'. Dalrymple was made to suffer for his family's unpopularity, and what was probably his own and his father's questionable advice, by finding himself one of the chief targets of the club's venom. When, in debating terms, he had the better of the argument, as sometimes he did, it made the situation worse rather than better. His very presence in parliament as an officer of state was an affront, and when his mental agility proved superior to that of his opponents the latter were incensed. The animosity against the Dalrymples could not help but show itself when Sir John appeared in the parliament house as lord advocate and virtually the sole spokesman for the court. Melville had stayed in London. Crawford, apart from being hampered by his position as president, was not at any time particularly effective in parliament. So for the most part Dalrymple spoke for the court unaided whilst the committed opposition numbered about seventy in a parliament of roughly 130.[8] Such a large proportion of the house had been alienated that professed courtiers were frequently awed into silence or occasionally into voting with the club. Even members of the newly appointed privy council joined in opposition, in most instances understandably. Over a topic such as the abolition of the articles on which the will of the estates was already known the court was in a minority of, at the most, twelve.[9]

The virulence of feeling against the Dalrymples was one of the elements which unified the club.[10] Opposition to them was turned into a shibboleth. One ground for condemnation of the new privy council was that only two of the members had voted for Dalrymple's opponent, Hamilton of Whitelaw, as the burghs' delegate from the convention.[11] What is remarkable, in view of all this, is the fact that Dalrymple had been elected at all. Most probably in the knowledge of Stair's influence with William some burgh members, usually susceptible to court influence, were hedging their bets by voting for Dalrymple and afterwards doing their utmost to neutralise the consequences of their vote. Even when Dalrymple had been chosen there had been an intrigue both in Scotland and between Argyll and Skelmorlie, his two colleagues in London, to prevent his exercising any influence at court.[12] Stair, his father, was also in ill odour, being held responsible for the proposed nomination of the new lords of session, described with some injustice as the 'dross of the nation'.[13] Nevertheless, some of the parliament were prepared, if it should be unavoidable, to tolerate Sir James as president of the session. But even their resistance was provoked by his son's appointment as lord advocate. Others steadfastly objected to the appointment of a Dalrymple to any post.[14] Apart from major attacks, sniping at the family became routine. An apparently formal motion in 1690 for the adjournment of all courts whilst parliament was sitting gave Ludovic Grant the opportunity to introduce a prearranged act disqualifying any temporal peer from being president of the court of session. The intended victim of this stratagem was the elder Dalrymple, recently raised to the peerage as viscount of Stair. The act was blocked only with difficulty.[15] The Dalrymples were made acutely aware of the feeling against them but attributed it all to jealousy.[16] They were not fully justified in doing so, but this animosity was one reason why throughout the session of 1689 the court teetered from one defeat to another. Any move against the royal prerogative or any proposal with an anti-Dalrymple flavour — one frequently involved the other — was assured of overwhelming support. Many apparently innocuous proposals proved to conceal traps for the Dalrymples. So, as the effects of the miscalculations made by William's advisers began to appear, the court was systematically humiliated by an organised opposition.

The importance attaching to the grievances had been grossly underestimated. William and his advisers had chosen to interpret them as guidelines only, not as literally binding, and to be moved by the spirit rather than the letter according to their own inclinations. This difference of view emerged over the articles. The advantages of some kind of steering committee were apparent to any parliamentary manager, so the court's intention was to retain the articles in some form, the grievances notwithstanding. William was set on the retention of the articles as an elective rather than a nominated body, thinking that no exception could be taken to this.[17] However, the grievances had complained not of the constitution of the articles, but of their existence, so the opposition was presented with an opportunity for harassing the court too good to miss. In even more express terms a large majority of parliament reaffirmed the articles to be a grievance. There was to be no standing committee at all, merely elected *ad hoc* committees from which officers of state were to be excluded.[18] An act to this effect was voted. When Hamilton announced this to be beyond the scope of his instructions, a further vote authorised him to send parliament's reasons to the king.[19] William then attempted a further concession, proposing frequent re-election in order to maintain the articles in some form, but the bulk of the parliament would have none of it.[20]

The recent nominations to the court of session were attacked, not with reference to individuals, but indirectly. Parliament began to discuss the general principle of how the session ought to be re-established after what was described as 'a total vacancy'. Club spokesmen contended that such a resettlement required the authority of parliament, not a mere nomination by the crown. The lords of session ought to be appointed first, afterwards electing a president from their own number. This was a blow at the royal prerogative and was intended as such. Even more it was designed as an obstacle to the ambitions of Sir James Dalrymple. Parliament accordingly voted an act in these terms but since there was no instruction for such a measure, nor ever likely to be, royal assent was not forthcoming.[21]

An oblique attack was made on Sir John Dalrymple for his behaviour as one of the commissioners for taking the offer of the crown to London. He was alleged to have given William advice on safeguarding the prerogative. Argyll accused him by implication of acting against the will of the convention by not ensuring that the oath taken by William and Mary on their accepting the throne was subsequent to their acceptance of the grievances and the claim of right. Dalrymple was very pleased at the good account he considered he had given of himself over this. He does seem to have won the bout on a technicality and the club, having other weapons at their disposal, let the topic fall.[22] A measure had been voted which, had it ever become law, would have sufficed to deal not only with the Dalrymples but with any others considered undesirable. This 'incapacitating act' was voted on 2 July 1689.[23] In its final version it debarred from office not only those involved in any of the actions complained of in the grievances, or who had opposed any aspect of the revolution since it had taken place, but anyone seen as 'a retarder or obstructer of the good designs of the ... estates ... '[24] As Dalrymple noted, such a law could exclude anyone the opposition did not like. Such was its intention and there was no doubt that he would have been amongst its first victims.[25] The motives of most opposition spokesmen in pressing for the act were personal and even unwholesome. One of the foremost proposers of the act was James Ogilvy, one of the five to vote against the 'forfaulture' of King James under whom 'the former evil government' had been carried on. And amongst those who had most vigorously supported the act were others who were in a very short time to place themselves within its intended scope.[26]

After this spasm of militancy the opposition could do little but wait on developments. Nor was Hamilton able to think of much in the way of business. After some attempts to propose supply, effortlessly brushed aside by the club, he gave some attention to the future government of the church. Several points were involved. Episcopacy had been declared a grievance, but what form of organisation was going to replace it? And what was going to be the extent of its powers? Which ministers were to be admitted to the church? Were the conforming clergy to be allowed in or not? Were patronages to be retained? Hamilton put forward the draft of an act prepared, it is to be supposed, in London, which would have provided a moderate settlement. The church would be restored to its state of 1592 save that all acts in favour of episcopacy would be rescinded. Conforming clergy would be reinstated and patronages, by implication, were to be allowed to stand.[27] But with Hamilton's proposal the court seemed to be declaring its intentions towards the church settlement, thus providing the opposition with something precise to attack and allowing them to regain some impetus. At once members of the club, whatever their religious persuasion, could feel safe in pressing for extremes of presbyterianism, merely to embarrass the court, in full confidence that their demands would be resisted. An immediate result was a succession of acts aimed at setting up the full presbyterian apparatus and rigour, at the abolition of lay patronages and confining reinstatement to those ministers deprived in 1661-2.

But it was plain that even in the 1689 parliament much of the demand for a presbyterian settlement was in origin quite irreligious. As soon as the club leaders arrived in London after the parliamentary session was over they began intriguing with James Johnston and Gilbert Burnet. Johnston, of course, was a presbyterian of some kind. Burnet was an episcopalian, newly created bishop of Salisbury, and strange company for members of the club as self-styled presbyterians of the utmost rabidity. The fact was that persons were far more important than principles. Johnston, like others who had been in Holland before the revolution, had hoped for office in Scotland and had seemingly been overlooked.[28] Burnet at the time was working closely with English court tories to secure, if not an episcopalian settlement in Scotland, then at least reasonable treatment of episcopalian and conforming clergy. Later he was exerting himself to limit the power in Scotland of Melville and other presbyterians.[29] One thing Johnston, Burnet and the club leaders all had in common was a strong antipathy to the emergent court interest in Scotland. It is difficult, though, in this curious subterranean alliance, to say who was using whom.

However, in 1689 all the club's ecclesiastical demands fell into a between-sessions limbo when parliament was adjourned. By then business had reached a complete *impasse*.[30] Court proposals had been rejected. Acts voted by parliament were blocked by the withholding of the royal assent followed by the adjournment. This state of affairs was directly attributable to two consequences of the court's inept management: Hamilton's behaviour as lord high commissioner and the size and virulence of the opposition.

Throughout the session Hamilton's attitude to business had veered between ambivalence and something which closely resembled direct support of the opposition. After the court's defeat on the articles he took the view that committees were not permissible and that henceforth business could be dealt with only in full parliament. The privy council, in which the club was strongly represented, formalised this decision. So the club had not only a majority in the house but the great tactical advantage of being able to introduce proposals at will, by surprise, their contribution to the debate already scripted and edited. Nevertheless Hamilton could have done much more to hinder them than he did. His task, had he taken it seriously, was admittedly not an easy one. But neither was that of the club leaders. They had to hold together a very mixed opposition for as long as pressure on the court needed to be maintained. The support they could command varied according to the issues involved. Areas of disagreement had to be avoided lest the cracks began to show. For instance, whatever they professed, the club was by no means agreed on church government, a weakness which presented Hamilton with a powerful weapon. He had been given an instruction on church government on which he could have proceeded. Had he chosen to do so opportunely, the king might not have been pleased but the club could have been disrupted. Dalrymple realised this and tried, vainly for the most part, to persuade Hamilton to make tactical use of the church settlement.

The duke proved too liberal in allowing general discussion to develop from the floor at the club's initiative, even on subjects for which he had no instructions. Such debates could end only in deadlock to the further detriment of the court's position. His reaction to Dalrymple's advice was wholly ineffective. Intermittently Hamilton mentioned church government but allowed himself to be easily deflected.[31] More usually he preferred to broach tentatively the subject of supply, which was always briskly overridden with much the same result: the club was again allowed a free hand to dictate proceedings. Hamilton was, of course, afraid of the topic. Church government was as much an embarrassment to him as it was to the club leaders. Whatever his instructions, Hamilton was afraid of being blamed for some development which William would find uncongenial. An act abolishing episcopacy could be tolerated by both sides since it lay within the scope of the grievances and so could receive the royal assent. But at the same time an act was voted to repeal the crown's ecclesiastical supremacy as established by the act of 1669.[32] Hamilton had an instruction which allowed the royal assent to this act, and had it been given it might conceivably have split the opposition. Hamilton for whatever reason refused assent. He had, of course, the king's preferences to keep in mind and their bearing on his own position. And if he thought that Dalrymple's motives in urging him to act on the subject of church government were not wholly disinterested, he could have been excused. Dalrymple's prospects could have benefited greatly from the disruption of the club and the discrediting of Hamilton at one and the same time. So the duke chose to exercise caution, thereby greatly increasing suspicion of the court's intentions.[33]

Trouble had been unavoidable from when Hamilton realised that the court was trying to use him without granting his demands. The king's advisers had then to live with the consequences of their own misjudgement. Hamilton's sole aim in the 1689 parliament was the advancement of his own interest in whatever way seemed to show most promise. He devoted little attention to the court's objectives, looking over his shoulder only to the extent of keeping within the limits of William's reservations over the articles and church government. As the author of a later, Dalrymple-inspired, memorandum observed, 'D[uke] Hamilton was not satisfied with his interest in the government, unless he had been chancellor, and had a greater share of his friends in the public judicatures . . .'[34] Towards the club opposition his attitude bordered on encouragement, though there were the inevitable inconsistencies in his behaviour. He had a deep mistrust of Argyll and

Skelmorlie, whom he scented as possible rivals and threats to his position. When this idea possessed him he became ill-disposed towards the club. Otherwise he allowed them great and quite unnecessary latitude. Dalrymple began to realise the magnitude of the mistake that had been made and tried, too late, to bring some influence to bear on Hamilton. He told him he should either do his job as commissioner or otherwise, if dissatisfied with the conditions imposed, ask for changes in his instructions.[35] He made little impression, Hamilton conducting himself pretty much as before. Sometimes the duke took it upon himself to block whatever court strategy there was by ruling that no business could be transacted even in full parliament until the question of the articles was settled. Yet he allowed the club to raise business in full parliament and have it discussed and voted on, as with the 'incapacitating act' and the affair of the court of session,[36] either of which he could have stopped by applying the same rule or by announcing that he was not instructed.

Hamilton was clinging tenaciously to his earlier hopes of establishing his family as the major court interest. For too long he had fancied that he was invulnerable to attack. His belief in his own indispensability remained unwavering but, as the session continued, it was increasingly borne in upon him that he was badly in need of help from somebody. He appeared to be trapped between a court that had already stabbed him in the back and an opposition that seemed to be all but invincible. Yet he had no wish to come to terms with either of them whilst the other was still able to do him damage. As a way out of his predicament his thoughts turned to an adjournment. He began to seek precise definition of the circumstances in which he could adjourn the parliament and Dalrymple feared that he might choose to adjourn at a time disadvantageous to the court.[37] What few committed courtiers there were came to accept that Hamilton, far from being their leader, was not really on their side. The havoc this behaviour was creating drove Dalrymple some way to a realisation, at least in the abstract, of what was necessary in Scotland. Unless the goverment was 'all of a piece' — an expression to gain increasing currency in Scottish politics until the union — nothing could be achieved. In 1689 the court had to come to terms either with Hamilton or the club. Of the two, Dalrymple saw Hamilton as the lesser evil. A bargain with the club would involve major and permanent concessions, whereas anything given to Hamilton could be taken away if the king later saw fit. A group of courtiers — Dalrymple himself, Sir William Lockhart, Melville's sons and major-general Mackay, the commander-in-chief, Scotland — went to Hamilton offering him their full support in gaining the post of chancellor if he exerted himself properly as commissioner.[38]

Dalrymple had at last concluded that, if the court's business was to be done, Hamilton had for the time being to be satisfied. He had to be transformed from a lord commissioner on sufferance into the key figure of the new court interest. Of course it is conceivable, even likely, that Dalrymple had nothing in mind beyond finding some other way of temporarily misleading Hamilton for the court's convenience. Whatever the intention, the move had been left too late. Hamilton had already decided that his purpose would be better served by an adjournment and a visit to London. There were strong grounds for suspicion that Hamilton and the club leaders had been in collusion over the timing and circumstances of an adjournment. Much of the duke's routine correspondence became dominated by the prospects of adjournment and, as soon as an opportunity arose, he did adjourn, leaving the court with an accumulation of problems of which he himself was by no means the least.[39]

Whatever the provocation, Hamilton's behaviour in 1689 had come close to disqualifying him for reappointment as commissioner in any subsequent session of parliament, although his confidence in his destiny remained unshaken. Given a more moderate approach on his part to the distribution of spoils, his belief might have borne some relation to reality, but he showed no sign of lowering his demands. On the adjournment of the 1689 parliament he went to London, which from the beginning of the session had been his main objective. There he did all he could to eliminate opposition to his family's advancement, asserting his claim to a major share of influence.[40] Meeting with no discernible success, he returned to Edinburgh sour at not having been made chancellor, the great seal being instead put into commission. In Scotland he exerted himself vigorously for some time in council. His dissatisfaction at the disposal of the great seal was very explicit although he had been appointed one of the commissioners. He devoted no little time to what had become his favourite occupation, that of devising alternative schemes of government in which he increasingly figured as secretary of state.[41] Apprehension that Hamilton's efforts might succeed in prising something more out of the court led Argyll to issue a warning. He had been made one of Hamilton's colleagues in the great seal commission and now, with the passage of time, was more directly one of the duke's competitors. His recent appointment to the commission, together with some official encouragement, had lured Argyll from the opposition to which, in the 1689 parliament, he had appeared to be dedicated. Now he was prepared to tell Melville that Hamilton's dissatisfaction was notorious. If this drove the king to gratify him further at other people's expense, Argyll himself would be disobliged. Nor, he added, would he be alone.[42] Notice was being served that the court had to decide what they thought Hamilton was worth in view of the certainty of offending others.

Spectacular tantrums having produced no tangible result, Hamilton became discouraged and followed the path already trodden by Atholl and Queensberry. He left Edinburgh and, after his seeming determination in the 1689 parliament to obstruct the establishment of high presbyterianism, began to make overtures to the cameronians, announcing that his great ambition was to be a witness to a presbyterian settlement.[43] Dalrymple concluded that Hamilton was of no further use and recommended that Melville instead should be made commissioner to the next session of parliament.[44] Melville appeared reluctant, and with good cause. Acceptance of the post could have been a political suicide leap, the situation differing from that of 1689 only in that the problems were more clearly defined. A decision was postponed for a time by Melville's being sent to Scotland with a blank commission and power to give the post to Hamilton or, if he thought it necessary, to take it himself.[45]

One interview with Hamilton decided Melville to accept the post, after which, presiding for the first time in the privy council, he began to experience at first hand what hitherto had been merely the subject of reports: Hamilton asserting himself at the council table. Hamilton's objections to Melville's appointment were many and varied but his main complaint was that a peer lower in rank than a duke should not have been made commissioner. Then, despite all his attempts to engineer an adjournment in the previous session, he had come to believe, or at least declare, that the adjournment had been forced upon him. That most of those present knew the contrary to be true left him unmoved.[46]

But Hamilton was only one of the hazards which rendered negligible Melville's prospects of success in the parliament of 1690. The club which in the previous session had so battered what court interest there was remained largely intact. During the adjournment the leaders had tried to preserve the solidarity of their following to maintain pressure on the court. As soon as the 1689 parliament had come to an end the court had taken the opportunity of passing in haste the definitive commission for the new court of session. The signet office had opened in some stealth for that express purpose.[47] In retaliation the club's most prominent lawyers tried to disrupt the court of session's proceedings. Both William Hamilton of Whitelaw and James Ogilvy had nurtured hopes of being lords of session and had been alike disappointed. They did their best to discourage advocates from appearing before what they claimed was an illegally constituted court, but their colleagues had their fees to think of, so the campaign met with little success.[48]

The peak of club activity between the sessions of 1689 and 1690 was the address. In this document the opposition requested the king to give assent to all the acts voted in the 1689 parliament, a concession which would have irreparably damaged the power of the crown. Seventy-two persons were persuaded to subscribe.[49] Only an occasional signature was open to suspicion. Sutherland had been one of the court's most consistent supporters but somehow found himself adding his name to the address. Alexander Gordon, provost of Aberdeen and member for the burgh, appears to have signed under a misapprehension when drunk.[50] These apart, the signatories seem to have comprised the hard core of the opposition though one or two club members surprisingly did not sign. Subscription was, in fact, so substantial that initially even the club leaders were alarmed. They feared it might provoke William into dissolving parliament, which was the last thing they wanted at that stage, the existing one in which they had a majority suiting them very nicely. But finally it was decided to present the address, and Annandale, Ross and Skelmorlie took it to London.[51]

Opposition on such a scale in the Scottish parliament came as a surprise to many. It ought not to have done. As the behaviour of Hamilton, Queensberry and Atholl shows the nature of magnate politics, so the composition and conduct of the club illustrates political motivation and tactics at other levels. The club campaign can be represented as the product of frustrated ambition and, to an even greater extent, of downright resentment. And of this resentment there is this to be said: for the most part it was not petty. Many in the 1689 parliament had much to be resentful about. There were those who had suffered forfeiture and risked worse; there were men who, whatever the pretext, had been harried by the previous administration for no reason save personal enmity. Sir Patrick Hume of Polwarth had a place in the long queue of those waiting for forfeitures to be legally rescinded. He told Melville, ' . . . I know that this four and twenty years I have spent my life and estate, and went very near losing both . . . while some of them were at more ease, in more security . . .'[52] In exile he had been as much one of William's advisers as Sir James Dalrymple and Melville but seems for some reason to have been elbowed aside. All he received was the token seat on the privy council which seems to have been the court's idea of winning friends. Polwarth led a distinct section of the club, comprising such men as Forbes of Culloden, Thomas Drummond of Riccarton, John

Dempster of Pitliver and 'Commissary' Munro of Bearscrofts, the latter having without apparent reason lost his place as solicitor-general to Lockhart. These amongst many others found it difficult to stomach the sight of Sir John Dalrymple as lord advocate and the court's chief spokesman. For what had happened there should, it was felt, be some form of retribution even if it amounted to no more than disqualification from office. If every dog can be said to have his day, the Dalrymples were widely taken to have had theirs. Any concept of balancing interests left the bulk of parliament unmoved. Some of those who should have been out were still in and to many of the rank and file this in itself sufficiently justified opposition. A new court which could countenance such a situation was suspect. Its apparent policy drove a wide spectrum of members into opposition, predisposing them to agree on tactics, in order to squeeze out of the court every concession demanded by the votes of the convention and more. There was talk amongst the club of impeaching some who had been involved in the government before the revolution. In particular they had in mind Queensberry, Tarbat, Sir George Mackenzie and, significantly, the Dalrymples, father and son.[53] Queensberry was lying low in apparent safety; Mackenzie had got away to England to the chagrin of many; Tarbat was rightly thought to be worming his way back into favour and the Dalrymples had already succeeded. All this bred dark humours and closed up the rank and file behind the club leaders. But, despite the elevated language of opposition, they were as a body motivated by anger and frustration, not by dedication to principle and abstract constitutional ideas. They set out to demonstrate to William that his intended 'managers' were unable to manage.

A number of the club rank and file and all of its leaders were men who felt they had justifiable claims to places and influence which had been ignored. One afflicted with the most urgent sense of ambition was Sir James Montgomerie of Skelmorlie. Before the fate of the revolution had been decided, he had been involved in raising the western militia for William. At a crucial stage he had succeeded in cutting communications between James and his Scottish administration. In the convention he demonstrated zeal and capacity, being in consequence elected as the barons' commissioner to go to London with Argyll and Dalrymple, taking the offer of the crown to William and Mary. During this visit he was, he later claimed, promised the post of justice clerk. He had actually kissed hands on the appointment but subsequently found himself thwarted by persons unknown though not unsuspected. Dalrymple, his colleague as commissioner, told him his appointment was to be delayed and made consequent on his good behaviour in parliament. Montgomerie then discovered that the justice clerk's place was at the same time being offered to others, also as an incentive to co-operation in the 1689 parliament.[54] This episode, as Montgomerie described it, was typical of court management in 1689 — too clever by half. The aim of this particular instance of sharp practice is dubious. But whether it was directed towards managing parliament by spreading expectation thinly over a wide area, or to reducing competition within the court itself for the benefit, mainly, of the Dalrymples, it was an expensive mistake. All Montgomerie received was a place on the privy council — on a level with Melville's sons whose claims were not so readily apparent. Melville, deficient in most things, was sole secretary. Crawford, with little to commend him but zeal for the Lord, was president of the parliament. Dalrymple, a survivor from the previous administration, whom Montgomerie and Argyll had tried in

London to keep from any position of influence, was lord advocate. His father, as unpopular after exile as before it, was president of the session. To Montgomerie, fevered with ambition to the point of instability, as later appeared, it seemed that his only possible course was to make himself a nuisance and to render Dalrymple's life unpleasant if not unbearable.

Montgomerie and Argyll, Dalrymple's erstwhile colleagues, were fellow sufferers in disappointment whilst Dalrymple had carried off the prizes. Argyll's sole reward in 1689, like that of Montgomerie, had been a place on the privy council. They were not alone in their dissatisfaction. The earls of Annandale and Ross were men of more ambition than ability thirsting for place, influence and profit. Ross was not very much regarded either then or at any other time. Annandale, already embarked on his chosen career as a consistent turncoat, inspired little confidence.[55] Montgomerie was Argyll's cousin and Annandale's brother-in-law. They and Ross seemed to have succumbed to Montgomerie's dominant personality. For the rest 'Skelmorlie carried the bell, though he had neither skill of law, nor experience, never having made any public appearance, yet he was earnest, eloquent and was the chief contriver'.[56]

Significantly they were allied to a group of men who, in the last year of James's reign, had emerged or, as some would have had it, set themselves up, as leaders of the presbyterian interest. Balcarres listed them, adding that they ' . . . were the chief leaders amongst them, until their brethren from Holland met them at London and eclipsed them . . . ' Some evidently resented this. Of the twenty-six named by Balcarres, fourteen were members of the 1689 parliament. Only four of them were not with the opposition. Those four exceptions included Crawford, president of the parliament, and Moncrieff of Reidie who was absent.[57] It seems that, Montgomerie's major disappointment aside, those who had been at all 'eclipsed' went into opposition to make their mark. Amongst them was an extremely able lawyer of forceful personality, William Hamilton of Whitelaw, whose name was to figure prominently in Scottish political in-fighting until his death in 1704. During the whole of this time he was, according to his expectations of office, alternately for or against the court. In the convention he had been the favourite for election as the burghs' representative to take the offer of the crown. Instead Dalrymple had been chosen and in the following parliament Hamilton emerged as the leader of the burgh opposition. Associated with him was James Ogilvy, a younger son of the earl of Findlater, with nothing but legal training and a little family influence to assist him in making his way in the world. He needed to attract attention and on every possible occasion did so, first speaking and voting against James's 'forfaulture' and then achieving prominence in the club. He and Hamilton of Whitelaw were active in promoting the address of 1689 and in trying to sabotage the newly constituted court of session.[58]

Of the many who at this time were professing their allegiance to presbyterianism, not all were equally dedicated and many had no feelings one way or the other. However, there were men who had involved themselves with the club for wholly religious reasons. Zealous presbyterians in close touch with the deprived ministers were working for what they considered to be the rightful church establishment. They entertained a strong and wholly justified suspicion that without political pressure of some kind they would receive little or no satisfaction from William. The number who began to leave the club in 1690 when Melville made religious concessions provides some evidence for the reality of this group, although there were at the time other pressing reasons for joining the court. But in 1689 these presbyterians added voting strength to the club and lent some credibility to the opposition's demands concerning the church settlement. As activists in their own right, however, they were a negligible force, restrained from pressing their religious cause by blackmail on the part of the club leaders who were merely using their votes and reputation. So many shades of religious opinion were represented in the club that the future settlement of the church in Scotland was a divisive issue for the opposition. Until the club leaders had pushed their political offensive against the court as far as they could, they durst not risk any attempt to settle the subject in parliament. Meanwhile they kept the high presbyterians in a state of alarm with rumours of the court's intention of thwarting a presbyterian settlement so that the only hope for presbyterians seemed to lie in supporting the club and trusting them to help when the time came.[59] But the time was to be postponed as long as possible. When presbyterian ministers drew up an address to parliament asking for a church settlement, they were told quite bluntly by the club leaders to wait or they could expect no support either then or for the future,[60] a threat the high presbyterians could not afford to ignore. Their main reason for being in opposition was that they needed all the support they could muster. Crawford later acknowledged that '... the sober presbyterians [in parliament] are for their number so few and inconsiderable ....'[61] Earlier he had judged that throughout the whole of Scotland 'the prelatick party' would certainly be in a majority.[62] So, with a court prepared to resist their kind of settlement, the presbyterians were left with little choice but to stay with the club hoping to come later into their reward.

Another element is discernible in the opposition, although its importance is not easy to assess. Through the whole episode of the revolution and its aftermath there was an accumulation of feeling within the estate of barons against the nobility, the greater nobility particularly. Signs of this can be traced back at least as far as the interregnum.[63] The lairds seem increasingly to have realised that their weakness in relation to the peers could be remedied in parliament. This awareness of new opportunity achieved expression in the persistent demand for increased shire representation[64] and in warnings to the court against handing over the conduct of affairs to the magnates.[65] Holders of baron courts demanded, in 1690, individual votes in parliament as a claim of right notwithstanding their shire representation.[66] Later, at the union, the barons were involved in a manoeuvre to exclude peers' eldest sons from sitting in the United Kingdom parliament as shire representatives.[67] And so it is probably not wholly coincidence that from Darien to the union the estate of barons became the main voting strength of the country party as the nobles and burghs represented that of the court. It is too much to argue that the club could have been any more than a very pale reflection of this assertive attitude. After all, nobles and burgh members were also in support of the club. More probably the discontent had significance only when channelled by events, and only then if the barons were suffering one of their recurrent bouts of disenchantment with the peers. The mechanics of election might have more to do with the comparative independence of the barons, together with the fact that they were somewhat less vulnerable than the burghs to pressure from either the court or the nobles. But tensions certainly existed. If at any time circumstances caused noble opinion to be outweighed by the votes of men of inferior substance, the peers were quick to express resentment. This very likely in its turn angered some of the barons, who were better able than the burghs to express their feelings.[68]

So the opposition had its origins mainly in jealousy, frustration and resentment with a thin sprinkling only of more creditable motives. Mostly these last were religious, but there appeared also a shadowy concept of political, not to say moral, retribution in reaction against a court seemingly bent on the re-establishment of something very like the old firm. Yet the club leaders were able to impose a remarkable discipline on this variegated membership. A prerequisite for joining the club was acceptance of its majority decisions, arrived at in extra-parliamentary meetings, and a willingness to vote in the house accordingly.[69] Tactics were concerted in Penstoun's tavern, where the opposition met twice daily.[70] The absence of committees in the 1689 parliament was a great advantage to the club, enabling it to deprive the court of both initiative and breathing space. Because each operation had been planned in advance, speakers briefed and rising in a pre-arranged order, the court was mostly at a loss.[71] It was this organised opposition together with Hamilton's ambiguous attitude as commissioner which, from the court's point of view, reduced the 1689 session of parliament to a fiasco.

Melville's unenviable task as commissioner in 1690 was to get through parliament, despite the club, some kind of settlement acceptable to William. In his favour were some slight advantages but not many. The king sent him money for 'secret service' and for the payment of troops in Scotland. Unpaid troops were a liability to government and a grievance to the population at large. The Scottish forces had been at free quarter for too long. For fear of violent opposition some Flemish cavalry were moved north and Berkeley's dragoons were posted to the border.[72] After the 1689 parliament an attempt had been made to spread court influence further. Presumably to extend patronage whilst avoiding excessive concentrations of power, the chief offices of state — chancellor, privy seal and lord clerk register — had been put into commission, each set of commissioners representing a range of interests. This principle of 'balance' was applied to the treasury commission and to a range of individual offices from the governorship of Edinburgh Castle to the mastership of works.[73] But this was merely a continuation of the court's policy before the previous parliament. There was no reason why it should have been more effective than the earlier nominations to the privy council. Nor was it. Members of the various commissions did not regard appointment as in any way limiting their freedom of action. Probably more significant and in the long run more effective was the steady creep of the tendrils of patronage and coercion at the lower levels. Dalrymple had recommended for the commissariat of Dunblane provost Hugh Kennedy, member for Stirling, as a man who had been turned out of the magistracy and never failed in a vote. It was necessary, Dalrymple had urged, that members of parliament should be employed in such minor offices and, as far as possible, in the revenue collection.[74] More robust measures were to hand if needed. Should the lord provost of Edinburgh decline to abandon the club in which he had hitherto been prominent, then in Dalrymple's opinion he ought to be brought before the privy council on an excise illegality to tame him.[75] Even so, far too many people remained both dissatisfied and unsubdued.[76]

Melville was given, on paper, virtually full powers for the management of parliament to enable him to tackle this problem of the recalcitrant members. He was allowed to bargain for the support of leading men, 'and what other employment or other gratification you think to promise them in our name we shall fulfil the same . . . ' For taking off any shire or burgh members who seemed worthy of acquisition he had the same guarantee.[77] There is no evidence that he had any success by this means. Such noticeable inroads as were made into the opposition were the result of bargains at the centre. One of the club leaders to go to London after the adjournment of the 1689 parliament had been Hume of Polwarth.[78] His visit had wrought a dramatic change. Before leaving Edinburgh Polwarth had indulged in some rather wild talk about his intentions: that he would strive all he could for presbytery, that though he might be a friend of Melville he proposed to attack the secretary's office and all the prerogatives of the crown. If the king did not go further in redressing the grievances then, in Polwarth's opinion, it would come to cutting throats and the king could go back to Holland and stay there.[79] Yet it is clear that by January 1690 Polwarth had changed sides. By then he was a committed court man concerned to strengthen his own interest, as he said, for the sake of the king's service. Some of his followers went with him and he exerted himself to persuade the rest. Part of the bargain was that this change of sides should be secret, so that in 1690 the Polwarth group functioned as crypto-courtiers.[80]

In terms of management this was the sum of Melville's advantages. There was on the other hand a substantial debit column which seemed to render any court success highly improbable. Hamilton was by now notoriously disobliged. Not only had he been kept out of the chancellorship and whatever else he thought his due, the court had publicly saddled him with the entire blame for the *débâcle* of 1689. His instructions had been published to demonstrate the king's good faith and, as written, without the tacit reservations that had existed, they did seem to point to Hamilton as the sole obstacle to any settlement.[81] The blame was far from being his alone, but naturally Hamilton acknowledged no responsibility at all for the situation which had come about. Not surprisingly he was incensed. At once he entered into an alliance with the opposition, the chief object of which was the destruction of both the Melville and Dalrymple interests.[82] The duke was soon joined by the other magnate groups. After the 1689 parliament Queensberry had made approaches to the court through Murray of Philiphaugh, asking to be consulted before decisions were taken. Murray set out the advantages it was alleged Queensberry would bring to the court. Most discontents, according to this version, had been due to Hamilton, whom the country found intolerable, whereas Queensberry's claim was to be able to unite the nobility and the club in support of the court's measures, thus restoring Scottish affairs to tranquillity. All this was quite beyond the capacity of Queensberry or anyone else, but magnates were seldom disposed to underrate their own influence. Murray hinted that it might even be possible for Queensberry, episcopalian in his leanings, to ally himself with Melville and the presbyterians, healing old wounds in the process. In fact, all that was happening was that the eclipse of Hamilton as a court notable was leading Queensberry to indicate that he was open to offers.[83]

The court was not in the least impressed, so Queensberry changed his tactics. The engrossing of power remained his ultimate objective; it was merely that he proposed to reach it by a different route. He now intended to move against the club leadership with a view to displacing them and taking over the opposition. Success in this venture would damage any similar plans Hamilton might have and wreck Melville's prospects, at the same time enabling Queensberry to bring direct pressure to bear on the court.[84] Such intoxicating visions were premature. The plan's more prosaic outcome was that, before the 1690 session, the groups loosely categorised as 'episcopalian' — those of Queensberry and Atholl — had moved into active opposition as temporary allies of the club, for which purpose those of them who had not already done so brought themselves to take the oaths and enter parliament.[85] Drumlanrig, as Queensberry's Williamite insurance, could not step too far out of line with the court, but he became unmistakably two-faced. To Melville he was openly critical of his father; to other courtiers he was loud in Melville's praise.[86] But he told the king, 'the government is not in very good hands'. According to Drumlanrig, officers of state were inexperienced and oppressive to their political opponents and the episcopalian clergy. This was not the whole truth but it contained enough recognisable substance to appeal to the susceptibilities of William and the English. The object was to gain their support against Queensberry's Scottish rivals, for which purpose it was shrewdly contrived.[87]

For reasons which later emerged, the club's leadership was beginning a campaign aimed at the complete disruption of the 1690 parliament. Their intention was to press demands they were quite sure William would never concede. It was this scheme into which the Queensberry and Atholl interests were drawn.[88] The result was a highly improbable alliance of Queensberry and Atholl with their episcopalian followers, Hamilton in a newly aroused presbyterian fervour, and the club leadership pressing for the establishment of high presbytery in the conviction that it would be flatly refused. They assumed that such pressure on Melville would rapidly bring about his political demise.[89] Taken in conjunction with Queensberry's episcopalianism, his earlier offer of an alliance with Melville and Hamilton's opposition to high presbytery in the 1689 parliament, such manoeuvres have to be seen as nothing more than the magnates' ruthless pursuit of power and influence by whatever means were available.

Melville's task was made harder by the fact that almost his first official duty was to preside over a privy council meeting to issue a proclamation for parliament's further adjournment. Privy councillors with club connections took care to be absent that day and then, according to taste and disposition, blamed the adjournment on either Melville or Stair.[90] It was the fault of neither. Nor was any sinister design involved. The adjournment was due directly to the powerful influence English politics could exert on Scotland. William wrote to Melville: ' . . . You know that we must walk with great circumspection in relation to the parliament of this kingdom [of England]; and that some busy men will endeavour to use the proceedings of one or other of the parliaments to no good ends, if they can but wrest their actions to any bad aspect; and therefore, as our predecessors did, upon serious considerations, order so as that, for the most part, both parliaments should not sit at the same time . . . .'[91] Portland put it more plainly. It was advisable that the English parliament should rise before religion was settled in Scotland.[92]

And as far as religion was concerned, the court's freedom of action in Scotland was being steadily eroded. English politicians and convocation were worried by the fact and so, therefore, was William. To Scottish presbyterians of extreme dedication it had seemed plain that if they had correctly judged the court's intentions, the sort of settlement they wanted in Scotland would call for something close to a religious revolution, perhaps with measures even more drastic than those needed in the state. A movement to this end had already begun and, in the forefront of it, transformed into a key figure, was Crawford, president of the parliament. The earl's activities and correspondence show his religious views at this time to have bordered on the fanatical. He acknowledged the virtue of moderation but placed on it a highly individual interpretation. Extreme presbyterians were in the eyes of God the only ones fit to rule the church. Furthermore, they alone were politically reliable. To the achievement of a high presbyterian settlement all else must be sacrificed. So, to Crawford, 'moderation' meant little more than the avoidance of actual bodily harm to episcopalian or conforming clergy. The president was by no means an able man. Occasionally he bordered on the incompetent and his political weight was minimal, but in prejudging the Scottish church settlement his role was probably decisive. He posed as the personification of official integrity whilst in fact erecting a screen behind which zealous presbyterians, with his connivance and even active cooperation, purged the Scottish church.[93] The absence of any official settlement made their task easier if illegal.

Those who were not 'high' presbyterians, whether episcopalians or those who thought of church government as a 'thing indifferent', had cause to be worried. A minority of dedicated and resolute presbyterians, dominated by a conviction of the divine ordination of presbytery and the 'intrinsic power' of the church, were carrying out pre-emptive measures. Their conviction that they were chosen and that their hour had come fortified them for the struggle. Fears of an episcopalian reaction and English interference stimulated them to energetic, even desperate, proceedings. Conforming ministers in the south-west had already been 'rabbled' out of their churches and manses, but still it was clear that in any church assembly to which all clergy were admitted the high presbyterians would be a minority. For a group committed to a belief in the supremacy of general assemblies this was an embarrassment. They had to ensure that in any such gathering they were dominant, and only if the ministers deprived in 1661, and no others, were reinstated would this be possible. A high presbyterian rump of about sixty members could then control the church judicatories, using their power to exclude others looked on as undesirable. So ministers not finding favour with the rump had to be stigmatised as ungodly, disloyal or both.

Within the administration Crawford, who between sessions was acting president of the council, was a most zealous agent in carrying through an unofficial and illegal purge, odd though such terms may seem when used in connection with the privy council.[94] His views at this time were so extreme that they seriously worried William's closest advisers. Of the former *émigrés* who retained any influence, none was really an extremist. Generally they favoured a presbyterian settlement involving a compromise with the conforming clergy. All were careful to dissociate themselves entirely from talk of 'intrinsic power', accepting that no ecclesiastical claims incompatible with the royal prerogative ought to be tolerated. Nor did they relish any settlement by which extreme presbyterians were put in a position to harass or oppress episcopalians.[95] Melville, for instance, was a presbyterian but of fundamentally moderate inclinations, sufficiently close to the court in England and the lobbying in progress there to realise the need for caution. Continually he urged Crawford to exercise restraint.[96] Melville's own position at court was not completely secure and he was too closely identified with the presbyterian cause for him to want affairs taken to extremes. For the time being he enjoyed some court favour and retained a certain standing with the presbyterians. He had no desire to forfeit either.

Consequently he tried to curb underhand presbyterian activities in Scotland. With Carstares's support he warned Crawford of the necessity for circumspection and better public relations. Allegations were reaching London that the council was depriving ministers for reasons other than moral turpitude or mere inadequacy. It was even said that some were being turned out for very little cause at all. Since Crawford was alleged to be asserting in Scotland that he acted on orders from London, those at court wanted to know in more detail what was going on. Until some satisfactory answers were forthcoming it was difficult for Melville and Carstares to avoid, at the least, embarrassment.[97]

Greatly to their consternation, Crawford met all such exhortations with vague generalities transformed occasionally into flights of exaltation as he contemplated a vision of presbytery restored in all its rigour.[98] The rule of presbytery and its accompanying discipline was the will of God. No concessions to the conforming clergy were possible because they were a majority who could, and very likely would, prevent the establishment of a true church government. In fact in his opinion the council, hampered by episcopalians ill-advisedly appointed to it, were treating the conforming clergy, if anything, too leniently.[99]

Carstares let Crawford know of the climate of opinion in England where convocation and other influential groups were determinedly pressing the cause of the Scottish episcopalians. Crawford's accounts of merely routine and moderate investigations of the clergy were being flatly contradicted in London. Care was needed because the establishment of presbytery was by no means such a foregone conclusion as he seemed to assume.[100] Crawford remained unmoved. ' . . . The message you delivered by the secretary's order,' he wrote to Carstares, 'anent the pressures on our king by the adversaries to our interest is almost as weighty to me as that by Samuel to Eli, to which I shall give the same answer. It is the Lord, let him do what seemeth to him good; for though I laboured in vain, and have spent my strength for nought, yet I trust my judgement is with the Lord and my work with God . . . ,'[101] But this other-worldly tone did not preclude more practical calculations. If enquiry into Scottish proceedings could be staved off until convocation was dissolved, Crawford thought, subsequent clamour over a *fait accompli* would have less effect.[102] Meanwhile, behind all this dishonest and time-consuming verbiage, the court's chances of obtaining a moderate agreement based on a compromise over ministers and patronages were rapidly diminishing.[103] Some settlement had to be reached, since the situation in Scotland could not be allowed to slide any further. To obtain a settlement was Melville's allotted task.

In so far as Melville succeeded in anything in the parliament of 1690 — and his main achievements were a religious and constitutional settlement most unwelcome to the king followed by the eventual crippling of the opposition — it was for two reasons. An almost total capitulation to club demands over the settlement satisfied many of the rank and file, leaving them little else to ask for. And then the bulk of the club was sent running to the court for shelter at the discovery that their erstwhile leaders had been involved in jacobite conspiracy.

The lord commissioner began the parliament by giving royal assent to two acts which in the previous session Hamilton had refused to touch: those for the abolition of the royal ecclesiastical supremacy and the restoration of the ministers deprived in 1661.[104] The new Hamilton of the club had since proved to be very much in favour of both acts.[105]

The increased strength of the opposition, reinforced by jacobites, episcopalians and Hamilton, left Melville little choice but to give way. This apparent evidence of royal surrender together with Polwarth's undercover activities split the opposition and produced a realignment in parliament. A majority including fifty-two former members of the club and amounting, according to Polwarth, to 'about ninety-five in all' was now prepared to support Melville if he continued to give way on the major issues. In opposition remained twenty of the club joined by forty-six others, episcopalian and generally reputed jacobite. Polwarth thought the rumour had some substance in that all but twenty of them were jacobites. These figures indicate an influx into parliament since the previous session of something like thirty, an increase attributable directly to the tactics of the higher nobility. Most were undoubtedly members of the Queensberry and Atholl interests.[106]

Although the structure of the opposition had changed, Melville's predicament was still the same — he remained under strong pressure to give ground. He next signified assent to an act concerning parliamentary committees which came just within the terms of his instructions. The articles were to go, being replaced by *ad hoc* committees of which officers of state were to be non-voting members only.[107] At this the opposition showed signs of further debility. The election of committees which directly followed this act indicated a marked decline in the influence of the club,[108] but still, the main drift of affairs could not be mistaken. Tarbat wrote to William that had Melville not acceded to the club's demands he would have lost a large number of votes and unless he went further, establishing high presbyterianism and abolishing patronages, his newly acquired majority would disappear.[109] Tarbat was of course right.

The lord commissioner was himself uneasy, being conscious of having gone faster and further in concessions than some of the king's verbal restrictions permitted. William received Melville's apologies for his having given premature assent to the act abolishing royal ecclesiastical supremacy. The commissioner tried to put the blame on the repeated adjournments which had damaged his chances in Scotland however necessary they might have been for England. He continued: ' . . . for my part, I see no remedy, if your majesty do not speedily satisfy your people, but all must go in confusion . . . I am very positive in this, if all the statesmen in Britain should be of another sentiment, that it is truly your majesty's interest at this time not to displease the people on this head as to their church government, for nothing else can satisfy . . . ,'[110] The only way of achieving any kind of settlement whilst keeping his own head above water was for Melville to accept the strict presbyterian establishment that the opposition was still clamouring for as its last weapon. Not that the majority wanted an extreme settlement, but under strong pressure in parliament it was difficult to stand out for moderation. Despite his reference to 'your people', Melville must have known that the problem was a parliamentary rather than a national one, although naturally he was unwilling to admit this to the king. For his own political benefit as much as anything else he was being driven in one direction. He could not survive in politics without the high presbyterians, who would support him as long as he seemed to be doing their work within the court. And if he gave assent to a presbyterian settlement, moderate or not, he could hang on in parliament and he might be able to survive any consequent royal displeasure, particularly since the *émigré* lobby favoured a presbyterian settlement of some kind. But if he tried to block, or even moderate, the extreme demands being made in parliament, as a political figure he was finished. Accordingly the church settlement was proceeded with.[111] An act for a church establishment was drafted to meet opposition demands and a copy sent to the king. William, with Carstares's advice, found some fairly substantial criticism to make. A commentary was prepared for Melville's guidance which illuminates William's views on Scottish church government at the time. He was not by this stage concerned to obstruct any presbyterian settlement, but merely to inhibit presbyterian delusions of grandeur. He was opposed to encroachment on the royal prerogative by the establishment of anything like a rival authority, so there should be no hint in the settlement of 'intrinsic power'. Nor in the act should there be any assertion of the essentially presbyterian character of the Scottish reformation since this would constitute a gratuitous offence to those who did not share that view. And he wanted episcopalians to enjoy a degree of toleration no less than that granted to presbyterians in England.[112] William's views had no effect on events in parliament. The situation had already developed too far. On 7 June the act ratifying the confession of faith and settling presbyterian church government was passed[113], giving the general assembly, or others deputed by them, the right 'to try and purge out all inefficient, negligent, scandalous and erroneous ministers'. Time was to show that almost anybody could be brought within one or other of those categories. Patronages were abolished and an act passed abandoning the 'yule vacance'.[114] The disappearance of the Christmas holidays was always a mark of presbyterian ascendancy.

So it was in part by a wholesale surrender that Melville was able to bring the 1690 session to a close. In a tidy parliamentary sense it had been an achievement. There had been no *impasse*. A settlement had been reached and twenty-eight months' cess granted,[115] but the outcome was not at all satisfactory to William. From the point of view of Anglo-Scottish relations it was a near disaster. Melville realised how the settlement would look in London and towards the end of the session he wrote apologetically to the queen, William being then in Ireland, trying to convince her that no other course had been open to him.[116] And he was right, from both public and personal aspects. From the first, all that had faced Melville was a choice between two evils. Surrender was the only way of avoiding another disruption of parliament, which was not to be risked unless William was prepared to contemplate another election. For very good reasons he was not; he would merely have been exchanging one set of problems for another. Had earlier schemes of management been different, perhaps the situation could have been avoided, but all that was in the past. As far as Melville's own position was concerned, the original appraisal that had been behind his appointment as commissioner, namely that he was the man to take the edge off presbyterian demands, had proved wholly erroneous. By this time Melville's presbyterian support was dependent on how much he could deliver and without such support he was a political nonentity. Surrender was therefore in his own interest. It transformed him into the man on whom the presbyterians felt they could rely and conceivably, in the long run, this could increase his importance at court.

The other reason for the opposition's collapse was the near-farcical conspiracy known as 'Montgomerie's plot'. This scheme came to light as a consequence of internal bickering combined with a loss of nerve on the part of some of the conspirators. Skelmorlie, almost demented by frustration and the contempt with which he and the other club emissaries together with their address had been treated at court after the 1689 parliament, had converted some of his colleagues to a scheme by which they hoped to seize power. If something was to be done, then it was, as Skelmorlie saw it, an urgent priority since the managers might succeed in establishing a grip on parliament which would deprive him of the power even to be a nuisance. He abandoned his earlier fear of a possible dissolution. So, in 1690, the opposition set out to disrupt parliament by increasingly extravagant demands which they thought William would have to refuse. They had in mind not only the establishment of high presbyterianism and the abolition of the articles, but a demand for the appointment of lords of session by parliamentary vote, *habeas corpus* and free speech in parliament. Should these be blocked, then either parliament would turn back to James, after first bargaining with him for acceptable terms, or William would be forced to a dissolution and new elections which the club with jacobite support might hope to carry.[117] Those who went along with the scheme, whether tentatively or with zeal, were those who were becoming almost as frustrated as Skelmorlie himself: Ross, Annandale, Ogilvy and Hamilton of Whitelaw. Their understanding of the plan was that, on a promise of suitable gratification, they would be prepared to accept the principle of James's restoration and henceforth work to overturn the revolution. A proposed scheme of government was actually drawn up allocating their prospective rewards. All the plums were kept for Skelmorlie and his intimates. It was this germ of a conspiracy for which Skelmorlie then tried to enlist the support of Queensberry and other dissatisfied elements. Atholl was certainly involved to some degree. Meetings were held at which Queensberry was represented, but how far he was ever, if at all, committed is impossible to say. Men of his standing did not easily abandon themselves to projects with any element of risk. For them the crucial questions were: how much chance of success did the scheme have and how much were they going to get out of it? These were considerations which did not weigh so heavily with such reckless spirits as Skelmorlie, driven by forces beyond rational calculation. There was not, therefore, much common ground between the club leaders and others, and what little chance of cohesion existed was ended by the puerile episode of the black box.

Skelmorlie had been in touch with James, whose reply to the plotters' scheme, together with promises of office, commissions to act on his behalf and other such credentials were despatched to Scotland in a sealed black box. Skelmorlie opened the box, alone. He then confided to Ross, Annandale and Arran, all by this time in the conspiracy up to their necks, that there were items in the box which it would be inadvisable for Queensberry and his followers to see or know of; the Queensberry interest had been ignored in the proposed scheme of government and it was better that the duke should be kept in ignorance of the fact. Skelmorlie's inner circle agreed to the making up of another black box containing a selection, less controversial, of the papers from James. They then arranged a meeting at Atholl's lodgings where the box was to be opened formally and with all due propriety in the presence of the interested parties. The occasion was far from a success.

Almost inevitably there had been talk. Arran had discovered that the conspirators had not abtained James's commission for him to be a general as they had promised, consequently he stayed away from the meeting. Nor was Queensberry present. At the opening of the box, apart from the leading conspirators, none were there save Atholl, Linlithgow, Breadalbane and Balcarres. From the beginning of the proceedings these few collaborators suspected that the box had been tampered with, a suspicion later confirmed to Linlithgow by James's messenger.[118] Then when the contents of the box were examined, it appeared that Ross was to be designated chancellor, Annandale both lord commissioner and treasurer, Skelmorlie sole secretary of state and Ogilvy and Whitelaw were to be joint presidents of session. There was no inducement here for either Queensberry or Atholl. After the opening of the black box there remained only the barest shadow of a conspiracy. It was the old story of the plotters' being unable to resist making claims too greedy to be realistic. When the success of the entire scheme depended on magnate collaboration, this was an unfortunate temptation to yield to. Outside Skelmorlie's own group only Arran and Murray were unable to sever themselves completely from the plot. It would have been in character for Arran to be unable to stop meddling. Perhaps Murray had the same disease. Of the rest a later apologist wrote that in 1690 they ' . . . joined in several votes with the club, but when the rumour arose of their new set of state, wherein they were neglected, they abhorred both their treachery and the late king's ingratitude and declared they would neither be for concurring with a French or Irish invasion or a highland depredation but would support the present government . . . ,'[119]

Gossip and suspicion were quick to circulate in Edinburgh. Rumours reached Melville, and by June he was telling the queen of a conspiracy which was real enough though not provable in law.[120] Then, individually, Ross and Annandale cracked. They tried to insure themselves by confessing but preserving, as they said, their honour, by not turning crown evidence against their fellow conspirators.[121] Skelmorlie, too, promised to tell all, but by a mixture of brazenness and prevarication fended off enquiry until he was able to flee the country.[122] The conspirators were treated with far greater consideration than might have been expected and certainly more than they deserved. It is true that William was notoriously lenient to those caught plotting against him, but rumour had it that Melville and Dalrymple aimed at picking up some support from the splinters of the conspiracy and so were opposed to any retribution, however mild.[123] There is also the possibility that Melville was after bigger fish, holding off in the hope of some evidence against Queensberry. If so he was disappointed. Melville was rapidly learning the tricks of political combat in Scotland but Queensberry had been at it longer.

When the news of the plot broke, what was left of the opposition scurried for shelter. Towards the end of the session parliament had been reduced to a very thin house, down to sixty, dwindling steadily and prepared to vote almost anything the court wanted. Once in full control, the managers conducted themselves with some arrogance, rushing business through, often with scant regard for proper procedure. Sir Alexander Bruce remarked that the act providing for the visitation of universities 'was passed with such a precipitous haste as that it was read three times in half an hour and immediately passed . . . I never seen [sic] such a man in my life as this Earl Crawford is for fervour and warmth of zeal. No argument can hamper him. He calls incessantly for the vote even when an act is by order to be mended in some things yet will not have the patience to let it be read over again, and the clerks are prepared and fitted for the purpose, for they upon the first word of command start up to the reading of the roll. Then immediately is it interrupted and amendments sometimes made after it is begun to be voted. Never was there such informality in the world . . . ,'[124] It was in this sparse gathering that a vote of twenty-eight months' cess was pushed through and a list of forfeitures rescinded without, as some thought, the legal investigation and care necessary.[125]

So the parliament of 1690 did not end in further stalemate. A settlement of sorts was reached, though both the means and the result left much to be desired. Save on the part of a few dedicated presbyterians, there appeared virtually no consistency or adherence to any principle apart from that of self-interest. It is difficult to claim for the court a success in management or to attribute to dedication a high presbyterian church settlement forced through in part by episcopalians hoping for a totally different outcome. Presbyterian aims were achieved, but quite fortuitously. Their success was due to the close association of the Scottish bishops with James's government, to magnate jealousies, fumbling management, lack of a properly organised court interest, the resentment of the excluded and the determination of certain second rank families to establish themselves, if possible, as major ones. They owed their coveted settlement, in fact, to a combination of other people's ambition, ignorance and miscalculation.

To the political situation of 1689 and 1690, apart from the abolition of the articles and its consequences for the Scottish parliament, two significant developments can be traced. Curiously enough the most important result of the session of 1690 was the religious settlement — or if not the settlement itself, then at least the more unsavoury aspects of its enforcement. The presbyterians were never free from suspicion — too frequently justified — of harassing or even persecuting the episcopalian and conform clergy. Yet English sympathies were with the espiscopalians and it became too easy for dissatisfied Scotsmen seeking English support for changes in the Scottish government to take up the religious issue as a false beard, to pose as champions of a fair deal for episcopalians. Of course they were nothing of the kind. They were merely making use of an obvious tactic whilst at the same time trying to impart a shoddy veneer of respectability to the competition for self-advancement. That rivalry carried on in this way became so keen and malicious was a symptom of the second important consequence of the revolution. After the events of 1690 the magnates had fallen into some discredit and so found it inadvisable to appear in person on the political scene. This could have been seen as good riddance but the natural political ballast had been dangerously lightened, giving rise to an unstable situation. The problem of the future composition of the Scottish court party and the distribution of power within it became extremely complicated as men of lesser substance had to perform the tasks of management. Their lack of political weight made them in theory less troublesome to the crown, whose functionaries they were intended to be. William favoured this kind of delegation which could, although mistakenly, have been seen as a solution to the magnate problem. Such ministries constituted a permanent invitation to challenge, not only from magnates who resented exclusion, but from men with no more standing than themselves who would normally have been pecking on the fringes of schemes made by their betters. Such a situation gave hope to those who would not otherwise have entertained it. The spectrum of possible court arrangements became wider and consequently the choice seemed more unpredictable. In these circumstances ministerial concoctions could function with any degree of efficiency only if they were openly and firmly supported by a sovereign who knew his own mind and was determined to see his will complied with. William, through lack of attention, bad advice, his own ignorance and inertia, did not fulfil these requirements. As a result, then, of the peculiar development of the revolution settlement and the virtual royal abdication which, owing to William's other distractions, accompanied it, a major share of influence in Scotland fell into the hands of two of the lesser families each bent on establishing itself as a major power in the kingdom. The struggle between the Dalrymples and Melville's family for political dominance could not fail to provide opportunity to others standing in the numerous ranks of discontent.

NOTES

1. *APS*, ix, 98.
2. *CSP (Dom.), 1689-90*, 126-8, 31 May 1689.
3. *HMCR Johnstone MSS*, 144, Carstares to Crawford, 7 Dec. 1689; *ib.*, 149-50, Melville to same, 16 Jan. [1690]; *ib.*, 150, Carstares to same, 16 Jan. 1690; *ib.*, 146, draft of letter from Crawford to a minister, 26 Dec. 1689.
4. Hamilton's.
5. *Memoirs*, 50.
6. *Proceedings*, i, 119-20.
7. *APS*, ix, 98.
8. The 130 included Hamilton as commissioner and Crawford as president. It seems impossible to arrive at completely precise figures. The address was signed not only by people who afterwards disclaimed their action but also by members not apparently present in the parliament of 1689. Any statement of the total strength of parliament in 1689 has to be received with caution. Both *APS* and *Returns*, ii, when compared with each other and with literary evidence, leave doubt over whether particular members were present or not. There was very likely a significant amount of unrecorded intermittent absence apart from those members who merely went home. See Appendix A, column 1 and cf. Halliday, 'The club . . . ', 148. However, active club support seems to have been a majority: 69/129 (53.5%) if one disregards the commissioner.
9. Crawford thought ten: *Leven and Melville Papers*, 78-81, to Melville, 25 Jun. [1689]. Dalrymple claimed to recollect twelve supporters and three abstainers: *ib.*, 81-5, to same, 25 Jun. 1689.
10. Balcarres, *Memoirs*, 50.
11. *Leven and Melville Papers*, 23, James Stewart to Melville, 24 May 1689.
12. Macpherson, App., 189, Dalrymple to Hamilton, 18 May 1689.
13. *Leven and Melville Papers*, 52, Crawford to Melville, 11 Jun. 1689.
14. *Ib.*, 95, Polwarth to Melville, 27 Jun. [16]89.
15. NLS, MS 7012, 87, Sir F. Scott to Tweeddale, 7 Jun. [16]90.
16. *Leven and Melville Papers*, 87-8, Dalrymple to Melville, 26 Jun. 1689.
17. *Proceedings*, i, 133.
18. *Leven and Melville Papers*, 63, Dalrymple to Melville, 18 Jun. 1689; *Proceedings*, i, 135-7.
19. *Ib.*, 140-41, 146-7.
20. *Ib.*, 158-9. For William's letter: *APS*, ix, 102.
21. *Proceedings*, i, 176-8, 181. The final appointments to the court of session are listed in *Leven and Melville Papers*, 307.
22. *Ib.*, 166, Dalrymple to Melville, 12 Jul. 1689; *Proceedings*, i, 160, 163-5. See above, p. 9, n. 21.
23. *Ib.*, 141, 144-5, 149.
24. *Ib.*, 152.
25. *Leven and Melville Papers*, 138, Dalrymple to Melville, 2 Jul. 1689.
26. See below, pp. 39-41.
27. *Proceedings*, i, 172, 17 Jul. 1689.
28. He was instead sent for a period as envoy to Brandenburg: Foxcroft, *Halifax*, ii, 204.
29. SRO, GD26, xiii, 28, [D. Nairn] to [Leven?], 15 Oct. 1689. See below, p. 54.
30. NUL, Portland, PwA 2441/74q; *Proceedings*, i, 182, 184-5, 189-90, 192.
31. *Ib.*, 144-5, 163.
32. *Ib.*, 149-54 passim and 175; *APS*, ix, 104.
33. *CSP (Dom.), 1689-90*, 126-8.
34. NUL, Portland, PwA 2441/74q.
35. Fraser, *Melvilles*, ii, 111-13, Dalrymple to Melville, 23 Jun. 1689; *Leven and Melville Papers*, 81, same to same, 25 Jun. 1689.

36. *Ib.*, 58, Hamilton to same, 18 Jun. 1689; *ib.*, 181, Dalrymple to same, 20 Jul. 1689; NUL, Portland, PwA 2441/74q.
37. *Leven and Melville Papers*, 166, Dalrymple to Melville, 12 Jul. 1689; Fraser, *Melvilles*, ii, 136-7, Melville to Hamilton, 17 Jul. [1689]; *ib.*, 138-9, same to same, 27 Jul. [1689].
38. *Leven and Melville Papers*, 157, Dalrymple to Melville, 11 Jul. 1689; *ib.*, same to same, 20 Jul. 1689; *ib.*, 182, Sir W. Lockhart to same, 22 Jul. 1689.
39. *Ib.*, 201, same to same, 27 Jul. 1689; *ib.*, 203, Hamilton to same, 28 Jul. 1689; *ib.*, 214, Dalrymple to same, 30 Jul. 1689; *ib.*, 218, Hamilton to same, 1 Aug. 1689; *ib.*, 229, same to same, 2 Aug. 1689.
40. *Ib.*, 249, same to same, 13 Aug. 1689; *ib.*, 251, Dalrymple to same, 13 Aug. 1689.
41. *Ib.*, 398, Sir W. Lockhart to [James Melville], 8 Feb. [1690].
42. *Ib.*, 361, Argyll to Melville, 2 Jan. 1689/90; *ib.*, 409, same to same, 20 Feb. 1690.
43. *Ib.*, 367, Dalrymple to same, 10 Jan. 1690; *ib.*, 369, same to same, 14 Jan. 1690; *ib.*, 389, Crawford to same, 4 Feb. 1690.
44. *Ib.*, 404-5, Dalrymple to same, 15 Feb. 1690; *ib.*, 407, same to same, 18 Feb. 1690.
45. *Ib.*, 418, Melville to the king, 18 Mar. 1690.
46. *Ib*; *CSP (Dom.), 1691-2*, 200-204, same to same, 26 Mar. [1690].
47. *Leven and Melville Papers*, 299, Crawford to Melville, 12 Oct. 1689; *ib.*, 303, same to same, 15 Oct. 1689; *ib.*, 306, Melville to Crawford, 20 Oct. 1689; *ib.*, 312, Dalrymple to Melville, 2 Nov. 1689.
48. *Ib.*, 320, Sir W. Anstruther to same, 12 Nov. 1689.
49. Halliday, 'The club . . . ', 155. For the list of signatories: Fraser, *Melvilles*, iii, 209-12. See Appendix A and note 8 above.
50. *Leven and Melville Papers*, 345, Dalrymple to Melville, 8 Aug. 1689. As a former *émigré*, Sutherland might have found himself subjected to conflicting pressures: Sir W. Fraser, *The Sutherland Book*, 3 vols. (Edinburgh, 1892), i, 298.
51. *Leven and Melville Papers*, 251, Dalrymple to Melville, 13 Aug. 1689.
52. *Ib.*, 42-3, 6 Jun. 1689. Not all felt, or at least gave expression to, the same bitterness. Sir John Maxwell of Pollock had refused the test of 1681 and suffered imprisonment rather than pay the fine: Sir W. Fraser, *Memoirs of the Maxwells of Pollock*, 2 vols. (Edinburgh, 1863), i, 80-85. Nevertheless he was steady in support of the administration in 1689 and remained so, earning his appointment to the court of session and the post of lord justice clerk in 1699.
53. *Leven and Melville Papers*, 52, Crawford to Melville, 11 Jun. 1689.
54. *Ib.*, 189, Montgomerie to same, 23 Jul. [1689]. G. W. T. Omond, *The Lord Advocates of Scotland* (Edinburgh, 1883), i, 236-7, has it that Montgomerie refused the post but gives no reference.
55. Balcarres, *Memoirs*, 10-11, 13, and see below, pp. 113, 126.
56. NUL, Portland, PwA 2441/74q.
57. *Memoirs*, 12-13. Those in the 1689 parliament and not members of the club were, in addition to Crawford and Moncrieff, the earl of Tarras and William Anstruther, younger, of Anstruther. With the opposition were Glencairn, Ross, Bargany, Montgomerie of Skelmorlie, William Hamilton, Thomas Drummond of Riccarton, Patrick Murray of Livingston, George Stirling, Alexander Spittall of Leuchat, Adam Cockburn of Ormiston.
58. See above, p. 29.
59. *Leven and Melville Papers*, 90-92, Crawford to Melville, 27 Jun. 1689.
60. *Ib.*, 87-8, Dalrymple to same, 26 Jun. 1689; *ib.*, 100-103, same to same, 28 Jun. 1689.
61. *HMCR Johnstone MSS*, 156-7, to a minister, 26 Feb. 1690.
62. *Ib.*, 153-4, 31 Jan. 1690. On this topic see Thomas Maxwell, 'Presbyterian and Episcopalian in 1688', *RSCHS*, xiii, 25-37. There was propaganda and wishful thinking on both sides, but it seems clear that presbyterians were in a minority when measured against episcopalians and those who did not greatly care.
63. See, e.g., T. G. Snoddy, *Sir John Scot, Lord Scotstarvit* (Edinburgh, 1968), chap. 8.
64. Formal proposals for increased representation were made in 1690, 1704 and 1705. The first became effective: *APS*, ix, 152.
65. E.g., *Leven and Melville Papers*, 29, Polwarth to Melville, 27 May 1689.
66. *CSP (Doml.), 1690-91*, 17, 24 May 1690.
67. *Marchmont Papers*, iii, 444, Seafield to [Godolphin?], 28 Jan. 1707.
68. Some significance, however, could be read into the relative strength of the club in the three estates although this could be misleading. Subject to the qualifications made in n.8 above, the club strength was made up as follows: peers: 10/33 (30.3%); barons: 25/42 (59.5%); burghs: 34/54 (63%). There is perhaps not much that can usefully be said about the club's geographical distribution. Not all members of the club shared the same motives for opposition, which confuses any geographical analysis. Low attendance probably distorts the picture, too. The north was generally under-represented. There were no members at

all from Caithness or Cromarty. Elsewhere, Kinross and Clackmannan provided no representatives. Numerical comparisons can become ludicrous when a 50% club return from one district means no more than that one member out of two was in opposition. The shires of Inverness, Peebles, Perth and the stewartry of Kirkcudbright came into this category. But the club was quite strongly represented (over 50%) in some S.W. districts (Ayr, Dumfries, Dumbarton, Lanark), in some border districts (Berwick, Roxburgh, Selkirk), the Firth of Forth and east coast (Edinburgh, Fife and Linlithgow) where the numbers were greatly swollen by the Fife members — ten out of fourteen of whom were in opposition — and a few northern patches (Banff, Elgin and Sutherland). Yet some of this was due to local political interest as much as to anything. The earl of Argyll was with the club and so were the two members from Argyll. Led by James Ogilvy, the Banffshire contingent of three were with the club. Taken together, the outlook and behaviour of Queensberry and Annandale could explain the return of four club members out of the five from Dumfriesshire. *Cf.* below, pp. 179-80.

69. NUL, Portland, PwA 2441/74q.
70. *Leven and Melville Papers*, 81-5, Dalrymple to Melville, 25 Jun. 1689.
71. *Ib.*, 90-92, Crawford to same, 27 Jun. 1689. See above, pp. 25-6.
72. *Ib.*, 427, Ranelagh to same, 19 Apr. 1690; *ib.*, 427-9, Portland to same, 22 Apr. [1690].
73. *Ib.*, 340, 7 Dec. 1689, lists the commissions.
74. *Ib.*, 369, Dalrymple to Melville, 14 Jan. 1690.
75. *Ib.*, 362, same to same, 4 Jan. 1690.
76. *Ib.*, 372, same to same, 16 Jan. 1690; *ib.*, 387, same to same, 30 Jan. 1690; *ib.*, 388, same to same, 31 Jan. 1690; *ib.*, 402, Polwarth to the king, 11 Feb. 1690.
77. *Ib.*, 417, Melville's instructions, Feb. 1690.
78. *Ib.*, 261, Polwarth to the king, 20 Aug. 1689.
79. *Ib*; *ib.*, 269, T. Dunbar to Melville, 4 Sep. 1689; *ib.*, 291, Sir W. Lockhart to same, [Sep. 1689].
80. *Ib.*, 365, Polwarth to same, 7 Jan. 1690; *ib.*, Sir W. Lockhart to same, 30 Dec. 1689; *ib.*, 407, Dalrymple to same, 18 Feb. 1690; *CSP (Dom.), 1689-90*, 495-6, Polwarth and Culloden to the king, 6 Mar. 1690; *ib.*, 510-11, Polwarth to same, 14 Mar. 1690.
81. *Leven and Melville Papers*, 311, Melville to the presbyterian ministers, Oct. 1689; Fraser, *Melvilles*, ii, 144-5, 9 Jan. 1689/90; Balcarres, *Memoirs*, 50.
82. *Ib.*, 56-8.
83. *Leven and Melville Papers*, 284, Philiphaugh to Melville, 12 Sep. 1689; *ib.*, 285, same to same, 14 Sep. 1689.
84. *Ib.*, 357, Crawford to same, 26 Dec. 1689, reporting what Strathmore had told his son, Glamis.
85. NUL, Portland, PwA 2441/74q.
86. Macpherson, App., 193-5, Melville to the king, 20 Mar. 1690; *Leven and Melville Papers*, 444, D. Nairn to Leven, 19 Jun. 1690.
87. *CSP (Dom.), 1689-90*, 530, Drumlanrig to the king, 29 Mar. 1690.
88. Balcarres, *Memoirs*, 56-8.
89. Macpherson, App., 200-201, Polwarth to the king, 25 Apr. 1690. Wodrow's view was that Queensberry, Hamilton and Atholl favoured the highest degree of presbyterianism in the hope that its rigours would alienate many from it: *Analecta*, i, 197, 7 Apr. [1690].
90. *CSP (Dom.), 1691-2*, 186-8, Melville to the king, 20 Mar. [1690].
91. *Leven and Melville Papers*, 420, 20 Mar. 1690.
92. *Ib.*, 427, Portland to Melville, 22 Apr. 1690.
93. See below, n. 94 and pp. 55-6.
94. Balcarres, *Memoirs*, 52-3; *The Register of the Privy Council of Scotland, 1689*, series 3, xiv, Intro., xvii-xxi *et passim*. Most deprivations seem to have been on the ground that the incumbent had omitted or refused to pray for William and Mary, a requirement imposed by the convention. The charges brought cannot always be taken at face value, being technicalities which would otherwise have been ignored. Both Carstares and Melville were worried about these measures, which could lead one to suppose that there was something to worry about. By 7 Nov. 1689, 182 ministers had been deprived, officially at any rate, for neglecting to pray for William and Mary: Dunlop, *Carstares*, 67. For specific examples: Drummond and Bulloch, *The Scottish Church*, 5-7. D. H. Whiteford, 'Jacobitism as a factor in Presbyterian-Episcopalian relationships . . . ', *RSCHS*, xvi, in claiming that ministers were expelled only for refusing to pray for William and Mary, seems to overlook the 'conform clergy' whose treatment caused the greatest concern in both Scotland and England. He seems, too, to place too much reliance on presbyterian justifications of proceedings and on council records which represent the official version only. The concern of Melville and Carstares, together with Crawford's attitude, seem to indicate proceedings at variance with the official record.

95. Japikse, ii, 599-603, Polwarth to Bentinck, 8 Feb. 1688; *Carstares S.P.*, 38-42, 'Hints to the King'. For Portland's views: *Leven and Melville Papers*, 435, Portland to Melville, 15/25 May [16]90.
96. E.g., *ib.*, 210, to Crawford, 30 Jul. 1689; *HMCR Johnstone MSS*, 140, to same, 10 Aug. [1689].
97. *Ib.*, 139-40, to same, 30 Jul [1689]; *ib.*, 142, to same, 31 Oct. 1689; *ib.*, 144, Carstares to same, 7 Dec. 1689; *ib.*, 145-6, same to same, 12 Dec. 1689.
98. *Leven and Melville Papers*, 105, Crawford to Melville, 29 Jun. 1689; *ib.*, 139, same to same, 6 Jul. 1689; *ib.*, 171, same to same, 18 Jul. [1689]; *ib.*, 187, same to same, 23 Jul. 1689; *ib.*, 273, same to same, 5 Sep. 1689; *HMCR Johnstone MSS*, 152-3, same to [Carstares], 30 Jan. 1690; *ib.*, 156, same to [Melville], 20 Feb. 1690; *ib.*, 149, same to Carstares (draft), 4 Jan. 1690.
99. *Ib.*, 163, Crawford to the king, 1690 (draft) adequately expresses his views.
100. *Ib.*, 144, Carstares to Crawford, 7 Dec. 1689.
101. *Ib.*, 144-5, 10 Dec. 1689 (draft).
102. *Carstares S.P.*, 125-7, to Carstares, 19 Dec. 1689.
103. *Leven and Melville Papers*, 430, Sir W. Lockhart to the master of Melville, 29 Apr. 1690; *ib.*, W. Cunningham to Cardross, 9 Aug. 1689; *ib.*, 435, Portland to Melville, 15/25 May [16]90; *HMCR Johnstone MSS*, 161-2, Linlithgow to Strathmore, 20 Nov. 1690; *ib.*, 163-6, Crawford to the king, [c. late 1690?].
104. *APS*, ix, 111, 25 Apr. 1690.
105. *CSP (Dom.)*, *1691-92*, 256-8, Melville to the king, 27 Apr. [1690].
106. Macpherson, App., 200-201, Polwarth to same, 25 Apr. 1690. See Appendix A. There seems to have been an effective increase of 31 members between 1689 and the first parliament of 1690. 36 new members appeared, whilst five of the previous parliament were missing. Newcomers amongst the nobility are easily identified and number 16, including Rutherfurd who had already signed the address though absent from the 1689 session. Members of the other estates who had attended specifically to reinforce the club cannot be identified with any certainty.
107. *APS.*, ix, 113, 8 May 1690.
108. Halliday, 'The club . . . ', 158.
109. Macpherson, App., 201-204, 13 May 1690.
110. *Ib.*, App., 195-8, 29 Apr. 1691 [*sic* for 1690].
111. *APS* ix, 117-31.
112. *Leven and Melville Papers*, 436-8, the king to Melville, 22 May 1690.
113. *APS*, ix, 133-4.
114. *Ib.*, 196, 19 Jul. 1690.
115. *Ib.*, 134.
116. *Leven and Melville Papers*, 456-7, 2 Jul. 1690.
117. Balcarres, *Memoirs*, 56-8.
118. *Ib.*, 61-3. Balcarres was in the plot although Skelmorlie was one of the privy councillors who had earlier refused him bail: *Leven and Melville Papers*, 372, Dalrymple to Melville, 16 Jan. 1690.
119. NUL, Portland, PwA 2441/74q.
120. *Ib.*, PwA 2337, 24 Jun. 1690.
121. *Leven and Melville Papers*, 453, Jun. [1690]; *ib.*, 484, Jul. 1690; *ib.*, 506-13, Aug. 1690. The giving of full information was one condition of Annandale's pardon: Fraser, *Annandale Book*, ii, 17.
122. *Ib.*, 478-9, Melville to Skelmorlie, 26 Jul. 1690; *ib.*, 479-80, same to the queen, 29 Jul. [1690]; *ib.*, 492-3, same to same, 16 Aug. 1690; *ib.*, 523-5, 6/16 Sep. 1690.
123. *Ib.*, 499, Sir W. Lockhart to Melville, 24 Aug. 1690.
124. NLS, MS 7012, 98, to Tweeddale, 28 Jun. 1690; *ib.*, 102, same to same, 1 and 3 Jul. 1690.
125. *Ib.*, 87, Sir F. Scott to same, 7 Jun. [16]90; *ib.*, 102, Sir A. Bruce to same, 1 and 3 Jul. 1690.

3
Melville and the Dalrymples

FROM 1690 onwards the full impact began to be felt of the deficiencies in the Scottish political system and the crown's weakness in the face of them.

Whatever opinion one might hold of the way in which it had been concluded, the religious settlement itself was not indefensible. It had, admittedly, placed episcopalians at a grave disadvantage, but after Scotland's recent history that would have been difficult to avoid. Episcopalians were, with varying degrees of justification, open to suspicion of being jacobite.[1] In a situation where compromise between two parties seems impossible, then, failing the imposition of a settlement from above, it seems that civil strife can be avoided only by the rapid domination of one group by the other, however repugnant to the liberal outlook such a solution might be. One can argue that this is what was attempted in Scotland. The big mistake lay in the alienation of religious moderates, the 'conform clergy' and their sympathisers, who would have accepted most settlements. They were cut off by a combination of doctrinaire theology, an unchristian desire for vengeance and the opportunism of a relatively small group of Scots prepared to extend their own influence by acting as political mentors and guardians to the high presbyterian ministers.

The initial identification of the ruling group with harsh discrimination against episcopalians and conforming clergy dictated the tactics of their opponents when appealing, as they were bound to do, for English help in remodelling Scottish ministries. It was their pretence that they were interested merely in restoring the religious balance and establishing some more tolerant system in Scotland. This religious pretext for interesting the English in Scottish affairs introduced into Scotland complications even more extraordinary than hitherto. Yet, despite all their posturing, Scotsmen, whether as individuals or in groups, showed themselves quite uninterested in the solution of the kingdom's problems. Their aim lay in merely using them to their opponents' disadvantage. The less powerful families were dissatisfied, restless and concerned to improve their status. Those in office were determined to defend their positions, accumulating more power if it was at all possible. Scottish politics became a jousting ground for rival families. Behind all this conflict there brooded the magnates, temporarily in disrepute, resenting their exclusion and resorting to subterranean intrigues to secure the re-establishment of their influence. Such was the reality of Scottish politics in spite of the myth that political divisions were due to the animosity between presbyterians and episcopalians. This fiction took a long time to dispel, proving, as it did, useful to so many people.

After the first parliament of 1690 the main rivals within the Scottish court were the two families who, with more or less enthusiasm, had collaborated in establishing the revolution settlement — the earl of Melville's family and the Dalrymples. Now they were to embark on a struggle for predominance within the administration. This situation was allowed to arise because William had no liking for the magnates whose conduct had put them out of royal favour and the king had decided to employ families of lesser rank, more ready, in theory, to carry out his wishes. But in the framing of this policy too many Scottish realities had been overlooked. Had William been more aware of the situation in Scotland, more diligent in enquiry and more ready to insist on obedience from his servants, the administration would not have decayed so rapidly. If functionaries are to be delegated to control a kingdom they ought not to be left completely unsupervised. William used rival 'trusties' and left them to it, an admirable recipe for the trouble that developed.

Oddly enough the pivot of this conflict between Melville and the Dalrymples was a peer who had not been in the forefront of politics since the end of the convention. He was now destined to become a man of some significance. The career of John Hay, second earl and later first marquess of Tweeddale, was to influence Scottish politics up to and beyond the union. Echoes of his short-lived pre-eminence in Scotland were still thinly vibrating long after 1707. Tweeddale had only once before approached the threshold of predominance in Scottish politics but had been stopped short through challenging Lauderdale prematurely. He had never enjoyed that long period of influence and high office necessary for establishing his family as a great interest. In 1688 he was already an ageing man and, although a member of both the treasury commission and the privy council, he had been for the past eighteen months an absentee. This semi-retirement was due partly to political caution and partly to illness. He had the gravel and was troubled by headaches for which consignments of pills and 'cephalic powders' were despatched to him from London.[2]

Tweeddale was in most respects a reasonable man. He was intelligent, a good husband and father and beloved of his grandchildren. Politically he inclined to moderate courses, composing for observers an image of complete integrity and steadiness of purpose. Within his own family this was his reputation. Perhaps this was how he thought of himself; yet outsiders had categorised him as a shifty politician—'selfish and pliant'.[3] He was certainly not, as for example Annandale, a blatant and unrepentant turncoat. Nevertheless he was prone to glissade on political slopes, coming to rest wherever it seemed most secure. Burnet characterised him fairly charitably: ' . . . He understood all the interests and concerns of Scotland well: he had a great stock of knowledge, with a mild and obliging temper. He was of a blameless, or rather an exemplary life in all respects. He had loose thoughts both of civil and ecclesiastical government, and seemed to think that whatever form soever was uppermost was to be complied with. He had been in Cromwell's parliament, and had abjured the royal family, which lay heavy on him. But the disputes about the guardianship of the duchess of Monmouth and her elder sister, to which he pretended in the right of his wife, who was their father's sister, drew him into that compliance which brought a great cloud upon him: though he was in all respects the ablest and worthiest man of the nobility he was too cautious and fearful...'[4] Perhaps the root of the matter was that, like many others, he was too impecunious for much of the time to afford principles, although he tried, whenever possible, to behave temperately.[5]

Parts of Tweeddale's career illustrate perfectly the tenuous threads which kept some

Scotsmen bound to the idea of union with England. It seems that, having once been involved in a union project, they tended to return to the idea as a possible way out of every crisis. As one of Lauderdale's henchmen in the earlier years of the restoration, Tweeddale, with Kincardine, had become involved in the secretary's abortive union scheme.[6] Trade seemed to be Lauderdale's motive in pursuing a union but this was merely a cover for political ends. His intention was to strengthen the English monarchy, an aim which might even have originated with Tweeddale, whose influence over Lauderdale at that time was considerable.[7] In 1689, certainly, Tweeddale's resurrection of the idea of union owed nothing to trade and was due to his avowed priorities of military and political security and a moderate religious settlement. It may have been that the Cromwellian union under which he had served his political apprenticeship, and to which he occasionally referred with something like nostalgia, had made a lasting impression on him. His enthusiasm for union never died though his hopes must have come perilously close to doing so. Union, in fact, manifested itself to Tweeddale as the solution to almost any problem.

Like other Scottish politicians, Tweeddale initially saw William's intervention in 1688 as likely to modify James's position rather than altogether dislodge him. Unlike others he felt no call to take hasty action. There was in fact really very little he could do, being out of circulation and lacking the weight to compete with the magnates for political influence. When it became clear that William had come to stay, Tweeddale accepted the fact, having no patience with scruples over loyalty to James, especially when they appeared within his own family.[8] Tweeddale's political leanings at the start of the revolution were determined largely by his personal animosities. He bore malice to Sir George Lockhart, the president of the court of session, and his predecessor, Stair, who had both, as he saw it, denied him justice in his litigation before 1688. For the same reason he was disinclined to co-operate with either Queensberry or Hamilton. And, whatever the extent of Melville's influence, collaboration between him and Tweeddale was out of the question, the two of them being involved in a long-standing territorial rivalry, later to impinge seriously on national politics. On the whole, until developments proved him wrong, Tweeddale was inclined to see an alliance with Atholl as his best route back to influence. Nevertheless, when Atholl allowed himself to be outmanoeuvred, Tweeddale was very quick to abandon any association with such a sinking interest.

Although ready to deplore unbridled self-seeking in others, Tweeddale did his utmost for himself and his family. His best proved to be not good enough. Other politicians were able to pursue their own interest in London. Tweeddale had to depend on his eldest son, Yester, who was sadly out of his depth at court and, for that matter, in most other places. From William's arrival to the meeting of the Scottish convention, Tweeddale was a diligent but frustrated correspondent. He glimpsed the opportunities as they seemed to open, knew whom to lobby, whose friendship ought to be cultivated and how to set about attracting favourable attention at the new court. His aim was to restore his own finances and to provide for his family throughout its entire ramifications. On all this he laid emphasis in his letters to Yester. Out of the pickings available his son had to get something for himself: the governorship of the Bass Rock was spoken of, the mint or even the sheriffdom of East Lothian. Tweeddale's other sons, David and Alexander, needed to be pushed in their military careers. The scruples David had developed about his oath of allegiance to James had to be overridden and kept quiet. Tweeddale himself felt he had claims to a pension and to a more important post than a seat at the treasury board.[9] Under his father's guidance from Edinburgh, Yester was expected to achieve all this. Tweeddale found it like digging with a wet sponge. Yester was, and to the end of his life remained, almost entirely devoid, not of ambition, but of the necessary drive and initiative for political success. Outside his own family he was stiff and unbending in personal relations which, in seventeenth-century politics, rendered him ineffective. A certain degree of correctness in his political behaviour gained him, in time, some respect, but long before that his immediate political associates looked on him as one of the crosses they had to bear. In 1689-90 Tweeddale needed all the patience he could muster to cope with his eldest son. After providing him with all the advice, ammunition and encouragement he could, but to no avail, he was driven to lamenting what he described as Yester's 'abstraction from persons'. Tweeddale knew that unless the right people were solicited one did not get a job.[10] So Yester was doomed to disappointment.

Meanwhile Tweeddale made use of such tactics as were possible in Edinburgh. As one of the treasury lords remaining in Scotland, he firmly declined to warrant expenses at the rate of £400 per head for each of the privy councillors going to London for no other reason than to advance their own interest. Tweeddale argued that he had no power to warrant anything during the emergency. The privy councillors had to go at their own expense and were not pleased,[11] but Tweeddale had evaded the responsibility for an improper use of public money. The legalistic argument he had used was not, however, necessarily binding in all circumstances. He was quick enough to warrant the despatch of powder to Londonderry, taking care to let William know of it. Shrewsbury sent him formal thanks for the prompt service rendered.[12]

Tweeddale put his English friends and acquaintances to as much use as he could. Some he had corresponded with regularly. He had exchanged letters with Fauconberg since they had served on their respective union commissions in the 1660s. He had been less frequently in contact with others though, as usual, bearing them in mind on convivial occasions when toasts were drunk: Halifax, Devonshire, Preston, Sir James Hay, Henry Sydney and, at a price, everybody's recourse in time of financial need, Sir Stephen Fox. Schomberg, he fancied, might be useful, especially for military advancement. He urged Yester to cultivate his acquaintance for the sake of the family's prospects in the army. Of the people who had been in exile, he knew several well from the old days. Polwarth had been formerly a political ally but in 1689 Tweeddale must have regarded him as otherwise committed. Burnet was well enough disposed. Then, although bearing animosity towards him, Tweeddale was well acquainted with Sir James Dalrymple of Stair and was realistic enough to overlook their quarrel if circumstances required it, as they seemed to do. As a comparatively minor peer he could signify nothing outside an organised interest. An alliance with the Dalrymples would make a useful start. And whilst not personally acquainted, he had heard that James Johnston would be a significant voice to have in one's favour. Tweeddale indicated all these possibilities to Yester, though without discernible effect.[13]

But it stands to Tweeddale's credit that he concerned himself seriously about the wellbeing of Scotland. He was one of the few Scottish politicians to do so. What frightened him was the likely prospect of a breakdown of government, or the seizure of power by some extreme party leading almost inevitably to violence.[14] Two courses of action occurred to him to be used in conjunction: the formation of a moderate group to hold the balance in the convention and the disinterment of his old policy of union with England. A centre party could, he thought, be created from the moderate elements of both presbyterians and episcopalians — the 'anti-testers' as he categorised them. He had talked to many of them about it before they left for London: Scott of Thirlestane, Murray of Blackbarony and others. His decision to make his peace with Dalrymple of Stair was part of this scheme. Tweeddale thought of the Dalrymples as essentially voices for moderation in that, with their own welfare at stake, they would always be unwilling to commit themselves too far to any one side. What he knew of the post-revolution attitude of Sir John supported this view. The news from London that Sir James was involved with the high presbyterians — the 'violent party' — greatly disturbed Tweeddale when he overcame his initial incredulity.[15] However, the centre party failed to materialise. Those Tweeddale expected to compose it were either not elected to the convention at all or proved to be absentees. He deplored the calculated withdrawal of Queensberry and Atholl who could have brought some weight to a moderate party, but the magnates, of course, were not thinking in those terms.

It began to look as though Tweeddale would have to rely completely on the union project as the only available solution to Scotland's problems both immediate and long-term. Typically, he did not lack personal motives. A union might dilute the power of the magnates in Scotland and men of lesser status would then count for more, as they did in England. Tweeddale nurtured hopes that a revived union project would move him, as a former union man, to the centre of affairs. It did, indeed, bring him some increased though very short-lived attention.[16] But Tweeddale had powerful reasons for union quite unconnected with his own private interest. It seemed to him the only way in which violence in Scotland could be contained. Any attempt to settle Scottish church government whilst so many things were still in doubt could hardly do other than lead to trouble. Constitutional rule in Scotland, rather than a permanent state of emergency, and a moderate church settlement could be achieved, he thought, only within an Anglo-Scottish union. He was right. A separate kingdom of Scotland was too small to reduce violent factions to size, there being too many with the ambition to be big fish in a little pond. Neither presbyterians nor episcopalians felt secure enough either to tolerate or ignore the other. So a new union project was to become a necessity and Tweeddale was one of the first with the prescience to realise it. He was sure that a union would provide a structure within which both moderate presbyterians and episcopalians could again achieve unity.[17]

Tweeddale's initial moves in this project were coy rather than clandestine. He wanted the source of the proposal to be as far as possible secret, he said. Yet, to provide Yester with an opportunity of speaking to William, since he seemed incapable of creating his own chances, Tweeddale concocted an address from East Lothian for his son to present. The style and origin of the address must have given at least some of the game away but it was in this that the proposal was first aired. William was asked to propose a union '... that we be not hereafter left open by the advantage may be taken of our distinct and different laws and customs and exercise of government whereby methods are taken by the enemies of our peace and tranquillity to raise standing armies in either kingdom by which the other may be threatened or enforced to submit to alterations in their religion or diminution of their liberty or foreign forces be brought in either for the subversion of the religion and liberty of both which were a work worthy of your highness . . .',[18] Tweeddale obviously appreciated the close connection between English and Scottish affairs and had taken the opportunity of expressing it, though perhaps rather extravagantly.

Yester was instructed to show the address to Halifax, Fauconberg and Sir James Hay before presenting it, in the hope that they could be persuaded to broach the topic to William as if independently.[19] Meanwhile Tweeddale himself wrote to a variety of people to enlist their support. He thought the proposal for union would come better from English sources: then the convention would debate it more readily than a suggestion originating in Scotland.[20] Another idea which Tweeddale fancied would improve the project's chances in the convention was an increase in the representation of the estate of barons. It would help to counter the influence of the nobility whose titles, he thought, made them sluggish over issues such as union which would affect their status.[21] This seemed a reasonable conjecture at the time but curious in view of the voting pattern of 1706-7, when a majority of the nobles voted for union whilst a majority of the barons opposed it. Tweeddale was correct in assuming that self-interest was the main determinant. He could hardly have been expected to predict that in 1706 it would point in a different direction.

William's subsequent letter to the Scottish convention did recommend union to them in terms which reflected Tweeddale's line of thought: security, religion and liberty. Tweeddale was delighted, detecting signs of Fauconberg's and Sir James Hay's having used their influence with William in favour of union.[22] Significantly, trade seemed to have no part in the calculations of 1689. Tweeddale's motives were entirely political and religious. Likewise the attitudes of others to union were determined by its probable effect on their own aims, personal, political or religious. Trade was not mentioned.

Tweeddale thought that the union project should receive priority in the convention, preceding any religious settlement and creating a better atmosphere in which such a decision could be taken. The revolution had provided an opportunity for union to be settled whilst there was no certainty of good prospects under the new dispensation, whereas any delay would lead to the project's being strangled by the growth of vested interests in a separate kingdom. A proposal was, in fact, made in the convention to proceed with the union scheme before any other aspect of a settlement was attempted, but the motives behind it were different from Tweeddale's. The suggestion emanated from elements who wanted an excuse for indefinite delay and recognised in union an excellent device for the purpose. As Balcarres later told James, this move was defeated because each group in the convention acted strictly in accordance with its own sectional interest and complete priority to union seemed of tactical benefit to few.[23] Balcarres's observation was, arguably, applicable to all attempts at union but it was certainly accurate for 1689. When the topic was first broached Hamilton, then in London, took an immediate and well-publicised dislike to it [24] which Balcarres attributed to his hopes of dominating a separate Scottish kingdom — a not unlikely explanation. The presbyterians, obsessed by one of their recurrent fears of the Church of England, had no great hankering for union with a bishop-ridden kingdom. They took alarm at the East Lothian address, which they were inclined to regard as a move in an episcopalian plot.[25] Not until the convention and the revolution itself seemed to be under threat from Gordon and Dundee did they change their minds, beginning then to share Tweeddale's conviction that only union could preserve them from invasion and counter-revolution. More politically-motivated 'revolution men' also went along with the plan for fear Scotland should become jacobite and completely independent of England.[26] Even so, both these groups were determined that priority should be accorded to other safeguards — the abolition of episcopacy, for instance, lest any union treaty should have the effect of preserving episcopacy in Scotland and hence the possibility of increasing the power of the crown.[27] But, not surprisingly, those who first embraced the idea of union in 1688-9 were episcopalian in sympathy, such as Tarbat and Queensberry, connected in various ways with the late administration.[28] In the existing political climate their prospects in a separate Scottish kingdom could not have been very highly rated. Tarbat, of course, always welcomed any tactical diversion for its own sake, but that aside, their probable calculation was that within a united kingdom the atmosphere would be more congenial to their views and their chances of regaining influence greatly improved.

For such a variety of reasons, once the crown was settled, the convention voted an act naming commissioners to negotiate for a union, the question of church government being made, on presbyterian insistence, a reserved topic.[29] But the project was killed in England, where parliament made no attempt to follow the Scots' initiative. With the settlement of the Scottish succession there was less immediate incentive for England to attempt a union and other business seemed more pressing. The Scottish parliament of 1689, moreover, had presented a spectacle so unedifying that it could only have reinforced any English reluctance to join in a union.

But before the union scheme had completely lost its momentum Tweeddale had taken what, in retrospect, was a significant step which made him briefly a key figure in Scottish politics. Moments of pessimism apart, he never abandoned hope of squeezing from the revolution something substantial for himself and his family,[30] though he knew that few, if any, influential Scots would go out of their way to oblige him. Much to his chagrin, Hamilton, as lord commissioner, even had Selkirk's name given precedence over Tweeddale's on the roll of parliament. This set him brooding on the family's fortunes. Perhaps, he mused to Yester, it was time they sought promotion in the peerage, being a more ancient family than many with superior titles.[31] But his ability to exercise influence in or from Scotland was negligible whilst Yester in England remained ineffective. Finally Tweeddale concluded that the best course was to concentrate his scheming on England, where his influence was probably greater than at home. Anyone wanting to leave Scotland when it was not strictly allowable usually planned a visit to 'the bath', and Tweeddale could with reason plead that he was in need of the waters. His visit was organised with an eye to strict economy. Yester was deputed to make arrangements in London, his father apparently trusting him in domestic organisation. Tweeddale wanted an unfurnished house further out of town than was fashionable, but for that reason cheaper. Linen, tableware and other necessary accoutrements could then be sent down from Scotland, a more economical arrangement than renting furnished lodgings. Tweeddale obviously had in mind something more than a visit to a spa.[32] He was to stay in England for two and a half years, during which period his solicitations were most effective. When he returned to Scotland it was on the eve of his appointment as lord chancellor.

Tweeddale's decision to go to England seems to have been at first a private venture — an attempt to acquire at least something for his family after Yester's failure. It seemed hard that, out of what had promised to be a great political upheaval, neither Tweeddale nor any of his connections had benefited and he was not prepared merely to accept such a situation. So his original plan was to solicit in person where he could be most effective. But, once in England, he found himself involved in a scheme to modify fundamentally the management of Scotland. The project was variously motivated. There lay behind it, naturally, the same resentments that had produced the 'club' opposition. Those with jobs were, if possible, to be deprived of them for the benefit of others. Another aim, the official one, spoken of rather more than felt but at least partially sincere, was to secure better treatment for episcopalian and conforming clergy, for whom a toleration was sought equal to that enjoyed by presbyterian dissenters in England. When this topic was kept in the forefront of lobbying, the Anglo-Scottish political network was at its most effective. Burnet with his customary energy busied himself in this campaign.[33] Nottingham was notoriously disturbed about proceedings in Scotland 'which did much affect the conformists here'[34] and wherein they would concern themselves . . .'[35] Convocation in its generally angry mood had been outspoken on this amongst other topics. Even Crawford was driven to take note of 'the concern of those in England that our [church] government be modelled with some charity to such as only differ from us in the constitution of our church'.[36]

To the English members of this lobby at least Tweeddale seemed an ideal choice to act as a brake on any acceleration towards immoderate policies in Scotland. In office he could provide a much-needed extra channel of information concerning events there. Should the suspicions entertained by the English prove to be well-founded, then they would have grounds for some action. As it was, their efforts to find out what was going on were always blocked by Melville's equivocation and Crawford's strenuous denial, as acting president of the council, of the disturbing unofficial accounts — for they were more than rumours — in continual circulation. Nevertheless, this English lobby was active enough to be regarded in Scotland as a threat to the fate of presbyterianism. Hume of Polwarth wrote from London, where he had gone after the 1689 parliamentary session: 'Our parliament is basely misrepresented by Tarbat, Tweeddale and folk of that gang . . . They and the English junto, viz., Halifax, Danby, Shrewsbury, Nottingham and Portland, are taking methods for breaking our parliament, calling a new one, and reducing what is done in our church government . . .'[37] This was little more than a scare story, however, since a dissolution of parliament was one of the last things the court wanted.

But one aim of the 'toleration' lobby was to have Tweeddale appointed joint secretary of state as Melville's colleague. Rumours of this design had been strong enough to disturb and even alarm Crawford and others during and after the 1689 parliament, making them apprehensive for the fate of presbytery.[38] Such talk was current until early in 1690. By February the plan seems to have collapsed completely, since William thought the appointment of two Scottish secretaries an unnecessary complication.[39] In the face of this obstacle the forces ranged behind Tweeddale were probably not sufficiently strong nor in great enough earnest. Aside from his English acquaintances, Tweeddale had little interest of his own and not much support from any Scottish group. Such as there was came only from his personal friends or a few others touting for English support. There was no other reason why significant numbers of discontented Scots should push Tweeddale's fortunes when his advancement seemed unlikely to lead to more general changes. To the Dalrymples he could represent only a threat. Queensberry, Atholl and Hamilton had other schemes for the parliament of 1690 — tactical support for a presbyterian settlement being one — and their prospects did not yet appear as bleak as they were later to become.[40] So Tweeddale was given a place on the treasury commission in December 1689 as a consolation prize and was expected to be satisfied,[41] Yester having already been put on the privy council. These two appointments represented the total gain made by Tweeddale's family as an immediate consequence of the revolution. Tweeddale valued his new appointment so little that he decided he would be better off in England, where he could still command some influence, rather than in Scotland, neglected and open to systematic misrepresentation by those who resented his presence in the treasury.

For some time after the settlement of 1690 William virtually ignored Scotland. Affairs there were seemingly to be left to sort themselves out, which they did but in a fashion most unwelcome to the excluded, even oppressed, Scottish interests and to Englishmen with some concern for Scotland. Amongst the many uncomfortable consequences of the Scottish parliaments of 1689 and 1690 was the rise to power of a very narrow clique. To the English the most obvious sign of this was the severity of the presbyterian reaction after the church settlement of 1690. Episcopalians and conforming clergy found it galling and even moderate presbyterians thought much of what was done ill-advised.

Amongst the last group was Melville who knew very well what was taking place, but there was little he could do to moderate high presbyterian zeal without risk to his own position. As the man who had touched with the sceptre the act setting up the presbyterian establishment, he had acquired for himself a political strength which he had never before possessed and which he was reluctant to forfeit. Most of his new-found influence depended on his standing with the strict presbyterians whom he durst not alienate any more than he durst offend the political 'revolution men' to whom they were firmly linked. Any offence to either would deprive him and his family of the power and profit to which they were rapidly becoming addicted. All he could do was urge moderation, privately and ineffectually, inside Scotland whilst doing what he could to keep such domestic scandals from the neighbours.[42] Behind this protective screen the presbyterian vendetta against the episcopalian and 'conform clergy' tended to run to extremes. Some presbyterians were eager to pounce on conforming clergy for minor technical breaches of the law whilst themselves showing scant respect for the civil power. There were ministers who declined to read parliament's proclamation for a fast, denying the competence of any secular authority in such a field. On the wilder fringes there was earnest talk of the covenant with declarations of intent that, as a religious duty, the reform of the Church of England should be embarked upon as soon as possible.[43] A purge of the entire ministry of the church and the staffs of schools and universities was instituted.[44] There were frequent allegations that exemplary ministers were being ejected on trumped up charges, despite the king's stated wishes when the act for church government had been passed. Since then William's views had been once more set out in Carmichael's instructions as commissioner to the general assembly of 1690, the first to be held after the settlement. Its composition served merely to emphasise the limitations of the church establishment. The 'general assembly' consisted of the sixty restored ministers — the 'Antediluvians' — with fifty-six other ministers they had handpicked and forty-seven elders. A majority of parishes was unrepresented and whole areas were ignored.[45]

The echoes which reached England of proceedings against episcopalian and other ministers and caused disquiet were no more than a part of the story, connected with the religious revolution to which Melville had found himself an accessory. There were other developments which seemed on the way to changing the character of the revolution settlement itself. As Melville and his family began to show signs of ambition and determination to rise, they sought to restrict power to an increasingly tight circle quite contrary to William's original intention of creating a balance of political forces. The administration seemed to be turning into the exclusive preserve of the Melville family and those prepared to follow their lead in claiming a monopoly of devotion to the new king. It was also marked by a surprising degree of pettiness and incompetence springing from ambition outstripping ability.

Skelmorlie's plot provided the initial impetus towards this government by clique. It became easy to label any kind of opposition as disaffection, so extending Melville's power inside and outside parliament.[46] In the name of the emergency, measures could be taken against individuals who were merely personal enemies or family rivals. Melville and his sons took full advantage of this to harass Tweeddale's family and connections. The two peers nurtured rival claims to property and superiorities in Dunfermline, in Fife and Midlothian. Such local rivalries exacerbated this notorious family feud which in one form or another continued until after the union.[47] Tweeddale's daughter, Margaret, countess of Roxburghe, was convinced that Melville's family were her father's irreconcilable enemies,[48] and her opinion seemed to be justified by events. At the revolution the rivalry became even more bitter. Apart from Melville's animosity to Tweeddale himself, he was engaged in a permanent competition with the Rothes interest for the political control of Fife[49] and with the Roxburghe interest in East Lothian. In 1690 lord Leslie and Roxburghe were both minors and under Tweeddale's wing. Hence for the time being he was virtually the political head of the three combined interests. And petty though it seems, the fact that Tweeddale's younger sons and his older grandsons were professional soldiers was also important. Melville's son, Leven, had military pretentions and gave the impression of bearing malice to others in the military trade as potential rivals.

Such scores were paid off during the security measures following the discovery of Skelmorlie's plot. Tweeddale's son, David, had resigned his commission in the horse guards through scruples over his oath of allegiance to James. This could have left him open to reasonable suspicion although in fact he had remained quite passive and had neither done, nor had any intention of doing, anything remotely savouring of plotting against the revolution. He was knocked up at five in the morning by Leven's troops, arrested and confined in the Edinburgh Tolbooth — an uncommon experience for one of his rank, even when under suspicion.[50] Yester was accused directly to the king of being involved in the club opposition within the privy council. Both he and his brother were the subjects of ill-founded rumours of sedition.[51] On the pretext that the Roxburghe territory of Teviotdale was a hotbed of conspiracy, the government selected it for special attention. Troops were quartered there.[52] Dragoons from Cardross's regiment were searching in and about Kelso, one of the centres of Roxburghe influence, taking parole extensively and seizing horses and arms for no very good reason. Mail was indiscriminately broken open in a way which occasioned comment even at a time when all private letters were regarded as insecure. In the meantime Melville caused some consternation in England by abandoning his routine reports to the court, which was kept in ignorance of Scottish developments.[53] Such rigour seems excessive when one recalls the consideration extended to Ross and Annandale as self-confessed conspirators.

The main object of all this seemed to be the crippling of rival interests. Despite Tweeddale's place on the treasury commission and Yester's in the privy council, they were to be regarded as competitors and outside the administration. But signs of tension had appeared within the ministry itself. Melville's family and the Dalrymples, the two interests which had originally formed the nucleus of the new court, had become overtly antagonistic.[54] After the settlement of 1690 the administration of the kingdom seems quite rapidly to have been drawn into the hands of a so-called 'secret committee', an inner clique of Melville, his sons and their anti-Dalrymple allies: Cardross, Ruthven, Polwarth, Forbes of Culloden and James Stewart.[55] Melville's political and religious stance virtually ensured him the support of those who had no time for the Dalrymples. So, whatever his private inclinations, Melville would probably have been drawn into the anti-Dalrymple group. The signs are, though, that neither Melville nor his sons showed any reluctance at the breach between the two families. Somewhat later Tweeddale complained to James Johnston, justifiably, of Melville's growing monopoly in the administration and the profit he and his family were making at the expense of the public interest.[56] There is no doubt that the Melville interest was determinedly on the make and that after the other interests had been subdued the Dalrymples were one of their biggest obstacles. But the latters' ambition was not in the least quenched by the caballing that was taking place against them, so inevitably the struggle between the court and the opposition was transformed into a tension within the court itself. In the late summer and autumn of 1690 the full strength of the Melville faction was exerted to squeeze Sir John Dalrymple from the innermost processes of government. Sir John was said to be trying, in retaliation, to build up a party against Melville.[57]

To remove friction from the Scottish court, changes were necessary. Each side, of course, saw itself as the natural vehicle of government and its opponents as the disruptive force. The administration could begin to make a show of working only if it were composed in the first instance of men prepared to co-operate. Not that that was the end of it but it was the necessary starting point. The officers of state had either to be dragooned into collaboration, which was hardly possible, or reshuffled, to reduce internal conflict. For changes to be secured, of whatever kind, William had to be persuaded either that Scotland had become a nuisance or that unless action were taken it would quickly become one. The latter was a forlorn hope. William had no desire to know what was happening in Scotland, much less what could conceivably happen. For that reason he had left management under the general oversight of Portland advised, as always, by Carstares. Both knew of the king's lack of interest in Scottish affairs and so were determined not to trouble him if they could help it and, moreover, other things being equal, they favoured the Melville group which was undoubtedly Williamite. For that assurance they were prepared to overlook a great deal. As long as major scandals could be avoided they would continue to support Melville, allowing William to think all was, if not altogether well, at least not far wrong. So any opposition to Melville had some very arid terrain to cross before it could hope to bring about changes.

Yet, though circumstances had combined to entrench Melville deep in the administration, it had become increasingly difficult for anyone to defend his conduct. It was not only his attitude to church affairs which invited attack. Scotland's financial state, never healthy, was being rapidly worsened by incompetence, or at least inexperience, and excessive self-seeking.[58] A second parliament had been found necessary later in 1690, the grant made by the first having proved inadequate.[59] Despite this augmentation of revenue there was at no time much money available for public needs. What cash appeared was collected by Melville directly from the receivers.[60] Sizable arrears must have been due to him from his allowances as commissioner and his salary as secretary of state. But the salaries of most other officers of state were also unpaid whilst Melville's demands were granted a higher priority even than the army, which lacked both pay and subsistence. Troops had been for too long at free quarter to the great dissatisfaction of landowners and tenants. In November 1690 the muster-master reported that over a period of twelve months the army had received only four months' subsistence and two months' pay. As a result the condition of Scottish troops was quite deplorable.[61] During the same period, however, the treasury's squandering of money was notorious.[62]

This lack of concern for the army led to a major quarrel between Melville and Mackay, the commander-in-chief. So many obstacles to efficiency were being erected in Mackay's path that there were rumours of a deliberate attempt to discredit him so that his job would be available for Leven. Melville was very free with criticism of Mackay, behind his back, for allowing too many abuses to arise in the army,[63] but abuses and the army were inseparable in the seventeenth century and that issue was largely irrelevant. At length Mackay was driven to request permission to go to London to state his and the army's grievances. Leave was granted, but to delay the general's departure Melville held up the warrant as long as he could.[64]

Such contrivances, charges and counter-charges became weapons in the struggle between Melville and those trying to dislodge him. In so far as the latter were all opposed to Melville, they drifted into a very loose alliance. Sir William Hamilton summed it up for Ogilvy: ' . . . The breach between the two Dalrymples and M[elville] is greater than ever. Young D[alrymple] they say has joined with d[uke] Q[ueensberry] and m[arquess] Atholl for breaking down of M[elville] and presbytery together; and yesterday eight days they sent Douglas of Gogar to the king to negotiate with lieutenant-general D[ouglas] in their behalf with the king. The morrow after W. Carstares was sent by Melville to counter them . . . '[65]

In fact, solidarity was not one of the opposition's most prominent characteristics. Sir John Dalrymple was concerned, for his own benefit, to organise resistance to Melville and, as existing circumstances seemed to demand, he concentrated his recruiting efforts on the excluded 'episcopalian' groups, or those willing to pose as such. He aimed always at the advancement of his own family, a cause in which he was willing to cultivate anybody, even jacobites, in the hope that they would serve his purpose.[66] However, apart from a desire to remove Melville and a willingness to profess 'episcopalian' sympathies to gain the support of English ministers, Dalrymple and his allies had little in common. Dislike of the Melville clique was widespread, especially amongst the nobility who felt their claims to influence were being ignored.[67] But there were serious, even insuperable, obstacles to any really close alliances — between Queensberry and Atholl, for instance, who were implacable rivals. Even during this period of limited collaboration the Queensberry party tried to damn Atholl by the assertion that he had yet to exert himself in any cause and 'Besides in God's name what would it cost to engage him? The nation is too little to satisfy that family . . .'[68]

However, at the end of 1690, whatever Dalrymple's contribution as co-ordinator, the main weight of opposition seemed to be that of the Queensbery interest together with the duke's immediate allies. Using as his agent Sir Alexander Bruce, and hoping to work through his own brother, lieutenant-general Douglas, in William's entourage, Queensberry was pushing for as much political advantage as possible. Openly he did little, screening himself behind Linlithgow and Balcarres, the jacobite remnant from the first parliament of 1690, and Tweeddale, who found himself drawn into the alliance.[69] Tweeddale shared some of the aims of this faction and since he was in London, in touch with Carmarthen and abreast of feeling at court, he came to be looked upon by the Queensberry group as a key figure. Drumlanrig was deputed to keep in touch with him.[70]

Tweeddale complained of his isolation in London, lacking the support to carry much weight in pressing for changes. He asked for more people to join him so that his representations would make more impression, though preferably those who came should not in the recent past have been active jacobites. For this reason he was reluctant to be associated with some of those who did make the journey. He certainly refused to trust them, as it happened justifiably, since some proved later to be serious enough jacobites to go into exile.[71] An accumulation of such rifts deprived the opposition alliance of substantial force. Many, including Queensberry himself, concluded that going to court was not worth the effort, believing Melville's position to be unassailable.[72] This lethargy drove Linlithgow to complain. The opposition, he said, was too poorly represented in London, which gave William no encouragement to make changes. When the king asked to see Linlithgow and Balcarres to hear their version of Scottish affairs, Melville, backed by Portland, did everything possible to prevent their audience taking place, whilst the opposition in London had been scarcely influential enough to overcome such obstruction.[73] Linlithgow did at last see William, afterwards reporting his impressions to Queensberry. In the end, he thought, the king would do nothing but appoint Dalrymple as joint secretary with Melville. With that he would merely announce his disapproval of parties and his intention of employing any he thought fit from amongst those prepared to assert the supremacy of the crown over the church.[74] Linlithgow was proved right. William must have been aware, if only from English sources, of the unsatisfactory situation in Scotland but contented himself with this one adjustment. Considerations of policy could have entered into this severely limited change. William could not afford to tolerate the full pretensions of the high presbyterians but neither could he afford to show them marks of active displeasure without creating even greater trouble. But Dalrymple's appointment typified William's caution, even sluggishness, in the face of complications in Scotland, where he seemed to observe the general rule of doing nothing if it was at all possible. With Dalrymple's appointment he must have overcome his aversion from conflicting advice, but he still seemed unaware that, if it was peace and quiet he wanted, his disregard of parties was unlikely to provide it. The ministry was still composed of rival factions.

So after all their lobbying, Tweeddale and the Queensberry group had achieved nothing more than the advancement of Sir John Dalrymple. It came as no surprise to Dalrymple's friends in Scotland who for some time had been talking of his becoming secretary.[75] And presumably it had come as no shock to Dalrymple himself. To Tweeddale and Queensberry's group, however, the appointment, though doubtless expected, was quite unwelcome. Although they had been willing to make use of Dalrymple, the realisation that he had made use of them caused some dissatisfaction. Even before the new joint secretary was appointed, Tweeddale, on the strength of rumours from Scotland, wrote to Carmarthen about the dangers of giving too much power to one family,[76] a view which put him out of sympathy with all his allies, since Queensberry's group was contemplating the duke's appointment as a permanent lord commissioner in Scotland, a development even more alarming to Tweeddale than what had come to pass.[77] Such conflicting aims deprived the opposition alliance of any cohesion.

In this politicking, Dalrymple gives the impression of having had little in mind but using other people's backs to reach higher and higher ledges. Tweeddale's vision had been wider-angled. He had correctly identified as one of the strengths of the Melville interest their virtual monopoly of the king's counsels thanks to the influence of Portland and Carstares. Information to William was filtered through them and in turn they felt free to disseminate their version of the king's views. Since, in the last resort, only the king could take decisive action, this arrangement was a crucial element in the maintenance of Melville's position.[78] Tweeddale had aimed at neutralising the influence of Portland and Carstares and at undermining the other bases of Melville's power by the appointment of James Johnston as joint secretary — a change he had been urging on an apparently sympathetic Carmarthen. With Johnston — of impeccable presbyterian and revolutionary antecedents — as co-secretary, the Melville group could no longer lay claim to be the sole representatives of presbyterian and loyal opinion. Until the field of advice available to William was considerably broadened, Tweeddale had little hope of any major shift of power in the Scottish administration. He recommended to Carmarthen that when William went abroad a Scottish secretary should go with him and he reported the conversation to Johnston. Carmarthen thought: '. . . there was little Scots business to be done abroad, to which I replied that he[79] had not committed the government of that kingdom when he went to Ireland to the queen, and that the greatest affairs of Scotland were then transacting and, as I heard, by the correspondence of one Carstares, a minister of no good report sent by commissioner Melville to the king . . .'[80] This was a somewhat dismissive way in which to speak of Carstares, but unless the English ministry forced a change in the conduct of Scottish business there would be none, regardless of their sympathy for the Scottish 'episcopalian' opposition,[81] so the Carstares channel had to be made to appear muddier than it was.

Tweeddale's perception was in this respect sharper than William's. William had almost certainly appointed Dalrymple as joint secretary in January 1691 with no other motive than that of placating Scottish and English episcopalian interests or, at least, of giving them less ground for complaint. Limiting adjustment to Dalrymple's function seemed one way of achieving this without damaging Melville's position to any great degree, so avoiding a presbyterian outcry. William was, in fact, 'balancing' again but in the process he had gone further than he either intended or was aware of. The appointment of a joint secretary brought about a change of perspective. Although Dalrymple was far from being Tweeddale's choice, his preferment could conceivably be turned to the opposition's advantage. Contrary to William's hopes the change could, in the short term, produce only further discord in the ministry. In the long term it could lead to a serious upheaval which would force on the king sweeping and, to him, unwelcome changes. Dalrymple's promotion could not help but appear as the establishment of a bridgehead in Melville's territory.

This was the idea that Dalrymple, after his appointment, began to publicise as offering the best chance of recovering the support his success had alienated. His objective was still to increase his power within the ministry at the expense of Melville or, for that matter, of anyone else, and he needed the backing of the 'episcopalian' groups. After all, although it had not been their intention, their lobbying of the English ministry had put him in the secretary's office. The logic of this Trojan horse strategy which Dalrymple had now expounded was inescapable and in time it became clear that most Scots opposed to the Melville administration were prepared, with whatever private reservations, to give the new secretary some support.[82] Even Tweeddale came to look on the appointment as a gain.

In order to demonstrate that his promotion had some significance, Dalrymple had to impress both William and the opposition. If he could show himself to be more effective in carrying out the king's wishes than his rivals had proved to be, William might reward him further. To retain the opposition's support Dalrymple would have to keep Melville under visibly strong pressure, so the weak spots of the existing administration had to be probed for and exposed. The result was that some of the main issues in government were fought over with control of the Scottish administration as the possible prize. Three problems were opened up to scrutiny: the conduct of church affairs in Scotland, the settlement of the highlands, and the apparent inability of Melville's eldest son and his supporters to manage the business of the treasury. The resulting conflict and its incidental consequences brought the entire kingdom into a state of administrative paralysis.[83]

The struggle between Melville and the Dalrymples dominated Scottish affairs between 1690 and 1692. It involved major policy clashes and seemingly endless administrative needling. The families were in dispute over almost everything, from the election of a new lord provost of Edinburgh, which assumed the aspect of a Melville-Dalrymple confrontation,[84] to disputes over official correspondence and the disposal of the secretaries' black box.[85] When Carstares felt obliged to deny, with some asperity, a rumour that he had been seen in Rotterdam with the master of Stair, the atmosphere had clearly become very tense.[86] The pettiness for which Melville's sons, Leven in particular, were noted, showed in their persecution of anyone they looked upon as an ally of the Dalrymples. The treasury commissioners refused to give Bruce, as muster-master, any pay and without apparent reason dismissed his brother from a revenue collectorship at

Kelso. From the hindrances he met with Bruce began to suspect that the work of the muster-master's office was being deliberately sabotaged.[87] But all this was mere skirmishing. There were more crucial issues.

The affairs of the Scottish church were clamouring for attention. Parochial organisation had drifted out of control even where it existed. Pastoral functions were often inadequately provided for as a result of the uncertainties inherent in the new settlement. In some ways the future of the church in Scotland was at risk especially in northern parts of the kingdom. But it was really the political uses to which church affairs in Scotland could be put which made the religious issue important in Edinburgh and London. English concern over the fate of episcopalian and conforming clergy made the subject worth the investment of time and trouble. Anyone who seemed ready to promote the cause of toleration or reunification could rely on the goodwill of Carmarthen and Nottingham, to name only two of the English ministers who had no faith in Melville's moderating influence. Since the bulk of Melville's support was presbyterian, he could afford to do nothing but utter the mildest of restraining noises as the thorough purge of the Scottish church was attempted. Soon, he ceased to do even this, concentrating instead on concealment of what was happening from the English. Dalrymple, as others, saw that this issue, properly handled, could become one of Melville's most vulnerable points. He set out to exploit it. But at the same time, true to the family tradition, his father continued, verbally at least, to espouse the presbyterian cause.[88]

Without doubt the new presbyterian establishment had determined to grant no quarter to the clergy who had conformed. Their object was to carry out a thorough religious revolution in Scotland, creating a committed presbyterian establishment from top to bottom. Much of the impetus was generated at the level of the local judicatories. The motives, however much deplored by saner presbyterians, ranged from sheer fanaticism and a desire for vengeance to an attempt to provide security against any religious counter-revolution. All the ministers in whose hands the establishment had been placed evinced a firm determination to create a godly church in Scotland. Yet they realised that the nature and extent of their activities had to be disguised as far as possible from the English lest attempts should be made to check them. There was no lack of will at the court in London to restrain the immoderate. Apart from his original reluctance to agree to the full presbyterian demands for the church settlement William, in 1690, had made a further attempt to influence the way in which it functioned through representations to the first general assembly since the revolution. He appointed as commissioner Carmichael, an undoubted presbyterian but no zealot, and counselled the assembly to moderation.[89] In the royal letter to the assembly William declared, ' . . . we expect that your management shall be such as we shall have no reason to repent of what we have done . . . we never could be of the mind that violence was suited to the advancing of true religion, nor do we intend that our authority shall ever be a tool to the irregular passions of any party. Moderation is what religion enjoins, neighbouring churches expect from you and we recommend to you . . . '[90] The underlying message was that if the assembly embarked on extreme courses it would embarrass William in his relations with the English parliament and very likely lead to political repercussions in Scotland.[91]

The assembly's reaction was to stonewall. Their reply to William equated loyalty to God and the kingdom with support of the presbyterian establishment. Nevertheless it appeared that they too were in favour of moderation and despite what they had been called upon to suffer for conscience's sake they would give the king no cause to repent. But, their letter continued, 'Great revolutions of this nature must be attended with occasions of complaint, and even the worst of men are ready to cry out of wrong for their justest deservings. But, as your majesty knows these things too well to give us the least apprehension of any impression evil report can make so we assure your majesty . . . that we shall study that moderation which your majesty recommends . . . '[92] Having thus attempted to forestall any complaints, they adopted the strategy of confining the assembly's proceedings to prayer, expressions of good intent and largely formal and uncontroversial business. It was the moderator's hope that the assembly would ratify no ejections of ministers purely on the grounds of their views on church government nor press anyone to be reordained.[93] A few clear cut and seemingly unexceptionable cases were dealt with. Several ministers were reinstated after they had made a humiliating recantation of 'those courses which we understood to have been corruptions and defections in this Church . . . '[94] Appeals against sentences of deprivation passed by lower courts were dismissed when the appellants, as John Mackenzie, expelled from the parish of Kirkliston,[95] failed to present themselves for re-examination, which seemed a fair procedure. Even a Mr James Forsyth, a former incumbent of St. Ninians, deprived for officiating at an incestuous marriage despite previous admonition, had his case reconsidered and referred back to the presbytery of Stirling[96] The purpose of all this was to avoid taking cognizance of controversial business in full assembly which would have made their attitude public and plain. Instead they delegated their powers to two commissions of visitation — one for north and one for south of the Tay. Their official instructions were quite innocuous, even redolent of christian charity. However, the commissions were specifically intended to carry through extreme policies, after the assembly adjourned, more unobtrusively than would otherwise have been possible.[97] The powers so delegated were speedily put to use. A general fast was decreed on such terms — atonement for breaches of the covenant and the like — as no episcopalians and few conforming clergy, however well-affected, could comply with, so providing legal grounds for proceedings against them.[98]

Such tactics produced a quick reaction from Dalrymple after his appointment as secretary in January 1691. It was not that he was able to effect any change in policy even if that had been his intention. Rather he provided a brisker channel of communication than had been available hitherto, making the royal will plain when and where necessary. The king's expressed intention had been that the commission of the assembly, which usually functioned in a caretaking capacity during adjournments, though with substantial powers, should neither sit nor act whilst he was out of England. His instructions had been disregarded. The commission had not only met but removed five ministers in one sitting. Even the privy council had found this too much and put a stop to the proceedings despite Crawford's protests but now, instead of nothing emanating from above but silence, the council's order was swiftly backed by a letter from Dalrymple to Hamilton. He reiterated the king's instruction that the commission should not sit and enjoined that the presbyterians were to unite with any episcopalian clergy worthy to be retained.[99] As the commission tried to think of ways of circumventing William's instructions, Tweeddale *via* Carmarthen brought their deliberations to the king's notice and once again Dalrymple forcibly stated the king's intention: he wanted union amongst the clergy. This carried a message for both parties: to the presbyterians to exercise restraint and to the episcopalians to abandon hope that they would do better with a separate church and toleration.[100]

The struggle was carried on at many levels and with a great deal of subterfuge. Officially, whatever he knew or suspected of their real intentions, the king could take cognizance only of the commission's formal pronouncements. The commissioners remonstrated mildly with the king for having stopped their examination of episcopalian clergy whilst he was out of the country, since it had been their intention to accept on their merits such of them as were qualified.[101] There was little the king could do but express pleasure at their disposition and hope that they would make progress to union on the basis of the confession of faith.[102]

But William and some of his ministers had also been engaged in a discreet manoeuvre. After reaching agreement with the episcopalian clergy on a petition they were to present to the commission asking to be accepted into the church, he sent a letter to the commissioners asking them to receive qualified episcopalian ministers.[103] This tactic was intended to drag the issue into the open, making it more difficult for episcopalian ministers to be excluded secretly. The commissioners were too shrewd to be trapped in this way. The petition was referred to the commissions for visitation. That for the north replied that having delegated their powers to a committee they were not themselves competent to receive the petition.[104] The commission for the south produced what Sir William Lockhart called 'a disingenuous cunning paper' to justify their not receiving any episcopal clergy in that region. The report, apart from taking refuge in technicalities, was certainly less than honest.[105]

Consequently, in the view of the court, there had been no progress at all and the commission was made forcibly aware of it. As a result presbyterian ministers were despatched to Flanders to state their case to the king but they found little favour with him. He saw them once only. Their letter 'was so very impertinent that the king had much to do to get it digested, but he would not take off the stop he put upon them not to meddle with the episcopalian clergy'.[106] Even Melville and Carstares, considerably embarrassed by the king's views and the attitude of the English, felt driven to rebuke their co-religionists with some solemnity. None of this had any effect on presbyterian intentions but it was not to be expected that it would. In fact had it done so it would probably have come as a disappointment to Dalrymple, since presbyterian compliance would have upset the wider scheme, disarming a major weapon against the Melville clique. The point which Dalrymple and the 'episcopalians' were continually making was the need, in the interest of royal authority, for a change in the Scottish government. In the opinion of Sir Alexander Bruce too much defiance of the king's will was being tolerated. What could be expected when the king wrote letters to Scotland and 'a company of greasy stinking fellows' wrote to him in answer? Or when the commission of the assembly had its requests for fasts refused by the privy council and held them nevertheless on their own authority, no action being subsequently taken against them?[107] Tweeddale's grandson told him that since Melville's party had a majority on the privy council, only a purge of the government would be effective.[108] The theme was taken up by Carmarthen, who complained that the church was being given an equal voice in the king's business.[109] The point of the campaign was made by Dalrymple's contention that a proper church settlement depended on people's being in the government who would not provoke the presbyterians but who would not tolerate their 'rash humours'.[110] Melville's grip, that is to say, had to be slackened if not broken, though the opposition had yet to agree who was to benefit from such a change.

On both sides there was delusion and dishonesty, although as time went on the element of dishonesty increased. Presbyterian ministers, or some of them, were driven forward by a vision of a divinely ordained church which it was their duty to establish. There were, of course, more unworthy motives but the outcome would have been much the same. This aspiration was unrealisable even in the south of Scotland where presbyterianism was strongest. In the north, what existed of christianity was largely episcopalian and the support of the congregations for their ministers made it difficult for them to be ejected. The church establishment had to tolerate this state of affairs although events were to show that it was merely biding its time. Full advantage was taken of circumstances after the 'Fifteen rising to purge the north. Between 1688 and 1716, 664 ministers of 926 parishes had been deprived on one pretext or another.[111] But in the early 1690s Melville and his allies, with no power base other than support from presbyterians, would not have dared to disillusion them even had they themselves known better. In Melville's favour there was the undoubted fact, sometimes overlooked, that as the only safeguard against jacobite reaction Scotland had to be ruled by a party which fully accepted the revolution. From the convention to 1703 the reality of this was forced upon Scottish politicians, whether or not they relished or even admitted it. Melville and his supporters naturally interpreted this as a justification for their monopoly of power though, of course, they were not the only supporters of the revolution.

The king and the English tory ministers, for their part, pursued a mirage of a unified, comprehensive Scottish church, comprising presbyterian, episcopalian and conforming clergy. An occasional Scotsman might have been found who shared their belief in this possibility, but those concerned with the practical conduct of Scottish affairs recognised it as the chimera it was. The gulf between presbyterian and episcopalian had become politically, if not theologically, too wide to be bridged. Presbyterians were committed to the revolution and looked on toleration as ungodly. The episcopalians had acquired an ambition to be tolerated as a separate church. In politics many of them were, or were to become, jacobites.[112] Whilst Scotland remained separate, the national religion had to be forced into one mould or the other. There could be no generally accepted workable compromise. Yet, although Scottish politicians were fully aware of this, the temptation to repeat the old argument about comprehension to gain English support for ministerial changes was too great for them to resist. Their sole object was to gain office, and once that was attained episcopalian sympathisers could be left to their inevitable disillusionment. Other than conformity — and many were not allowed even that option — there was no hope for episcopalians in the early 1690s nor for some time after that.

The church settlement was one of the few problems in Scotland which could be dignified by the term 'national issue', justifying the adoption of differing attitudes whether emerging from principle, prejudice or private interest. Another major issue was the settlement of the highlands, where most of the clans had not submitted to William since the collapse, after Killiecrankie, of Dundee's rising. There was scope enough for a variety of opinions over methods of pacifying the highlands. But policies were immaterial. What counted were personalities and self-interest. And, like the problem of the church settlement, that of the highlands became closely linked with the composition of the civil government and for much the same reason. The opponents of the administration needed a weapon and Dalrymple fancied he had devised one. His scheme depended largely on the success of a particular highland policy which he had adopted whilst still lord advocate.[113]

No matter who was on the throne there had always been trouble in the highlands, so the connection of the highland problem with jacobitism was at bottom tenuous if not altogether incidental. James himself had had his share of difficulties with highland chieftains. However, William's highland problem had taken on a jacobite complexion. It flattered the self-esteem of the chiefs to defy a distant government as long as they appeared to be beyond its reach. The revolution presented them with excellent opportunities. Once established in defiance, the chieftains enjoyed making a flourish of the punctilios of war, the sanctity of oaths of allegiance and the like. A tendency on the part of some in both the Scottish and English administrations to oversimplify the problem into a single issue of allegiance made the problem more rather than less intractable. The root causes of the problem lay deeper. Activities which made the life of the highlander appear lawless to outsiders — cattle-stealing, the levying of 'blackmail' or protection money — were, in the highlands, sensible ways of making a living; the blood feud was a part of their existence and a useful means of maintaining what peace there was. Yet more was involved than a way of life. Friction developed when a part of a clan had to accept the feudal superiority of another, often a rival, clan chieftain, as some Macleans and Camerons had had to accept the superiority of the Argyll Campbells as a result of the latters' expansionist policies. The Campbells had extended their empire as far as they could, particularly in the 1670s, to the great resentment of those brought under their jurisdiction. James had at length come to accept a policy whereby the crown would buy up feudal superiorities and reallocate them in accordance with clan loyalties. But the plan came to nothing. Now for the highlands the revolution seemed to involve little more than the restoration, or even the aggrandisement, of the house of Argyll. Such indeed was the ambition of Archibald Campbell, the tenth earl. The clans exerted the only pressure open to them, namely, violence, but now they were able to invoke in its justification their loyalty to King James.[114]

William's government considered various approaches to the problem, policies which became aligned with the splits within the Scottish administration and inseparable from the struggle for its control. There was general agreement that the highlands stood in need of pacification, but this inclined no-one to tolerate another's success in actually pacifying them if it could be at all avoided.

Limited military presence became the standard policy of the government, largely because that was all and almost more than all it could afford. Under Mackay a fort was established at Inverlochy — Fort William — with command given to colonel John Hill, who had with some success served the Cromwellian administration in a similar capacity. With adequate support Hill was probably the best man for the job. He knew the problem and the terrain and had established an effective style of relationship with the clan chieftains, who respected him even when they despised the central government. But

Hill's men were too often unpaid, hungry and ragged, a condition due in part to the inadequacy of the Scottish treasury. Not enough money was forthcoming and the army was neglected, having been accorded in Edinburgh a very low priority.[115] Hill himself, merely to keep his job, had to spend too much time looking over his shoulder to assess the political situation lest he should be stabbed in the back without warning. He badly needed his command at Fort William for the sake of the pay. The struggle to make ends meet explains much of seventeenth-century Scottish politics. Since the first master he had in Scotland after the revolution was Melville, as secretary and commissioner, Hill was drawn by circumstances and by inclination into the Melville network. He came to believe that his tenure at Fort William depended on Melville's continued favour. Dalrymple's appointment as secretary dismayed Hill, who expressed alarm at the encouragement seemingly given in London to those in league with the Church of England.[116]

As far as the highlanders were concerned, Hill thought that excessively harsh treatment of them was a mistake, in the long run making things worse.[117] This inclined him to favour a scheme put forward by George Mackenzie, viscount of Tarbat: pacification through the distribution of money and honours amongst the chieftains and the purchase of superiorities for reallocation. Others did wonder whether Tarbat, slippery and widely distrusted, was the right man for any such task, but in 1689 and 1690 Hill was disposed to co-operate with him. His proposals seemed sensible and, most important to a colonel in need of favour, his current standing with both the court and Melville was high. By some means Tarbat had inveigled himself into a position of special trust with William.[118] Melville was related to him and, regarding him as a possible ally, had sponsored the claims of his brother, Roderick Mackenzie, to a vacancy in the court of session.[119] Most important of all, Melville had a clear interest in any scheme which reduced the influence of Mackay, saved money on the army and would be financed from England. If the scheme succeeded it might add to Melville's prestige, whilst if it failed the blame would clearly be Tarbat's. A project with so much to commend it could not be too highly rated.

So, in 1689 Tarbat had been allowed the money to embark on his scheme,[120] but his efforts were inconspicuously though effectively sabotaged. Too many people wanted to see him fail, particularly those with a vested interest in the existing highland situation, however disturbed.[121] Two such were Argyll and Atholl, who both contributed to ruining the project.[122] Hill had complained that some members of the privy council were encouraging the highland lairds in their resistance.[123]

Although under Tarbat the project lost momentum, the scheme itself was not abandoned.[124] Its possibilities had been appreciated by Dalrymple, when lord advocate, as a means of achieving his own objectives. His first priority was not the pacification of the highlands but the dislodging of the Melville family. On his becoming joint secretary in 1691 he had intensified his attempts to ease out the Melville interest and the pacification of the highlands was to be one of his instruments. The pacification was not to be achieved by Tarbat with the credit, if any, going to Tarbat himself and perhaps Melville, but by Dalrymple's nominee Breadalbane, whom he had succeeded in recruiting as a member of the somewhat diffuse 'episcopalian' interest.[125] The credit would go largely to Dalrymple.

John, first earl of Breadalbane, was the chief of the Breadalbane Campbells, with highland interests of his own and a sharp eye for profit and the political main chance. During the revolution he had been cautious though determined to find himself, when all the noise had died away, on the winning side. But always, if he scented the probability of success, he was prepared to play for high stakes. In this spirit he had dabbled in Skelmorlie's plot. Breadalbane was the man selected by Dalrymple to advance the cause of peace in the highlands and the victory of the Dalrymples within the administration.

When Dalrymple's alternative scheme was first mooted there had been obstacles. Tarbat had not yet abandoned hope and had to be allowed to continue until he conceded failure. Breadalbane was unable to venture to Edinburgh without official protection from his creditors.[126] Such odds and ends had to be tidied away. But on Dalrymple's recommendation, William had made the first moves early in 1690. He warranted Breadalbane to negotiate with the highland chieftains, allowing him money for the purpose.[127] In 1691, when Tarbat's efforts had come to nothing and Breadalbane was ready to begin operations, Dalrymple was already secretary of state and fully embattled with the Melville interest. A loose plan was in existence for securing changes in the Scottish ministry, though of necessity there was no specific agreement on the actual changes to be attempted. A political network with links in England, Scotland and Flanders was to put the plan into operation. The London group consisted of Nottingham, Carmarthen, Tweeddale and, surprisingly, the queen, whose sympathies were wholly episcopalian. The Scottish section of the network involved Breadalbane and his highland project, with the Queensberry group waiting to take advantage of any opportunity this might create. Lockhart, the solicitor-general, was the link between the Scottish operation and Nottingham in London. Dalrymple was with the king in Flanders keeping him informed of developments and making what impression he could.

In the correspondence of this network there is continued reference to the importance of the highland scheme for the projected political changes but little mention of its significance for the future of the highlands. Dalrymple represented the purpose of the scheme to Nottingham as providing the opportunity to show that the 'episcopalian' interest was willing to serve the king. He warned him: ' . . . If these who have given this evidence of their capacities and readiness to serve their majesties be neglected and matters in Scotland stand as they now do, can men assure the success of the king's affairs contrary to the violent inclinations of these he only entrusts there? This obliges me to tell you that if no motions from you comes to the king of the great advantage to England in this settlement and what further is necessary to Scotland, all will lie over and those who are most capable to serve the king will have absolute conviction that it's impossible to do what may recommend them to the king's favour, whereby affairs there will again go wrong . . . I believe it's plain and necessary for the king to settle the government there in the hands of men of sense that are not enemies to government in general, and who have power to influence others and something of their own to hazard.'[128] The same message was preached from Edinburgh by Lockhart.[129]

When it appeared briefly that Breadalbane might have succeeded, Dalrymple hastened to re-emphasise the point to Nottingham and hold out to him the prospect of being able to do something about church affairs in Scotland.[130] Such was the extent of the investment in Breadalbane's highland project. The entire 'episcopalian' interest was to be rescued from the suspicion of jacobitism and put forward as a loyal but moderate alternative to Melville and the 'presbyterians'.

But substantial powers were ranged against Breadalbane as earlier they had been against Tarbat. They were closer to the scene of action than London and ably supported by persons with access to William, namely Portland and Carstares. Melville seems to have remained passive, carrying out orders and hoping devoutly for spectacular failure. So many people were already exerting themselves to sabotage the scheme that little more was needed. Few other highland chieftains wanted Breadalbane to succeed, least of all Argyll whose own interests were threatened.[131] A majority of the privy council were opponents of Breadalbane and his backers. At one stage Cassillis was organising a semi-official deputation to London to complain of his activities.[132] Hill, fearing for his own position at Fort William, was actively against the new highland scheme though it was quite in accordance with his earlier views. Breadalbane had been ordered to correspond only with Nottingham, an arrangement to which both Melville and Hamilton objected, resenting their exclusion.[133] He arrived in Scotland to find that the nature of his secret mission had been leaked by members of the privy council. To wreck negotiations the council was also doing its utmost to embroil the highlanders with the army in the hope of creating incidents despite the king's express prohibition of military activity during the talks.[134] Army officers showed a strong disposition to start trouble, and advantage was taken of a brawl between some of Hill's men — out on a drinking spree in Inverlochy — and a few of Stewart of Appin's men to arrest Stewart and some of his followers, which seemed more than likely to ruin the project.[135] Hill himself did what he could to cast aspersions on Breadalbane's competence and integrity.[136]

Despite all this Breadalbane had obtained a limited and conditional agreement from the chieftains about their taking the oath of allegiance. The king pronounced himself satisfied that Breadalbane had so far done his best and accordingly gave him an official discharge. To discredit him and his party, therefore, the opposition to Breadalbane had to produce something quite dramatic, and quickly. After a meeting between Breadalbane and the chieftains at Achallader in June 1691, copies of a document were put into circulation by Macdonald of Glengarry. The document purported to show that to make some appearance of obtaining results Breadalbane had entered into a secret bargain by which he pledged his own loyalty to James. It is difficult to think of any reason why Breadalbane should have done this in writing unless he were a fool, which he was not. It seems very likely that the documents distributed by Glengarry amongst members of the government were 'copies' of a non-existent original. Both Atholl and Glengarry were involved in this scheme to discredit Breadalbane.[137] On the strength of a copy of this document, and with considerable alacrity, Hill lodged information against Breadalbane who was greatly aggrieved.[138] William, by ignoring the allegations then and subsequently, indicated that he did not believe them.[139] Lockhart wrote to Nottingham,' . . . The plain English, my lord, of all this matter is the apprehension some men are under that Breadalbane and others may come to have share in the government, and therefore find it useful to defame him as actor, and the secretary as giving the measure of bringing the highlanders in this method to the king's obedience.

'We who serve the king heartily do admire that hitherto he hath made no alteration in his council, for as we are weary in struggling, so his affairs suffer every day . . . .'[140]

There were no changes, however, and the chief reason was the strong support on which Melville could rely from Portland and Carstares, never far from William's side. During the conflict of 1691 Portland blandly told Nottingham that he was not aware of any party animosities in Scotland.[141] It could, of course, have been that they saw Melville and the presbyterians as the best hope of stable government in Scotland and so thought their position worth preserving. If so they were ignoring completely and unwisely the excluded magnates and their ambitions. Later events seem to indicate that Portland was tied to Melville by blind loyalty, ignorance and gross miscalculation. And what applied to Portland was true also of Carstares who advised him.

Meanwhile, under the impression that the highland affair was being successfully concluded, Dalrymple continued his exertions. A visit to Flanders was arranged for Breadalbane to give the king an account of his negotiations in the hope of some promise of reward.[142] Dalrymple exhorted Queensberry and Linlithgow to greater efforts.[143] It is quite apparent that to Dalrymple and others Breadalbane's highland scheme was no more than a means to an end, as was the subject of church government. In quarters where he thought one or the other topic likely to be politically useful, Dalrymple made a point of emphasising them. There were less devious motives. As an administrator Dalrymple was irked by the high presbyterians' defiant prevarication and the reluctance of the government to interfere with them, but he was also trying to improve his own position. Both aims could conceivably be achieved by a demonstration that his opponents were inefficient, recalcitrant or both, coupled with proof of his own superior capacity. The line between his two motives is not easy to draw and to the man himself they might well have been indistinguishable.

The change in Dalrymple's attitude during the latter part of 1691 shows his interest in the highland problem for its own sake to have been slight. When there was still hope of success he bombarded Breadalbane with advice, criticism and warning.[144] But more complications emerged than either Dalrymple or Breadalbane had ever dreamed of. Opposition came not only from the threatened Melville interest; others, too, had doubts. It was very easy to upset one's apparent friends. The 'episcopalian' alliance aimed at dislodging Melville was still in being, but no nearer agreement on what was to happen if they succeeded. No one was anxious to incur risks, or even exertion, for the advancement of others. Queensberry had reservations about the drift of affairs, especially if Breadalbane's power was intended to become inflated to the extent hinted at by persistent rumour. Talk of any increase in another's influence was bound to set any Scottish magnate's teeth on edge. Breadalbane thought it advisable to write to Queensberry in the hope of soothing him.[145] Tweeddale, apart from being jealous and mistrustful of Breadalbane, lacked any faith in negotiations with highlanders.[146] But although sharing few common aims, members of the Scottish 'episcopalian' lobby were at one in having confidence in their English sympathisers. Breadalbane wrote to Nottingham that he knew he ought to be on his way to London to support the general interest and, ' . . . to satisfy some of my friends who are going up, whose concerns as to the public I value equal with myself, D[uke] Queensberry, Earl Linlithgow and Earl Kintore . . . These lords are encouraged by me to this journey by the accompt I give to them of my lord president[147] and your lordship's firm friendship to them and to their and our interests.'[148]

But the English ministers did not altogether share the Scottish opposition's sense of urgency. Nor, in spite of their naivety over Scottish religious divisions, were they totally inclined to take at face value everything they were told about Scotland. Both Nottingham and Carmarthen were rather less committed to particular persons than some of the Scots imagined. Nottingham mentioned to Portland 'the several schemes proposed by Sir John Dalrymple from D[uke] Hamilton on the one hand, and several of the Scotch nobility on the other, for the administration of the government in Scotland . . . ' His own view was that some changes ought to be made in view of the damage being done to the power of the crown by the Melville group. He claimed to have no partiality for any set of men, but whether the king decided to make changes at once or delay them, he thought Breadalbane ought to be given some grounds for hope.[149] Obviously when writing to a committed supporter of the very interests under attack in Scotland, Nottingham had to proceed warily, but his attitude was considerably more detached than Breadalbane and some of his allies thought. Carmarthen's views were also cautious. He committed himself only to the statement that if Scotland remained free from disturbances some changes should be made in the ministry to include some who were not of the presbyterian interest.[150] Obviously he, too, shared the delusion that the rival interests in Scotland were capable of collaboration.

Dalrymple knew of all these reservations. The fact was that, by the end of November 1691, decisions concerning changes in the Scottish ministry had already been taken, if only in principle, so that for this purpose the highland project had lost its importance. From this point onwards Dalrymple's only interest in the highlands was to extricate himself from the pacification project without incurring allegations of jacobitism. He began to think of insuring himself in case the clan chieftains had still not taken the oaths by 1 January 1692, the date they had agreed with Breadalbane. There had to be a conclusive demonstration that neither he nor Breadalbane was excessively lenient towards highlanders.[151] If they failed as 'doves', they had to achieve a rapid transformation into 'hawks'. Dalrymple told Breadalbane that he expected to hear from him either news of success or, failing that, a scheme for 'mauling' the clans.[152] The secretary himself entertained thoughts of making an example of the Macdonalds or of Lochiel.[153] At the same time he prepared Breadalbane for the news that he was not to be given such an important post as he had expected, at the same time implying that Breadalbane could consider himself lucky to be getting anything at all.[154]

Apart from the highland business and the church settlement, Dalrymple's attack on the Melville family had a third prong: an attempt to expose malpractice, inefficiency, or some combination of both, in the treasury as it was being administered by lord Raith, Melville's eldest son, treasurer-depute, with his supporters. Dalrymple employed his brother Hugh to pass on to him such evidence of bad financial management as he could find.[155] The maladministration in the treasury was notorious. Much was due to ineptitude and idleness; some of it to greed. Although the cess was coming in well, there was never enough money to supply the army, payments to individuals being given priority without any set policy. Patronage requirements and the mere whim of the commissioners seemed to be decisive. When the army clamoured for its arrears, enough money was borrowed from the hearth tax to prevent disorder and all other payments had then to be suspended. The treasury commissioners, without any obvious reason, allowed the excise roup [156] to be lowered, after which they adjourned for a lengthy period, making it impossible for any treasury business to be transacted. [157] The treasury was, in fact, in no fit state to account to anybody.

Accusations were freely made that Melville and his family were feathering their nests. It seems highly likely. Melville, pushed by his sons, seemed to be trying to make a fortune and lay the foundations of a magnate interest. [158] Such ambitions needed the profits and perquisites of office and some of their activities were rather blatant in view of the known poverty of the treasury. Melville gave priority, as a matter of course, to his own salary and arrears. [159] Financial administration seemed to be directed towards making a profit for himself and his connections: an unnecessary minting of copper coinage to benefit the family, inflated tax collecting allowances, skimping on pay in Leven's regiment which provoked a mutiny, the disappearance of the pay for four whole regiments and the sale of blank signatures which Melville had by some means procured from William. It was thought noteworthy that the family had suddenly become very rich. Although their former penury was notorious, they had all taken to buying land. Raith, for example, had bought some property, paying £7000 down, which was remarkable. [160]

Much of this evidence comes from hostile sources which could render it suspect but, on the other hand, it was not likely to come from anywhere else. The allegations are consistent and reinforced by other circumstantial evidence, the episode of the Edinburgh bond for instance. By what amounted to administrative sharp practice and misrepresentation Melville had got his hands on a bond for £3000 payable by the city of Edinburgh. When the details of the transaction attained some notoriety, the king, after showing his habitual reluctance to take action, ordered Melville to deliver up the bond. For some time, in spite of the king's order, Melville declined. Even after complying, he still tried to squeeze the money out of the town unofficially. Possibly he had come to look on the bond as an official payment of his arrears and allowances regardless of the fact that these had nothing at all to do with Edinburgh. [161] To the end, though quite unjustifiably, he seems to have thought he had been cheated out of something to which he had a perfect right.

It was this sordid aspect of the financial administration that finally enabled Melville's opponents to achieve some success. The main agent of the opposition proved to be none other than Tweeddale. After his years of waiting and intrigue he now reaped the reward. Since leaving Scotland in 1689 he had moved between London and Tunbridge Wells, taking the waters and cultivating a variety of persons, some episcopalian, such as the English ministers and Burnet, some presbyterian: the Johnston brothers, James and Alexander. All of them were opposed to Melville and working through the English court to secure his removal. [162] He had had little to show for his efforts. Some of his former associates in Scotland had come to terms with Melville and advised Tweeddale to do the same or retire from politics. [163] His political future had seemed desolate.

The first step foreshadowing the changes of 1692 had come in the previous October, just as Dalrymple was deciding that the highland project had ceased to be relevant to his main purpose. What enabled action to be taken was the Scottish treasury's reduction in the excise roup. Dalrymple produced a plan based, like the ill-fated highland scheme, on the chance of making an impression by success in some relatively spectacular achievement which would expose the deficiencies of the existing administration. For this purpose someone was needed in the treasury with power to transact business swiftly and efficiently. Whether because Tweeddale had acquired sufficient backing to make him an unavoidable choice or whether his administrative experience made him the obvious man for the job, Dalrymple settled for Tweeddale. The only other man whose treasury experience exceeded Tweeddale's was Queensberry, whose demands would have been excessive and who was unacceptable to many. Tweeddale, moreover, could not have seemed to Dalrymple a potentially dangerous rival.

The plan involved careful preparation, in that a suitable situation had to be contrived. Dalrymple obtained private assurances that an offer would be forthcoming for the excise representing an increase of £5000 on the existing roup. Tweeddale was to be provided with a commission empowering him to act over the excise roup as if he were a quorum of the treasury and sent to Scotland to bring off this financial *coup*. Frantic last-minute efforts were made to obstruct this scheme, but Tweeddale obtained his commission in spite of it all. Since Dalrymple had virtually assured success in the excise negotiations, all that remained was for Tweeddale to conclude the bargain, as it were off-hand, demonstrating at one and the same time the inadequacies of the existing treasury commission and his own capacity for business.[164]

Tweeddale went to Edinburgh and did what was expected of him, much to the mortification of Melville and Raith. Melville tried to belittle the achievement. According to him the king could have made a much better bargain, at which William, quite competent at judging specific performance, was moved to observe that if so it was a pity Raith had not managed to make it. At this Raith left in haste for Scotland to see if he could disrupt the arrangement.[165] He had no immediate success.

Thus the way was cleared for a ministerial reconstruction, not by moderating the church establishment or through a dramatic solution to the highland problem, but by some administrative sleight of hand. However, the long-sought reconstruction, despite the efforts of Dalrymple and the presence in London of Queensberry, Linlithgow, Strathmore and Kintore, did not involve the purge that the 'episcopalian' party had hoped for.[166] Portland and Carstares had played a big part in preventing this. In the apparent belief that any change would upset stability in Scotland, they applied their full strength to propping up the tottering Melville interest.[167] And, of course, William still cherished the delusion that it was possible to achieve a balance between parties — a concept which proved even less successful when applied in Scotland than it did in England. Therefore, although Melville had not at any time given full satisfaction and had even fallen into something approaching disgrace, he and his family were not completely removed from the government.[168] The scheme of reconstruction had, in fact, gone off at half cock and its failure, sooner or later, was guaranteed. At the same time it must be conceded that by this stage no other scheme was likely to have been any more successful.

The original project had envisaged Tweeddale as lord chancellor and Melville as privy seal, with Dalrymple and Carmichael as joint secretaries. Lothian was to act as commissioner to the next general assembly.[169] A lengthy delay followed this decision, Carmichael having, in an attack of nerves, refused to accept the post. He was not capable of being a secretary, he said, an excuse with which Dalrymple had little patience, putting it down to false modesty. He regretted Carmichael's decision since there was nobody else in his opinion so universally acceptable.[170] Certainly Carmichael would have been a quiescent colleague and no competitor for Dalrymple. The post of secretary was finally given to James Johnston, an appointment of more significance than appeared at the time. The rest of the commissions were issued in March 1692. Tarbat, fully restored to grace, appeared in his old post as lord clerk register. A new treasury commission was appointed in which Drumlanrig represented the Queensberry interest with the addition of Linlithgow and Breadalbane as a gesture to the 'episcopalians'. Raith, however, remained as treasurer-depute. A new privy council list was warranted with an increased 'episcopalian' representation.[171]

What had emerged was a combination which did not even begin to resemble a 'balanced' ministry, much less one which would accord a high priority to co-operation. It comprised a group of men, each highly charged with ambition, dissatisfaction or both. Yet, although the new administration did not satisfy the 'episcopalians', it was much more in their favour than the king had originally intended it to be. In June 1691 Dalrymple had written to Nottingham about the king's views on ministerial changes: 'I have shown him both D[uke] Hamilton's scheme, which appears too narrow and more calculate for his grace's interest than his majesty's. The other[172] as being more comprehensive, takes better, but the objection still sticks that it's undecent [sic] and unsecure to assume persons immediately from getting their pardons to trusts and places . . . '[173] William, in short, wanted no former jacobites in office, at least not for some time, and would have preferred to pacify the 'episcopalians' by taking the edge off Melville's predominance rather than by making them too powerful in the administration. But, according to Johnston, between the planning of the original scheme and the issue of the commissions, hasty changes had been made as a direct consequence of William's angry reaction to the general assembly's behaviour in January and February 1692. There had taken place a confrontation between church and state.

Lothian as commissioner had been instructed to procure the admission to the church of a significant number of episcopalian and conformist ministers. William's letter deplored that, despite the assurances given by the commissioners of the assembly that they would admit conformist clergy, ' . . . there hath not hitherto been such progress made in that as we could have expected. It is represented to us that you are not a full General Assembly, there being as great a number of ministers in the Church of Scotland as you are who are not at all allowed to be represented though they were neither purged out upon the heads mentioned . . . ' The king requested that 'conform' clergy who applied to be admitted should be tried immediately in full assembly and allowed in if not found scandalous. If this proved impossible in the time available, then the task should be delegated to commissions for north and south of the Tay. Each commission should be composed half of 'old presbyterians' and half of 'conform' clergy against whom no fault had been proved. These commissions were to complete the task of examining ministers so that the next general assembly was fully representative.[174] After replying suitably, the assembly spent much of the next four weeks on provision for the care of records and other routine business. An address from Robert Meldrum and other conforming clergy was read only at the commissioner's direction. All this increased Lothian's impatience at the nature and pace of proceedings, leading to high words being exchanged.

Finally, on 13 February, immediately after prayers, the commissioner acted briskly.

He addressed the assembly through the moderator: ' . . . What I said last had so little success that I intend to give you no more trouble of that nature, only this. You have now sat about a month which was a competent time both for to have done what was the principal design in calling this assembly (of uniting with your brethren) and to have done what else related to the church. But his majesty perceiving no great inclination amongst you to comply with his demands hath commanded me to dissolve this present assembly...' In the king's name Lothian accordingly declared the assembly dissolved, omitting to announce the date of the next meeting. This gave rise to a disturbance during which the moderator found himself invoking the intrinsic power of the assembly to meet and, in spite of the commissioner, fixing the date.[175] William had been annoyed — so annoyed that he had abruptly changed his mind over the ministerial changes and taken them further than he had intended.[176]

The reshuffle originally projected in the ministry had been based on a limited and controlled dilution of the presbyterian interest. 'Presbyterians' were to dominate the administration in the proportion of two to one. The government was to be left in what Portland and Carstares thought of as safe hands whilst the supposed 'episcopalian' interest was to be reconciled by one or two concessions. As a result of William's fury at the assembly's tactics and its ultimate defiance of the royal will, what had emerged was little more than a cobbling together of interests. Yet the selection had not been entirely random, though it might well have been for all the difference that it made. Even during William's bout of table-thumping some key considerations had been borne in mind. The 'presbyterian' interests could not be ignored and were still strongly represented, claiming a monopoly of loyalty to the revolution. Johnston had even been added to them although he, of course, stood well outside the Melville clique. Most probably his appointment was intended to put in a royal servant who could be trusted and yet not be repugnant, as was Dalrymple, to the presbyterians as a body. Others, Tweeddale, Tarbat, Linlithgow and the rest, had been put in to pacify the 'episcopalians' and to disturb presbyterian complacency after the general assembly of 1692. Yet both schemes, that originally planned and that actually put into effect, were based on the misapprehension that the problem was one of reconciling two religious interests.

So, although the new administration was the product of scheming, hard bargaining and royal outrage, it did not lack a *rationale*, though one some way removed from reality. What had been flung together was a highly improbable combination. No interest was completely dominant; none remotely satisfied. And still personally excluded, jealously and closely watching their inferiors, were the magnates. With hindsight it is easy to see that further trouble was unavoidable and that religion would have comparatively little to do with it. Even at the time this ought perhaps to have been prophesied.

NOTES

1. D. H. Whiteford in his two articles on the theme 'Jacobitism as a factor in Presbyterian-Episcopalian relations . . . ', *RSCHS*, xvi, is concerned to establish that episcopalians were theologically bound to be jacobite. Whether this was true of episcopalians or not, it could hardly have applied to the conforming clergy who were pragmatists almost by definiton.

2. NLS, MS 7026, 89, Tweeddale to Yester, 22 Dec. 1688; *ib.*, 151, May 1687.
3. J. R. Jones, 'The Scottish constitutional opposition in 1679', *SHR* (1958), 39.
4. Burnet, i, 188-9.
5. For his tortuous past: P. J. Pinckney, 'The Scottish representation to the Cromwellian parliament of 1656', *SHR* (1967), 107; Sir W. Fraser, *The Scotts of Buccleuch* (Edinburgh 1878), i, 312-54; NLS, MS 7014, 63, [J. Dickson] to Tweeddale, 5 Apr. 1692. For his moderate attitudes after the restoration: G. Donaldson, *Scotland: James V to James VII* (Edinburgh, 1965), chap. 19; Burnet, i, 210, 229 and John Patrick, 'The origins of the opposition to Lauderdale in the Scottish parliament of 1673', *SHR* (1974). Patrick, *art. cit.*, also refers to Tweeddale's estate difficulties. For a summary of his embarrassment over the affair of the £10,000 bond, see NLS, MS 7026, 61, [Tweeddale] to Yester, 3 Mar. [16]68 [*sic* for 86]. This episode can be traced in *ib.*, *passim* and reflects little credit on anybody involved.
6. This episode is reconstructed in Maurice Lee, jr., *The Cabal* (Urbana, 1965), 43-69. For a summary of the negotiations: J. Bruce, *Report on the . . . Union* (London 1799), i, 185-230.
7. John Patrick, *art. cit.*, n.5 above.
8. NLS, MS 7026, 106, Tweeddale to Yester, 19 Jan. 1689.
9. *Ib.*, 91, same to same, 27 Dec. 1688; *ib.*, 121, same to same, 2 Feb. 1689; *ib.*, 79, same to same, 8 Jan. 1688[/9]; *ib.*, 139, same to same, 19 Feb. [16]89; *ib.*, 141, same to same, 21 Feb. [16]89; *ib.*, 122, same to same, 2 Feb. [16]89. For the other half of this correspondence, see HLRO, Willcocks MSS, 3/17-97.
10. NLS, MS 7026, 110, same to same, 24 Jan. 1689. It is fair to say that Yester saw no need for haste over place-hunting or a settlement: HLRO, Willcocks MSS, 21, 11 Feb. [16]89 and 22, 19 Feb. [16]89 to Tweeddale.
11. NLS, MS 7026, 85, same to same, 16 Dec. 1688; Balcarres, *Memoirs*, 18.
12. NLS, MS 7026, 127, Tweeddale to Yester, 7 Feb. [16]89; *ib.*, 129, Tweeddale to William, [Feb. 1689]; *CSP (Dom.), 1689-90*, 5, 21 Feb. 1689.
13. NLS, MS 7026, 90, Tweeddale to Yester, 23 Dec. 1688; *ib.*, 92, same to same, 28 Dec. 1688; *ib.*, 100, same to same, 3 Jan. 1689; *ib.*, 105, same to same, 17 Jan. 1689; *ib.*, 106, same to same, 19 Jan. 1689. Yester mentions his own soundings: HLRO, Willcocks MSS, 24, 23 Feb. [16]89, to Tweeddale.
14. NLS, MS 7026, 90, same to same, 23 Dec. 1688: *ib.*, 105, same to same, 17 Jan. 1689; *ib.*, 112, same to same, 29 Jan. 1689 and *ib.*, *passim*.
15. *Ib.*, 108, same to same, 22 Jan. 1689; *ib.*, 77, same to same, 5 Jan.1688[/9]; *ib.*, 119, same to same, 31 Jan. [16]89. Stair was later reported to have issued a print — *Stair's Apology* — in two versions, one for England recommending an episcopalian settlement in Scotland, and one for Scotland in favour of presbyterianism: HLRO, Willcocks MSS, 61, 20 Mar. 1690, [David Hay] to Tweeddale.
16. NLS, MS 7026, 176, same to same, 30 Mar. [16]89.
17. *Ib.*, 94, same to same, 29 Dec. 1688; *ib.*, 149, same to same, 2 Mar. [16]89.
18. *Ib.*, 94a, [1689].
19. *Ib.*, 92, Tweeddale to Yester, 28 Dec. 1688.
20. E.g., *ib.*, 135, same to Halifax, undated; *ib.*, 116, same to Stair, 29 Jan. [16]89.
21. *Ib.*, 134, same to Yester, 14 Feb. [16]89; *ib.*, 75, same to same, 4 Jan. 1688[/9]; *ib.*, 77, same to same, 5 Jan. 1688[/9].
22. *APS*, ix, 9; NLS, MS 7026, 160, Tweeddale to Yester, 16 Mar. [16]89.
23. *Memoirs*, 32-3.
24. NLS, MS 7026, 147, Tweeddale to Yester, 28 Feb. [16]89.
25. *Ib.*, 95, same to same, 31 Dec. 1688.
26. *Ib.*, 219, same to same, 25 Apr. [16]89; SRO, GD26, xiii, 125, [Memorial of 1704].
27. NLS, MS 7026, 209, Tweeddale to Yester, 15 Apr. [16]89.
28. *Ib.*, 156, same to same, 12 Mar. [16]89.
29. *Ib.*, 184, same to same, 4 Apr. [16]89; *ib.*, 209, same to same, 15 Apr. [16]89; *APS*, ix, 60, 23 Apr. 1689.
30. NLS, MS 7026, 161, Tweeddale to Yester, 20 Mar. [16]89; *ib.*, 184, same to same, 4 Apr. [16]89.
31. *Ib.*, 190, same to same, 6 Apr. [16]89.
32. *Ib.*, 219, same to same, 25 Apr. [16]89; *Proceedings*, i, 35, 12 Apr. 1689.
33. *HMCR Johnstone MSS*, 150, Carstares to Crawford, 16 Jan. 1690.
34. I.e., members of the Church of England.
35. *HMCR Johnstone MSS*, 149-50, Melville to Crawford, 16 Jan. [1690]
36. *Ib.*, 144, Carstares to same, 7 Dec. 1689; *ib.*, 146, draft letter from Crawford to a minister, 26 Dec. 1689.
37. *HMCR Marchmont MSS*, 118, Polwarth to Culloden, 22 Aug. 1689.
38. *Leven and Melville Papers*, 171, Crawford to Melville, 16 Jul. 1689; *ib.*, 277, same to same, 10 Sep. 1689.
39. Foxcroft, *Halifax*, ii, 218.

40. See above, pp. 34-5.
41. *Leven and Melville Papers*, 341, 7 Dec. 1689; Foxcroft, *Halifax*, ii, 217.
42. *HMCR Johnstone MSS*, 158, Melville to Crawford, 4 Jul. [1690]; *ib.*, 159, same to same, 11 Oct. [1690].
43. NLS, MS 7012, 92, Sir A. Bruce to Tweeddale, 26 Jun. 1690; *ib.*, 102, same to same, 1 and 3 Jul. 1690.
44. *Ib.*, 123, countess of Roxburghe to same, 23 Jul. [1690]; *ib.*, 167, same to same, 5 Sep. [1690]; *ib.*, 173, same to same, 27 Sep. [1690]; *ib.*, 156, Bruce to same, 28 Aug. 1690 for its local manifestations.
45. Drummond and Bulloch, *The Scottish Church*, 9; *HMCR Johnstone MSS.*, 159-60, [Oct] 1690. See HLRO, Willcocks MSS, 40, 20 Sept. [16]89, [Yester] to Tweeddale; *et passim*.
46. See above, pp. 41-2 and NLS, MS 7012, 187, [Bruce] to Yester, 15 Oct. 1690. Melville was said to be 'as much master of this country as any secretary ever we had . . .' (HLRO, Willcocks MSS, 63, 22 Mar. [16]90, [Yester] to [Tweeddale]).
47. E.g., Melville's protest against the ratification of Tweeddale's lordship of Dunfermline: *APS*, ix, 332-3, 15 Jun. 1693 and below, *passim*.
48. NLS, MS 7012, 123, countess of Roxburghe to Tweeddale, 23 Jul. [1690].
49. See below, p. 92 and Fraser, *Cromartie*, i, 119-20, Tweeddale to Yester, 8 Feb. 1696.
50. NLS, MS 7027, 1-2, Tweeddale to Sir R. Southwell, 30 Jun. 1690. For David's account of his arrest: HLRO, Willcocks MSS, 64, 22 Jun. 1690. Leven opposed his release on bail.
51. *Ib*; *Leven and Melville Papers*, 384, Sir W. Lockhart to Melville, 25 Jan. 1690; NLS, MS 7012, 89, countess of Roxburghe to Tweeddale, 12 Jun. 1690; *ib.*, 161, same to same, 5 Sep. [1690]. Yester had told his father his intention of 'living abstractly' and minding 'our private affairs': HLRO, Willcocks MSS, 37, 13 Aug. [16]89. See also *ib.*, 41, 23 Sep. [16]89.
52. NLS, MS 7012, 81, same to same, 3 Jun. 1690.
53. *Ib.*, 117, same to same, 16 Jul. 1690; *ib.*, 96, same to same, 27 Jun. 1690; *ib.*, 106, J. Aikenhead to Yester, 1 Jul. 1690; *ib.*, 7013, 3, countess of Roxburghe to Tweeddale, 10 Feb. 1691; Browning, *Danby*, ii, 166-8, Carmarthen to [   ], 23 Jun. 1690; *ib.*, 168-9, same to the king, 26 Jun. 1690.
54. *Leven and Melville Papers*, 378, Dalrymple to Melville, 21 Jan. 1690; *ib.*, 384, Lockhart to same, 25 Jan. 1690.
55. NLS, MS 7012, 156, Bruce to Tweeddale, 28 Aug. 1690. Cf. *Seafield Correspondence*, 62-3, [Sir W. Hamilton] to Ogilvy, 2 Aug. 1690.
56. SRO, SP3/1 (unpaginated), Tweeddale to [Johnston], 23 Feb. 1692. See also NLS, MS 7028, 52, same to same, 15 Mar. 1694.
57. NLS, MS 7012, 156, Bruce to Tweeddale, 28 Aug. 1690. For one symptom of the division: NUL, Portland, PwA 216, countess of Kincardine to Portland, 1 Sep. 1690.
58. See below, pp. 71-3.
59. NLS, MS 7012, 156, Bruce to Tweeddale, 28 Aug. 1690; *ib.*, 167, J. Aikenhead to same, 5 Sep. 1690; *APS*, ix, 236. So thinly attended apart from Melville courtiers that Hamilton proposed fines.
60. NLS, MS 7012, 151, Bruce to Tweeddale, 9 Apr. 1690. Private statements of account for 1691-2 and 1692-3, for what they are worth, show that the revenue was not fully meeting expenditure even on paper without arrears in collection or leakage; Buccleuch (Drum.), Church and State, 'The Revenue and Burden thereupon from November 1691 to November 1692' and a similar statement for the succeeding twelve months. The statements were obviously for Drumlanrig's use.
61. NLS, MS 7012, 214, Bruce to Tweeddale, 15 Nov. 1690; *ib.*, 228, same to same, 8 Dec. 1690.
62. *Ib.*, MS 7027, 2, Tweeddale to Sir R. Southwell, 30 Jun. 1690; *ib.*, MS 7012, 156, Bruce to Tweeddale, 28 Aug. 1690; *ib.*, 145-8, same to same, 7 Aug. 1690. For Crawford's confused defence of the treasury: *HMCR Johnstone MSS*, 163-6.
63. *Ib*; *CSP (Dom.), 1691-2*, 540, Melville to the king, 3 Apr. [1690 or 1691]; *ib.*, 4 Apr. [1690 or 1691]; SRO, GD26, xiii, 15, ' . . . a History of Scotland from Charles I and afterwards' — an attempted justification of Melville's conduct.
64. NLS, MS 7027, 4, Tweeddale to Carmarthen, 12 Nov. 1690; *ib.*, 7012, 197, Bruce to Tweeddale, 4 Nov. 1690.
65. *Seafield Correspondence*, 62-3, 2 Aug. 1690.
66. NLS, MS 7012, 156, [Bruce] to Tweeddale, 28 Aug. 1690. The term 'episcopalian' was used to include genuine episcopalians, moderate presbyterians and would-be compromisers. Likewise 'presbyterian' denoted both religiously and politically motivated presbyterians. Both terms will therefore be qualified by inverted commas where it seems appropriate.
67. Sir J. Dalrymple, *Memoirs of Great Britain and Ireland*, 2 vols. (London 1771-3), ii, 107-10, Nottingham to the king, 15 Jul. [16]90.
68. NLS, MS 7012, 197, Bruce to Tweeddale, 4 Nov. 1690; *ib.*, 203, same to same, 8 Nov. 1690.
69. Buccleuch (Drum.), Queensberry Letters, ix, Linlithgow to Queensberry, 27 Sep. 1690; *HMCR Johnstone MSS*, 161-2, same to Strathmore, 20 Nov. 1690.

70. *Ib.*, 177, same to same, 1 Oct. 1690; NLS, MS 7012, 183, Bruce to Tweeddale, 6 Oct. 1690.
71. *Ib.*, 209, [Bruce] to Yester, 14 Nov. 1690; *ib.*, 203, [same] to Tweeddale, 8 Nov. 1690.
72. *Ib.*, 177, same to same, 1 Oct. 1690; *ib.*, 222, [same] to same, 29 Nov. 1690.
73. HMCR *Johnstone MSS*, 161-2, Linlithgow to Strathmore, 20 Nov. 1690; Buccleuch (Drum.), Queensberry Letters, ix, same to Queensberry, 25 Dec. 1690.
74. *Ib.*
75. NLS, MS 7012, 195, [Bruce] to Tweeddale, 1 Nov. 1690; *ib.*, 197, same to same, 4 Nov. 1690.
76. *Ib.*, 7027, 4, 12 Nov. 1690.
77. *Ib.*, 218, Bruce to [Tweeddale], 18 Nov. 1690; *ib.*, 7013, 41, same to [same], 6 Apr. 1691; *ib.*, 5, [same] to [same], 19 Jan. 1691.
78. *Ib.*, 7012, 226, Charles Hay to Yester, 2 Dec. 1690.
79. I.e., William.
80. NLS, MS 7027, 6, Tweeddale to [Johnston], 28 Nov. 1690.
81. *Ib.*, MS 7012, 226, Charles Hay to Yester, 2 Dec. 1690; Buccleuch (Drum.), Queensberry Letters, vi, James Douglas to Queensberry, 12 Aug. 1690; *ib.*, ix, Linlithgow to same, 25 Dec. 1690.
82. NLS, MS 7012, 226, Charles Hay to Yester, 2 Dec. 1690.
83. HMCR *Finch MSS*, iv, 3-5, [Memorial from A. Higgins, 1691].
84. NLS, MS 7013, 53, countess of Rothes to Tweeddale, 21 Apr. 1691; Fraser, *Melvilles*, ii, 160-5, [Crawford] to Carstares, 16 Jun. 1691; Browning, *Danby*, ii, 201-2, Carmarthen to the king, 14 Jul. 1691.
85. *Caldwell Papers*, pt. i, 181, J.E. to undersecretary Hamilton, 27 May 1691.
86. Fraser, *Melvilles*, ii, 172, 22 Jul. 1692.
87. NLS, MS 7013, 41, [Bruce] to [Tweeddale], 6 Apr. 1691; *ib.*, 67, [same] to same, 26 May 1691; *ib.*, 69, [same] to same, 11 Jun. [16]91; *ib.*, 55, [same] to [same], 21 Apr. 1691.
88. *Ib.*, MS 7012, 214, [same] to same, 15 Nov. 1690.
89. HMCR *Johnstone MSS*, 159, Melville to Crawford, 11 Oct. [1690]; *ib.*, 159-60, Instructions to Carmichael.
90. SRO, CH1/1/12, 19, 10 Oct. 1690, read on 17 Oct.
91. NLS, MS 7012, [Bruce] to Yester, 15 Oct. 1690.
92. SRO, CH1/1/12, 23.
93. *Ib.*, 26, 22 Oct. 1690.
94. *Ib.*, 32-5.
95. *Ib.*, 44.
96. *Ib.*, 53, 62.
97. *Ib.*, 78-82; NLS, MS 7012, 218, [Bruce] to [Tweeddale], 18 Nov. 1690; *ib.*, 189, [same] to [same], 16 Oct. 1690; *ib.*, 195, [same] to same, 1 Nov. 1690; *ib.*, 203, [same] to same, 8 Nov. 1690.
98. *Ib.*, 214, [Bruce] to Tweeddale, 15 Nov. 1690; *ib.*, 218, [same] to [same], 18 Nov. 1690.
99. *Ib.*, MS 7013, 5, [Bruce] to [Tweeddale], 19 Jan. 1691; Macpherson, App., 190, Dalrymple to Hamilton, 13 Feb. 1690/1; *CSP (Dom.), 1690-91*, 257, the king to the Scottish privy council, 13 Feb. 1691; *ib.*, 257-8, same to the general assembly, 13 Feb. 1691.
100. NLS, MS 7013, 16, [Bruce] to [Tweeddale], 26 Feb. 1691; *ib.*, 18, Dalrymple to Tweeddale, 27 Feb. 1691; Browning, *Danby*, ii, 197-8.
101. HMCR *Finch MSS*, iii, commissioners to the king, 24 Apr. 1691.
102. *CSP (Dom.), 1690-91*, 414-15, the king to the commissioners, 15/25 Jul. 1691.
103. HMCR *Finch MSS*, iii, 168, 20 Jul. 1691.
104. *Ib.*, 160, Lockhart to Nottingham, 16 Jul. 1691.
105. *Ib.*, 186, same to same, 29 Jul. 1691, enclosing a report by the 'commissioners for visitations on the south side of the Tay', 22 Jul. 1691.
106. *Ib.*, iv, 2, Dalrymple to Nottingham, 8/18 Jun. 1691; NLS, MS 7013, 71, C. Hay to Tweeddale, 25 Jun. 1691.
107. *Ib.*, 59, [Bruce] to Tweeddale, 9 May 1691.
108. *Ib.*, 71, C. Hay to Tweeddale, 25 Jun. 1691.
109. Browning, *Danby*, ii, 201-2, Carmarthen to the king, 14 Jul. 1691.
110. Buccleuch (Drum.), Union, i, Dalrymple to [Queensberry], 2/12 Oct. 1691.
111. Drummond and Bulloch, *The Scottish Church*, 8-9; F. C. Mather, 'Church, parliament and penal laws: some Anglo-Scottish interactions in the eighteenth century', *EHR* (1977).
112. For the arguments which bound convinced episcopalians to jacobitism see D. H. Whiteford, 'Jacobitism as a factor in Presbyterian-Episcopalian relations in Scotland, 1689-1714', *RSCHS*, xvi.
113. Buccleuch (Drum.), Union, i, Dalrymple to Queensberry, 13/23 Jul. 1690 [*sic* for 1691]; Ferguson, *Scotland*, 18, dates the Breadalbane scheme as early as August 1689.

114. *Ib.*, chap. i.
115. See above, p. 58.
116. *HMCR Johnstone MSS*, 166, Hill to Crawford, 16 Jan. 1691.
117. *Leven and Melville Papers*, 425, Hill to Leven, 17 Apr. 1690; *ib.*, 611, same to Melville, 12 May 1691; *ib.*, 612, same to Tarbat, 12 May 1691; *ib.*, 617, same to Melville, 3 Jun. 1691.
118. See, e.g., *CSP (Dom.), 1689-90*, 550-51, Tarbat to the king, 13 Apr. 1690; *ib.*, 551, same to same, 14 Apr. 1690; Balcarres, *Memoirs*, 56-7.
119. NUL, Portland, PwA 216, countess of Kincardine to Portland, 1 Sep. 1690.
120. *Leven and Melville Papers*, 422, 25 Mar. 1690; Ferguson, *Scotland*, 17 and n.
121. *Ib.*
122. Macpherson, App., 217, letters from Tarbat to the king, [1691]; *CSP (Dom.), 1691-92*, 60-62, Tarbat to the king, [1691].
123. *HMCR Johnstone MSS*, 161, Hill to Crawford, 16 Nov. 1690.
124. *HMCR Finch MSS*, iii, 42, 'The Affaire of Scotland', [received] 1 May 1691.
125. Buccleuch (Drum.), Union, i, Dalrymple to Queensberry, 13/23 Jul. 1690 [*sic* for 1691].
126. *Leven and Melville Papers*, 530, Breadalbane to Melville, 17 Sep. 1690.
127. *Ib.*, 421, the king to Melville, 20/30 Mar. 1690; *ib.*, 429, warrant to Breadalbane, 24 Apr. 1690; *ib.*, 434, the king to Melville, 2 May 1690.
128. *HMCR Finch MSS*, iii, 166, 20/30 Jul. 1691.
129. *Ib.*, 135, Lockhart to Nottingham, 2 Jul. 1691.
130. *Ib.*, 213-14, 17/27 Aug. 1691. See above, pp. 62-5.
131. *Ib.*, 174, Dalrymple to Breadalbane, 23 Jul. 1691; Macpherson, App., 208-9, same to Hamilton, 17/27 Aug. 1691.
132. NLS, MS 7013, 82, [J. Dickson] to Tweeddale, 24 Sep. 1691.
133. *HMCR Finch MSS*, iii, 159-60, Lockhart to [Nottingham], 16 Jul. 1691.
134. *Ib.*, 100-101, Breadalbane to same, 5 Jun. 1691; *ib.*, Lockhart to [same], 16 Jul. 1691; *ib.*, 171-2, Nottingham to Lockhart, 22 Jul. 1691; *ib.*, Leinster to Livingston, [Jul. 1691]; *ib.*, 184, Lockhart to Nottingham, 29 Jul. 1691; *ib.*, 194, same to [same], [c. 4 Aug. 1691]; *ib.*, 204, same to [same], 13 Aug. 1691; Macpherson, App., 210, Dalrymple to Breadalbane, 15/25 Jun. 1691; *CSP (Dom.), 1690-91*, 413, the king to the privy council, [15 Jun. 1691]; NUL, Portland, PwA 2429, privy council to the king, 3 Aug. 1691, Fraser, *Annandale Book*, ii, 52-3, [Whitelaw] to Annandale, 6 Aug. [1691].
135. *HMCR Finch MSS*, iii, 184-6, Lockhart to Nottingham, 29 Jul. 1691; *ib.*, Nottingham to Lockhart, 1 Aug. 1691; *ib.*, 190, same to Dalrymple, 3 Aug. 1691.
136. *Leven and Melville Papers*, 625, Hill to Melville, 26 Jun. 1691; *HMCR Johnstone MSS*, 173-4, same to Crawford, 14 Sep. 1691; *ib.*, 175-6, same to same, 19 Oct. 1691.
137. Ferguson, *Scotland*, 17-20; NLS, MS 7013, 82, [Dickson] to Tweeddale, 24 Sep. 1691; Macpherson, App., 216-17, Dalrymple to Breadalbane, 3 Dec. 1691. Tarbat had earlier professed good will to the project: *CSP (Dom.), 1690-91*, 208-10, to the king, [1690].
138. *Leven and Melville Papers*, 643, 645; *ib.*, 647, Breadalbane to Hill, 10 Oct. 1691; *ib.*, 648, Hill to Breadalbane, 17 Oct. 1691; *ib.*, 649, same to lord Raith, 29 Oct. 1691; *HMCR Johnstone MSS*, 170-71, same to Crawford, 18 Jun. 1691.
139. See below, pp. 94-5.
140. *HMCR Finch MSS*, iii, 241, 28 Aug. 1691.
141. *Ib.*, 211, Portland to Nottingham, [17/]27 Aug. 1691.
142. Buccleuch (Drum.), Queensberry Letters, vi, J. Douglas to Queensberry, 22 Jul. 1691.
143. *Ib.*, Dalrymple to [Queensberry], 24 Aug. O.S. 1692 [*sic* for 1691]; *ib.*, Union, i, same to [same], 2/12 Oct. 1691.
144. Macpherson, App., 210, 15/25 Jun. 1691; *ib.*, 211-12, 18 Sep. 1691; *ib.*, 212-13, 20/30 Sep. 1691; *HMCR Finch MSS*, iii, 174-5, [Dalrymple] to Breadalbane, 23 Jul. 1691.
145. NLS, MS 7013, 79, [Bruce] to [Tweeddale], 13 Aug. 1691; Buccleuch (Drum.), Queensberry Letters, ix, Breadalbane to [Queensberry], 10 Sep. 1691.
146. NLS, MS 7027, 12, Tweeddale to Yester, 28 Jul. 1691; *ib.*, 20, same to the king, 16 Feb. 1692.
147. Carmarthen.
148. *HMCR Finch MSS*, iii, 280, Breadalbane to [Nottingham], 3 Oct. 1691.
149. *Ib.*, 172-3, Nottingham to Portland, 23 Jul. 1691
150. Browning, *Danby*, ii, 200-201, Carmarthen to the king, 22 May 1691.
151. Macpherson, App., 213-14, Dalrymple to Breadalbane, 24 Nov. 1691; *ib.*, 214-16, same to same, 2 Dec. 1691.
152. *Ib.*, 216-17, same to same, 3 Dec. 1691.

153. *Ib.*, 213-14, same to same, 24 Nov. 1691; *ib.*, 214-16, same to same, 2 Dec. 1691; NLS, MS 7014, 5, Dalrymple to Tweeddale, 11 Jan. 1692.
154. Macpherson, App., 214-16, 2 Dec. 1691.
155. NLS, MS 7013, 41, [Bruce] to [Tweeddale], 6 Apr. 1691. See above, p. 58 and n. 60.
156. I.e., farm.
157. NLS, MS 7012, 151, Bruce to Tweeddale, 9 Apr. [*sic* for Aug?] 1690; *ib.*, 228, [same] to same, 8 Dec. 1690; *ib.*, MS 7013, 14, [same] to [same], 29 Feb. 1691; *ib.*, 24, [same] to same, 17 Mar. 1691; *ib.*, 114, Dalrymple to same, 27 Oct. 1691.
158. Buccleuch (Drum.), Queensberry Letters, xiv, [Hamilton?] to [Queensberry], 29 Jul. 1691.
159. See above, p. 58.
160. NLS, MS 7012, 181, [Sir F . Scott] to Tweeddale, 1 Oct. [16]90; *ib.*, MS 7013, 16, [Bruce] to [same], 26 Feb. 1691; *ib.*, 14, [same] to [same], 29 Feb. 1691; *ib.*, MS 7012, 228, [same] to same, 8 Dec. 1690; *ib.*, MS 7013, 33, [same] to same, 2 Apr. 1691; *ib.*, 37, [same] to [same], 4 Apr. 1691; *ib.*, 55, [same] to [same], 21 Apr. 1691; *ib.*, MS 7028, 130v., Tweeddale to Johnston, [Aug.] 1694; *ib.*, 137, same to same, 25 Aug. 1694; *ib.*, 148, same to same, 17 Sep. 1694.
161. Fraser, *Melvilles*, ii, 47-8, 15 Oct. 1690; NLS, MS 7014, 8, Dalrymple to Tweeddale, 16 Jan. 1692; *ib.*, MS 7028, 100, Tweeddale to [   ], 14 May 1694; *ib.*, 148, same to Johnston, 17 Sep. 1694; *ib.*, MS 7029, 9v., same to same, 1 Dec. 1694; SRO, SP3/1, [Johnston] to Tweeddale, 1 Dec. 1692; *APS.*, ix, 408-10.
162. NLS, MS 7013, 120, [Dickson] to Tweeddale, 29 Oct. 1691.
163. See the series of letters to him from the countess of Roxburghe, e.g., NLS, MS 7012, 171, 25 Sep. 1690; *ib.*, 212, 15 Nov. 1690; *ib.*, MS 7013, 8, 24 Jan. 1691. See also *ib.*, MS 7012, 169, Murray to Tweeddale, 22 Sep. [16]90.
164. *Ib.*, MS 7013, 114, Dalrymple to same, 27 Oct. 1691; *ib.*, 126, same to same, [31 Oct.] 1691; *ib.*, 128, Sir P. Murray to Tweeddale, 2 Nov. 1691; *ib.*, 136, Dalrymple to same, 10 Nov. 1691.
165. *Ib.*, 142, [Dickson] to same, 14 Nov. 1691; *ib.*, 146, [same] to [same], 17 Nov. 1691.
166. *Ib.*, 120, [same] to same, 29 Oct. 1691.
167. *Ib.*, 146, [same] to [same], 17 Oct. 1691.
168. A great deal of trouble was taken to justify Melville's conduct in presbyterian terms and to stigmatise his enemies as jacobites: SRO, GD26, xiii, 15, 69, 120-24.
169. NLS, MS 7013, 158, Dalrymple to Tweeddale, 26 Dec. 1691.
170. *Ib.*, MS 7014, 2, same to same, 5 Jan. 1692.
171. *Ib.*, 19, [Dickson] to Yester, 3 Mar. 1692. New privy council list: NUL, Portland, PwA 2442, Mar. 1692. New commissions: *CSP (Dom.), 1691-92*, 166-7, 3 Mar. 1692.
172. I.e., Dalrymple's.
173. *HMCR Finch MSS*, iv, 2, 8/18 Jun. 1691.
174. *CSP (Dom.), 1691-92*, 92-4, 11 Jan. 1692. For the king's speech: SRO, CH1/1/12, 106-9, 7 Jan. 1691/2.
175. Ferguson, *Scotland*, 108; SRO, SP3/1, [Johnston] to James Stewart, 10 Mar. 1691/2. SRO, CH1/1/12. 152-4, 13 Feb. 1692.
176. SRO, SP3/1, [Johnston] to James Stewart, 5 Mar. 1691/2.

4
Johnston, Tweeddale and the Magnates

EVEN in 1692, when it was being constructed, the new 'motley ministry' seemed certain to generate further agitation. The probability was that dissatisfaction and intrigue would increase rather than diminish. It remained only to be seen what alignments would develop and how the tension would find expression.

One 'trigger' of the subsequent trouble — in a situation so fundamentally unstable as that of 1692 one cannot really say 'cause' — was the appointment of James Johnston whose ambitions and temperament were incompatible with those of Dalrymple. This is not to blame Johnston. Anyone of ambition would have found himself in conflict with Dalrymple. Given other circumstances, either of the secretaries would have been to William's taste, brisk transactors of business with a mastery of detail. As it was, the animosity between the two secretaries became the pivot for all the existing rivalries in Scotland. Both Johnston and his brother Alexander were restless, energetic men, concerned to make their way in the administration and through their activities in Anglo-Scottish affairs to gain some security and influence. Their efforts were not expended entirely on selfish ends. In everything they did they were zealous servants of the crown, but if William's service seemed to call for the humiliation of their personal rivals it gave them satisfaction. Johnston's own determination to succeed was the greater for the long period of what seemed to him deprivation, when he had been kept out of domestic politics after the revolution and shunted instead into the diplomatic service.[1] Dalrymple's ambition had been manifested continuously before and since the revolution. So to contain both Johnston and Dalrymple for any length of time within one administration was not feasible. Nor could conflict between them have been long postponed. Whilst Dalrymple had his family connections in Scotland and other alliances contracted since he had been in office and scheming against Melville, Johnston was starting from scratch. His priority was the rapid accumulation of an interest which, in the nature of things, could not be directed other than against Dalrymple. From the moment of Johnston's appointment, lord Stair, Dalrymple's father, had been afraid of such a development.[2] Other issues, of course, polarised round this personal conflict. The various contenders for power aligned themselves with one or other of these rival court factions as private interest seemed to dictate.

In this situation Tweeddale's position was from the start uncomfortable. Nominally, as chancellor, he was head of the ministry and co-ordinator of policy, but his appointment was unwelcome to many. Hamilton, for one, had long coveted the post of chancellor and looked on Tweeddale as having been placed 'over his head'.[3] Until the following year he resolutely fended off all attempts to placate him.[4] Nor had Tweeddale's appointment pleased the more aggressive 'episcopalians' any more than it had the Melville interest, still represented in the ministry. He was sniped at from all sides and quite soon his commonwealth past was being resurrected to discredit him.[5] Dalrymple's attitude to him was initially one almost of condescension as he did his best to convey the impression to Tweeddale that his tenure of office was precarious and dependent on Dalrymple's support.[6] And it was true that Tweeddale had no personal following worth speaking of. His position was in fact quite unenviable.

To Tweeddale's credit he was prepared to try to make the administration work despite the absence amongst its various elements of any willingness to co-operate. But the Melville family was unlikely to rest until it had regained its former position or at least inflicted damage on its rivals, and Tweeddale realised that unless the administration was purged of that entire interest he would have no peace. He was even desperate enough to think of cultivating Hamilton as an ally against Melville.[7] Restlessness and disharmony, wholly personal in origin, prevailed throughout the court. Sir William Hamilton told Ogilvy: ' . . . These that are in court think never to be out of it; and these that are out are still hoping to be in. It is thought by some that there will be some alterations when the king return. This is hoped and feared by different parties . . . '[8]

Amidst this discord Johnston determined to construct his own interest and consequently to define his position. The problems faced by the new government made the task easy for him. Johnston's views had the support of the king, and their nature, together with Johnston's office as secretary, dictated the extent of his future following. The secretary had come in partly on the strength of a promise to Tenison, archbishop of Canterbury, to do what he could for the episcopalian clergy. Tenison had been greatly exercised in finding some formula which would allow the episcopalian and conformist clergy to gain official recognition in Scotland. Johnston was a presbyterian of strictly regular private life but largely untroubled by theological niceties. This outlook enabled him to sympathise with Tenison's aims.[9] The new secretary was clearsighted enough to see that the previous ministry had shown far too much weakness over the church settlement. There had been a point, just after the new establishment had begun to operate, when a much firmer line could have been drawn for the benefit of both crown and conforming clergy, but instead there had been vacillation and connivance at presbyterian irregularities. Yet it was also apparent to him that episcopalians had been most recklessly encouraged by court intrigues to hold out for a separatist settlement when, in 1692, in Scotland, toleration for an episcopalian church was no solution. As Johnston saw it the only hope for a tolerable religious peace was some measure of comprehension within a presbyterian settlement which had to be forced, if necessary, on both parties. To accomplish this and, at the same time, to demonstrate Johnston's efficiency as a manager, there had to be a parliament. After undertaking to carry a parliament he would have a much better claim to request further ministerial changes to strengthen his position in relation to the estates. His views were kept no secret. He told James Stewart that the recent changes had put the government out of step with the church: 'The present state of things is an unnatural state. The church must go to the civil government or the civil government return to it, as I am confident it will if people be wise, for the king declares to me that he has not the least thought of changing the church government . . . ' But there had to be moderation: ' . . . I always reckoned the point of church government to be the rock on which the presbyterian interest in Scotland would split itself. That interest is now upon that rock and it's plain enough that without wisdom and moderation, it will not, at least for some time, get off again . . .'[10] His aim was the cultivation of the presbyterian interest to win them over to moderation. A more broadly based 'presbyterian' group in church and state might give less excuse for opposition, a possibility which provided Johnston with an argument for securing changes in the government. He seems to have envisaged a ministry moderate enough to reduce religious antagonism but, ultimately, strong enough to withstand a parliamentary attack. The odds were heavily against him.

From the outset Johnston had looked upon Tweeddale's appointment as no more than a stop-gap measure. In fact the secretary was never unreservedly allied to the lord chancellor until four years later when, willy-nilly, they found themselves in the same predicament. He was, however, concerned to cultivate Tweeddale's son, Yester, to gain if possible the assistance of the Tweeddale political strength without Tweeddale, though as long as he had to put up with the chancellor he did all he could to associate him with his own interest.[11] He felt, too, that he needed the support of a magnate, to which end he paid court to Hamilton. Before the parliament of 1693 Hamilton, during the chancellor's absence, was allowed to preside in the privy council instead of Melville, lord privy seal. Hamilton was also chosen as commissioner to the parliament. At the same time, by way of insurance, Johnston embarked on the advancement of Annandale, newly rehabilitated after the fiasco of Skelmorlie's plot. In 1693 he was put on the privy council and made an extraordinary lord of session. Apart from such efforts to gratify a few nobles of worthwhile interest, most of Johnston's influence was exerted in favour of those who were presbyterian by inclination but outside Melville's sphere. He induced Campbell of Cessnock to resign from the post of justice-clerk —voluntarily, Johnston said, but later, beset by creditors, Cessnock denied this — and his place was given to Adam Cockburn of Ormiston, now considered presbyterian in religion, and in politics a 'loner'. Sir James Stewart, an able lawyer with a dubious past and a well-founded reputation for venality, was brought in as lord advocate. Two intimates of the Dalrymples were put out: Sir Patrick Murray for conversational indiscretions and Sir William Lockhart, accused of taking bribes, offences rarely punished by dismissal without some political motive. On this occasion Johnston wanted them both out.[12]

This rivalry continued to be presented as a religious conflict. Johnston was not blind to the dangers of ignoring the plight of episcopalians. Although he knew they were being used as political tools, he saw the sense and justice of placating them as far as possible. But the forthcoming parliament was to be that same convention parliament which had made the original church settlement. Giving reassurance to the presbyterians offered a chance of managing parliament, whereas concessions to episcopalians offered no such hope. Johnston himself thought the best religious solution would be to unite both groups of clergy in one church establishment, but when he suggested it both Crawford and Tarbat appeared simultaneously in London to protest. The only course open appeared to be the imposition of moderate presbyterianism. The presbyterian establishment was to be exhorted to moderate courses and to be closely supervised, whilst the episcopalians were eventually to be offered fair terms for acceptance. It had to be made plain that, whatever had been allowed in the past, the church establishment was no longer to be permitted to defy the royal will. Meanwhile, until after the parliament, the council was not to interfere in church business unless it became absolutely necessary.[13] This instruction led the newly appointed 'episcopalians' in the ministry to make what capital they could of their being restrained from acting in religious issues. A chorus of complaint was as usual directed to their English sympathisers.[14]

Unfortunately for both his own position and that of the government Dalrymple, self-appointed spokesman of the 'episcopalian' party, had left himself open to attack by the final consummation of his highland venture. Breadalbane's arrangements with the chieftains had virtually excluded all courses but one if the government were not to be discredited. The ministry would have to resort to punitive action against any chieftains not taking the oaths. Since Dalrymple's involvement in the highland scheme had been incidental, its conclusion had become for him a peripheral matter and he saw no reason to hesitate over the infliction of punishment. He was not alone in thinking this way. Many who were later to express their abhorrence of what took place would earlier have been heartily in favour of it, not only to teach the highlanders a lesson but even more to sabotage Breadalbane's scheme. Punitive actions were a fairly routine occurrence in the highlands, and Dalrymple was looking for someone to serve as an example. He had in mind the Macdonalds of Glencoe.

The massacre itself on 13 February 1692 and the way in which it was carried out by Campbell troops was a sickening affair, especially since MacIain's offence was merely technical. He had not refused the oath but had been late in taking it, and not altogether through his own fault. The offence was no more than an excuse for the killing. In the light of what happened in Glencoe the utterances of Dalrymple have a brutal ring about them. ' . . . I am extremely glad,' he wrote to Tweeddale, 'that the murderer MacIain of Glencoe did not accept the benefit of the indemnity. I hope care will be taken to root out that thieving tribe . . .'[15] And afterwards he wrote: '. . . It's true that affair of Glencoe was very ill execute but it's strange to me what means so much regret for such a sept of thieves . . . '[16] At no time did he appear repentant.[17] The Macdonalds, of course, had themselves been responsible for barbarities in the usual highland style. Not all of the clan were completely innocent victims, a fact well known to those who shouted most loudly for retribution. A nauseating aspect of the whole affair was that people who had associated themselves with the massacre and, like colonel Hill, hastened to report how efficiently the order had been carried out, [18] later put the blame on Dalrymple. In fact the outcry was more against Dalrymple than the crime. Feeling against the Dalrymples had not at all disappeared since the revolution; it had merely, in the absence of a parliament, been muted. Now in some quarters there was a determination to place on the master of Stair the blame for ordering the massacre, in an attempt to force him out of the government. Quite early there were signs that Johnston was looking for a way of attacking Dalrymple over Glencoe whilst avoiding any criticism of the king, who bore the ultimate responsibility.[19]

On the surface it seemed that Dalrymple had agreed to the changes of late 1692 and early 1693 engineered by Johnston, although they had had a 'presbyterian' flavour.[20] At least he had appeared to co-operate. He was, however, fully aware of the trend of events. Already he had made an alliance with Tarbat and various English sympathisers against both Tweeddale and Johnston.[21] The latter's proposal for a session of parliament in 1693 alarmed him and he insisted that a parliament was quite unnecessary. His official arguments against it were mostly practical ones of little substance, although his contention that instructions could not be drafted in the commissioner's absence was not without irony since the commissioner was to be Hamilton.[22] This time, however, Hamilton was not disposed to quarrel, looking on his appointment as a step to further advancement.[23] What Dalrymple was really afraid of was the advantage Johnston would try to extract from a parliament. The long-prophesied effects of a split between the secretaries were becoming apparent, aggravated by William's style of government which subordinated the secretaries to Portland. This, by inserting an extra stage in the reaching of decisions, provided almost unlimited opportunity for court intrigue.[24]

But Johnston was choosing his ground well. Dalrymple's 'episcopalian' interest in the convention parliament was neither extensive nor popular, and a further session was likely to demonstrate this conclusively. Furthermore the position his party had taken up was shaky. Dalrymple and the 'episcopalians' were contending that the root of the trouble in Scotland was the intransigence of the high presbyterians and their vindictiveness in persecuting the episcopalian clergy.[25] Great political capital had been made out of the need to make the presbyterians comply with the king's wishes. There was some truth in all this. Ostensibly it had been the point of urging changes in 1691-2. Dalrymple had written to Tweeddale on the latter's appointment as chancellor, ' . . . There's nothing now in Britain that's more the subject of men's observation than whether the presbyterians will comply with the king's desires in assuming their brethren or not. If they be obstinate I fear they repent it.'[26] Throughout this campaign the underlying contention was that, treated properly, the episcopalian clergy were ready to take the oaths. English tories had to be convinced that the only men willing to bring this about were Dalrymple and his allies. But one major circumstance did not fit very well into this picture. Episcopalian ministers, whatever their earlier views, had by this time no wish to be 'assumed' except on their own terms. If parliament forced the issue by compelling the church establishment to accept episcopalian clergy, subject to their being qualified, and the dissenting clergy still refused to apply for admission or even to qualify, then the argument of the political 'episcopalians' was likely to be exposed for what it was — a confidence trick on the English court. Should they, on the other hand, take the oaths at Johnston's behest, Dalrymple's claim to a special relationship with the episcopalians would seem feeble. Dalrymple knew this and so did Johnston, who now aimed at ensuring that what had hitherto been royal instructions were given the force of law. Johnston was quick to point out that the 'episcopalians' would be given a chance to show that they could deliver by bringing in the episcopalian clergy to take the oaths.[27] If the government determinedly embarked on a unification policy and it subsequently appeared that the royal will was no longer being defied by the presbyterian establishment but by the episcopalian clergy, then the Dalrymple group's argument would boomerang. Yet, having staked almost everything on the assertion that dissenting ministers, if not actively discouraged, would take the oaths, Dalrymple had little choice but to accept its being put to the test,[28] though utterly without relish. When his objections to a parliament were overridden he was rancorous.[29] And all the time, whether or not he suspected it, his difficulties were being increased by Tarbat, always a dangerous ally. Far from attempting to reconcile the episcopalian clergy to the establishment, Tarbat and some of his followers were vigorously encouraging them to refuse the oaths. The bait was the prospect of their being either tolerated as a separate church or received into the general assembly not as individuals but *en bloc*. All this was to be consequent upon the political 'episcopalians' securing predominance in the government.[30] If he believed this, Tarbat was mistaken, although he was probably indifferent to its truth or otherwise. Dalrymple certainly knew better.

Beyond doubt Johnston was the chief manager of the 1693 parliament. Dalrymple, having done what he could by raising awkward issues to obstruct the preparation of business, had then declined to attend.[31] Johnston, therefore, sat in parliament as lord secretary and chief manager. Even Tweeddale, although presiding as chancellor, does not seem to have wielded much influence. Nor was he in full co-operation with Johnston and perhaps not altogether in his confidence.[32] The lord secretary's handling of parliament was robust. He turned to his purpose a recently uncovered invasion threat, citing some apparently genuine evidence from intercepted letters. He played this for all it was worth, and possibly more, to secure a grant of supply on account of the alleged imminent emergency.[33] The test of any Scottish management was whether or not it could produce supply, and Johnston was determined not to fail in that respect.

Also ready to hand was a strong current of antipathy in the parliament to the Dalrymples. Dalrymple himself was unpopular on account, as it was said, of Glencoe. At least it gave his opponents what they had hitherto lacked — something specific to charge him with. Stair, his father, was thought to have established too great an ascendancy over the court of session. In an attempt to weaken if not destroy his position, a precise allegation had been levelled against him, as president of the court, and one of his other sons, a clerk of session, namely that of altering the court's official judgements.[34] The convention parliament's hostility also encompassed Linlithgow and Breadalbane as displacers of presbyterians and enemies of the revolution. Johnston tried to turn this to account. To those 'presbyterians' in parliament who were not bound to Melville he held out the hope that with their backing he would be able to press more strongly for the dismissal of their rivals and the curbing of Stair's ascendancy by the appointment of Hamilton of Whitelaw to the court of session. He succeeded in mobilising 'presbyterian' support to some purpose. By the end of 1693 he had achieved Whitelaw's promotion to the bench.[35] Getting rid of Dalrymple was a more difficult proposition, although Johnston made what use he could of the 1693 parliament. To the court he claimed credit for protecting Dalrymple and his allies, as royal servants, from parliament's wrath but at the same time urged their dismissal as the only way to gratify members and prevent further trouble.[36] He assured his own supporters that Dalrymple's dismissal was his first priority. The parliamentary session of 1693 was Johnston's first major *putsch* within the ministry.

Parliament split cleanly. On one side were the Dalrymples allied to the Linlithgow-Breadalbane interest. With this strange company, in uneasy collaboration, was the Melville family. This was a small minority in the convention parliament. Against them was the bulk of the house, either indulging its animosity towards the Dalrymples or carried along by the apparent authority of the managers. The 'episcopalian' minority stood no chance of carrying any votes.[37] All they could hope to do was manufacture as much ammunition as possible to discredit Johnston after the session. Their own inconsistencies of behaviour left them untroubled. Presumably they hoped such lapses would be lost to sight in the general flurry of slander. For instance, Johnston's opponents initially tried to limit the vote of supply but, finding this impossible, they abruptly changed tactics and with some fervour proposed a vote of supply for life. As both the managers and they knew, this had no hope of success, but it was an opportunity of introducing some confusion with no risk to themselves. Subsequently they were to claim the credit for such a loyal proposal and put the blame on the managers for discouraging it.[38]

Johnston pursued a determined policy aimed at unifying the church by law. The act for settling the peace and quiet of the church laid down the terms of the revised settlement.[39] It confirmed the existing church government. A minister was to be considered qualified if he took the oaths of allegiance and assurance and accepted the confession of faith 'as likewise that he owns and acknowledges presbyterian church government as settled by the . . . fifth act of the second session of this parliament to be the only government of this church . . . ' All ministers possessing churches but not having been admitted to membership of church courts could, if qualified, make individual application to a general assembly to be received. Failure to qualify or make application to be received into church government within thirty days of the meeting of an assembly would involve deprivation. In an attempt to clear up the situation left by the disorderly adjournment of the last general assembly, the act made provision for the summoning of another assembly. Meanwhile, as a token of impartiality, the qualifying oaths were to be imposed on all the clergy, presbyterian as well as episcopalian.[40] The aim was to make clear who exactly was refusing to accept the settlement and why.

In absolute terms, those who were episcopalians by conviction had grounds for objecting to these provisions. They would be accommodating themselves to a presbyterian establishment and, greatly to the concern of some, recognising William as king *de jure*. The issue was not seen in these terms by the managers. For them the question was political, not religious. The position of the Dalrymple group was that the episcopalians would take the oaths if the presbyterians stopped harrying them, a claim now in danger of being exposed as spurious. Episcopalian clergy for the most part had, at that time, no intention of taking the oaths. They and their political mentors had been hoping to be saved from their dilemma by the refusal of parliament to sanction the 'erastian' imposition of oaths on presbyterian ministers. As far as parliament was concerned they were disappointed, but Johnston's aims were defeated and the problem left unsolved by the intransigence of many of the presbyterian clergy themselves. The latter had no scruples about imposing oaths on episcopalians, but regarded such civil requirements, when applied to themselves, as 'erastian'. This attitude made the issue less clear-cut than it might otherwise have been. Efforts had, in fact, been made to persuade presbyterian clergy to refuse the oaths, a campaign supported by the Melville family whose real aims were becoming apparent with their rapidly accelerating slide into an 'episcopalian' alliance. In parliament, when the question of oaths had seemed about to come to a vote, Melville's family withdrew in some haste but prematurely, since the vote was not taken then. Finally, when voting did take place, Melville was present and declared himself *non liquet*.[41] A 'presbyterian' family in alliance with the 'episcopalian' party and engaged in equivocation about the oaths was only one curious aspect of the parliament. The house also witnessed the spectacle of two leading 'episcopalians' posing, in the hope of preventing any settlement at all, as stalwart defenders of the rights of presbyteries and synods.[42]

The managers made what were represented to parliament as 'concessions'. There was an act to encourage foreign trade, allowing the establishment of companies to trade with all places within the law, promising them a royal charter and the protection of the crown.[43] As a further carrot Hamilton, as commissioner, and Johnston promised to make representations to the king about some things 'that are heavy and uneasy to your people', namely the continued presence in office of the Dalrymples. Tweeddale thought action was needed to implement at once the laws relating to the church and trade, or parliament would not again meet in such a good temper.[44]

The parliament of 1693 had defined even more firmly the division in Scottish politics and within the government. Against Johnston and the growing number of his allies, attracted to his interest by his role of manager, his vigour and his anti-Dalrymple sentiments, were arrayed the political 'episcopalians' including Dalrymple and the now ambivalent Melville family. Johnston, by this time completely identified, publicly at least, with the 'presbyterian' cause, was ripe for portrayal to the king and the English as a 'hot man' and a 'bigot'. An alternative 'episcopalian' version of the recent parliament was swiftly manufactured. Dalrymple went as far as to misrepresent the church act to Englishmen as an extreme presbyterian measure. Certainly it was presbyterian in intent but it was also the first determinedly constructive move towards some kind of comprehension, however slight, since 1689, and Johnston had inspired it. Somehow Dalrymple secured an inaccurate version of the act in which it was asserted that presbytery was the only divinely ordained system of church government. He showed this to the archbishop of Canterbury, who was understandably outraged at the Scottish ministry, the Scottish parliament and their act. Only later, when he discovered that the act had very carefully avoided saying anything of the kind, was he very annoyed with Dalrymple.[45] Dalrymple made no secret of what he had done, nor did he attempt to rectify the mistake, if that is what it was. Johnston wrote to him fairly bluntly on the subject.[46] It is possible that initially Dalrymple had received the inaccurate version in good faith from Tarbat, who had been sending to London unofficial minutes of parliamentary proceedings. Tarbat was quite capable of modifying the act if he thought his own interest or some related cause would be advanced thereby. During the session he had again been caught, for the third time in his career as lord register, falsifying official minutes. Because he was unable to think of any excuse and made no attempt to defend his action, parliament did not proceed against him. Instead members found themselves almost sympathising with him in his affliction.[47] Nevertheless, whatever its source, this spurious copy of the act was put into circulation and the fullest possible use made of it. Linlithgow and the others were lauded for, it was said, standing out boldly in the teeth of the managers' displeasure for a grant of cess for the king's lifetime.[48]

The breach between the secretaries was now quite irreparable.[49] The Scottish administration was split in a way which paralysed effective government. More energy and ingenuity went into manoeuvring to score points off rivals than into the conduct of everyday business. Sniping between the two secretaries was continual and blatant.[50] William's reaction to this state of affairs was to let things drift to the detriment of both his own power and Scotland's welfare. He might have felt that there was nothing he could usefully do and was tacitly admitting it. If that were so, then he should have made use of the standard recipe, that of doing nothing, but with a show of vigour and determination. But the impression he gave for much of the time was one of near-abdication, avoiding Scottish affairs whenever he could, settling them in haste when something had to be done and then hoping for the best. Consequently, to Scotsmen, William appeared almost inert.

Johnston found himself with a growing interest reinforcing his pressure for more changes in the government. Dalrymple and his allies concentrated on keeping a foothold until what seemed the current trend at court could be reversed. The former party affected to believe the revolution itself to be in danger whilst Dalrymple, Linlithgow and Breadalbane were in office. The latter group continued to pose as protectors of the northern clergy against a small group of presbyterian 'bigots' with power out of all proportion to their numbers.[51] Johnston thought the chief trouble with the Scottish government was that it comprised a mixture of these two groups, which he referred to as 'presbyterian' and 'espicopalian', not even pretending to co-operate. Always keenly aware of the connections between English and Scottish politics, he drew the parallel for the benefit of Polwarth: '. . . The case with you and here [in England] is the same, such a mixture in councils of men directly opposite to one another will never do. I think indeed the king would do better to have them all either white or black . . . .'[52] Naturally he was hoping for a purge in his own favour, but his conclusion was the one sooner or later forced on most Scottish politicians – the government had to be 'of a piece'. As he had earlier told Queensberry, ' . . . we are the tail which will move as the body here [in England] moves . . . ', and he scented things in England – as it happened prematurely – moving in favour of the whigs. His feeling was that this could do nothing but improve his own position in Scotland.[53] Meanwhile he tried to counter Dalrymple's influence by keeping in close touch with Carstares, the usual channel of communication with the king.[54] Their relations were most cordial until their notorious quarrel, immediately damaging to Johnston and subsequently, for whatever reason, heavy on Carstares's conscience. To rebut the charge that his interest was composed of narrow-minded presbyterians, Johnston worked to broaden his ostensible political base. As part of this scheme he had cultivated Hamilton, helping to secure his appointment as lord commissioner in 1693, a task which the duke seems to have performed in a relatively unobtrusive and quite uncharacteristic fashion. Encouraged by this, Johnston, after the session of parliament, tried to fortify what he regarded as a promising alliance.[55] But he had a great deal to learn about Hamilton. Being commissioner to the 1693 parliament had revived all Hamilton's delusions of grandeur. The whole panorama of his claims once more unfolded itself. He wished to be an overlord in Scotland, if not as permanent commissioner, then at least by presiding in the treasury as well as in the council. Report had it that he was at court every day with new and contradictory propositions.[56] He pressed for another parliament with himself as commissioner; he fancied being granted a general commission to farm the maintenance of Holyrood and all the royal castles; he tried to eject Tweeddale from his lodgings at the Abbey.[57] By 1694 he was very free with criticism of the previous year's parliament as if he had had no part in it and consequently was being taken for one of the Dalrymple party. In fact his continued presence at court was an embarrassment to both secretaries alike. Johnston had completely recovered from his delusion that an alliance with Hamilton was possible. 'I would rather be a porter than live such another winter with him,' he wrote to Annandale. That problem was solved by

Hamilton's death in 1694, which produced suitable expressions of sorrow but widespread relief.[58]

Annandale had appeared to Johnston to be another possible recruit for his new court interest, so the secretary, encouraged by some nagging, bursts of temper and threats of resignation from his *protégé*, continually pushed the earl's claims for preferment. Johnston's life as a parliamentary manager was never an easy one. When the lord chancellor was called to London, Annandale was voted into the presidency of the privy council, in preference to Melville, by a handsome majority. He then pressed to be formally appointed president of the council. With Johnston's support he succeeded. In the 1695 parliament, when Tweeddale served as commissioner, Annandale was president of the parliament. Rumour had it that Johnston was grooming Annandale as his candidate for the post of chancellor should Tweeddale die or have to be supplanted.[59] Circumstances certainly made it seem plausible.

The bulk of those who ranged themselves in support of Johnston were men who, for whatever reason, religious or political, were content to be labelled 'presbyterian', or courtiers advancing their careers by what they calculated to be the most promising route. In the first group could be placed such as Polwarth, Carmichael, Ormiston, Baillie of Jerviswood, Crawford and, possibly, Hamilton of Whitelaw, who never let slip a chance of any kind. In the second group were, amongst others, Ross, Annandale, Murray of Livingston, Murray of Blackbarony and Sir James Ogilvy.[60] Johnston was committed to this company by his aim of purging the government of its 'episcopalian' element, comprising for the most part personal rivals of himself and his allies.[61]

The 'episcopalian' party was a loose grouping of political interests by no means homogeneous in religion, which is not at all surprising since religion had been an excuse rather than a reason for their existence. The party included the entire Dalrymple family, although viscount Stair's task had been to make presbyterian noises to ensure for them a line of retreat should it become necessary. Breadalbane and Linlithgow were generally looked upon as the leaders, or at least the most strident, of the group. Tarbat, too, was heavily involved. All had conformed to the church settlement, their religious professions notwithstanding.[62] Malcontents within the court, whatever their religious views, tended to join this dissident group, however unhallowed the resulting alliance might appear. Tarbat had been instrumental in recruiting the Melville family so that, although professing to be presbyterians, in council and treasury they had a firm working alliance with Linlithgow and the Dalrymples, their former enemies.[63] Lothian was also involved with them, having been deprived of what he considered his fair share of influence.[64] And significantly, though under an effective camouflage, Queensberry was in close collaboration with Johnston's opponents. Drumlanrig was professing friendship to Tweeddale but was at the same time allied to Dalrymple. On the occasions when he was present at the treasury he invariably supported Breadalbane and Linlithgow.[65] For some time, as Johnston warned Tweeddale, he had been pursuing equivocal policies.[66]

Tweeddale was left perching uneasily between these two parties. After the 1693 parliament he had been left in something like isolation. Whatever intrigues Johnston and Dalrymple were conducting, he as chancellor bore the responsibility for administration, which might have discouraged him from taking sides. He was certainly not regarded by Dalrymple as a committed enemy until later. In fact Dalrymple continued for some time to write to him as one who hoped to retain his support,[67] until, as disillusionment set in, his correspondence tailed off into purely formal letters. At the end of 1693 Tweeddale had even seemed set on an alliance with Queensberry, probably against Hamilton, who might then have seemed to be posing the most immediate threat.[68] The Johnston group for its part was prepared to make use of Tweeddale, though regarding him as not wholly to be relied upon. They subjected him to a barrage of persuasion and attempted to disillusion him concerning the views of his English tory friends.[69] Sir Archibald Murray of Blackbarony repeatedly exhorted him to join the 'presbyterians' and throw in his lot with Johnston since he had no one else to trust.[70] Tweeddale remained uncommitted and temporarily seemed to have no firm allies. Queensberry and Dalrymple, his former friends, had tried, he said, to cut his throat, but it was clear that if he moved decisively towards Johnston it would cost him any English tory support he might still retain. Already Carmarthen, his former champion, had been heard to refer to him as a 'dumbstick'.[71] And yet there were those with Johnston who, if they saw the opportunity, would drop him not only without compunction but gladly. Tweeddale took refuge in a somewhat vague and obscure mode of speech which made him all but unintelligible.[72] Nobody knew how the king stood in relation to all these divisions and, until affairs erupted in some immediate crisis demanding action, it hardly mattered.

From time to time Tweeddale made tentative moves to strengthen his personal interest as distinct from those of the contending parties, perhaps to diminish his increasing isolation. He began a rather disingenuous correspondence with Portland aimed at increasing his own influence by flattering the great. He tried to obtain various jobs for Yester. None of this came to anything.[73] He was very disheartened when the king refused to allow Yester to be a member of the treasury board on the principle that two of the same family ought not to be concerned with the finances.[74] Yet it was in the treasury, and for purely administrative reasons, that Tweeddale needed support.

In the latter part of 1694, after the death of Hamilton, the chancellor, under pressure of circumstances, began to find himself drifting with Johnston and recommending a purge of the government. And, in truth, nothing but a purge, one way or the other, would save the administration of the kingdom. The processes of government had long ago reached a standstill and Tweeddale had come to accept the inseparability of politics and administration. By August of 1694 he was in favour of opposing Dalrymple and the other episcopalian lobbyists at court and had written to the king in measured terms about factions and humours. These were nurtured, he claimed, by non-jurant clergy and the disputes between persons in office, ' . . . partly from the difference of their opinions but more from discontent with their share in the government, and jealousies of the firmness of some employed in it which your majesty cannot be a stranger to . . . but above all the different sentiments of your secretaries gives good occasions of divisions amongst us . . . '[75] The 'presbyterians' began to think they were likely to gain his support and he now looked upon himself as an ally of Johnston and Annandale.[76] They did not view him in exactly the same light. Johnston told Annandale that he had no wish for a break with Tweeddale 'at present'. The chancellor's inclinations were right enough, but Johnston wondered how long he would retain them. Tweeddale and Johnston were not really committed allies until the parliament of 1695.[77]

Above all Tweeddale was an administrator. What had driven him closer to Johnston and the 'presbyterian' interest was the opposing party's success in paralysing the Scottish administration, which made his life as chancellor very difficult. Contributing powerfully to this situation was the personal enmity between Tweeddale and Melville's family. Although based mostly on local rivalries, its manifestations ranged over the entire field from petty spite in Fife to sabotage at the highest level of the administration. Feelings were so bitter and intense that on Tweeddale's appointment as chancellor Melville's family would certainly have begun a campaign of serious obstruction, even had they not at the same time suffered considerable demotion. A family which had seen bleak times before the revolution and then glimpsed the possibility of attaining fortunes and high status found it galling to see their hopes ruined. And it was not in their nature to accept failure philosophically.

Tarbat, in furtherance of his own scheme to ruin the Johnston interest, pleaded Melville's cause. It had been a big mistake, Tarbat argued, to remove Melville with marks of disgrace, subjecting his sons to undignified reductions in rank when Melville was the only man capable of managing the presbyterian party.[78] This was, of course, not true. And if it were, why Melville had not hitherto made more of his supposed influence and talents went unexplained. Tarbat was too concerned with the episcopalian sympathies of the English tories and with showing that Melville's opponents had no real claim to be considered 'presbyterian' to be worried about loose ends of that kind.

In Fife Melville indulged his enmity against Tweeddale's connections. Whilst lady Rothes and lord Leslie were holding a sheriff court, Melville and his sons burst in upon them in a rowdy and officious fashion and turned everybody out, ostensibly to make way for a meeting of the supply commissioners although their need for accommodation was hardly dire enough to warrant such action. Also with lady Rothes were the young peers Haddington and Montrose. Melville and family showed public contempt for them all. Lady Rothes decided to treat the incident as a riot and brought it before the privy council,[79] which ordered Melville and his sons to make public apology. They complied with very bad grace. Each in turn read out a form of words and then, refusing to speak further to anyone, they left for Fife in great anger. Tweeddale at once took the opportunity of settling any outstanding questions relating to Fife in a manner favourable to lady Rothes and Yester.[80]

With local feeling at this intensity there was little hope of collaboration between the two interests at a higher level. Just as privy council meetings were bedevilled by disputes between the two factions, decisions being changed according to whoever predominated on any particular day, so affairs in the treasury were paralysed. When Tweeddale had been made chancellor the treasury was in a poor state and, as a result of further royal grants which the treasury could not afford to pay, the situation had worsened.[81] Difficulties were made over clearing past accounts lest enquiry might unearth unpleasant details from the earlier administration. The hearth tax, for which Melville's brother had been responsible, was especially suspect since its yield had been very disappointing. But the main obstacle to efficient financial administration lay in the membership of the treasury board. In 1692 the aim of the reshuffle had been to balance interests, not to secure efficiency. Raith, Melville's son, remained on the board, conducting with Tweeddale an acrimonious dispute over the right to preside in the treasury.[82] Cassillis was in to placate the 'presbyterians', Linlithgow and Breadalbane were added to gratify the 'episcopalians' and Drumlanrig to represent his father's interest. There was no basis here for collaboration of any kind. Linlithgow, Breadalbane and Drumlanrig had come in as part of the same ministerial change as Tweeddale, nominally as his allies, but they were far from gratified at his becoming chancellor whilst they were merely lords of the treasury. When the alliance between Melville and the 'episcopalian' interest developed, Tweeddale's effectiveness was completely undermined although, as chancellor, he could be saddled with all the blame. Dissension stopped treasury business completely since for long periods the board lacked a quorum.[83]

In the latter half of 1694 the anti-Johnston interest felt itself strong enough to launch an offensive. A preliminary gathering of some of the leaders was held at Bath.[84] Their usual programme was to be adopted: complaints against the harsh treatment of the northern clergy and scorn for any counter-allegations of jacobite plotting. The immediate aim was to force a new parliament in which they would undertake to get supply or at least claim credit for any supply which was forthcoming.[85] Dalrymple and his party were said to be offering to get William a grant of cess for life, promising that, even if they failed in the existing parliament, they would certainly succeed after new elections. In something like panic at being outbid their opponents began to think in the same terms.[86] Johnston told Polwarth: '... You mistake the state of the question. It's not if a cess during life should be given or not, but whether knaves or honest men should have the merit of giving it? ...'[87]

Soundings on this topic took place as the Johnston group continued its campaign for dismissals before the next parliament. The need for such changes was constantly urged by members of the 'presbyterian' interest in London.[88] The ministry had to be remodelled in their favour, the argument ran, to make it more secure and efficient and to render parliament more manageable after the stir created in 1693. However, influences other than that of the Johnston group were also at work, in opposition to any alterations before a parliament. Johnston became convinced, it seems correctly, that one of the most important sources of opposition was Carstares. At the beginning of 1695 Carstares was in touch with the Dalrymples, affecting a very equivocal attitude to dismissals from the government.[89] The Atholl interest, represented by lord John Murray, was once more vigorous in politics much to Annandale's disgust, since he feared competition. Murray was also declaring himself against any ministerial changes before parliament met. Johnston suspected Carstares of having put him up to it,[90] but he had a suspicious mind and was quick to scent conspiracy. However, it seems likely that Carstares was disseminating his views as widely as possible. The commissioners appointed by the general assembly to settle the church in the north, whose conduct had been fiercely attacked by the episcopalians, had sent to court a deputation to justify themselves. Not surprisingly, as they took leave of Scotland, they had been solidly in favour of changes in what seemed to be their own interest. Amongst the deputation was Carstares's relative, Dunlop. After some time in London, much of it spent with Dalrymple and Carstares, the former being curious company for a visiting delegation of presbyterians, they began to hedge over whether changes in the government were needed after all. It seems that they had been given assurances for the church settlement and were prepared to accept them.[91]

William at length decided to make no ministerial changes in 1695 but nevertheless to hold a parliament with Tweeddale as commissioner.[92] Tweeddale's guess was that

William, convinced that all requests for dismissals were motivated by private animosity and greed, had decided not to give way to them. More probably William was suffering from his habitual inertia in the face of Scottish affairs. Whatever its cause, the decision was itself a recipe for further trouble. To leave the government and parliament unchanged, counselling them to 'no heats', betokened undue optimism.[93] The contestants were far from inert. At the beginning of the parliament Carstares went down to Scotland on some mysterious errand which involved his opening Johnston's mail. Tweeddale felt obliged to complain to Shrewsbury about it.[94] Both Linlithgow and Tarbat were keeping closely in touch with Portland and Carstares, proclaiming their own moderation and deploring the conduct of the 'hot men' in the ministry, such, that is to say, as were opposed to Melville and Carstares.[95] Such people were also rivals of Tarbat and Linlithgow. Portland, asserting his determination not to meddle in Scottish affairs, had not only come down firmly against changes but strongly supported Linlithgow's candidacy for the post of extraordinary lord of session.[96]

The active managers of the 1695 session were Johnston and his allies, with whom, by now, Tweeddale had become completely identified. The task was to obtain supply from a largely 'presbyterian' parliament which, despite its representation of 1693 against the Dalrymples and others, had still not been gratified by dismissals, prosecutions or even enquiries.[97] If the managers were to produce any results at all they were going to find it necessary to gratify the unabated virulence of the majority against the Dalrymples. Tweeddale had asked the king to do something for parliament's satisfaction: to dismiss Dalrymple or allow parliament to attack both him and his father. His feeling was that parliament would not otherwise be co-operative.[98] But nevertheless the only official concession allowed was power to set up a commission of enquiry into the Glencoe affair. Despite William's reluctance to make concessions to them, the managers would have been unrealistic had they not used their predominance in parliament to discredit their opponents, whilst the 'episcopalians' remained so much a minority that they could hope to do little but score enough points during the session to use at court against the managers in what, to the trade, was known as an 'after-game'. For both factions it seemed vital to force the issue to a resolution one way or another. Scottish opinion assumed that the parliament of 1695 would determine the future shape of the government.

The king's letter to the parliament had exhorted them to 'a disposition to moderation and union about church matters . . . ' and recommended to them 'calmness and unanimity' in their proceedings.[99] This was extravagantly optimistic. Parliament entered swiftly into business concerning the Glencoe episode, and an enquiry would have been instituted on parliamentary authority had not Tweeddale forestalled it by producing the royal commission to investigate. On the following day, as a direct result of William's concession, the committee resolved to propose to the house a vote of supply.[100] Tweeddale feared, he wrote to the king, that parliament would not be satisfactorily concluded unless he were empowered to tell some of the leading men privately that changes would be made after the session. William did not even acknowledge this strong hint.

Attempts were soon made to pay off old scores. Early in its proceedings the Glencoe commission exhumed the dubious allegations made against Breadalbane at the time of his highland mission,[101] as a result of which parliament instructed the lord advocate to proceed against him with a charge of high treason, committing the earl in the meantime to the castle at Edinburgh.[102] Johnston was surprisingly frank about the reason. It was, he told Portland, a device to get Breadalbane out of the treasury. If it had not been attempted this way, another method would have been tried.[103] But the reappearance of this charge irritated William who, soon after parliament had adjourned, ordered Breadalbane's release and gave him a pardon without mentioning it to Tweeddale. Breadalbane was thus in a position to use his royal pardon in a way carefully calculated to make Tweeddale appear as much of a fool as possible. He attended privy council, but not until Tweeddale had challenged his right to be there on the ground that a prosecution against him was pending and a lengthy altercation had ensued did he produce his pardon. Tweeddale was understandably annoyed.[104]

A further attempt was made to deal with the continuing problem of the episcopalian clergy. Johnston was following the policy which seems to have guided him from his first appointment as secretary — not only to settle the problem of episcopalian dissenters but to settle it in such a way as to take the issue completely out of politics. If episcopalians could be satisfied, and seen in England to be so, then dissident political factions would have to fabricate another, perhaps less persuasive, basis for opposition. So there emerged yet another church act which, although a further blow at Dalrymple, provided Johnston's opponents with additional cause for complaint. After the act of 1693 most of the episcopalian clergy had refused to take the oaths despite Dalrymple's apparent optimism. The issue had been blurred by the attitude of the presbyterian clergy to the taking of oaths and William's decision to allow presbyterian ministers to sit in the general assembly of 1694 without having sworn to either the allegiance or assurance.[105] Afterwards Dalrymple, after trying to discredit the act though without real justification, began to let it be known in circles where sympathy abounded and expectations were high that in his opinion the 1693 act 'against', as he put it, the episcopalian clergy would be suspended. This, presumably, would take place when his party was victorious in the battle for influence. According to Dalrymple, the whole question of the Scottish church would then be left to the king, since the English bishops could not decide whether they wanted the Scottish religious question to be settled by comprehension or toleration.[106] Again, by such half-promises, the impression was being conveyed that there was considerable English support for granting episcopalian demands in full, which unsettled the clergy even more.

The new church act extended to 1 September 1695 the time in which episcopalian ministers were allowed to take the oaths. Ministers who qualified themselves were then free to apply, if they pleased, for admission to church judicatures and the latter were allowed to admit them or not as they thought fit.[107] Presbyterian opinion was satisfied, since the church was not obliged to admit episcopalian ministers to membership. The latter on taking the oaths were assured of their churches and civil protection under the law.[108] After the parliament Johnston personally went north to persuade episcopalians to take the oaths, and numbers of them do seem to have qualified, whether or not as a result of Johnston's efforts.[109] By October 1695, 116 episcopalian ministers were reported to have complied with the law, but the entire project had been made harder by the false hopes circulated for political reasons.[110] Johnston had brought parliament to accept what was probably the best settlement possible under the circumstances. The presbyterian establishment was to remain unchanged but the position of episcopalian ministers was improved. They could not be ejected merely for being episcopalians, and as late as 1711 there were apparently 113 episcopalian ministers still in parishes. However, regardless of its effect, such an act could still be misrepresented in England and those who had the advantage of being first there with a story were likely to have the edge in propaganda.

During parliament's proceedings Tweeddale struck one or two blows against Melville and his allies. A petition from the town of Edinburgh over the affair of the £3000 bond effectively brought some of Melville's dirty linen into full view.[111] And, in Melville's first parliament of 1690, Lothian had been given precedence over Tweeddale's grandson, Roxburghe, a minor, much to his mother's chagrin. Now parliament voted that the precedence of Roxburghe, Galloway, Haddington and Kellie should be established over Lothian in the rolls.[112] It was not at all a coincidence that Lothian happened to be allied with Melville and the 'episcopalians'. The occasional power to inflict such humiliations was one of the things which lent spice to political life.

When the committee of security's resolution in favour of supply came before parliament it was unanimously accepted, but until the completion of the Glencoe enquiry the house proceeded very slowly over ways and means. It was fairly plain that there would be no supply until the report was published and discussed, as Tweeddale and the other members of the commission of enquiry realised. Tweeddale wrote asking the king to excuse his communicating the report to parliament without permission[113] and then promised the estates to lay the result of the enquiry before them. On 24 June, at the insistence of some members, Tweeddale produced the report and was at once rewarded with a vote of supply.[114] The parliament, with relish, sank its teeth into the report. It was an excellent opportunity to indulge in the favourite sport of Dalrymple-baiting. Stair himself had already been attacked over his conduct as president of session and now it was the master's turn.[115] Parliament voted the occurrence in Glencoe to have been murder. However, they absolved from blame the king and everybody else save lieutenant-colonel Hamilton, deputy-governor of Fort William — who had directed the operation and who failed to appear to give evidence when summoned — and Dalrymple. Obviously their accumulated venom was to be directed with some precision. They issued orders for the arrest of the former. An address to the king recommended the punishment of the latter.[116]

Then Tweeddale was able at last to adjourn parliament. He claimed to have done so by surprise to forestall an address requesting changes in the government to remove obnoxious persons.[117] William was to be left in no doubt of what Tweeddale and Johnston thought of some of their colleagues and of the concurrence of parliament in their opinion. Whatever personal satisfaction the managers derived from it, and it must have been considerable, the mood of parliament had made an attack on the Dalrymples unavoidable if supply was to be obtained. This was the only alternative to failure and adjournment. In the process the managers had overstepped the lines laid down by the king concerning the Glencoe report which was intended, initially, for the king alone. Yet in the general conduct of parliament there was little obvious ground for complaint. So much is indicated by Sir James Ogilvy, the solicitor-general, who, although currently attached to the Johnston-Tweeddale interest, had too much concern for his own welfare to take needless risks. He wrote to Carstares: '... I know endeavours will be used to misrepresent our proceedings but, when duly considered, I am hopeful the king will be satisfied. As to the earl of Breadalbane we will not proceed against him; it will be left to the king to order what he pleases. The master of Stair is indeed loaded to purpose, but thereby the king is most justly relieved of all the aspersions raised in that affair of Glencoe and I doubt not the master['s] letters and our votes, both in the commission and parliament, when compared, will justify us that we have proceeded impartially. And here I cannot but say that our carrying so great a plurality in parliament against an [sic] secretary of state, an [sic] lord of the treasury and an [sic] president of the session may convince anybody both of the strength of our party and that there was ground for what is done. I must tell you that all will bear me witness I have acted an [sic] moderate part in all this and, when it's over and represented to his majesty, I will be ordered by his majesty as to the method of serving him, as is my duty ... Our party, if well with the court, is able to serve the king to his satisfaction. Neither can it be proposed that all the other party be run down. All the alteration necessary may soon be found out, but I am afraid the king may be misinformed. It is now a proper time for you to do good to your country. Honest men expects [sic] your assistance and mistake will soon go over. You know the king has been much troubled about our church matters, but now we have prolonged the time to the ministers for taking the oaths and those take [sic] them are declared to be under his majesty's full protection within their churches ... ,'[118] For Ogilvy to have written in this fashion seems fair evidence that the general shape of the parliamentary session was thought satisfactory.

And perhaps it would have satisfied but for the fact that a step had been taken in parliament, the significance of which took everyone by surprise. Even Tweeddale's opponents had overlooked it when trying to devise allegations to discredit him in the eyes of the king. William seems to have ignored most of the accusations: immoderate courses over the church act, the Glencoe report, the charge against Breadalbane, Tweeddale's supposedly having let parliament sit beyond the permitted time which, if true at all, was true only in a niggling technical sense. The king was resigned to the Glencoe report and no more than irritated by the Breadalbane episode, and he had, in fact, warranted the extension of the parliament.[119] To the trade act of 1695, however, his attitude was markedly different because it produced a violent reaction in England. Subsequently it was to lead to more serious trouble over the Darien project.

A group of merchants whose interests linked Scotland and London had for some time been lobbying for an act which would allow them to set up a trading company. In the 1693 parliament the way was cleared by a general trade act to allow the formation of trading companies, promising them a royal charter and royal protection.[120] In 1695 the parliamentary committee for trade considered the draft of an act intended to make effective the 1693 provisions. Its details were finally settled by the committee, at the Abbey, in Tweeddale's presence. They approved the draft subsequently passed by parliament as the act for a company trading to Africa and the Indies, to which Tweeddale gave the royal assent.[121]

The apparent commercial implications of the act as indicated by the title were, in the minds of the projectors, quite secondary. They were really passing a law which would at one and the same time disguise their real purpose of founding a Scottish colony whilst legalising such a settlement. No one in the ministry seems to have thought that the act would have any effect at all on trade or, for that matter, produce a colony. In 1695 what mattered to the Scottish ministry were the act's attendant political advantages, although clearly they had to profess faith in its ostensible purpose.[122] One of their strengths in managing parliament seems to have been the grip that Hamilton of Whitelaw, as a court manager, had established on a block of burgh members, so it was always considered necessary for the burghs to be gratified whenever possible as one means of ensuring their support. Anything which seemed in theory likely to promote trade without favouring one burgh or any particular interest amongst them against the rest would be welcomed. Parliamentary votes rather than commerce were the managers' concern in 1695. The repercussions of these tactics proved to be more dramatic than anyone could possibly have imagined.

On the whole it seems that Tweeddale, though not blameless, was the victim of circumstances and double-dealing. The act was drafted by the lord advocate, Sir James Stewart, on whose legal advice Tweeddale relied. Its terms were wholly within the scope of the act of 1693, to which no one had taken exception, but they were almost certainly outside the intended limits of Tweeddale's instructions as commissioner. He was allowed to pass an act 'for the encouragement of such as shall acquire and establish a plantation in Africa or America or in any other part of the world where plantations may be lawfully acquired, with such rights and privileges as we grant in like case to the subjects of our other dominions, the one not interfering with the other'.[123] Such restrictions were very difficult to observe in practice, whether intentionally so or as the outcome of hasty drafting. However, having recited the earlier act, the trade act of 1695 set up a corporate body: the Company of Scotland trading to Africa and the Indies, granting it extensive powers. The company had the right to plant colonies and make treaties, together with the grant of a monopoly for thirty-one years of the trades in which it chose to engage. Its right to found colonies was accompanied by that of making trade regulations. For the first twenty-one years the company's trade was to be virtually exempt from customs and the power of the crown was pledged in support of the company and its claims.

Stewart drafted the act in full knowledge of the commissioner's instructions, and although Tweeddale bore the ultimate responsibility he was entitled to place some reliance on the advice of the crown's senior law officer in Scotland. In fact, Tweeddale did express some doubt concerning a customs exemption for twenty-one years, but support for it in the committee was unanimous and so strong that he withdrew his objection. Even so, as Tweeddale was to discover, he had been jibbing at a very minor brook only to leap head first into something very much deeper. In England, where a struggle was taking place for the control of the East India Company and perhaps even for its very existence, the news of the Scottish act came to a variety of parties as a tactical bonus. It created an outcry surprising even to Shrewsbury, who had at first welcomed it. A clamour was set up which took on the proportions of a full-scale parliamentary campaign, seriously embarrassing William who did not enjoy being harassed by the English parliament and whose displeasure was correspondingly acute. At a conference held subsequently between the opposing Scottish groups in the presence of the king to conduct a *post mortem* on the 1695 parliament, the only topic to arouse William's anger was the trade act. It granted such powers, he said, as if there had been no king of

Scotland.[124] The king felt driven to make a public disavowal of the affair: 'I have been ill-served in Scotland.'

English reasons for opposition to the trade act were varied and not at all as straightforward as they seemed. It did not, for instance, escape notice that heavily involved in the uproar were English politicians such as the duke of Leeds, formerly Carmarthen, by this time almost wholly estranged from the English court. Leeds had been one of Tweeddale's erstwhile supporters but had since come to oppose him as Tweeddale severed his connections with the Dalrymples and Queensberry. He had also become involved with the English East India Company's machinations to an extent exceeding both propriety and discretion. However, Tweeddale's Scottish rivals were in close touch with Leeds and other English interests attacking the trade act. Despite the risks involved, the temptation to use the act as yet another issue with which to discredit the ministry proved too great for them to resist. Most Scots in London resented the actions of the English parliament, the young earl of Roxburghe told his mother, except some of the Scottish statesmen.[125] Since, as commissioner, he was the most vulnerable to attack of all the officers of state, efforts were directed towards laying the entire blame on Tweeddale. It was even alleged that he had taken bribes, a charge which Tweeddale greatly resented and rightly so.[126]

A manoeuvre of this kind was not without dangers for Tweeddale's opponents. Most of them had been present at the passing of the trade act which had, after all, gone through parliament unanimously. As they knew, second thoughts on the act would do their interest no good in Scotland, so they tried to have it both ways and to some extent succeeded. Those in England deplored the act, attacking the ministry for passing it, whilst their colleagues in Scotland were insisting that in their support of the act and the proposed company they stood second to none.[127]

Tweeddale was not cut out to be an heroic figure. His first panic reaction was a readiness to say anything which seemed to offer a way of escape. He even had wild thoughts of pretending that the act was a rough draft passed by mistake.[128] However, finally he decided to take his stand on the act's legality, expecting the lord advocate's unequivocal support since the latter had drafted it. Whilst the lord advocate remained in Scotland, Tweeddale did receive at least his verbal backing. But when Stewart had left for England, ostensibly on a mission to support Tweeddale at court, he began to disclaim all responsibility. He denied that he had ever seen the commissioner's instructions on the trade act or that he had been at all involved with the act itself. There is no doubt that the lord advocate was a liar.[129]

The 'episcopalian' opposition to Johnston and Tweeddale had begun their serious campaign during the session of parliament and continued it afterwards. They aimed at creating in the English court an image of a parliament in which Tweeddale and Johnston with a group of a very few 'hot men' had embarked on immoderate courses, deaf to all supplication from the more balanced members. Tarbat's contribution was quite in character and typical of the opposition tactics. He implied that there had been no need at all to place the Glencoe report before parliament. Supply, according to him, could have been obtained much sooner had the managers not set out to attack their personal enemies first, thus creating unnecessary ill feeling. He drew up a list of these 'hot men' — all members of the Tweeddale-Johnston group, including, quite incredibly, the earl of

Findlater, who completely lacked interest in politics and was in parliament only at his son's request — and contrasted them with a further list of 'moderate men' who, not surprisingly, were all allied to Tarbat. Significantly, he complained that, although the nation's strength lay in its nobility, a burgh vote counted as much as that of a Queensberry or Argyll who were each worth twenty burgh votes.[130] An objection was really being lodged against Whitelaw's use of the burgh votes to support the managers, some of the nobility being dissatisfied with their own position in parliament. The church act of 1695 was misrepresented in exactly the same manner as that of 1693 had been.[131] What began to emerge from opposition reports was a fictitious large, silent and long-suffering majority dissociating itself from parliamentary business whilst a small and frenzied group carried things to extremes against Dalrymple, Stair and Breadalbane. This version of the 1695 parliament was quite ridiculous. There is no reason to doubt that in the 1695 parliament the opposition was a comparatively small minority which voted together, when it was thought advisable, throughout the session.[132] But, on the strength of this flood of rumour and denigration fed back through 'episcopalian' channels to William, attempts were made by Dalrymple and Breadalbane's son, Glenorchy, to rush the king into making changes in their favour whilst he was still in Flanders and before he could be exposed to any contrary arguments from Johnston and Tweeddale.[133]

Since it was not in William's character to be stampeded into action of whatever kind, they failed. But when he returned to London a *post mortem* was held at Johnston's insistence in the presence of the king. On this occasion each of the two groups attempted to justify its behaviour and its view of affairs. Despite his manifest annoyance over the trade act, William remained non-committal, dispensing little or no blame or praise, so that both factions retained some hope of increased favour. The Tweeddale-Johnston group seemed to remain on good terms with the king even after the English reaction to the trade act of 1695 had become apparent.[134] Sir James Ogilvy continued to expect some changes in their favour though not, he thought, as many as they had hoped for.[135] Tweeddale, however, began to feel harassed and expended much thought and most of his energies in trying to justify his conduct beyond all argument for the benefit of the king.[136] But all the signs were that the correctness or otherwise of Tweeddale's behaviour as high commissioner, or the rights and wrongs of the trade act, had ceased to be important for the future of the Scottish ministry. Wider issues were now involved.

Rumour had it, and coincidence seemed to provide confirmation, that Johnston and Tweeddale were eventually dismissed on account of their part in the trade act. The whole character of the ministerial change of 1695-6 and the way it came about belies this in spite of Carstares's assertion, some four years later, that the trade act and the prolongation of parliament were the causes of their dismissal.[137] The reason was quite other.[138] William had at last realised that stable government in Scotland had been made impossible because of the virulence of the faction struggle which had given him more trouble than he was prepared to tolerate. The entire scheme of government seemed to need resettling, though William still thought of the task in religious terms. It no longer seemed feasible to urge co-operation on a ministry which included Johnston and Dalrymple and then hope for the best. In fact, no matter what illusions the king and his advisers had nurtured, there had never been a time when this course had been a practical one. However complicated the proposed solutions sometimes were, the problem of

Scottish government as analysed by William and his advisers appeared, in essence, simple. It was also, even in those terms, virtually insoluble, but the king had yet to reach that conclusion. As viewed from London or Flanders, the Scottish kingdom and parliament were split into two opposing groups: 'presbyterians' and 'episcopalians'. Given the composition of the convention parliament, due to the circumstances of its election, a ministry of 'episcopalians' would have been an invitation to disruption. 'Presbyterian' government had been safe but, as practised by the Melville ministry, oppressive. William's attempted solution in 1692 had been to combine elements of both, seeing in this device the discouragement of faction and the mollifying of dissident groups. But mixed or 'motley' ministries containing strong and restless characters such as Johnston and Dalrymple did not function because they were soon paralysed by internal rivalry.

Johnston's personal achievement had been considerable. He had produced a relatively moderate group in the court commanding the support of presbyterians committed in varying degree, of most 'revolution men' and of some episcopalians. Given time he might even have gone some way towards depriving opposition groups of any credible religious pretext. Even so his achievements could never have been other than severely limited. As the active, managing section of the court which it became, this Johnston group could produce a majority in parliament but it was quite obviously no more than a parliamentary majority. Everyone was conscious of interests that were either under-represented or not represented at all. It was made to appear to William that the 'presbyterian' element had got out of hand again and was trying to establish a total domination of the court interest. Such government by 'presbyterians' to the exclusion of others provided opposition groups with too much leverage at the English court. In William's view the time had come for another mixture of the two parties, purged this time of the more restless spirits. Whatever the rights and wrongs of the 1695 parliament and all its acts, for reasons of temperament if for no other, the secretaries had to go. Both men were quite beyond the forgiveness of their opponents, so for the time being neither was of any use to the crown. 'Motley ministries' were unworkable, however. The very idea of collaboration was seen by most Scottish politicians as an intolerable obstacle to self-advancement and therefore as a challenge. Neither William nor his advisers fully realised this.

Tweeddale seemed not at all to appreciate the reappraisal taking place at court towards the end of 1695. He saw himself as beleaguered by an alliance of hostile factions which, in the interests of sound administration, had to be purged from the ministry.[139] The death of the first viscount of Stair, president of the court of session, in November 1695, seemed to him to present an opportunity for sweeping changes. His thinking on this topic was far removed from anything envisaged at court. To both Johnston and Shrewsbury, he denounced in some detail the influence of all those he saw as his enemies and proposed a clean sweep, the vacancies to be filled by his own and Johnston's supporters. He wrote to the king in the same strain but Johnston, who presumably knew how things were developing at court, decided that the letter would be safer undelivered.[140] Others of their party thought it worthwhile appealing to Portland and Carstares, though suspecting that neither was really on their side.[141] Their suspicions were justified. The views of Portland and Carstares had for some time been at variance with those of the Tweeddale-Johnston interest, though their thinking seems to have been even more unrealistic than Tweeddale's. Many more mistakes had to be made before William and his advisers approached anything like an appreciation of the true nature of the trouble in Scotland.

NOTES

1. See above, p. 25, n. 28. Fletcher of Saltoun said later that Johnston became secretary by interest of 'the late archbishop of Canterbury, my lord Romney and others he could name': SRO, GD124, Box 16, 'An Account of what past in the Parliament of Scotland 1704', 16, 25 Jul. 1704.
2. SRO, SP3/1, Stair to [Johnston], 3 Mar. 1692.
3. Macpherson, App., 204, lord B. Hamilton to Hamilton, 12 Dec. 1691.
4. Ib., 206-7, same to same, 10 Apr. 1692; ib., 207, same to same, 7 May 1692; ib., 208, same to same, 19 May 1692.
5. NLS, MS 7014, 63, [Dickson] to Tweeddale, 5 Apr. 1692.
6. Ib., 77, [Dalrymple] to [Tweeddale], 30 Apr. 1692.
7. Ib., 16, Tweeddale to the king, 9 Feb. 1692.
8. Seafield Correspondence, 91-2, 23 Sep. 1692.
9. Dunlop, Carstares, 89 n.5. Foxcroft, Supplement, 370.
10. SRO, SP3/1, [Johnston] to J. Stewart, 10 Mar. 1691/2.
11. Ib., [Johnston] to Tweeddale, 2 Dec. 1692; ib., [same] to lord Easter [sic for Yester], 14 Mar. 1691/2. Yester declined to accept even a place on the privy council. NLS, MS 7014, 27, [Murray of Blackbarony] to Yester, 8 Mar. [16]92.
12. SRO, SP3/1, [Johnston] to Hamilton, 10 Mar. 1691/2; ib., [same] to Portland, 8 Mar. 1691/2; Caldwell Papers, i, 184, W. Stewart to W. Hamilton, 3 Jan. 1692/3; HMCR Johnstone MSS, 59-60, A. Johnston to Annandale, 2 Feb. 1692/3; Buccleuch (Drum.), Union, i, J. Johnston to Queensberry, 1 Feb. 1692[/3]; Carstares S.P., 188-9, A. Johnston to Carstares, 4 Aug. 1693; ib., 161-6, J. Johnston to same, 6 May [1693]; ib., 184, same to same, 27 May [1693].
13. SRO, SP3/1, [same] to Mr Weyly [sic for Wyllie?], 7 Apr. [16]92; ib., [same] to Portland, 8 Apr. [1692]; Buccleuch (Drum.), Union, i, same to Queensberry, 1 Feb. 1692[/3].
14. HMCR Finch MSS, iv, 212, Tarbat to [Nottingham], 8 Jun. 1692; ib., 253, same to same, 21 Jun. 1692; ib., 364-5, Lockhart to [Nottingham], 3 Aug. 1692; ib., 392-3, Breadalbane to [same], 14 Aug. 1692.
15. NLS, MS 7014, 8, Dalrymple to [Tweeddale], 16 Jan. 1692. The action taken was based ultimately on the king's orders to Livingston: CSP (Dom.),1691-2, 94, the king to the privy council, 11 Jan. 1692; ib., 94-5, the king to Livingston, 11 Jan. 1692; ib., the king's instructions to Livingston, 16 Jan. 1692.
16. NLS, MS 7014, 77, [Dalrymple] to [Tweeddale], 30 Apr. 1692.
17. Ib., MS 7015, 7, same to same, 14 Jan. 1693.
18. Ib., MS 7014, 13, Hill to same, 14 Feb. 1692.
19. SRO, SP3/1, [Johnston] to same, 26 Mar. [16]91 [sic for 92]; ib., [same] to Portland, 1 Apr. 1692; ib., [same] to Tweeddale, 9 Apr. [16]92.
20. Buccleuch (Drum.), Union, i, same to Queensberry, 1 Feb. 1692[/3].
21. SRO, SP3/1, [same] to Tweeddale, 2 Dec. 1692 (not sent).
22. NLS, MS 7015, 11, Dalrymple to same, 13 Jan. 1693; ib., 17, same to same, 26 Jan. 1693; ib., 23, same to same, 21 Feb. 1693; ib., 25, same to same, 28 Feb. 1693.
23. SRO, SP3/1, [Johnston] to Ormiston, 27 Dec. 1692; ib., [same] to lord advocate, 27 Dec. 1692; ib., [same] to Hamilton, 27 Dec. 1692.
24. Ib., 'Memoirs of some things to be considered by Secretary Johnston . . . ' [from lord Hailside], 15 Mar. 1691/2.
25. Carstares S.P., 170-77, Johnston to Carstares, 16 May 1690 [sic for 1693]; SRO, SP3/1, [same] to viscount Sydney, 18 Oct. 1692.
26. NLS, MS 7014, 5, [Dalrymple] to [Tweeddale], 11 Jan. 1692.
27. SRO, SP3/1, [Johnston] to Portland, 26 Jul. [1692]; ib., [same] to 'My Lord', 2 Aug. 1692; ib., [same] to Nottingham, 13 Aug. 1692.

28. *Ib.*, [same] to Tweeddale, 24 Nov. 1692; Buccleuch (Drum.), Union, i, same to Queensberry, 1 Feb. 1692[/3].
29. NLS, MS 7015, 40, Dalrymple to Tweeddale, 15 Apr. 1693.
30. *Carstares S.P.*, 170-77, Johnston to Carstares, 16 May 1690 [sic for 1693]; *ib.*, 181-3, same to same, May 1693; Fraser, *Cromartie*, i, 102-103, Breadalbane to Tarbat, 7 Dec. [16]93.
31. *CSP (Dom.), 1693*, 450-51, 'Memorandum of business to be done at the next session of parliament', 1693.
32. SRO, SP3/1, [Johnston] to Portland, 22 Apr. [1693]; *Carstares S.P.*, 184, same to Carstares, 27 May 1693.
33. Johnston believed in the reality of the plot: Foxcroft, *Supplement*, 392.
34. SRO, SP3/1, [Johnston] to Portland, 22 Apr. [1693].
35. *Ib.*, [same] to Sir. W. Hamilton, 19 Dec. [1693].
36. See Johnston's letters to Carstares throughout the session of parliament: *Carstares S.P.*, 154-5, 157-8, 161-6, 170-77, 184.
37. See below, p. 100, n. 132.
38. *APS*, ix, 253-4, 254-5; *Carstares S.P.*, 158, Johnston to Carstares, 29 Apr. 1693; *ib.*, same to same, 6 May [1693]; *ib.*, 184, same to same, 27 May 1693.
39. *APS*, ix, 303.
40. *Ib.*, 262-4.
41. I.e., abstained: *Carstares S.P.*, 170-77, Johnston to Carstares, 16 May 1690 [sic for 1693]; *ib.*, 178-81, same to same, 19 May 1693.
42. SRO, SP3/1, [Johnston] to Burnet, 1 Jul [1693].
43. *APS*, ix, 314-15.
44. NLS, MS 7027, 49, Tweeddale to the king, [1693].
45. *HMCR Johnstone MSS*, 60, c. Jul. 1693; *Carstares S.P.*, 185-6, A. Johnston to Carstares, 7 Jul. 1693; NLS, MS 7015, 51, Dalrymple to Tweeddale, 22 Jun. 1693. Fraser, *Annandale Book*, ii, 60, Johnston to Annandale, 29 Jul. [1693].
46. SRO, SP3/1, [Johnston] to the master of Stair, 30 Jun. [1693].
47. *Carstares S.P.*, 170-77, same to Carstares, 16 May 1690 [sic for 1693].
48. NUL, Portland, PwA 2445, 11 Jul. 1693.
49. *Seafield Correspondence*, 115, 11 Aug. 1693; SRO, SP3/1, [Johnston] to Tweeddale, 29 Jul. [1693].
50. NLS, MS 7015, 102, Fauconberg to Tweeddale, 19 Sep. [1693].
51. Fraser, *Cromartie*, i, 93-4, Dalrymple to Tarbat, 20 Jul. 1693; *ib.*, 101, same to same, 24 Nov. 1693; *ib.*, 102-3, Breadalbane to same, 7 Dec. [16]93; NLS, MS 7015, 122, Dalrymple to Tweeddale, 5 Oct. 1693.
52. SRO, SP3/1, [Johnston] to Polwarth, 21 Oct. [1693].
53. *Ib.*, [same] to Ormiston, 20 Dec. 1692; Buccleuch (Drum.), Union, i, same to Queensberry, 1 Feb. 1692[/3]; *HMCR Johnstone MSS*, 61, same to Annandale, 24 Aug. 1693; *ib.*, same to same, 19 Oct. 1693; *ib.*, 96, same to same, 22 Mar. 1694.
54. *Carstares S.P.*, *passim*, the numerous letters from both Johnstons, 1693-4.
55. *Ib.*, 187-8, A. Johnston to Carstares, 14 Jul. 1693; *HMCR Johnstone MSS*, 61, Johnston to Annandale, 19 Oct. 1693.
56. NLS, MS 7016, 19, Blackbarony to Tweeddale, 16 Jan. [16]94; *ib.*, MS 7028, 3, Tweeddale to Blackbarony, 13 Jan. 1694; *ib.*, MS 7016, 25, Blackbarony to Tweeddale, 23 Jan. 1694.
57. *Ib.*, MS 7028, 25, Tweeddale to Blackbarony, 15 Feb. 1694; *ib.*, 29, same to Johnston, 19 Feb. 1694; *ib.*, MS 7016, 56, Blackbarony to Tweeddale, 22 Feb. 1694.
58. *Ib.*, MS 7028, 54, Tweeddale to Blackbarony, 17 Mar. 1694; *ib.*, MS 7016, 93, Blackbarony to Tweeddale, 24 Mar. 1694; *HMCR Johnstone MSS*, 96, Johnston to Annandale, 22 Mar. 1694; *ib.*, same to same, 29 Mar. 1694; *ib.*, 65, Annandale to Johnston, 17 Apr. 1694; NLS, MS 7028, 87, Tweeddale to the king, 18 Apr. 1694.
59. *Ib.*, MS 7029, 8, same to Johnston, 29 Nov. 1694; *ib.*, MS 7018, 28, Annandale to Tweeddale, 17 Jan. [1695]; *HMCR Johnstone MSS*, 64, same to Johnston, Mar. 1694; *ib.*, 67, Johnston to Annandale, 11 Dec. 1694.
60. The evidence for this is scattered throughout NLS, MSS 7016, 7018, 7028 and *HMCR Johnstone MSS*.
61. *HMCR Johnstone MSS*, 177, Johnston to Crawford, 6 Dec. 1693; *ib.*, same to same, 2 May 1694.
62. *Carstares S.P.*, 188-9, A. Johnston to Carstares, 4 Aug. 1693; Fraser, *Cromartie*, i, 101, Dalrymple to Tarbat, 24 Nov. 1693; *ib.*, 102-103, Breadalbane to same, 7 Dec. [16]93.
63. NLS, MS 7028, 48, Tweeddale to Blackbarony, 10 Mar. 1694; *HMCR Johnstone MSS*, 63, Annandale to Johnston, 15 Mar. 1694.
64. NLS, MS 7018, same to Tweeddale, 2 Jan. 1695.
65. *Ib.*, MS 7016, 83, Queensberry to same, 12 Mar. 16959 *ib.*, MS 7017, 109, same to same, 16 Nov. 1694;

ib., MS 7016, 103, Drumlanrig to same, 3 Apr. 1694; *ib.*, MS 7017, 17, Queensberry to same, 21 Jun. 1694; *ib.*, MS 7028, 125v., Tweeddale to Carstares, 28 Jul. 1694; Fraser, *Cromartie*, i, 106, Queensberry to Tarbat, 19 Mar. 1694; Buccleuch (Drum.), Queensberry Letters, xiv, Dalrymple to Drumlanrig, 30 Mar. 1695.
66. SRO, SP3/1, [Johnston] to Tweeddale, 20 Dec. 1692.
67. E.g., NLS, MS 7015, 122, 5 Oct. 1693; *ib.*, 138, 4 Nov. 1693.
68. *Ib.*, MS 7015, 136, Blackbarony to Tweeddale, 11 Nov. 1693; *ib.*, MS 7016, 5, Queensberry to same, 4 Jan. 1694; *ib.*, MS 7015, 171, Blackbarony to same, 26 Dec. [16]93.
69. SRO, SP3/1, [Johnston] to Ormiston, 20 Dec. 1692; *ib.*, [same] to Tweeddale, 28 Mar. [1693].
70. NLS, MS 7015, 136, Blackbarony to Tweeddale, 2 Oct. [16]93; *ib.*, 146, same to same, 11 Nov. 1693; *ib.*, MS 7016, 93, same to same, 24 Mar. 1694.
71. *Ib.*, MS 7028, 22, Tweeddale to Blackbarony, 10 Feb. 1694; *ib.*, MS 7016, 23, Blackbarony to Tweeddale, 18 Jan. [16]94.
72. *Ib.*, MS 7015, 155, seme to same, 12 Dec. 1693; *ib.*, 157, same to same, 14 Dec. [16]93.
73. *Ib.*, MS 7028, 1, Tweeddale to Portland, 13 Jan. 1694; *ib.*, 3, same to Blackbarony, 13 Jan. 1694; *ib.*, 117v., same to Johnston, 7 Jul. 1694.
74. *Ib.*, 9, same to same, 27 Jan. 1694; *ib.*, 76v., same to same, 10 Apr. 1696; *ib.*, 16, same to Blackbarony, 3 Feb. 1694.
75. *Ib.*, 133, same to the king, 20 Aug. 1694.
76. *Ib.*, 148, same to Johnston, 17 Sep. 1694; *ib.*, MS 7029, 5, same to same, 24 Nov. 1694; *HMCR Johnstone MSS*, 66, Ross to Annandale, 27 Nov. 1694; *ib.*, 68, Tweeddale to Annandale, 17 Dec. 1694.
77. *Ib.*, 70-71, Johnston to same, 19 Jan. [1695]; *ib.*, 73-4, Ormiston to same, 16 Feb. 1695.
78. *Carstares S.P.*, 233-5, Tarbat to Carstares, 25 Jun. 1695.
79. NLS, MS 7029, 103, Tweeddale to Johnston, 8 Nov. 1695.
80. *Ib.*, 88, same to Annandale, 10 Oct. 1695; *ib.*, 108, same to same, 14 Nov. 1695; *ib.*, 110, same to same, 16 Nov. 1695; *ib.*, 113v., same to same, 21 Nov. 1695.
81. *Ib.*, MS 7027, 16, same to the king, 9 Feb. 1692; *ib.*, MS 7028, 2, same to Johnston, 13 Jan. 1694; *ib.*, 52, same to same, 15 Mar. 1694; *ib.*, 160, same to same, 16 Oct. 1694; *Carstares S.P.*, 161-66, Johnston to Carstares, 6 May [1693].
82. NLS, MS 7014, 174, Dalrymple to Tweeddale, 17 Nov. 1692; *ib.*, MS 7027, 22, Tweeddale to Yester, 14 Mar. 1692; *ib.*, MS 7028, 44, same to Johnston, 10 Mar. 1694; *ib.*, 125v., same to Carstares, 28 Jul. 1694; *ib.*, 133, same to the king, 20 Aug. 1694.
83. *Ib.*, 170, same to Johnston, 9 Nov. 1694; *ib.*, MS 7017, 117, Ormiston to Tweeddale, 11 Dec. 1694; *ib.*, 119, Annandale to same, 11 Dec. 1694; *ib.*, 133, Ormiston to same, 22 Dec. 1694.
84. *Ib.*, MS 7028, 126v., Tweeddale to Johnston, 1 Aug. 1694; Buccleuch (Drum.), Queensberry Letters, xiv, R. Seton to Drumlanrig, 4 Aug. 1694. Fraser, *Annandale Book*, ii, 81, Livingston to Annandale, 16 Dec. 1694.
85. NLS, MS 7028, 172v., Tweeddale to Carstares, 1694; *ib.*, 144, same to Johnston, Sep. 1694; *ib.*, 174, same to same, 15 Nov. 1694.
86. *HMCR Marchmont MSS*, 125-6, Jerviswood to Polwarth, 8 Nov. 1694.
87. *Ib.*, 126, Johnston to same, 4 Dec. 1694.
88. *Carstares S.P.*, 203-204, A. Johnston to Carstares, 20 July 1694; *HMCR Johnstone MSS*, 61, Ross to Annandale, 11 Dec. 1694; Fraser, *Annandale Book*, ii, 102, Ogilvy to Annandale, 26 Feb. [16]95; *ib.*, same to same, 28 Feb. [16]95.
89. *HMCR Johnstone MSS*, 70-71, Johnston to same, 19 Jan. 1695; *ib.*, 98-9, same to same, 12 Jan. 1695; *HMCR Marchmont MSS*, 126-7, Jerviswood to Polwarth, 12 Jan. 1695; Fraser, *Annandale Book*, ii, 81, Livingston to Annandale, 11 Dec. [1694].
90. *HMCR Johnstone MSS*, 65, Annandale to Johnston, 13 May 1694; *ib.*, 76, Johnston to Annandale, 13 Apr. 1695.
91. *Ib.*, 98-9, same to same, 12 Jan. 1695. See also n. 89 above.
92. *Ib.*, 74, Ogilvy to same, 5 Mar. 1695; Buccleuch (Drum.), Queensberry Letters, xiv, Dalrymple to Drumlanrig, 30 Mar. 1695.
93. NLS, MS 7029, 22, Tweeddale to Shrewsbury, 19 Apr. 1695.
94. *Ib.*
95. NUL, Portland, PwA 713, Linlithgow to Portland, 25 May 1695; *Carstares S.P.*, 229-31, Tarbat to Carstares, 16 May 1695.
96. *HMCR Johnstone MSS*, 72, Johnston to Annandale, 24 Jan. 1695; *ib.*, 74, Ogilvy to Annandale, 5 Mar. 1695; Buccleuch (Drum.), Queensberry Letters, xiv, Ranelagh to Queensberry, 4 May 1695.
97. See above, p. 88.
98. NLS, MS 7029, 33, 16 May 1695.

99. *APS*, ix, 350-51, 17 Apr. 1695.
100. *Ib.*, 353, 21 May 1695; NLS, MS 7029, 34, Tweeddale to the king, 25 May 1695.
101. See above, p. 69.
102. *APS*, ix, 366, 10 Jun. 1695; NLS, MS 7029, 36, Tweeddale to the king, 11 Jun. 1695.
103. NUL, Portland, PwA 699, Johnston to Portland, 11 Jun. 1695; *HMCR Buccleuch MSS*, ii, 194, same to [Shrewsbury], 21 Jun. [16]95.
104. NUL, Portland, PwA 223, Breadalbane to Portland, 4 Jul. 1695; NLS, MS 7018, 108, R. Pringle to Tweeddale, 11 Jul. 1695; *ib.*, 134, same to same, 18 Aug. 1695; also Tweeddale's series of letters from 10 Oct. 1695 in *ib.*, MS 7029, 79, 81v., 84v., 89v., 94v., 117v., 146v., 149v., 155.
105. There are versions of the way in which William reached this decision which border on fantasy (e.g., Dunlop, *Carstares*, 87-9). They may be discounted. William was merely taking the easy way out. See T. Maxwell, 'William III and the Scots Presbyterians', *RSCHS*, xv, for a critical examination of the folklore.
106. Buccleuch (Drum.), Queensberry Letters, xiv, Dalrymple to Drumlanrig, 30 Mar. 1695.
107. *APS*, ix, 449-50, 16 Jul. 1695.
108. *Carstares S.P.*, 254-6, D. Blair to Carstares, 18 Jul. 1695.
109. NLS, MS 7029, 59, Tweeddale to A. Johnston, 17 Aug. 1695; *ib.*, 68, same to same, 29 Aug. 1695; *ib.*, 69, same to Pringle, 5 Sep. 1695; *ib.*, MS 7018, 161, A. Sinclair to Tweeddale, 31 Aug. 1695; *ib.*, MS 7019, 113, G. Seton to Tweeddale, 30 Oct. 1695.
110. *Carstares S.P.*, 263, Ogilvy to Carstares, 26 Oct. 1695; Dunlop, *Carstares*, 89. The capture of Namur had the effect of encouraging episcopalian compliance: *ib.*, n. 5. Tweeddale received thanks from episcopalian ministers: NLS, MS 7019, 113, G. Seton to Tweeddale, 30 Oct. 1695.
111. See above, p. 72.
112. *APS*, ix, 389-91, 1 Jul. 1695.
113. NLS, MS 7029, 38, Tweeddale to the king, 20 Jun. 1695.
114. *APS*, ix, 371-6.
115. For the report: *Carstares S.P.*, 236-54.
116. *APS*, ix, 376-7, 388, 408, 421, 424-5.
117. NUL, Portland, PwA 549, Tweeddale to the king, 19 Jul. 1695.
118. *Carstares S.P.*, 257-8, Ogilvy to Carstares, 23 Jul. 1695.
119. The extending of the parliamentary session involved a disproportionate amount of correspondence: NLS, MS 7029, 36, 40, 44v., 51, 57v., 61v; *ib.*, MS 7018, 119, 134.
120. See above, p. 88.
121. *APS*, ix, 367, 377-81.
122. This will be documented in a forthcoming work.
123. Quoted by T. Keith, *Commercial Relations of England and Scotland, 1603-1707* (Cambridge, 1910), 167.
124. NLS, MS 7019, 153, Annandale to Tweeddale, 9 Dec. 1695.
125. *Ib.*, MS 7029, 95, Tweeddale to Johnston, 19 Oct. 1695; *ib.*, 108, same to same, 14 Nov. 1695; Roxburghe MSS (Floors Castle), bundle 19, Roxburghe to the countess, 19 Dec. 1695.
126. NLS, MS 7019, 157, Annandale to Tweeddale, 19 Dec. 1695; *ib.*, MS 7029, 134, Tweeddale to Johnston, 14 Dec. 1695; *ib.*, 137v., same to same, 19 Dec. 1695.
127. *Ib*; *ib.*, 139, same to same, 19 Dec. 1695; *ib.*, MS 7030, 6v., same to Fauconberg, 31 Dec. 1695.
128. *Ib.*, MS 7028, 36, same to Johnston, 15 Oct. 1695; *ib.*, MS 7029, 123v., same to the king, 28 Nov. 1695; *ib.*, MS 7030, 1, same to same, 20 Dec. 1695.
129. NLS, MS 7030, 8v., same to Yester, 7 Jan. 1696; *ib.*, 27, same to same, 23 Jan. 1696; *ib.*, 29v., same to Johnston, 23 Jan. 1696; *ib.*, 42v., same to the king, 30 Jan. 1696; *ib.*, 43v., same to Yester, 1 Feb. 1696.
130. NUL, Portland, PwA 842, Tarbat to Portland, 25 Jul. 1695; *ib.*, PwA 713, Linlithgow to same, 25 May 1695; *Carstares S.P.*, 232-3, Argyll to Carstares, 21 Jun. 1695; Buccleuch (Drum.), Queensberry Letters, xiv, Boyle of Kelburn to Queensberry, 25 Jun. 1695.
131. NLS, MS 7018, 76, A. Johnston to Tweeddale, 18 May 1695.
132. *Ib.*, MS 7029, 134, Tweeddale to Johnston, 14 Dec. 1695. Melville strove hard to justify his collaboration with this party in a lengthy memorandum: SRO, GD26, xiii, 94ff., [1695]. Some guide to the relative strength of the parties can be provided by the figures available, for what they are worth. The allegiance of every member of the Scottish parliament cannot be ascertained so we are left with a sample determined by the survival of evidence. Although the survival seems to have depended entirely on accident nevertheless it does not provide an acceptable statistical sample. On the other hand if the sample contains any bias it is not easy to detect what it is. The relevant figures for the strength of parties for the period between 1692 and 1696 can be tabulated as follows:

Size of sample:

	Nobles	Barons	Burghs
	50/64 (78.1%)	44/84 (52.4%)	36/67 (53.7%)
Parties:	Johnston	Dalrymple	Transferred from Johnston to Dalrymple over the period
Nobles	22/50 (44%)	28/50 (56%)	4
Barons	30/44 (68.2%)	14/44 (31.8%)	—
Burghs	26/36 (72.2%)	10/36 (27.8%)	1

A majority of burgh members always followed the court after 1689. Their support of Johnston was probably due to nothing more than his seeming to represent the active court management.

133. NLS, MS 7029, 43, Tweeddale to Pringle, 29 Jun. 1695; *ib.*, 75, same to Shrewsbury, 10 Sep. 1695; *ib.*, MS 7019, 77, Pringle to Tweeddale, 3 Oct. 1695.
134. For the *post mortem*: *ib.*, MS 7027, 39, Johnston to same (enclosed by Tweeddale in a letter to Yester), 3 Dec. 1695; *ib.*, MS 7029, 134, Tweeddale to Johnston, 14 Dec. 1695; *ib.*, MS 7019, 109, A. Johnston to Tweeddale, 26 Oct. 1695; Fraser, *Cromartie*, i, 117-18, Tweeddale to Yester, 8 Dec. 1695; *Carstares S.P.*, 269-70, [   ] to Carstares, 10 Dec. 1695.
135. *Seafield Correspondence*, 174, Ogilvy to Findlater, 8 Nov. 1695.
136. NLS, MS 7030, 12v., Tweeddale to Yester, 9 Jan. 1696; *ib.*, 39v., 40v., same to same, Jan. 1696; *ib.*, 42v., same to the king, 30 Jan. 1696; *ib.*, 56, same to same, 18 Feb. 1696.
137. Buccleuch (Drum.), Carstares, [Carstares] to [Queensberry], 9 Jan. 1700[/01].
138. *HMCR Johnstone MSS*, 81, Ormiston to Annandale, 11 Feb. 1696; NLS, MS 7020, 90, Dickson to Tweeddale, 7 Sep. 1696.
139. *Ib.*, MS 7029, 155, Tweeddale to [Yester?], 29 Dec. 1695.
140. *Ib.*, 105, same to the king, 13 Nov. 1695; *HMCR Buccleuch MSS*, ii, 242, same to Shrewsbury, 24 Oct. 1695. For Tweeddale's other reflections: NLS, MS 7029, 108, 116v., 117v., 123v., 124v.
141. NUL, Portland, PwA 293, Ormiston to Portland, 29 Oct. 1695; *Carstares S.P.*, 265-6. Carmichael to Carstares, 7 Nov. 1695; *ib.*, 270, Ogilvy to same, 10 Dec. 1695.

5

The Magnate Resurgence

PORTLAND and Carstares had become completely opposed to Tweeddale and Johnston. There had been a period when Carstares had reconciled himself to their administration. In day-to-day business he had collaborated well enough with Johnston himself and his brother, Alexander. But sometime in 1694 Carstares had quite broken with them and begun to envisage some reconstruction of the ministry, though what changes he contemplated remained undefined. From 1694 at least he had been engaged in intrigues against Johnston and the chancellor but the nature of his activities suggests that he was not altogether aware of the problems existing in Scotland.

To a quite extraordinary degree he remained convinced of the utility of Melville and his family to the court, whatever their past sins were thought to have been. In October 1695 he had organised a trip for Melville to London in the hope that he would seize some chance of recovering royal favour.[1] At the beginning of the 1695 parliament, before leaving Edinburgh for London, Carstares had been in close touch with Melville's 'episcopalian' allies.[2] Consequently he seems to have proposed that Tweeddale be replaced as chancellor by Melville, but no one took this seriously. William had not recovered from his dissatisfaction with Melville's earlier conduct. To the English ministry the suggestion appeared ludicrous.[3] The fact that the proposal was made at all should seriously damage Carstares's reputation for sagacity.

But what happened to Melville, though it might have been important to Carstares, was only a minor aspect of a scheme of government which was beginning to emerge. The signs are that some change was becoming urgently necessary, whatever views were entertained by William, Portland and Carstares. One of Scotland's major problems, quite unsuspected at court, was becoming critical. Stronger pressures had been generated in Scottish politics than had existed for some time. Scottish governments since the revolution had been extraordinary in that they had virtually dispensed with magnates as officers of state. Governments had, of course, been contrived to meet extraordinary circumstances. Neither Queensberry nor Atholl had been trusted. Argyll, when it suited him, had shown extreme self-assertion on limited and personal issues but very little application to business. Hamilton had energetically involved himself in public affairs, much to everyone's discomfiture and his own ultimate dissatisfaction. The result of the court's policy had been that the magnates were left brooding on their exclusion, however justifiable it had seemed to others. In fact, one of the main forces behind the 'episcopalian' opposition was the resentment of the magnates, virtually disabled from holding office although itching for more influence. Dalrymple and others had sought to harness this dissatisfaction for their own purposes, yet, in a sense, he, Breadalbane, Linlithgow and their like had been 'front men' for the magnates. But none of the greater nobles had so far met with much success.

A completely different situation had now arisen. Something like a second generation of magnates had appeared. Hamilton had died in 1694. The family interest remained intact to be exercised by his eldest son, Arran, though he had been too notoriously involved in jacobite schemes to be immediately acceptable to the court. Atholl himself remained *persona non grata* but the political interest of the family was taken over by his eldest son and heir, lord John Murray. Argyll, to the surprise of most people, developed a sudden taste for business and began to push his claims with almost random self-assertiveness. More important still, before the parliamentary session of 1695 the first duke of Queensberry died, to be succeeded by his son, James Douglas, earl of Drumlanrig, as the second duke. So the circumstances which had led to the eclipse of some of the magnate interests since 1688 had passed. Henceforward it would be folly to assume that these men could be ignored. This, though, was exactly the mistake made in the first reshuffle of the ministry following the 1695 parliament. Throughout the long period of this readjustment in 1695-6, the belief seemed still to be cherished at court that it was aimed at reconciling the 'presbyterian' and 'episcopalian' interests, a largely imaginary problem. It is true that even the Scots most intimately involved in the changes spoke in those terms, though it is unlikely that they thought in them. One of the results of the court's wrong appraisal was that the scheme of readjustment seriously underestimated the power and determination of two figures who, whatever reputations they enjoyed, were outside these religious categories, namely Queensberry and Argyll. It is significant that in the 1695 parliament Argyll was part of the 'episcopalian' opposition.

Murray, despite his occasional involvement in jacobite conspiracy, had always been available as the Williamite arm of the Atholl interest.[4] During the general lobbying in London in 1694-5 he had been very active. He could have been, and apparently was, mistaken by some for the ideal agent for reconciling the two religious groups. Although representing an episcopalian family, he had himself recently professed presbyterianism. He seems to have aimed at attracting to his family interest some additional support from persons of both persuasions. Johnston and Tweeddale eyed him with no great favour. Annandale, whose political advancement he was trying to prevent, was bilious. Murray concentrated on cultivating second-rank political figures lacking any sizable political interest in their own right, for example Cockburn of Ormiston.[5] Before the parliament he had opposed the kind of changes in the government Johnston wanted and spoke instead in terms of an accommodation with the 'episcopalian' interests[6] — that is to say he had wanted changes of a kind and at a time more advantageous to himself and tailored his argument to suit the court's predisposition. After the session he was brought into the ministry as the basis of a new administration aimed at securing collaboration between the supposed two religious parties.[7]

Both Dalrymple and Johnston were dismissed, the latter, at least, solaced with a pension of £4000 a year. To replace them, lord John Murray and Sir James Ogilvy were appointed secretaries: one the representative of a magnate interest who saw himself as the controlling influence in the ministry, the other an administrator thought to be innocent of political ambition and therefore likely to give no offence. Linlithgow had died and Breadalbane was dismissed to remove a possible irritant in the new scheme. Tweeddale was left, for the time being, as chancellor to lead a new treasury commission composed of Queensberry, Argyll, Annandale, Raith and Sir John Maxwell. The first three were in the treasury in the hope that it would satisfy their pretensions. Raith represented the Melville interest — his father remained privy seal — and Maxwell of Pollock was a presbyterian who had for the time being attached himself to lord John Murray. In an attempt to placate the Hamilton family, Selkirk, son of the late duke, was appointed lord clerk register in the place of Tarbat who resigned.[8] The lord advocate, up to his neck in intrigues against Johnston and Tweeddale despite his professions of friendship, was rewarded by being allowed to keep his job. His abandonment of Tweeddale had been brazen and his lying unashamed, but the advocate was notoriously thick-skinned.[9] He was known to covet the president of session's place and had very likely received assurances of support for the contest. So now, with the disruptive influence of the old leaders removed, their followers within the court might the more easily coalesce. Such at any rate seems to have been the official reasoning. There were doubtless more personal motives. William had given the general oversight of Scottish management to Portland, which clearly added to the latter's prestige, but since 1692 the control he had been able to exercise over Scottish affairs had patently slackened. Johnston was not the most tractable of men. According to Burnet, he 'had not been so obsequious and dependent as the court expected . . . ' It is possible that any change would have been for the better from Portland's point of view. Burnet's interpretation of the changes was that 'a new set of men are put in who will generally depend on Portland . . . ' and those appointed certainly contrived to give this impression.[10]

In such a relationship as existed between Portland and Carstares as advisers to the king it is impossible to determine which of them initiated this or any other scheme and at what level. On this occasion Carstares had at some stage been deeply involved in the disposal of offices, setting out in writing his detailed suggestions. His views are interesting. He was fully capable of intrigue and misrepresentation, but in this affair his comments seem devoid of personal animosity. He particularly wanted Portland to intercede with the king for Johnston, no friend of his, so that he could be given hope of other employment for, he said, 'I should be sorry to see him reduced to straits'.[11] But in terms of policy Carstares had gravely miscalculated. He shared the belief that the principal object of remodelling the Scottish ministry was to reconcile members of the two religious interests to which even the magnates were taken as belonging. Apart from the special role accorded to Murray, he thought it sufficient for the other magnate interests merely to be associated with the administration. This view produced his rather dismissive attitude to Queensberry. The death of Linlithgow and Stair, and the dismissal of Stair's son, seemed to have weakened the 'episcopalian' party, so Carstares thought them worth correspondingly less consideration. He judged it sufficient for Queensberry and Breadalbane to be seen by the king before decisions were announced. Any audience granted to them was clearly to be a formality, which was most unwise, for Queensberry was getting not only far less than he thought his due but less even than he expected.[12] It did not take long for the major Scottish problem, which Carstares — and presumably Portland and the king — had either underestimated or been unaware of, to come to the surface.

As a result of the reconstruction all four magnate interests were now represented but the ministry was still a 'motley' one of irreconcilable factions and the magnates were far from satisfied. Divisions were wide and fundamentally unbridgeable because they concerned personal influence rather than policy. Consequently these rivalries were the source of further trouble. William hoped, as always, that exhortations to unity would suffice. He had come to realise their inefficacy with the old administration but seems to have been more optimistic about their effect on the new one. When the assassination crisis developed in February 1696 he had further recourse to talk of co-operation,[13] failing to take any account of the magnate pressure which had been building up for far too long and which the recent changes had done nothing to lessen. Queensberry and Argyll had first of all allied themselves against the Johnston-Tweeddale group.[14] They were now ready to concert their efforts against both the remnant of this interest within the ministry, and against Murray whose advancement was an affront which poisoned both of them with jealousy and frustration.

Murray, on the other hand, was out to recruit what remained in the ministry of the Tweeddale-Johnston group. He exerted himself to establish a good understanding with Tweeddale with the advantage that Murray's rivals were also hostile to the chancellor.[15] When it came to keeping Queensberry and Argyll from the centre of power, then Murray was on Tweeddale's side. Such consideration for Tweeddale in eclipse was also likely to create a good impression amongst those who had previously looked to him and Johnston for leadership. Ostentatious trust was placed in the chancellor. On the exposure of the assassination plot he was put in charge of security measures in Scotland. The responsibility of reporting on the affairs of the treasury was also left to him.[16] Later, when Tweeddale was finally removed from office, Murray told him that although it was the custom of the country for those dismissed to be insulted by those newly appointed, Tweeddale could rely on his protection. He claimed the credit for Tweeddale's having remained in office for so long.[17] But, from the end of 1695, in or out of office, Tweeddale seemed not to care very much. The strains of age and responsibility had taken heavy toll and he was glad to let events follow their course.[18]

Argyll's determination to uproot every interest from the ministry but his own and Queensberry's had merely been intensified by the changes of 1695. Before and after Tweeddale's dismissal his clamour was incessant. He was re-entering politics with great impetus after a period of detachment from national business. And once Argyll got the bit between his teeth he was not easy to live with. He magnified and boasted of his part in the opposition in the 1695 parliament.[19] He began a petty dispute, the first of several, with the commander-in-chief, Scotland, Sir Thomas Livingston, which had to be settled by the arbitration of a privy council committee.[20] Underlying all these squabbles was the mere fact, which the earl found hard to bear, that Livingston was senior to Argyll in military rank.

Argyll's appointment to the treasury commission found him in full rant. He bombarded Carstares with manic abuse of everyone who crossed him, straining in the process his credibility, one would have thought, to breaking point, despite his assertion: 'So averse am I from making complaints, that often I choose rather to suffer . . . .'[21] Nevertheless, Livingston was 'but a fresh-water sojer',[22] an 'imperious, ignorant, freshwater Crumdell general'. Tweeddale was an 'old weather-beaten decayed doge'; Murray a 'silly piece of a secret statesman . . . who can never purge the Gillicrankie blood, taken in either sense'. But the main burden of his complaint was that 'those of the first magnitude are neglected'. 'I would have the nation,' he said, 'ruled by such as are most able to support the government if the worst of times should come; for, were there invasion, we should be obliged, either to take it upon us, or run for it and let all go to ruin, which God forbid.'[23] His complaints were continuous and not infrequently inconsistent: the treasury was short of money because Tweeddale had applied most of the money to himself; alternatively the treasury was short of money and Tweeddale had not even had the sense to pay his own salary.[24] The only immutable point of reference was Argyll's resentment of all obstacles to his own advancement. Of course the treasury was in a bad way and Tweeddale had been well aware of it. Most of the trouble had been due to the continued absence of a quorum of which he had repeatedly complained. Two of the most culpable commissioners had been Argyll's allies, Queensberry and Raith.[25] At the end of 1695 Tweeddale had reported that owing to the lack of a quorum there had been no sittings of the treasury or exchequer that session, which had never happened before in forty years.[26]

Queensberry was not as clamorous as Argyll but equally relentless. He had joined the opposition in the 1695 parliament, claiming that this was because he was kept in ignorance and treated with contempt, and because Tweeddale's private interest was given preference over the king's service.[27] In the first two allegations there might have been some little truth. As far as the last was concerned, Tweeddale's period of office had been marked by a degree of self-restraint in the advancement of his personal interest rare in Scotland and utterly foreign to Queensberry. After the changes of 1695, when Queensberry found himself still a mere treasury lord, he joined in attacking those of the old Tweeddale-Johnston group still holding office. Some of them were so far gone in faction, he complained, that they were impossible to work with. Without a purge men of honour could not serve the king. If confusion were to be avoided changes would have to take place before the king went to Flanders. Furthermore, if Queensberry were not appointed to his father's place as extraordinary lord of session people would justly conclude that the king had no desire to have service done him.[28] Queensberry's frame of mind at this time had been such that even Ogilvy had thought fit to exhort him to 'abstain heats and divisions'.[29] Nevertheless, threats were being made and Queensberry and Argyll were going to have to be placated. The real nature of the Scottish problem was being revealed. It was not, as William and his advisers had seemed to think, the finding of a *modus vivendi* between presbyterians and episcopalians but of satisfying the growing demands of the magnates and coping with their rivalries.

The bickering, which was all too likely to increase, had already been demonstrated over the 'association'. At the news of the assassination plot of 1696 Annandale had proposed an association based on the English model, members of parliament pledging themselves to the defence of William's person. The proposal was taken up by Carmichael, Ormiston, Livingston and other survivors of the Tweeddale-Johnston interest within the ministry for reasons similar to those motivating the whigs in England. They aimed at stigmatising as disaffected those who were reluctant to sign it, and the chances were good that some followers of both Queensberry and Murray would be unenthusiastic. Murray was as yet regarded without affection and had much work to do before being accepted as leader of the Tweeddale-Johnston group. So a split appeared between the old and new interests. Argyll, Queensberry and Murray, none of whom wanted the embarrassment of exposing divisions on pro- and anti-revolution lines, vied with each other to delay the association until the king had been consulted, thus passing on the responsibility and gaining time. Their delaying tactics were successful. Argyll denounced the association as something plotted by a 'drunken club'. Since the official project had been unsuccessful, he complained, 'those noble drunken patriots', Annandale, Yester and Livingston, were starting an unofficial movement for the same purpose. Those who favoured an association were to wear blue ribbons, a tactic which Argyll deplored as divisive.[30] William's cautious ruling was that he favoured an association provided that it aroused no discords,[31] at which the project had to be dropped temporarily, the king's stipulation being impossible to meet.

The secretaries tried to impress on the court the need to tackle the main problem of Scottish government, of which both Murray and Ogilvy had some appreciation. They recommended as a priority that the 'nobility of the first rank' should be gratified. A significant change was involved in this suggestion. The plan was to make the magnates the basis of a court party drawn from the more moderate politicians, thus building the administration on real political interests instead of a fictional reconciliation of 'presbyterians' and 'episcopalians', even though the secretaries still occasionally used the religious terminology. Tweeddale was to be removed. To replace him as chancellor lord Polwarth[32] was chosen as a man committed to the revolution and, since leaving the club, a political moderate with some claim on the allegiance of Johnston's former group. On his appointment Tweeddale wrote with something like relief to congratulate him.[33]

Even then the court was slow to take the point. Polwarth's preferment was one of the least of the proposed changes. Ogilvy wrote to Portland, ' . . . It is known that my lord Polwarth is chancellor; some are well satisfied with it but I am afraid the nobility of the first rank be displeased unless there be alterations made in their favours. My lord Murray and I did both propose them to the king and we spoke of them to your lordship and the long [sic] I think on it I am the more convinced that they are necessary for his majesty's service for nothing is more desirable than that those entrusted live well together and take joint measures in the management of the government . . .'[34] Murray stressed the same point about the need to satisfy the nobility 'of the first quality'. He continued, ' . . . if it be objected that there are others of the nobility who may pretend also to be considered I must say by looking over the list of those who are presently in his majesty's service one may be easily satisfied that those who are of the ancient nobility as the marquis of Douglas, the earls of Sutherland, Erroll and Morton are not very fit for higher stations and for others they have places and pensions which ought to satisfy them as the earls of Melville and Lothian and their families and the lord Carmichael. It's true the earl of Annandale might pretend on the accompt of his parts which yet are better in public than private, but it's thought his majesty will not think of advancing any to greater trusts in the government who are capable to act for the late King James after they had sworn to be faithful to his majesty . . . '[35] Coming from Murray, whose circumstances were little different, this was somewhat brazen. But by focussing attention on the need to satisfy the nobility, both Ogilvy and Murray were rendering a service.

Ogilvy's recommending further gratification for Queensberry and Argyll is understandable, Murray's less so. Possibly he saw that some concessions were inevitable and wished to seem to initiate them rather than have them forced upon him. He doubtless hoped that in the long run he would be able to outmanoeuvre them both. The proposed scheme was modest enough. Queensberry and Argyll were to receive preferment in an attempt to satisfy them whilst co-ordination of the ministry was entrusted to a reliable and relatively innocuous chancellor. Queensberry was to have Melville's post of privy seal, Melville becoming president of the council. Argyll was to take over the troop of guards from Queensberry. James Baird reported the general aim to Ogilvy's father: ' . . . by this settlement and the other alterations I gave your lordship an account of formerly, they have broken the interest of both the divided parties, and brought all into one united party who I hope will continue in union and follow that which is for his majesty's service with closeness . . . '[36] Ogilvy himself was more specific: ' . . . I am still of the opinion I was of that the making those alterations in favours of Q[ueensberry] and Arg[yll] which we proposed to the king will in all probability unite those of both parties [who] are valuable . . . '[37] The religious designation had been dropped from this talk of parties but there seemed to be no realisation that the parties themselves were transient groupings and that rivalries would emerge in some other form. The court, for its part, was so far from appreciating the importance of the magnates that its acquiescence in the gratification of Queensberry and Argyll was not easily forthcoming. But the changes were at last agreed.

Since there was going to be no complete purge, efforts were made to mollify Queensberry; Murray wrote to him in placatory terms which indicated the intensity of pressure Queensberry had been exerting for sweeping changes: ' . . . and you know the king is not hasty in making alterations. Annandale being newly put in he would not so soon lay him aside but I am persuaded his own carriage will soon do it. Besides when a president of council is named he will demit or else he is much foresworn. Sir Thomas [Livingston's] carriage I am convinced is very disobliging, but the king will make no changes in the commands as I think till his return . . . I hope your grace will carry fair to the new chancellor which is expected here especially since you were desirous to be rid of the last and if you say anything of this in some of your letters it will not be amiss . . . '[38] Since Queensberry was never satisfied with words, his attitude boded ill for the future of co-operation.

But, even the planned adjustments did not prove easy to make, and that entirely for personal reasons. Melville's immediate assumption on being asked to change posts was that he occupied a good bargaining position of which he tried to take full advantage. He declined to transfer from one post to another unless his family was given its 'due' and until he had received his £3000 bond back from the town of Edinburgh.[39] A contingency plan had hastily to be devised whereby if Melville should prove adamant, Queensberry would become president of the council instead of privy seal. Some were naive enough to think that, since Queensberry was going to keep his place in the treasury, his bedchamber place and his recent appointment as an extraordinary lord of session, he would look upon his new post as a political promotion and accept a reduced salary which he could notoriously afford to do.[40] Portland and the secretaries were soon disabused of this idea. Queensberry was surprised, he said, though prematurely — no changes having yet been made — at being moved about from one post to another, which looked very much like a mark of displeasure. However, rather than take a lower salary for the presidency of the council, he would keep the troop of guards which was worth more.[41] Unless Queensberry had exactly what he wanted, then he was going to make sure that Argyll would be disappointed and the entire scheme wrecked. Murray concluded that if it should be necessary to make Queensberry president of the council, then he would have to be paid the full salary.[42] Portland, Murray, Ogilvy and Carstares pleaded with Melville to exchange one post for another without demanding conditions[43] and finally he agreed, though he did insist on the receipt of his new commission before surrendering his old one.[44] Somewhat later and under different circumstances Ogilvy remarked to Carstares, '. . . As for *Melville* and his family, they are . . . after their old manner, complaining of injuries.'[45] They had clearly acquired a reputation.

Simultaneously further attempts were being made to placate the Hamilton family who, apart from Selkirk's recent appointment, were unrepresented in the government. Lord John Hamilton was made general of the mint, foregoing the salary in view of the low state of the revenue, and his brother, lord George Hamilton, was created earl of Orkney.[46]

The nobility of the first class were assured that Polwarth would not tread on their toes. Murray hoped he would carry with 'deference', and Ogilvy was certain he would not behave undutifully to Queensberry.[47] Polwarth's correspondence seems to indicate that at the time he shared this view of his status and function: ' . . . I will set myself with all earnestness to endeavour the reconcilement of parties and the removal of animosities and the preventing of heats among those whom the king employs to bring them to a pleasant concurrence in his majesty's service; and I hope to carry so fairly and live so well with the noble persons your lordship mentions as shall engage them. I do believe the duke of Queensberry may by this post intimate to your lordship his noticing the beginning of it.'[48] It was odd that so much importance was attached to whether Polwarth would be tolerable to Queensberry and Argyll but nobody questioned whether collaboration was possible between them and Murray.

For a time, as far as could be judged on the surface, it seemed that a new court interest had at last been established. Three magnate interests seemed to be united in one administration — four if the Hamilton family were counted, but to do that would have been optimistic in the extreme. If one thought in religious terms, as the court still seemed to do, then presbyterians at all levels were represented: Annandale, Polwarth, Ormiston, Sir James Stewart, Sir John Maxwell and Argyll, even if the last had come in under 'episcopalian' auspices. Murray had been raised an episcopalian but had embraced presbyterianism, whilst Queensberry's advance had always been with the 'episcopalian' party, his family being regarded in that light although he himself conformed. Perhaps William hoped that this new arrangement he had so painfully and reluctantly entered into would provide some stability in the northern kingdom and relieve him of Scottish troubles for some time to come. If this were so he was to be very disappointed. The magnate interests had come out into the open and the task of their reconciliation merited the intercession of St. Jude.

NOTES

1. Fraser, *Melvilles*, ii, 173, Carstares to Melville, 17 Oct. 1695.
2. NUL, Portland, PwA 222, Breadalbane to Portland, 1 Jun. 1695.

The Magnate Resurgence 115

3. Buccleuch (Drum.), Queensberry Letters, xiv, lord John Murray to Queensberry, 7 May 1696; *HMCR Johnstone MSS*, 99-100, Johnston to Annandale, 18 May 1696.
4. *Ib.*, 76, same to same, 13 Apr. 1695. See above, pp. 11-13.
5. *HMCR Johnstone MSS*, 75, Johnston to Annandale, 9 Apr. 1695; Fraser, *Annandale Book*, ii, 110-11, same to same, 13 Apr. [16]95.
6. *HMCR Johnstone MSS*, 77-8, same to same, 23 Apr. 1695.
7. *NLS, MS* 7029, 157, Tweeddale to [Yester?], 29 Dec. 1695.
8. *Ib.*, MS 7020, 10, lord John Murray to Tweeddale, 1 Feb. [1696].
9. *Carstares S.P.*, 262, Sir J. Stewart to Carstares, 17 Oct. 1695; NLS, MS 7029, 155, Tweeddale to [Yester?], 29 Dec. 1695; *HMCR Johnstone MSS*, 81, Ormiston to Annandale, 11 Feb. 1696.
10. Foxcroft, *Supplement*, 415. See below, pp. 130-1.
11. R. H. Story, *William Carstares* (London, 1874), 252-4, [1695].
12. *Ib*.
13. *HMCR Hastings MSS*, ii, 256, [Dr N. Johnston] to Huntingdon, 18 Feb. [16]95[/6].
14. Buccleuch (Drum.), Queensberry Letters, xiv, Argyll to Queensberry, 31 Jul. 1695; NUL, Portland, PwA 308, Queensberry to Portland, 12 Aug. 1695.
15. A series of letters from Murray to Tweeddale: NLS, MS 7020, 4, 6, 10, 14, 18 (Jan.-Feb. 1696); *ib.*, 16, Ogilvy to same, 18 Feb. 1696.
16. See *ib.*, 20-63, *passim*.
17. *Ib.*, 90, Dickson to Tweeddale, 7 Sep. 1696.
18. See his letters of Jan.-Feb. 1696: *ib.*, MS 7030, 12, 18v., 45, 51, 66v., 67v.
19. Buccleuch (Drum.), Queensberry Letters, xiv, Argyll to Queensberry, 31 Jul. 1695; *Carstares S.P.*, 232-3, same to Carstares, 21 Jun. 1695.
20. NUL, Portland, PwA 952, lord John Murray to Portland, 12 May [1696]; *ib.*, PwA 954a, same to same, 29 Jun. 1696; Buccleuch (Drum.), Queensberry Letters, xiv, Ogilvy to Queensberry, 14 May 1696; *Carstares S.P.*, 274-6, Argyll to Carstares, 21 Mar. 1696.
21. *Ib.*, 277-8, same to same, 16 Mar. [1696].
22. *Ib*.
23. *Ib.*, 274-6, same to same, 21 Mar. [1696]; *ib.*, 277-8, same to same, 16 Mar. 1696; *ib.*, 279-82, same to same, 23 Mar. [1696].
24. *Ib.*, 272-4, same to same, 19 Mar. [1696].
25. *Ib; ib.*, 274-6, same to same, 21 Mar.1696; NLS, MS 7030, 20, Tweeddale to Johnston, 18 Jan. 1696; *ib.*, MS 7029, 72v., same to the king, 5 Sep. 1695.
26. *Ib.*, 121, same to Johnston, 27 Nov. 1695; *ib.*, 134, same to same, 14 Dec. 1695.
27. NUL, Portland, PwA 364, Queensberry to Portland, 11 Jun. 1695; *ib.*, PwA 365, same to same, 25 Jun. 1695; *ib.*, PwA 366, same to the king, 25 Jun. 1695; *ib.*, PwA 367, same to Portland, 2 Jul. 1695; *ib.*, PwA 369, same to same, 2 Nov. 1695.
28. *Carstares S.P.*, 291-2, same to Carstares, 14 Apr. 1696; *ib.*, 292-3, same to same, 30 Apr. 1696.
29. Buccleuch (Drum.), Queensberry Letters, xiv, 5 Mar. 1696.
30. For this whole episode: *Carstares S.P.*, 282-9, *passim*.
31. NLS, MS 7020, 57, Ogilvy to Tweeddale, 4 Apr. 1696.
32. He had been created first baron Polwarth in 1691: *HMCR Marchmont MSS*, 119-21.
33. NLS, MS 7027, 44, 14 May 1696; *ib.*, MS 7020, 69, 13 May 1696.
34. NUL, Portland, PwA 976, 12 May 1696.
35. *Ib.*, PwA 952, 12 May [1696].
36. *Seafield Correspondence*, 197-8, J. Baird to Findlater, 2 May 1696.
37. NUL, Portland, PwA 977, to Portland, 22 May 1696.
38. Buccleuch (Drum.), Union, i, [1696].
39. SRO, GD26, xiii, 66/9, Melville to [   ], [1696]; Fraser, *Melvilles*, ii, 175, Melville to Ogilvy, 15 May 1696.
40. NUL, Portland, PwA 976, Ogilvy to Portland, 12 May 1696.
41. *Ib.*, PwA 371, Queensberry to same, 14 Jun. 1696.
42. *Ib.*, PwA 953, 20 Jun. 1696.
43. Fraser, *Melvilles*, ii, 174-8.
44. NUL, Portland, PwA 954a, Murray to Portland, 29 Jun. 1696. To retain his support every appearance had to be made of meeting Melville's wishes: letters from Ogilvy to Melville (SRO, GD26, xiii, 99/2,4,6; *ib.*, 103/1).
45. *Carstares S.P.*, 335-8, 31 Aug. 1697. Words italicised were in cipher in the original.
46. NUL, Portland, PwA 952, Murray to Portland, 12 May [1696]; *ib.*, PwA 976, Ogilvy to same, 12 May 1696; NLS, MS 7030, 13v., Tweeddale to Yester, 11 Jan. 1696.

47. Buccleuch (Drum.), Queensberry Letters, xiv, Murray to Queensberry, 7 May 1696; *ib.*, Ogilvy to same, 22 May 1696.
48. *Marchmont Papers*, iii, 103-104, Polwarth to Murray, 14 May 1696; NUL, Portland, PwA 682, same to Portland, 16 May 1696.

6
The Establishment of the Queensberry Interest

WHATEVER the reality of the situation in Scotland as it had begun to strike the secretaries, William, Portland and Carstares regarded the ministry as having been reconstructed for the better accommodation of two religious factions. Argyll was taken to be firmly presbyterian, Queensberry as having episcopalian leanings but a committed revolution man nonetheless, whilst Murray was a presbyterian convert from an episcopalian and, as many suspected, crypto-jacobite interest. Marchmont, Stewart and Melville represented the *émigré* old guard which continued to flaunt its presbyterian allegiance — even Melville in spite of his recent 'episcopalian' entanglement. Ogilvy was the sort of man of business William favoured and had already, though unsuccessfully, in the persons of Dalrymple and Johnston, tried to employ, though his appointment at this time was due rather to his status as a functionary who would get in nobody's way. The ministry seemed to comprise a wide enough spectrum of religious views to attract the support of a majority in parliament whilst avoiding charges of religious bigotry and persecution, but there were ample signs that more than religion was involved. Religious affiliations did exist but the main determinants of Scottish politics were the magnate interests and the attitudes of lesser families to them.

This reconstructed ministry of 1696 demonstrated beyond doubt the utter incompatibility of the great nobles and the lengths to which they were prepared to go in order to dominate the administration. The first manifestation of this in the new ministry was the rivalry between Murray on the one hand and the Queensberry-Argyll alliance on the other, an episode which greatly accelerated the seepage of the discontented into active opposition.

But first the new court coalition had to face the parliament of 1696 as a public test. Some indication of the court's calculations appeared in the appointment of Murray as commissioner to the parliament. Clearly he had been selected as the man most likely to succeed in spanning the gap between the two supposed groups. Almost immediately the failure of the scheme was signalled by the very briskness with which the new commissioner tried to squeeze out of his nomination the greatest possible advantage to himself.

Custom ruled that only a peer could represent the king in parliament and Murray, as no more than Atholl's eldest son, had to be raised to the peerage in his own right. His claims were high. He wished to be a marquess, his argument being plain if lacking cogency. Already there existed an earldom of Moray, so raising him to the peerage as earl of Murray would lead to confusion. Since Murray had no wish to change his name, the simplest solution was to make him a marquess, thereby distinguishing the two. On the death of his father he was going to be a marquess anyway, so he could envisage no objection to such a proposal.[1] Objections were raised nevertheless and Murray finally agreed to be earl of Tullibardine,[2] changing his name with apparent equanimity, as he was to do again on succeeding to his father's title.

The ministry, in the parliament of 1696, had one real aim: to obtain a grant of supply for the forces.[3] But Tullibardine's instructions also allowed him to accept other measures, church acts, for instance, aimed at composing differences between presbyterian and other clergy provided that they were not inconsistent with the royal prerogative or the privileges already granted to episcopalian ministers. This was a gesture to those who had attacked Johnston's acts as too harsh but intended at the same time to avoid offence to the presbyterian establishment. Under the circumstances it is difficult to see how it could have been any other than the meaningless formula which emerged. Acts for the encouragement of trade were also allowable as long as they were not likely to annoy the English.[4] Tullibardine showed himself particularly anxious to avoid any such offence to the English parliament, almost abasing himself to give assurances on this point.[5]

Apart from the new commissioner's importunity over his title, everything in September 1696 favoured a peaceful session. Each man with a share in the government or hope of acquiring something of the sort knew he was on trial and had a strong incentive to co-operate. Circumstances combined to make the task of parliamentary management easier than it might have been. Dalrymple, who had become a peer on his father's death, did not attend the parliament. Of the old managing interest, Johnston had sat formerly only as lord secretary and was in England, Tweeddale had asked to be excused on the grounds of infirmity,[6] whilst Yester as a peer's eldest son was not entitled to attend. Annandale, sulking over Melville's appointment as president of the council, stayed away. The absence of such spectres made the feast a more relaxed occasion. Yet in parliament there were still remnants of the old Tweeddale-Johnston interest. Some were within the ministry and some outside it, but all viewed the new managers with a mixture of suspicion and hostility. Those out of office formed the nucleus of a new opposition which made its appearance in this parliament. In view of the ministry's limited aims they had not much choice over what to oppose, so they took issue over taxation, declaring their readiness to vote a year's supply but objecting to the two years proposed by the managers. For the behaviour of their former colleagues, showing their zeal as members of the new court, they affected the utmost contempt. Cockburn of Ormiston wrote of it to Annandale: ' . . . The first year['s cess] passed unanimously enough, but the second met with great opposition. In the committee Grant, Culloden and Whitelaw wrought it through. In the parliament the chancellor pressed it and Commissary Munro second[ed] him. No men so forward as the *nouveaux convertie* [sic].[7] When it came to be voted, though only 3 or 4 of the nobility (whereof Lauderdale and Ruthven were two) were against it, yet it was lost when it passed the barons. But Whitelaw and his burghs carried it. Whitelaw has lost himself in the esteem of all honest men, except the above named...'[8] So the ministry obtained its two years' cess for the army. For the rest they were content with voting the formerly controversial association which all members signed[9] and passing an act of security to ensure continuity of government on the death of William.[10] It was plain that the new court had retained the support of most former Johnston men, who had decided to go in with Polwarth, though others bore malice whilst Ormiston held on to his job and grumbled.

Despite all that had been said in the past about the immoderate nature of Johnston's church acts, no attempt was made to modify the church settlement or make any further provision for the admission of ministers. It was not that the new ministry regarded the church settlement as unimportant — church affairs comprised one of the planks along which some had recently edged themselves into office. But no subsequent ministry in an independent Scotland, whatever professions it made before or after taking office, did anything to change the arrangements made for the church between 1690 and 1695. Criticisms continued to be expressed for largely political reasons but almost everyone tacitly recognised the fact that, once the initial settlement had been completed, the church establishment as it remained after Johnston's act of 1695 was realistically based and dangerous to tamper with.

The session ended on 12 October 1696.[11] Such of the Johnston-Tweeddale interest as followed Polwarth and, in particular, Hamilton of Whitelaw with his grip on the burgh members, had given the new managers their majority. Polwarth's group were hoping for reward in the aftermath of his promotion and were concerned to acquire merit at the earliest opportunity. Whitelaw, for example, was serving in expectation of being made president of the court of session now that Stair was dead. With such co-operation it could easily have been assumed that the new ministerial mixture had succeeded, since it had passed its first test in the 1696 parliament. In fact it was unlikely in the extreme to outlive its infancy. Linking the interests of Queensberry and Argyll together with that of Atholl whose objectives were incompatible with theirs was doomed from the very beginning. Eventually one or other of them would have to go and for reasons quite unconnected with religion. The rival interests were brazen in pursuit of private advantage, whatever protestations of innocence were made when accusations of 'entering into a party' were bandied about. What was at stake was the predominance of one or other of the magnates within the kingdom. The administration was not big enough to hold them all, particularly after Tullibardine had been favoured by appointment as secretary of state and commissioner.

The eventual trial of strength took place over the post of president of the session. Whitelaw's pretensions to the post were fully recognised and he had Tullibardine's firm support. Tullibardine had even taken to Scotland Whitelaw's commission as president, conditional presumably upon his behaviour in parliament. Despite Whitelaw's great service to the court in the parliament of 1696, at the end of the session Tullibardine found the commission inexplicably obstructed.[12] Whitelaw's expectations became the pivot of the contest between Tullibardine and the rival interests. Queensberry accused Tullibardine of 'entering into a party', in opposition, presumably, to himself and Argyll. Tullibardine emphatically denied the charge unless, he added, attempting to keep his promises to Whitelaw came into that category.[13] It was, of course, about this very point that Queensberry was complaining. Queensberry's strong feelings over Whitelaw's candidature were due to his concern for his own interest, Whitelaw having always been opposed to him. In Stair's time the Dalrymple and Queensberry influence had dominated the court of session. For Tullibardine to succeed in procuring the job for Whitelaw would have been a major defeat for Queensberry in fact as well as in prestige.

There was another aspect to this issue which produced consternation even amongst the relatively uncommitted. The appointment of president of the session was of more than legal significance. As the civil court, the session was responsible for decisions affecting property rights and was thus able to exert great pressure on individuals, a power which there were no scruples about using. All landed interests in Scotland were acutely conscious of this, so it was generally thought highly desirable that some balance should be preserved amongst the judges. Though all save the extraordinary lords were lawyers, they had nevertheless been appointed as a reward for political services and loyalty to a particular interest. If one interest should predominate, the chances of any other receiving justice, saving the intervention of parliament, were slight. Some of the great animosity shown towards Stair was due to this although, of course, past resentments had been involved. But Stair's legal authority had been so great and his persuasiveness so notorious that he had come to dominate the court. Allegations were persistently made that he exercised his power unfairly.[14] Whitelaw had in part owed his original appointment as a lord of session to the need for some check on Stair. Under the Tweeddale administration a commission on judicatures had been set up to consider, amongst others, this very problem. One of its recommendations had been that there should be no permanent presidency. The king should either name three judges to serve in turn, or appoint presidents for one year of office only, to avoid any such personal ascendancy as Stair had exercised and the consequent dissension in the court as the minority of judges tried to obstruct the president's will.[15]

But Whitelaw also was a man of dominant character. Even one of Ogilvy's detachment was influenced by this. Ogilvy wrote to Carstares that he would never agree to anything which would be to Whitelaw's prejudice, ' . . . But I am sure it will never be the interest of *the king* to make *Whitelaw* independent. He is a good servant, but when he is a master he is furious . . . '[16] Queensberry was primed with similar arguments against the appointment of Whitelaw as well as with some curious reflections concerning judical appointments in general. According to Queensberry's adviser, Sir James Stewart, notoriously corrupt, was preferable to Whitelaw untrammelled and rampant.[17]

Queensberry, though, wanted the appointment of Hugh Dalrymple, Stair's son. His choice was quite unconnected with Dalrymple's legal ability or concern for the efficiency of the court. He wished merely to maintain his own influence in the session through his own post of extraordinary lord and the preservation of the Dalrymple interest which was allied to him.[18] Too much was at stake for Queensberry even to contemplate Whitelaw's appointment.

Tullibardine, too, was unable to compromise, being widely known as Whitelaw's sponsor. He was driven to offer Queensberry a bargain: ' . . . If you will yield Whitelaw, my lord Tullibardine says he shall be ready to do anything for you that you can propose, that is he will counsel and advise him to be your grace's servant . . . '[19] But Queensberry was not interested in promises, especially those as little likely to be honoured as this one. So the ministry staggered through a blizzard of accusations and counter-accusations which made relations between the magnate groups even worse until the issue of the presidency was decided in 1698.[20]

During this period Tullibardine worked assiduously to reduce his undoubted disadvantages. Within the ministry he was the odd man out, not having belonged to Queensberry's branch of the 'episcopalian' opposition before the reshuffle of 1696. Nor had the 'presbyterian' interest, formerly associated with Johnston, much reason to be grateful to him.[21] His task was to recruit for himself an interest comparable to that of Queensberry and Argyll. He resorted to all the usual tactics. As secretary in waiting he was tireless in his solicitation of favours to secure the alliance of one person or another. Ogilvy viewed this morosely: ' . . . I am sure he has this year thrice as much from the king as I have got. He will improve all these favours for establishing his own power...'[22] Tullibardine told Ogilvy plainly not to encroach on magnate preserves. It did not at all become Ogilvy, he said, to oppose anything Tullibardine might do, 'neither was it expected of him'.[23] Tullibardine denounced, as was his habit, anyone of whom he disapproved in such comprehensive terms that even the king began to think him 'too ready to give such characters of those who are not of his party'.[24] With this propensity for denigrating his rivals went a strong determination to claim the credit, whether justifiably or not, for any ministerial achievements, however meagre.[25]

By the end of 1697, through sheer persistence in such tactics, Tullibardine had had some degree of success in building up a party. As the most favourably placed of Queensberry's opponents he proved able to establish a working relationship with the remnants of the old Johnston group, given by the Queensberry alliance the pejorative nickname of 'the club'. Such members of the administration as had no liking for either Queensberry or Argyll seemed willing to be associated with him: Annandale, for example, and Sir Thomas Livingston, recently created viscount of Teviot. Consequently, as these two poles exercised their respective attractions, the groups became more rigidly aligned.[26]

Tullibardine said he was driven to such manoeuvres only because Queensberry and Argyll were intriguing behind his back, a notion at which Argyll professed himself astounded since, he said, it was untrue. Furthermore ' . . . we may the more easily be believed, since it is not our interest, besides not our inclination, to make division. We are all satisfied with the posts we are in. We envy nobody . . . ' This declaration formed the prelude to a further tirade of abuse against Teviot, whose post as commander-in-chief Argyll greatly coveted.[27] The prospect of Tullibardine's gaining support from presbyterians moved Argyll to wrath as being an encroachment on his preserve: ' . . . I am heartily sorry to hear that any presbyterians of the Church of Scotland can be prevailed upon (by a runegado Church of England man and a presbyterian but of two years' standing) . . . I think it a very bad measure to set up a pretended presbyterian, who wants but an opportunity to return to the mire when once he has established himself. And lest by my friendship with some, I mean the duke of Queensberry in particular, it may be thought I must go another way, his family having been reputed episcopal, I dare answer for him he will be ready to embark heartily with the presbyterians if they will cordially accept them [sic]; and when I am guarantee, I think you have better security for his grace than any is yet got of our two-year old presbyterian, the marquis of Atholl's son, the earl of Tullibardine . . . '[28] Quite clearly no prospect of co-operation existed.

Stepping uneasily between the interests were those trying either to preserve some detachment or to appear members of both sides at once. Sooner rather than later the coalition would break down and those who wanted to keep their jobs would need to have been on the winning side or at the least have given no gratuitous offence. Sir James Ogilvy for various reasons appeared to be on Queensberry's side but in reality was padding unobtrusively through the administrative undergrowth on his way to becoming, in English eyes, the indispensable Scottish minister. Ormiston had no liking for Queensberry but, although assiduously cultivated by Tullibardine whom he made no effort to discourage, he nevertheless covertly signalled his independence.[29] The lord advocate characteristically tried to give the impression of belonging to all parties at once. He leaned towards Queensberry and Argyll whilst professing friendship for Tullibardine though sniping at him from behind. Meanwhile he recommended to Carstares changes of his own devising and calculated entirely for his own benefit. Nobody completely trusted him, and wisely.[30]

Most delicately balanced of all was the chancellor, committed by the terms of his appointment to the maintenance of unity in the ministry.[31] However, as an ally of Whitelaw and a supporter of his candidacy for the post of president, he found himself drawn towards Tullibardine, to whom he wrote with extravagant expressions of loyalty, referring to Tullibardine's rivals as 'the siding, party-disposed men'.[32] At virtually the same time he made appeals to Ogilvy for unity, complaining of being criticised for having sided too much with Queensberry and Argyll,[33] though Carstares, at least, regarded him as an ally of Tullibardine.[34] There were good reasons for Carstares's opinion. Many of Tullibardine's new supporters were Polwarth's former colleagues of the old Johnston interest and the chancellor might well have felt the pull of old friendships and allegiance. He also felt the need for some allies of his own, since he wanted to keep his post of chancellor and Tullibardine was making his flesh creep with stories of a conspiracy to remove him in favour of Argyll.[35]

Finally, before crossing to Holland in 1698, William made Hugh Dalrymple president of the court of session.[36] On the surface this was no more than a limited victory over one issue for Queensberry and Argyll. In fact, by the time the decision was made, so much had come to hinge upon it that it proved to be decisive for the future of the ministry, disrupting the reorganised court interest of 1696. At the time of Dalrymple's appointment, William had said that he looked on Whitelaw as an honest man whom he would reward, but not by making him president of session. As a temporary consolation prize Whitelaw was given a pension[37] which failed completely in its intended purpose of retaining Whitelaw's support. The chancellor had been committed to Whitelaw's appointment, but this and his earlier protestations of loyalty to Tullibardine notwithstanding, he swallowed his mortification and accepted the *fait accompli*.[38] Not so Tullibardine and Whitelaw, both proud men who were not prepared to suffer humiliation passively. Tullibardine, rightly or wrongly, blamed the influence of Portland and Carstares.[39] Both he and Whitelaw were full of resentment and were encouraged by Annandale and Ruglen to make a display of it, but perhaps they needed no such urging. Annandale thought the only possible course for Tullibardine to take was resignation. Tullibardine came to the same conclusion and went to resign but seems to have been very surprised when William did not ask him to stay in office. Whitelaw refused the pension he had been offered[40] and broke with the court completely. Polwarth as chancellor was left behind in office, in very cool company and irritable, deploring the decisions of both Tullibardine and Whitelaw.[41]

Although Tullibardine was very much put out by Dalrymple's appointment, his resignation did not spring merely from a huff over the loss of one prize. He had lost a whole campaign of which the disposal of the presidency was the climax. Since the reconstruction of 1695-6 he had been working to improve his interest the better to compete with

Queensberry and Argyll. Over the same period Queensberry and the Dalrymples had also maintained a steady pressure to increase their power within the administration and with some success. A sustained growth of the Queensberry interest had occurred to the detriment of all who did not openly accept the duke's leadership and patronage. Gritty elements were to be prised out and supplanted by his allies and followers. Both he and Argyll pressed implacably for their own interests, reacting immediately to apparent slights for the sake of expressing displeasure. Ceaselessly they kept watch against any advancement of the house of Hamilton.

Shortly after his appointment as privy seal Queensberry had prepared to justify his further promotion. The king's service had suffered more, he thought, ' . . . for not seeming to care for the prerogative and for his advancing everybody who were known to be against it than by jacobitism and this with the former methods have brought his authority so low that it's hardly possible to retrieve it, at least not suddenly . . . My present character of privy seal does not lead me to have great burden or influence.'[42] So he continued to push. He agitated successfully for the elevation to the peerage of his brother, lord William Douglas. Lord William selected the title earl of Peebles. At the same time, Sir Thomas Livingston, in process of becoming a viscount, was also choosing the title Peebles. After much acrimony the dispute was resolved by each taking a completely different title, earl of March and viscount of Teviot respectively. Queensberry let it be known that he would bear no malice if his brother were, in addition, put on the privy council.[43] March was made a privy councillor to keep Queensberry quiet and there followed a whole succession of appointments for the duke's benefit. Murray of Philiphaugh, one of the duke's close advisers, was added to the council and exchequer. Mar and Boyle of Kelburn were put on the council.[44] Tullibardine's resignation brought no slackening of the pressure and, as a result, by the time of the Africa Company crisis in 1700 and 1701, Queensberry, with Portland and Carstares as his chief advocates, had achieved something close to predominance in the Scottish court. But the cost had been high. Portland and Carstares, in pursuit of some chimera, destroyed, instead of prolonging, what little inclination to co-operate existed within the court. As his victory over Tullibardine forced the latter out of the ministry and, with Whitelaw, into opposition, so each Queensberry advance increased the resistance to him within and without the ministry. Consequently the Scottish court party began to show signs of imminent collapse and a point was reached at which William had to question whether he could afford continually to gratify Queensberry's ambitions. But in 1698 there was still some way to go before this stage was reached and fundamental questions had to be faced.

NOTES

1. NUL, Portland, PwA 956a, to Portland, 21 Jul. 1696.
2. Japikse, i, 189-91, Portland to William, 7/17 Aug. 1696.
3. *APS*, x, 9.
4. NUL, Portland, PwA 957, enclosed with 957a, includes formal and secret instructions.
5. *Ib.*, PwA 956a, 21 Jul. 1696.
6. NLS, MS 7020, 90, Dickson to Tweeddale, 7 Sep. 1696.
7. All members of the former Johnston interest who had gone expectantly into the new court.

8.   *HMCR Johnstone MSS*, 82, 29 Sep. 1696.
9.   See above, pp. 111-2. Those refusing to sign had their seats declared vacant.
10. *APS*, x, 10-11, 25, 59-60.
11. *Carstares S.P.*, 112.
12. *ib.*, 338-41, Sir J. Stewart to Carstares, 4 Sep. 1697; *HMCR Johnstone MSS*, 99-100, Johnston to Annandale, 18 May 1696.
13. Buccleuch (Drum.), Queensberry Letters, xiv, [Tullibardine] to [Queensberry], 23 Dec. 1696.
14. See above, p. 96.
15. NLS, MS 7028, 150, Tweeddale to Johnston, 22 Sep. 1694; *ib.*, 167, same to same, 3 Nov. 1694.
16. *Carstares S.P.*, 349-51, 1 Oct. 1697.
17. Buccleuch (Drum.), Col., bundle i, fragment of a memorial to [Queensberry], [1697-8].
18. See below, Chaps. 7 and 8, *passim*.
19. Buccleuch (Drum.), Queensberry Letters, xiv, Ogilvy to Queensberry, 26 Dec. 1696.
20. *Carstares S.P.*, 338-41, Stewart to Carstares, 4 Sep. 1697; Buccleuch (Drum.), Queensberry Letters, xiv, [Ogilvy] to [Queensberry], 15 Jan. 1697 and below, p. 122.
21. *HMCR Johnstone MSS*, 82, Ormiston to Annandale, 29 Sep. 1696.
22. *Carstares S.P.*, 297-9, to Carstares, 27 Apr. 1697.
23. *Ib.*, 319-21, Ogilvy to same, 24 Jul. 1697.
24. *HMCR Marchmont MSS*, 133-4, Pringle to Polwarth, 15 Apr. 1697.
25. See, e.g., *Carstares S.P.*, 312-13, 314-15, 315-16, 480.
26. Buccleuch (Drum.), Union, i, [Tullibardine] to [Queensberry], [2 Feb. 1697]; *Carstares S.P.*, 307-8, Ogilvy to Carstares, 8 Jun. 1697; *ib.*, 309-10, same to same, 18 Jun. 1697; *ib.*, 316-18, Argyll to same, 10 Jul. 1697; *ib.*, 319-20, Ogilvy to same, 24 Jul. 1697; *HMCR Johnstone MSS*, 100-101, Teviot to Annandale, 30 Oct. 1697; *ib.*, same to same, 19 Nov. 1697.
27. *Ib.*, 316-18, Argyll to Carstares, 10 Jul. 1697.
28. *Ib.*, 370, same to same, 26 Feb. 1698.
29. Buccleuch (Drum.), Union, i, [Tullibardine] to [Queensberry], [2 Feb. 1697]; *Carstares S.P.*, 335-8, Ogilvy to Carstares, 31 Aug. 1697.
30. See his letters to Carstares, 1697: *ib.*, 322-4, 325-6, 338-41, 354-5, 363-4; *ib.*, 335-8, Ogilvy to Carstares, 31 Aug. 1697; *ib.*, 368, Pringle to same, 10 Feb. 1698.
31. *Marchmont Papers*, iii, 130-32, Polwarth to Johnston, 15 Mar. 1697.
32. *Ib.*, 120-22, 5 Jan. 1697; *ib.*, 126-7, same to same, 30 Jan. 1697.
33. *Ib.*, 124-5, Polwarth to Ogilvy, 23 Jan. 1697.
34. Fraser, *Melvilles*, ii, 178-9, Carstares to Leven, 10 Mar. 1698.
35. *HMCR Marchmont MSS*, 139, Tullibardine to Polwarth, 16 Dec. 1697. Ogilvy denied the rumours: *ib.*, 140, to same, 21 Dec. 1697.
36. SRO, GD26, xiii, 99/8, Ogilvy to Melville, 17 Mar. 1698.
37. *Marchmont Papers*, iii, 150, Polwarth to Whitelaw, 31 Mar. 1698.
38. *HMCR Johnstone MSS*, 105, Polwarth to Annandale, 31 Mar. 1698; *Marchmont Papers*, iii, 151, same to Sir D. Hume, 31 Mar. 1698.
39. *Ib.*, 146, Tullibardine to Polwarth, [c. 20 Feb. 1698].
40. *HMCR Johnstone MSS*, 105, same to Annandale, 3 Apr. 1698; *ib.*, 104, Annandale to [Tullibardine], 24 Mar. 1698; Japikse, i, 282-3, the king to Portland, 11 Apr. 1698.
41. *Marchmont Papers*, iii, 153, to Whitelaw, 19 Apr. 1698.
42. Buccleuch (Drum), Union, i, memorial by Queensberry, [1697-8].
43. *Ib.*, Queensberry Letters, xiv, [Ogilvy] to [Queensberry], 5 Dec. 1696; *ib.*, [   ] to [Queensberry], 8 Dec. 1696; *ib.*, Ogilvy to [same], 24 Dec. 1696; *Carstares S.P.*, 304-5, same to Carstares, 1 Jun. 1697.
44. *Ib.*, Union, i, [Philiphaugh] to [Queensberry], 12 May [1696]; *Carstares S.P.*, 297-9, Ogilvy to Carstares, 27 Apr. 1697; *ib.*, 307-8, same to same, 8 Jun. 1698.

7
Queensberry and the Rise of the Country Party

THE success of Queensberry and Argyll in driving out Tullibardine not only disrupted the reconstructed court interest of 1696, it also produced, as a direct result, a more active and concentrated opposition than the somewhat scattered voices of dissent which had been heard in Tullibardine's parliament. This became apparent almost immediately in the parliamentary session of 1698 which, the comparative murmurs of 1696 apart, marked the first stirring of that 'country party' which was to plague the administration till the union.

This country party originally comprised some of the remnants of the Tweeddale-Johnston group who had remained unreconciled to the changes of 1696 and had quietly festered ever since. They had kept up regular communication with Johnston himself, by then in England, tending his gardens and loitering at court in search of gossip and opportunity. As a leader, for want of better, they had Tweeddale's son, formerly the proud but diffident Yester who, on the death of his father in 1697, had become the no less proud and diffident second marquess of Tweeddale. On Hugh Dalrymple's appointment as president of session they were joined in opposition by Tullibardine, Whitelaw and such others as they took with them. There was no doubt why they were in opposition – resentment and pride made it impossible for any of them to accept the new leadership at court after the humiliation they felt they had suffered at the hands of Queensberry and Argyll.

In opposition their difficulty was the usual one of finding some motive more creditable than resentment to parade in public. Like most country parties they affected concern over the ministry's alleged neglect of Scottish interests and in 1698 an issue came ready to hand. The country was suffering yet another bad harvest – one of the lean years of King William – and neither had a monopoly of concern at the consequences. The chancellor left Carstares in no doubt about the country's condition,[1] but although Polwarth and other officers of state might express private disquiet, the opposition as always was in a better position to make capital out of it. Ogilvy, created in 1698 viscount of Seafield, wrote: ' . . . I find we will meet with difficulty [in parliament], but I assure you it is not that Tullibardine or his friends signify anything. It proceeds only from this, that there is almost a famine in the country and that there is an appearance of an extraordinary bad crop. And, therefore, a great many say that they are not able to give subsidies . . . '[2] The peace of Ryswick had created the usual pool of unemployed officers – and presumably of other ranks although they were not mentioned – which aggravated the situation. And it was well known that, though feeling in England was strongly in favour of cutting down the standing army in peacetime, supply was to be requested for the upkeep of forces in Scotland.[3] On all this material the opposition hoped to work and the signs were unmistakable that they were well embarked on preparations for the 1698 parliament.[4] A version of Tullibardine's resignation had been circulated which presented him in a most favourable light. The king, it was claimed, had pressed him to stay and serve him but he had resigned rather than oppress his compatriots — 'his conscience and his love to his country would not allow him . . .'[5]

Plain words between Seafield and Tullibardine epitomised the situation: 'I find my lord Tullibardine is positively resolved to oppose . . . He said plainly he could not in conscience burden the country with so much money as the expenses of the establishment would require, but that he would do as much for the king now as if he were in his service. I answered him that the country was poor when he was commissioner, for that year there was [sic] vast quantities of victual imported both from England and Ireland and above £100,000 exported in specie, whereas there had been little or no victual imported this last year. He said then it was time of war and I told him then he was commissioner and now he was not. I told him also that we had more need of forces now for our security than we had in time of war, for then in the case of necessity the king could have sent his regiments to our assistance . . .'[6]

Court preparations for managing parliament defined even more sharply the composition of the opposing forces, though even then there were some who managed to preserve an ambiguous attitude. Polwarth accepted the post of commissioner and the earldom of Marchmont that went with it but he was uneasy, feeling obliged to defend his decision to the small group of his followers who continued to sympathise with Tullibardine and Whitelaw. In 1696 they had exerted themselves as prominent courtiers in hope of better things but had since become alienated. Marchmont asked them to keep their minds free from 'prepossessions' till he saw them.[7] Nevertheless from their point of view his position was open to criticism. He had been in alliance with Tullibardine, or at least had succeeded in giving that impression, when the latter was in the ministry. Now Marchmont's own following seemed to have considerably more sympathy with the opposition than with a court dominated by Queensberry and Argyll, whether Marchmont were part of it or not. So the commissioner's allies either voted in parliament with the opposition or stayed away, which Queensberry, Argyll and Seafield all made a point of reporting.[8] Annandale had been a very prominent supporter of the Tullibardine faction and the one who had ultimately encouraged the earl to resign although himself feeling under no such obligation. When the managers made it quite clear that any opposition would result in the loss of places and pensions, Annandale silently changed sides and stayed unobtrusively with the court.[9] The Melville family, too, were placed in difficulties. Despite their links with the 'episcopalian' opposition to Johnston and Tweeddale, and Tarbat's use of Melville's name to establish the opposition's credit with Carstares, the family had gained nothing from the reconstruction of 1696. Nor had Melville met with any success in recovering the Edinburgh bond which had developed into something of an obsession with him.[10] Melville had also been far from pleased at Dalrymple's appointment. His objections to the new president implied no preference for Whitelaw — indeed he disliked both candidates. It seemed rather that he had come round again to fearing the Dalrymples. As a result, in the 1698 parliament the family acted most equivocally. Raith, Melville's eldest son, had died, but Melville and Leven confined themselves to silent voting with the court whilst privately encouraging the opposition to press their more embarrassing 'popular' acts. Their few followers, led by Mr James Melville, voted against the court — 'the little thing, the brother, has voted wrong in almost all the votes . . .'[11] And, significantly, associated with the opposition was the earl of Ruglen, the sole representative in parliament of the late duke of Hamilton's family. It was plain how the house of Hamilton regarded a court dominated by Queensberry and Argyll.[12] The feeling was shared by most of the opposition and even by some who were still managing to keep a foothold inside the court.

Parliament's business was planned to be uncomplicated: supply, with permission granted for the passing of trade acts and some provision for disbanded officers as long as the standing forces were given priority.[13] From the beginning the court's numerical superiority was apparent, every conceivable pressure having been exerted to ensure it. Tullibardine was removed from the privy council, for instance, though greatly against Marchmont's inclination.[14] Once the session had started, the second marquess of Tweeddale made an unhappy debut as an opposition leader, acting with all the rashness of an opinionated introvert under some compulsion to make a mark in public. Others took advantage of this, which seemed to be his invariable fate. Argyll reported to Carstares: 'As for the marquess of Tweeddale, he has acted a foolish part, for they have made him give in all the foolish proposals . . .'[15] But Tweeddale was subdued by the introduction of a private act relating to lady Dalkeith's jointure and involving the principle of entails on a point which Tweeddale thought might be disadvantageous to him. The act was not proceeded with but kept deliberately 'as a whip over his head' to moderate his opposition.[16]

Amongst the nobles the court had a large majority, a smaller one in the estate of barons but, managed by commissary Smollett under the guidance of president Dalrymple, the burghs were almost all for the court. Whitelaw's earlier grip on them had clearly been official, as a court manager, rather than personal. The burghs' allegiance seemed open to negotiation for substantial benefits which only the court was in a position to supply. Argyll remarked, '. . . the tack [of the customs] to the burghs has been of good use upon this occasion . . .'[17] Consequently, even at its strongest, the opposition mustered no more than about fifty votes and for the most part as few as thirty. The thirty represented the hard core of opposition which, on particular votes, was joined by others not utterly committed against the court. This latter group, willing to show some, but not too much, independence, exerted itself over relatively fine distinctions, for instance the amount of cess to be voted — the firm opposition wanting to vote none at all whilst the others would have preferred eighteen months' supply to the court's proposed two years' — and a procedural vote concerning an Africa Company petition.[18] It could be argued, but not very convincingly, that the increased vote on these two issues illustrates the appeal of the country cause. For two ready-made country issues to attract a mere twenty votes extra at a time when the ministry had just suffered a shock through the departure of Tullibardine and Whitelaw hardly indicates strong country feeling. More probably a few members wished to show their disquiet over developments in the court but without adopting a full opposition stance. So despite the fact that the opposition had chosen its ground with skill — the bad state of the country, demands for a prohibition on English cloth and all French imports, for a habeas corpus act, for the Scots guards to be given their rightful precedence when serving abroad and for the support of the Africa

Company — they were so overwhelmed by the court majority that none of these issues was allowed to come to a vote.[19]

The only question which could have caused trouble was that of the Africa Company, whose project to found in Darien a Scottish colony had already become a national cause, supported by courtiers as well as opposition and even by some who thought the company's venture ill-advised. But the Scottish ministers were not yet in the invidious position in which the fate of the project was later to place them, so the question at this stage could not be turned into a serious issue between court and opposition. An address in support of the company was rendered as innocuous as possible and approved *nem con*.[20]

The session of 1698, largely as a result of Seafield's management and his capable performance as president of the parliament, had shown up the opposition for what it was, a disgruntled faction opposed to the prevailing interests in the court. However, it had also exposed weakness within the court party. Argyll had enthusiastically reported any defection or failure on the part of those courtiers he had no liking for. The equivocal behaviour of Melville's family and Marchmont's lack of control over his erstwhile followers were meat and drink to him.[21] Murray of Philiphaugh, a devoted Queensberry adherent, in a letter to Carstares gave vent to a denunciation of Tullibardine and pointed out what appeared to him to be the lesson to be learned from the session: ' . . . Is it not odd that a man[22] should join or aim at the like of such things, upon whom the king, after he had first brought him into his interests, and heaped favours on him from time to time. For my part, I wonder what the devil he saw in him. I hope it will teach his majesty to buy men again when he may have better without it . . . the king hath it now in his hands to manage his affairs in Scotland to his own ease and honour, and to our advantage . . . ' He continued with high praise for Queensberry, Argyll and Seafield, but made no mention of Marchmont.[23] In his opinion the time had come to make such errors less likely for the future by conducting another purge of the ministry. Nor was this a mere thought which had come into Philiphaugh's head, but a further application of the unremitting pressure for Queensberry's advancement. And now, as the 1698 parliament came to an end, demands multiplied and were orchestrated towards the same object. Philiphaugh and Boyle of Kelburn joined voices in Queensberry's praise.[24] Queensberry wanted peerages for Primrose of Dalmeny and Kelburn.[25] He itched to have Ruglen out of the mint and to have Philiphaugh made lord justice clerk.[26] George Ramsay was his candidate for the post of commander-in-chief, to replace Teviot against whom Queensberry's hatred was deep and black and his complaints unending.[27] Later, both Queensberry and Argyll agitated for the breaking of Teviot's regiment on the ground that the officers were disaffected, though the king seemed to think it a good regiment.[28]

Queensberry also intensified his campaign against the house of Hamilton and its clients. Of the recent parliament he remarked, ' . . . It is to be observed that all the opposers are either of the family of Hamilton by relation or other ties . . . ',[29] overlooking the fact that this was a wide category, including most of the court, even Queensberry himself. When Arran, the eldest son of the late duke of Hamilton, was granted the title as fourth duke, Queensberry was greatly incensed.[30] Both he and Argyll tried to inveigle Seafield into supporting their campaign for a purge of the ministry to discourage such as might be elated by Arran's new title.[31] Queensberry's eye for slights became even keener, surpassing even that of Argyll. Annandale's interest, as did Queensberry's, centred on

Dumfriesshire. When, at Annandale's request, extra assessment commissioners were appointed for the shire the duke looked upon it as an act of hostility.[32] Subsequently, as the earl of Morton, one of Queensberry's relatives, who had gone to London without permission, was ordered back by the king, Queensberry took it as a personal slight.[33] Before the next parliament, in 1700, he was considerably irked at not being given the garter. It was represented as the height of magnanimity that, in spite of his dissatisfaction, he consented to be lord high commissioner.[34] The duke's expectations were manifestly on the increase.

Argyll, too, raised his voice in support of what he imagined was a campaign to advance jointly his own and Queensberry's interest. His theme was that the government should be settled firmly in the hands of himself and Queensberry, a purge being conducted against the house of Hamilton and all its connections.[35] Only those who served well were to be rewarded.[36] But it was clear that, however exemplary the service, some were more worthy than others. Reward was to be selective and was to go only to those who met with Argyll's approval.'. . . If any mention be made of Sir John Home,' he wrote, 'beware of him, for he'll make mischief amongst us. And, though he went as to the cess alongst, yet, in the polls he opposed us. He is light in the forehead, full of notion, always talking and most uneasy to be in business with . . .'[37] Home might or might not have been 'light in the forehead', but his chief defect was that he was favoured by Marchmont and owed no allegiance to either Argyll or Queensberry.

Perhaps as a result of this agitation there was, at the end of 1698 and the beginning of 1699, a further reshuffle of the ministry. Apart from Selkirk, who remained as lord clerk register, it removed all trace of Hamilton influence. Carmichael was pitched on as an innocuous choice to act as joint secretary with Seafield and was this time persuaded to overcome his lack of confidence. But Queensberry remained dissatisfied. To his distress such persons as Annandale and Ormiston, unsympathetic to him, were left in the ministry and Marchmont continued as chancellor.[38] His attitude became notorious.

The urge to make his family interest predominant in Scotland drove Queensberry towards the idea mooted earlier by Dalrymple that the government should be 'of a piece'. The need to preserve harmony within the administration provided a sound argument for this objective but it was also a useful rationalisation for the Queensberry group. Queensberry and those of his following who urged the advantages of one group's monopolising the administration thought only in terms of their own interest, as appeared later when Queensberry began to direct his strength within the court against Argyll. From the point of view of efficient management the drawback to making the ministry 'all of a piece' was the practical one that no single interest was strong enough to control Scotland. Queensberry was, from selfish motives, attempting the impossible. Even to establish predominance needed considerably more support from the crown than Queensberry had so far received. In fact, his position and prospects of advancement depended largely on the peculiarity of William's arrangements for handling Scottish business. The king had chosen to delegate its oversight to Portland advised by Carstares, which meant that much depended on attracting their favourable attention. In this Queensberry proved remarkably successful, thus reducing the power of the secretaries who would normally have constituted the main channel of solicitation. As it was, the secretaries were largely by-passed, greatly to the benefit of Queensberry and Argyll, who had set up their own lines to the king. But there were risks. Queensberry and those associated with him knew that they depended almost entirely on the support given to them by Portland, prompted by Carstares. It was on these advisers that much of Queensberry's effort was concentrated and his persuasion continually brought to bear. More than a little alarm was felt, then, at the realisation that Portland's influence might not necessarily be permanent. The importance of the arrangement is adequately demonstrated by the despondency at the end of the close friendship between William and Portland as the latter became jealous of the new favourite, van Keppel. Queensberry and others were led to consider some fairly drastic expedients to preserve their position.

The power generally ascribed to Portland was not at all exaggerated. As the man 'interposed' between the king and the secretaries, he played a considerable part in Scottish administrative adjustments.[39] His influence had made a major contribution to the settlement of 1696, whatever his private motives. Hardly less important was the role of Carstares, trusted adviser to both William and Portland and unofficial intermediary between them and Scotland. Over the history of post-revolution Scotland his name is writ large. His attachment to Melville and his quarrel with Johnston had been significant if not decisive for the ending of the Tweeddale-Johnston ministry. Over the appointment of Tullibardine, for whom he had no liking, he was probably overridden by the king, following a whim of his own,[40] but Carstares was given the task of revising Tullibardine's instructions as commissioner in 1696.[41] At the end of 1697 Queensberry and Argyll thought it better that when Portland arrived in England to help in the settlement of Scottish business, Carstares should be there too, 'for it is not probable that we can come to a final conclusion without him . . . '[42] At a later stage Carstares was to function as something like Queensberry's personal agent at court.[43]

So Portland, guided by Carstares, was properly looked upon as the main anchor at court of the Queensberry-Argyll alliance. His good offices and his current standing with the king were of vital concern to the Scots, since anything which disturbed his position could unsettle Scottish politics. And, from about 1697, it began to seem that something of the kind might be imminent. William did not dismiss Portland and certainly did not abandon all faith in his judgement, but he had become involved with another favourite, van Keppel, earl of Albemarle.[44] In so far as Albemarle showed any political preferences at all, he inclined in England to the whigs as opposed to Portland's preference for the tories. There is little evidence that Albemarle had much interest in Scotland, though what leanings he had seem to have been towards Queensberry's opponents. He supported Teviot, for instance, throughout Queensberry's attempt to procure his dismissal.[45]

Faced with this new friendship of William's, Portland developed a bout of the sulks, talked of retiring from court and did resign his offices. But although he withdrew from active politics in England, he seems to have retained his influence over Scottish affairs. Nevertheless there was alarm in Scotland. Seafield, or Ogilvy as he then was, looked on his own prospects as bound up with Portland's standing. He wrote to Queensberry, ' . . . your grace knows that he has been a true friend to us all, and has had a great hand in our present settlement and his interest was sufficient to have supported it . . . ' Without Portland's influence, Seafield thought, the ministry would collapse.[46] Speculation and unease about the breach between William and Portland grew steadily in Scotland,[47] until officers of state afraid for their posts took to alarmist correspondence. They assured each other of loyalty and exhorted each other to solidarity in the face of whatever misfortune might befall. Seafield declared that he had nothing to hope for from Hamilton and Teviot, who seemed to be looked on as the most probable beneficiaries of any new arrangement.[48] Fear of desertion, dismissal or, at least, the infiltration into the ministry of discordant elements were rampant.[49] The tactical advantages of mass resignation were calculated, and its timing if things should ever come to that, to demonstrate the indispensability of the Queensberry-Argyll alliance. The likelihood of such an event taking place was remote and, probably to the relief of those who had first conceived the idea, Portland declared himself against it and counselled patience.[50]

Portland, in fact, radiated far more confidence than his Scottish dependents were feeling, but his attitude failed to reassure the Scots. President Dalrymple, in London for consultations about the Darien crisis, had also been deputed to investigate the situation at court. His views were not encouraging. He thought Scottish politics could be greatly affected by what was taking place there: '. . . it's visible the king is fond of Albemarle which 'tis just now as remarkable at Windsor since e[arl] P[ortland]'s retiring as ever so he must have suffered mortification which all courtiers must meet with at one time or another. Whether the king will still have some person interposed betwixt him and his secretaries or if they shall have that immediate influence that belongs naturally to their offices a little time will clear . . .'[51] Even the acquisition of more influence by the secretaries could be a dangerous development for Queensberry since they could conceivably become additional hurdles to surmount in his pursuit of the monopoly of influence in Scotland. But, whatever the administrative outcome, Dalrymple regarded Portland as finished. It was merely a question of whether he would be replaced at all and if so by whom. ' . . . I am satisfied e[arl] P[ortland] is not a foundation can support us long . . ,' he wrote to Philiphaugh. In the meantime his thoughts seemed to be moving towards some accommodation with Albemarle if that would save the Queensberry interest. He had also investigated the possibility of coming to terms with Hamilton but naturally discovered there was no hope in that direction.[52]

In fact, although the Scottish ministry was never free from the suspicion that its foundations were being undermined at court, William allowed the situation to remain largely unchanged. And if he was not quite so well disposed towards Queensberry in 1701 as previously, this was due to other, more practical, causes.[53]

But, protestations of loyalty and solidarity notwithstanding, events were to show that the Scottish ministry was not really able to withstand the strains of political crisis. In 1699 the conflicting pressures of English influence and Scottish opinion began to tighten on the Scottish courtiers as a consequence of the Africa Company's failure to establish a colony in Darien.

The directors of the Africa Company had gone ahead, despite shortage of capital, with what from the outset had been their intention, the founding of a Scottish colony at Darien. At that time the climate of the isthmus of Panama was notoriously unhealthy and the territory furthermore was claimed, if not by settlement at least with determination, by the Spanish king. As king of England, William's relations with Spain were going through a delicate phase owing to his involvement in arranging the succession to the Spanish throne, so that the activities of his Scottish subjects were a great embarrassment to him. What the Scots were attempting was also unwelcome to the English, who foresaw that a successful Scottish colony at Darien would knock a gaping hole in the navigation system. The English used some hectoring language, it is true, but they did not so much attempt sabotage as withhold co-operation and persuade others to do the same. William, despite his being king of Scotland, could hardly put his relations with both Spain and his English subjects at risk for what was undeniably a half-baked enterprise. Left to itself it could be relied upon to collapse, as it did, of its own accord. But in the meantime, William's — on this occasion, calculated — inactivity provided scope for the Scottish opposition and alienated some courtiers who had lost either relatives, money or both. The nation at large put the blame for the Darien failure on the English. It was easier to have a scapegoat, particularly one so satisfying as the ancient enemy, than to look for the causes of disaster nearer home where they were to be found.

From the start, none of the Scottish ministers had been enthusiastic over the project or its prospects, except for Annandale in the short-lived opposition phase from which he had recovered. Marchmont entertained little hope for the future of the colony.[54] He found it quite inexplicable that anybody should be prepared to go to Darien at all, still less with enthusiasm.[55] He was firmly of the opinion that the project's failure was due to Scottish mismanagement rather than English opposition.[56] A body of informed Scottish opinion supported him, from Seafield and the lord advocate, who had stayed at home, to Campbell of Finnab and William Paterson, one of the scheme's 'projectors', who had both been to Darien on the expedition. All agreed that blame rested almost entirely with the company's directors, and there is little reason to doubt that their view was justified.[57] The scheme was quite beyond the competence of the Africa Company.

Nevertheless, Scottish ministers, Seafield especially, pressed very strongly to the king the case for assistance to the Africa Company and full recognition of its colonising activities. President Dalrymple and the lord advocate went up to London to assist the Scottish secretaries in representing the company's interests. Although all the officers of state were satisfied that every possible effort had been made, the Scots' cause was quite hopeless.[58] William was concerned about the Scottish disaster[59] and its likely political consequences, but there was nothing he could do about it. If the king could do nothing it was certainly beyond the power of his Scottish ministers to achieve anything. All of them, though, and Seafield in particular, were subjected to some undeserved vilification.

The political aftermath of the Darien failure was serious. So many people had been involved in the scheme, if only through sentiment, that its collapse would very likely produce complications in the next parliament.[60] One significant fact was that, from almost the beginning, the organisation of the Africa Company had looked remarkably like the opposition going into business. This may in part have resulted from the circumstances in which the original act was passed in 1695 and the rôle played in it by men who subsequently left the court. Putting money in the company might well have been for some a gesture of loyalty towards the ministers dismissed in 1695-6 or a sign of resentment against the English parliament's attitude to the trade act.[61] Either would indicate that such subscribers were not inhibited by court pressures. Of course people with court connections also invested in the company — Queensberry himself subscribed £3000 — but the opposition seemed most active in the management. Sir Francis Scott, Tweeddale, Drumelzier and the 'country party' Annandale were all involved. Tullibardine bought himself into the company later, associating himself more closely with it after his resignation. Others were opposers of another kind, jacobites, such as Henry Maule and the earl of Panmure. Apart from the obvious grievances arising out of the Darien failure and loss of money, the opposition were in need of an issue which might increase their support, and it would have taken superhuman restraint on their part to refrain from making the company's cause a political weapon. The opposition had no motive for such self-denial. Even in the parliament of 1698 before the project had properly begun, opposition members, merely to embarrass the court, had tried to push the demands of the company far beyond what was reasonable. Marchmont wrote, ' . . . there are some amongst that council [of the company] who have designs quite cross to ours as to the country's interest and the king's service . . . ' Seafield had formed a similar opinion.[62]

The final collapse of the company's colonising project with the consequent loss of life and capital led to a widespread political agitation against the Scottish ministry on a scale which was to make their existence all but intolerable. This opposition to the ministry comprised various elements. There were the embittered strata of discontent left over from the changes of 1695-6 and the parliament of 1698 — the Tweeddale interest with that of Tullibardine and Whitelaw — together with such others as had taken umbrage since the adjournment for one reason or another. Amongst these more recent arrivals in opposition was, for instance, lord Ross. After the 1698 parliament, without having done much to earn it, he had wanted to be secretary of state. His pretensions were justifiably ignored and he was left bearing unutterable grudges.[63] Members of the Hamilton family and their wide connections, both presbyterian and jacobite, were in opposition, Hamilton having no more scruples than Queensberry about appealing to all at one and the same time. A further category was composed of men who were more usually courtiers and in normal times wholly amenable. But now they had lost capital and sometimes relatives in the Darien expedition, had taken it hard, and thought something should be done about it. Both their pride and pockets had been hurt and one of their most urgent needs was a scapegoat, the most convenient and attractive candidates being the link with England and the Scottish ministers involved in its operation.

The Tweeddale and Tullibardine groups were already allies in resentment and ambition. They were also firmly entrenched in the company and, although it would be unfair to Tweeddale and Sir Francis Scott to suggest that they lacked concern for the fortunes of the Darien colony, they were at the same time quite aware of its potentialities for political opposition and determined to exploit them. However, it would be no injustice to say that the appearance of some members of the Hamilton family in opposition was wholly due to their exclusion from influence and quite unconnected with the Africa Company. In the reshuffle of 1696 an attempt had been made to placate them, although Hamilton himself, then earl of Arran, was reputedly jacobite. The aim of this move had been to link this excluded magnate interest with the new ministerial coalition. To Queensberry their presence in the ministry had been a grievous irritant leading to his continual agitation for their dismissal, especially after Arran's elevation to the dukedom, which Queensberry took as a personal affront.[64] In the purge following the 1698 session, when the Hamilton family paid the penalty of opposition, his campaign succeeded.[65] Its only member remaining in office was Hamilton's brother, Selkirk, an absentee lord clerk register in attendance on the king.

Soon after his elevation, Hamilton met Seafield in London and indicated his position well enough by being slyly critical of proceedings in the 1698 parliament. At the time he seemed deep in collaboration with Johnston, who was still in touch with his former associates in Scotland.[66] Then the Darien agitation gave Hamilton, as a duke, the opportunity to seize the foremost role amongst the opposition leaders. It seemed a good political tactic to keep the feeling over Darien running as high as possible.[67] Lord Basil Hamilton became a key figure in co-ordinating the protest campaign and remained so until his death.[68] At the same time Hamilton was making approaches to Queensberry by way of president Dalrymple and Philiphaugh, indicating his willingness to be bought off. He offered an alliance should he be taken into the ministry and given a share of patronage. Dalrymple and Philiphaugh were so pessimistic about the chances of managing the next parliament that they advised Queensberry seriously to consider the proposal,[69] though the duke's fear of any threat to his own position led him to reject the overture outright. And whatever Queensberry's motives, the decision was correct in that it could have led to no more than a repetition of the Tullibardine episode, but with Hamilton as the enemy within. The episode is important only for the light it throws on Hamilton's position at that time.

Hamilton in the meantime kept up pressure on the ministry by making as much capital out of the Darien crisis as he could although, on his arrival in Edinburgh in 1699, he displayed rather embarrassingly his ignorance of the situation. Entering in great style, he issued a dramatic call to all men to pledge their purses for the salvation of the colony. It had to be pointed out to him that the colony was well beyond assistance of that kind, and only then did he begin to consider addresses.[70] With a keen eye for political advantage he began to promote the idea of presenting to the king an address concerning the company. For Hamilton the address and its content were immaterial. What mattered was the means by which the address was presented. Although the secretaries were the most effective channel of communication, it had at all costs to be kept out of their hands. If they should present it and the king returned a satisfactory answer, they would receive the credit which, from the opposition's point of view, would have been highly undesirable.[71]

The opposition, under Hamilton's leadership, tried with some success to attract presbyterian support. Presbyterians who had been loyal to the court at least since the parliament of 1690 were prevailed upon to sign the addresses.[72] The duke secured the collaboration of some presbyterian ministers, who tried the usual device of asking for a fast to be declared for the welfare of the company.[73] Portland's secretary commented to Carstares, ' . . . I don't question but it must be surprising to you, and all others, that duke Hamilton proves to be a zealous presbyterian and that something of great importance must lie at the bottom of his turning that way . . . '[74] Nor, as a consequence of his new friendships, did Hamilton allow his jacobite connections to atrophy. Jacobite interest in the company was remarkably strong.[75] At the time of the second parliament of 1700, when the crisis was at its peak, Hamilton and other opposition leaders made open appeals for jacobites to come into the house to give their support. Atholl presented himself without much scruple. The sheriff of Bute and lord Nairne were the objects of special pleas to help the opposition in parliament, 'for we have it now in our hands to preserve ourselves and support our country'.[76] Tweeddale and his family were not jacobites but were nevertheless anxious for jacobite reinforcements in parliament to swell the opposition quite regardless of any long-term consequences.[77] Queensberry remarked on this connection between jacobitism and support of the company. He wrote, '... it was evident that many who set most up for the company and for the privileges and independence of this nation as a popular handle had never taken the oaths and owned your majesty's government and especially several peers who had not taken the oaths did qualify themselves in this session and very many of the addressers both to your majesty and the parliament were such...'[78] He overlooked the fact that in the past he, too, had made use of jacobite support and without any qualms would do so again.

Contemporaries had little difficulty in distinguishing between those merely zealous for the company's welfare or wanting compensation for losses and those with ulterior motives. '... I don't doubt,' wrote Seafield, 'but a great many, especially the ringleaders, have other designs at the bottom ...'[79] These other designs included the disruption of government business and the creation of sufficient uproar to force the admission of the country leaders into the ministry as a means of quietening them. The jacobites were just beginning to adopt what was to become their customary pose as champions of Scotland's welfare, this time to obstruct business in parliament in the hope that it would force the disbandment of the army.[80]

In 1700 and 1701, the years of the last two parliaments of William's reign, the extramural exertions of the opposition were prodigious. They addressed for a parliament. Should a summons to parliament not be forthcoming, they talked of holding a convention of estates at Perth whether the king approved or not. For their security during this venture they proposed to rely on highland support.[81] All this was greatly disturbing to the court. The Scottish officers of state did not at all relish the addresses, but William very strongly objected to them and urged that the organisers be prosecuted, though any such action was quite impracticable. All that could be done was to ensure scant attention and a very dusty answer for those who took up the addresses to court.[82]

The opposition leaders remained undeterred either by the dangers of the popular feeling they were arousing or by court attitudes to their actions. In their usual meeting place at Steel's tavern they resolved on a boycott of foreign manufactures, French wines and brandy to reduce the customs revenue, thereby making the court's financial position worse than it already was. The court deemed this project to be an illegal combination and by so doing brought itself into some ridicule. A proclamation was issued against the boycott but it discouraged nobody.[83] Johnston and George Ridpath continued unperturbed their country party propaganda in support of the opposition's various schemes.[84] And schemes, both overt and otherwise, proliferated. A possible tory resurgence in England was a development the opposition devoutly wished for since obstructive tactics in the English parliament might contribute to the pressure for changes in Scotland.[85] The Scottish ministry started an addressing campaign pledging support for William's foreign policy with a view to strengthening his position in England. Opposition members ostentatiously dissociated themselves from it and instead addressed in their own terms as did Tullibardine after opting out of Mar's address from Perthshire.[86] Thus the opposition aligned themselves with the English tories on foreign policy as they had already done over the standing army. To embarrass the court, the opposition set out to generate extreme presbyterian demands in the 1700 parliament and in the general assembly of

1701.[87] In fact country party leaders exploited every tactical possibility to attack the court wherever a weakness might conceivably exist.

In this kind of campaign the opposition could make a nuisance of itself but it, too, had weaknesses. A perennial opposition problem was that of preserving solidarity in the face of court attempts to nobble its supporters. Patronage, a necessary bonding agent for political groups, was virtually unavailable to opposition leaders. They were conscious of this and tried to remedy it as far as they could by substituting private for crown patronage. There was an attempt to secure the allegiance of the duke of Lennox, hereditary but absentee lord high admiral of Scotland, whose acquaintance with Scottish politics was negligible. They hoped that some of the patronage at his disposal through the admiral's office could be put to opposition use[88] to stop up some of the leakage from their support. In the Darien agitation the possibility of losing members to the court was quite high, since some opposition supporters were really court men in temporary revolt through indignation at the loss of their money and frustration at the court's inability to help them. Such men were important to the opposition out of all proportion to their number and especially vulnerable to the court's blandishments.[89] Opposition leaders took what precautions they could. Members carrying addresses up to court were pledged not to see the king individually, even if he asked to see them.[90] Instructions were procured to members from their constituents with the aim of binding them to support Caledonia and oppose a standing army.[91] But these were routine measures for such a campaign. The opposition was strong in its own right, even without the discipline maintained by intimidation or appeals to personal loyalty. Sentiments which swelled the country party could not have been turned to political ends if they had not existed in the first place. Enthusiasm for the Africa Company was nationalist rather than economic in origin, if resentment at outside interference can be called nationalism. But even if 'nationalism' was the wrong word for the sentiment initially, the situation itself and the objectives of the country party could have done little else but transform the agitation, where it was spontaneous, into something like a nationalist movement. It could hardly have become a successful nationalist movement, since the leaders were not nationalists. They wanted merely to humiliate the court and get jobs for themselves. Only if pressure could be kept up against the ministry long enough to make its position untenable could these aims be achieved. With indignation over New Caledonia the only issue, their task was difficult, the problem of the leaders being that of maintaining a furious agitation whilst doing their best to avoid gaining any concessions. As Carmichael noted, ' . . . If his majesty could yield anything it might undeceive some honest men that are gone in that way.'[92] If they possibly could, the opposition leaders had to avoid that. But sooner or later when the project of Caledonia became an historical rather than a political question the main source of opposition strength would evaporate unless a further issue could be developed.

It is difficult to see where the argument could have led other than to the question of sovereignty, which was to become the mainstay of the opposition up to the union. The question emerged from agitation over the Africa Company and Caledonia. In fact the debate over Darien had always involved the issue of sovereignty as the basis of New Caledonia's right to exist. Melville told Carstares, summarising the opposition argument: the king must have reasons for his refusal to allow an act asserting Scotland's right to Darien. Then, ' . . . his reasons do either concern Scotland, or are exotic as to Scotland.

If the first let us know them; we will be ready to comply with his greater wisdom. If they do not concern Scotland, then, say they, this gives ground for an unanswerable argument, that the crowns of England and Scotland are incompatible, seeing it is not to be supposed that, where the interest of England and Scotland do irreconcilably interfere, the king must act in favours of England . . . ' Such arguments were uncomfortable for the court. When they were raised in parliament, adjournment was no answer, as Queensberry found, since it led only to the further issue of freedom of debate.[93] The drift to this position was apparent from England. As Vernon wrote to Shrewsbury: ' . . . The Scotch look as they were ready for any mischief, and that nothing will please them but setting up for themselves . . . they push for extremities and besides the support of Darien they aim at the removing the present ministry in Scotland, and that they may have no forces kept up in time of peace . . . '[94] The opposition leaders were moving naturally and perhaps inevitably into an anti-English posture as far as public disputation was concerned. They had set out to inflame resentment against England and were succeeding.[95] Yet with no more than one or two exceptions the opposition spokesmen lacked sincerity, incitement against England being no more than a means to an end: employment.

The struggle between court and opposition was fought out over two sessions of parliament in 1700, between the two sessions, through what remained of William's reign and then into Anne's. In the first session of parliament in May 1700, with Queensberry serving as commissioner for the first time, the court wanted only supply for the forces and an additional vote to make up a deficiency in the excise yield.[96] But, as Murray of Philiphaugh told Queensberry, unless substantial concessions were made over Caledonia, there was little hope of success, since there was no other way of detaching habitual court supporters who had been swept into the opposition.[97] Nevertheless there was little or no attempt made to achieve this end. Officially the court barely recognised the existence of the Scottish complaint. Few concessions were to be sanctioned, and even those were to be held in reserve. No act confirming the legality of the Darien settlement was to be permitted. A separate supply could be voted to subsidise legal trade, but if parliament wanted to use it for the benefit of the Africa Company it was to be specified as compensation for past calamities only, not used as capital for future projects. There was no possibility of the Darien project's being given official, even retrospective, recognition.[98] So the session was doomed from the start. The opposition whipped up feeling to the highest pitch. Hamilton and Tweeddale inflamed and exploited popular opinion in Edinburgh, always a dangerous city to arouse.[99]

The relative strength of the parties in the Scottish parliament usually appeared in the voting for committees. In 1700 it was significant. The court carried a majority amongst the nobles but the opposition controlled the barons. There was a court majority amongst the burghs but it was wavering. Several members who had been lobbied by the court with apparent success had since changed their minds. Queensberry felt very insecure and with good reason. The committee votes, as he said, seemed to produce 'greater boldness on the one side and diffidence on the other'.[100] Immediately after the committee elections the two prongs of the opposition attack developed: to disrupt the court over religion and to assert the company's right to Darien. When, at the outset, on 27 May, the lord advocate moved the usual ratification of laws in favour of presbytery, the opposition attempted to push the law to even greater lengths. It was proposed, for instance, that general assemblies should be allowed to meet without royal sanction. Even in 1690 and 1692 that had been resisted in both parliament and general assembly. But the opposition's support of high presbyterianism was a purely political tactic designed for one main purpose: to drive, if possible, a wedge between the 'presbyterian' and other elements of the court coalition. Failing that, the presbyterians in the court might discredit themselves through lack of zeal and the court might even become embroiled with the church to the country party's great satisfaction. This religious ploy was followed by Hamilton's proposal for an act asserting without compromise the company's right to Darien.[101] In the face of this the court had no hope of controlling parliament and, on 30 May, Queensberry decided to adjourn. The court had suffered a sizable and public defeat.

NOTES

1. *Carstares S.P.*, 385, Marchmont to Carstares, 12 Jul. 1698.
2. *Ib.*, 386, Seafield to same, 12 Jul. 1698. See also *ib.*, 408, Kelburn to same, 29 Jul. 1698; *ib.*, Seafield to same, 15 Aug. 1698
3. *Ib.*, 390, same to same, 14 Jul. 1698.
4. *Ib.*, 380, H. Dalrymple to Seafield, 21 Jun. 1698.
5. *Ib.*, 388, Argyll to Carstares, 12 Jul. 1698; *ib.*, 392, same to same, 16 Jul. 1698.
6. *Ib.*, 391, Seafield to same, 16 Jul. 1698.
7. *Marchmont Papers*, iii, 152, Marchmont to Sir A. Munro, 5 Apr. 1698.
8. *Carstares S.P.*, e.g. 393, 397, 400, 411, 421.
9. *Ib.*, 386, Seafield to Carstares, 12 Jul. 1698.
10. Fraser, *Melvilles*, ii, 179-80, Carstares to Melville, 10 May 1698; *ib.*, 179, Seafield to same, 28 Apr. 1698.
11. *Carstares S. P.*, 411, Argyll to Carstares, 4 Aug. 1698; *ib.*, 442, same to same, 14 Sep. 1698; *ib.*, 429, Seafield to same, 2 Sep. 1698. SRO, GD26, xiii, 35 ('Miscellaneous Manuscripts of little importance'), [Melville] to [   ], [1698] is an attempt to justify James Melville's conduct in parliament.
12. *Carstares S.P.*, 395, Seafield to same, Jul. 1698; *ib.*, 411, Argyll to same, 4 Aug. 1698.
13. *Marchmont Papers*, iii, 160, 26 Jul. 1698.
14. *Carstares S.P.*, 389, Argyll to Carstares, 14 Jul. 1698.
15. *Ib.*, 411, same to same, 4 Aug. 1698.
16. *Ib.*, 431, same to same, 3 Sep. 1698.
17. *Ib.*, 411, same to same, 4 Aug. 1698.
18. *Ib.*, 395, Seafield to same, Jul. 1698; *ib.*, 405, same to same, 27 Jul. 1698; *Marchmont Papers*, iii, 165, Marchmont to the king, 9 Aug. 1698.
19. *Ib.*, 169, same to same, 3 [sic for 2] Sep. 1698; *Carstares S.P.*, 429, Seafield to Carstares, 2 Sep. 1698.
20. *Ib.*, 405, same to same, 27 Jul. 1698; *APS*, x, 126, 134, 135.
21. See above, pp. 126-7.
22. Tullibardine.
23. *Carstares S.P.*, 381, 8 [sic for 28] Jul. 1698.
24. *Ib.*, 408, Kelburn to Carstares, 29 Jul. 1698; *ib.*, 381, Philiphaugh to same, 8 [sic for 28] Jul. 1698.
25. *Ib.*, 420, Queensberry to same, 8 Aug. 1698; *ib.*, 437, Seafield to same, 3 Oct. 1698.
26. *Ib.*, 452, Queensberry to same, 3 Oct. 1698.
27. Buccleuch (Drum.), Queensberry Letters, xiv, Seafield to [Queensberry], 29 Oct. 1698; *HMCR Johnstone MSS*, 106, Teviot of Annandale, 10 Nov. 1698. For the Queensberry-Argyll campaign against Teviot; *ib.*, 100-101; *Carstares S.P.*, 457, 465, 468, 469, 471, 475; Baccleuch (Drum.), Queensberry, Letters, xiv, [Carstares] to [Queensberry], 14 Feb. 1699; *ib.*, Union, i, draft, [Queensberry] to T. Deans, [1699]; *ib.*, draft, [same] to [H. Dalrymple], [1699]; *ib.*, draft [same] to Carstares, [1699]; NUL, Portland, PwA 372, same to Portland, 9 Mar. [1699].
28. *Carstares S.P.*, 565, Argyll to Carstares, 13 Jul. 1700; Buccleuch (Drum.), Queensberry Letters, xvi, [Carstares] to [Queensberry], 25 Jul. 1700.

29. *Carstares S.P.*, 400, Queensberry to Carstares, 24 Jul. 1698.
30. *Ib.*, 429, Seafield to same, 2 Sep. 1698. Arran was granted the title as fourth duke by an arrangement similar to that which his mother, duchess in her own right, had made in favour of her husband.
31. *Ib.*, 441, same to same, 10 Sep. 1698.
32. *Marchmont Papers*, iii, 136-7, Polwarth to Queensberry, 29 Apr. 1697; *Carstares S.P.*, 302-3, Ogilvy to Carstares, 29 May 1697.
33. *HMCR Johnstone MSS*, 103, Teviot to Annandale, 20 Jan. 1698.
34. Buccleuch (Drum.), Queensberry Letters, xvi, [Carstares] to [Queensberry], 10 Jun. 1700.
35. *Carstares S.P.*, 421, Argyll to Carstares, 8 Aug. 1698.
36. *Ib.*, 449, same to same, 27 Sep. 1698.
37. *Ib.*, 442, same to same, 14 Sep. 1698.
38. SRO, Paper Register of the Great Seal, 14, 233, 21 Oct. 1698; *HMCR Johnstone MSS*, 107, Seafield to Annandale, 31 Jan. 1699.
39. Buccleuch (Drum.), Union, i, [president Dalrymple] to [Queensberry], 11 May [1699].
40. See above, pp. 108-9.
41. *Carstares S.P.*, 293-5, 'Instructions proposed by Lord Murray amended by Mr Carstares'. See also Japikse, i, 180-3, Portland to the king, 28 Jul. 1696; *ib.*, 179-80, the king to Portland, 6 Aug. 1696; *ib.*, 189-91, Portland to the king, 7/17 Aug. 1696; *ib.*, 185, the king to Portland, 13 Aug. 1696.
42. *Carstares S.P.*, 355-6, Ogilvy to Carstares, 12 Oct. 1697.
43. Buccleuch (Drum.), Carstares, *passim*.
44. S. B. Baxter, *William III* (London, 1966), 384ff.
45. Buccleuch (Drum.), Queensberry Letters, xiv, [H. Dalrymple] to [Philiphaugh?], 13 May 1699.
46. *Ib.*, [Ogilvy] to [Queensberry], 23 Apr. 1697; *ib.*, [same] to [same], 25 Apr. 1697; *ib.*, [same] to [same], 4 May 1697.
47. *Carstares S.P.*, 368, Pringle to Carstares, 10 Feb. 1698; SRO, CH1/1/12, 78-82.
48. Buccleuch (Drum.), Queensberry Letters, xiv, [Seafield] to [Queensberry], 27 Apr. 1699.
49. *Ib.*, xvi, [Carstares] to [Queensberry], 27 May 1699; *ib.*, Union, i, draft, [Queensberry] to Argyll, [1699]; *ib.*, draft, [Queensberry] to L[ord] S[eafield], [1699].
50. *Ib.*, draft, [same] to same, [1699]; *ib.*, Queensberry Letters, xiv, [Seafield] to [Queensberry], 2 May 1699.
51. *Ib.*, Union, i, [H. Dalrymple] to [Queensberry], 11 May [1699].
52. *Ib.*, Queensberry Letters, xiv, [same] to [Philiphaugh], 13 May 1699.
53. See below, pp. 153ff.
54. *Marchmont Papers*, iii, 176, to Seafield, 3 Apr. 1699.
55. *Carstares S.P.*, 474, Marchmont to Carstares, 3 Apr. 1699.
56. *Marchmont Papers*, iii, 181, same to the king, 24 Oct. 1699; *ib.*, 178, same to Seafield, 18 Oct. 1699.
57. *Ib.*, 185, same to same, 28 Oct. 1699; *Culloden Papers*, 26, Seafield to Culloden, 24 Oct. 1699; *CSP (Dom.), 1699-1700*, 345-6, W. Harris to Vernon, 7 Jan. 1700; *Carstares S.P.*, 577, Seafield to Carstares, 24 Jul. 1700; *ib.*, 490, Stewart to same, 12 Aug. 1699.
58. *Ib.*, 476, Ormiston to same, 4 Apr. 1696; Buccleuch (Drum.), Queensberry Letters, xiv, [president Dalrymple] to [Queensberry], 22 Apr. 1699; *Culloden Papers*, 26, Seafield to Culloden, 24 Oct. 1699.
59. Japikse, i, 344-6, the king to Portland, 29 Sep. 1699.
60. *Marchmont Papers*, iii, 178, Marchmont to Seafield, 18 Oct. 1699.
61. See *A Perfect List Of the several Persons Residenters in Scotland Who have Subscribed as Adventurers In The Joint-Stock Of The Company of Scotland Trading to Africa and the Indies...* (Edinburgh, 1696).
62. *Carstares S.P.*, 414, Seafield to Carstares, 1 Aug. 1698; *HMCR Johnstone MSS*, 111-12, Marchmont to Annandale, 23 Oct. 1699. See below, pp. 134-5.
63. *Carstares S.P.*, 437, Seafield to Carstares, 6 Sep. 1698.
64. *Ib.*, 426, same to same, 20 Aug. 1698; *ib.*, 441, same to same, 10 Sep. 1698.
65. See above, p. 129.
66. Buccleuch (Drum.), Queensberry Letters, xiv, Seafield to [Queensberry], 29 Sep. 1698; *ib.*, [same] to [same], 15 Oct. 1698.
67. *HMCR Johnstone MSS*, 109-10, [   ] to Annandale, 15 Jun. 1699; *Marchmont Papers*, iii, 178, Marchmont to Seafield, 18 Oct. 1699.
68. NLS, MS 7104, 16, [lord B. Hamilton] to Gleneagles, 28 Dec. 1699.
69. BL, Add. MSS 6420, 3, president Dalrymple and Philiphaugh to [Queensberry], 12 Dec. 1699.
70. *Carstares S.P.*, 499, Ormiston to Carstares, 21 Oct. 1699.
71. NLS, MS 7104, 18, Hamilton to [Tweeddale], 3 Jan. 1700; *ib.*, 21, same to [same], 10 Jan. 1700.
72. *Carstares S.P.*, 520, J. Stewart to Carstares, 5 Jun. 1700; NLS, MS 7104, 17, W. Cochrane to [Hamilton], 14 Jan. [1]700.

73. *Carstares S.P.*, 505, [   ] to Portland, 31 Oct. 1699.
74. *Ib.*, 505, 31 Oct. 1699.
75. *Ib.*, 577, Seafield to Carstares, 24 Jul. 1700.
76. *HMCR Bute MSS*, 617, Hamilton to Bute, 2 Nov. 1700; *HMCR Laing MSS*, ii, Hamilton *et al.* to lord Nairne, 3 Nov. 1700.
77. Fraser, *Cromartie*, i, 147-8, Yester to Tweeddale, 22 Sep. 1701.
78. Buccleuch (Drum.), Col., bundle i, draft, [Queensberry] to [the king], 28 May 1701. Cf. *Marchmont Papers*, iii, 178, Marchmont to Seafield, 18 Oct. 1699.
79. *HMCR Johnstone MSS*, 115, to Annandale, 2 Jan. 1700.
80. *Carstares S.P.*, 626, J. Stewart to Carstares, 24 Aug. 1700.
81. *Ib.*, 570, same to same, 18 Jul. 1700.
82. *HMCR Johnstone MSS*, 112-14, *passim; Marchmont Papers*, iii, 193, 197; Buccleuch (Drum.), Queensberry Letters, xvi, Carstares to [W. Stewart?], 5 Nov. 1700; *ib.*, [same] to [same?], [1700]; *ib.*, [same] to [Queensberry], 16 Nov. 1700; *ib.*, Carstares, [same] to [same], 26 Nov. 1700.
83. *Carstares S.P.*, 560, 561, 573.
84. Fraser, *Cromartie*, i, 147-8, Yester to Tweeddale, 22 Sep. 1701.
85. *HMCR Bute MSS*, 617, lord Haddo to Bute, 30 Jan. 1701.
86. *HMCR Hamilton MSS, Supp.*, 146, Pencaitland to Hamilton, 30 Oct. 1701; Buccleuch (Drum.), Queensberry Letters, xvi, Tullibardine to [Queensberry], 3 Nov. 1701. For addresses: *HMCR Mar and Kellie MSS*, i, 223, 224; *HMCR Hamilton MSS, Supp.*, 147, 148; SRO, GD26, xiii, 103/6.
87. *Carstares S.P.*, 709, Carmichael to Carstares, 18 Aug. 1701.
88. *HMCR Hamilton MSS, Supp.*, 145, Pencaitland to Hamilton, 30 Sep. 1701; NLS, MS 7104, 26, H[amilton] to [Tweeddale], 19 Oct. 1701.
89. See Appendix A.
90. *Carstares S.P.*, 518, Philiphaugh to Carstares, 5 Jun. 1700.
91. *Ib.*, 514, Melville to same, 4 Jun. 1700.
92. *Ib.*, 524, Carmichael to same, 11 Jun. 1700.
93. *Ib.*, 514, Melville to same, 4 Jun. 1700.
94. Vernon, iii, 75, Vernon to Shrewsbury, 11 Jun. 1700.
95. *Marchmont Papers*, iii, 233, Marchmont to the king, 22 Oct. 1701.
96. BL, Add. MSS 6420, 26, public instructions to Queensberry, [25 Apr. 1700].
97. Buccleuch (Drum.), Queensberry Letters, xvi, 30 Apr. 1700.
98. BL, Add. MSS 6420, 28, 25 Apr. 1700.
99. Buccleuch (Drum.), Queensberry Letters, xvi, [Philiphaugh] to [Queensberry], 30 Apr. 1700.
100. *Ib.*, Col., bundle i, draft of a memorial by Queensberry, 28 May 1701 [*sic* for 1700].
101. Hume, *Diary*, 5. *APS*, x, 194-5.

8

Queensberry *versus* the Rest

THE defeat of the court in the first session of 1700, followed by the continued activity of the opposition, placed strains on the ministry which it was not able to bear. Riddled by internal dissension, the Scottish ministry found itself in no fit state to meet a crisis of any kind.

Since the original 'coalition' of 1695-6, the court had undergone successive movements of polarisation: between Queensberry and Tullibardine first of all, to be followed by a further division between the Queensberry interest and almost everybody else. It could seem that a constant feature of these developments was the position of Queensberry. An element did exist in the ministry, with sympathisers outside it, which seemed prepared always to go counter to Queensberry, whether their reaction was confined to murmurs or intrigue, or emerged as open defiance. Some of the people who comprised it could properly be described as 'old revolution men'. That would certainly have been how they saw themselves, though their number included such as Annandale, whose right to the title was dubious. However, all of them in some degree shared this antipathy towards the duke. The reasons for it need examination. In part it was a product of the reputation and equivocal behaviour of the first duke. But Queensberry's own revolutionary credentials seemed impeccable so, although Queensberry himself had kept some odd company and contracted some dubious alliances, the alignment against him has to be accounted for in terms other than long-standing grudges against his father.

This continual split between these 'revolution men' and Queensberry, on the ground that whilst they were loyal to the revolution they were not so sure about him, could easily be mistaken for an incipient party division rooted in principle. On one side were men who had either been in exile under James or had stuck their necks out at the revolution, and on the other were people who had done no more than come to terms with the events of 1688-9. Although no one would wish to deny such as Marchmont and Ormiston credit for their consistent Williamite allegiance, there are too many exceptions and transformations on both sides for this to be a sufficient explanation. It is not even possible to see the pattern as similar to that which emerged in England in the first part of William's reign, where, before the party structure became virtually rigid in 1696 under the impact of the assassination plot and the association, there were whigs and tories in both court and opposition. The terms 'country whig' and 'country tory' had some meaning. In Scotland the situation, with both court and country holding mixed views, superficially resembled that in England. Queensberry himself passed as a 'revolution man', being taken by some, including former *émigrés* such as Melville and Leven with others of undoubted Williamite loyalties, to be the leader of the 'revolution party'. For some time he enjoyed the support of Argyll. Marchmont had obeyed orders and treated him with deference. Queensberry's allies and followers, however, included elements whose credentials were considered to be not above suspicion — the Dalrymples, Philiphaugh, the sheriff of Bute and others who refused the oaths. The opposition, likewise, was mixed. It ranged from jacobites such as Lindores and Marischal, through Hamilton and Tullibardine whom one would hesitate to categorise, to such undoubted revolution men as Baillie of Jerviswood, Bennet of Grubbet and Burnet of Leys. Motives for opposition were predictably similar. Some, as Tullibardine, were in the country party having been pushed out of the court; others, Hamilton for instance, because they had never been allowed in. Blantyre had changed from court to virulent country because no effort had been made to pay his pension and other arrears due to him.[1] Sir John Home of Blackadder had been denied by Argyll and Queensberry any reward for his service in the 1698 parliament and at the next one was found in opposition.[2] Hamilton of Whitelaw was in the country party because he had not been given the job he wanted although he remained open to offers.[3] With others the process was not altogether completed in William's reign. Buchan was very dissatisfied at being neither paid the arrears on his pension nor given any other reward.[4] Till Anne's reign he stayed with the court in hope but then, deciding that the line had to be drawn somewhere, he joined the opposition and voted against the union.

These were individual decisions based on private self-interest or resentment, not, as they tended to become in England, party decisions arrived at for much the same reasons. In theory there was in Scotland at least as much basis for established parties, split ostensibly on principle, as there was in England. Some professed enthusiasm at the revolution. Others had been hesitant and remained inclined to quibble over details even when their ultimate allegiance was not jacobite. But in Scotland other necessary requirements were lacking. The ready-made stereotypes of whig and tory which had embedded themselves in the lore of English politics had no real Scottish equivalents. No major and nationally divisive issue existed to reinforce the separation of the groups and lend them respectability, a function performed in England by the war, particularly. In English politics, the party groupings as organised forces both influenced policy and accumulated patronage. Whilst magnates and managers retained their own channels of negotiation, the usual route to personal advancement lay through party loyalty. This resulted partly from the emergence of a stable leadership amongst the whigs, producing in reaction some solidarity in the tory party. A further consequence was a strengthening of the power of the leaders, thus making possible a greater degree of discipline until ultimately, for a short period, the choice facing the crown in England was between parties, not individuals. In Scotland individual competition was too intense for any single interest or even combination of interests to be able to monopolise the administration for very long. Outsmarting one's opponents was merely a preliminary to easing out one's allies, an approach which did not make for stability. In fact, in a system where politics were unrelated to decisions and divorced from responsibility, and where organisation and consolidation of interests were lacking, principle exerted little influence.

The self-styled 'revolution men', professed presbyterians, were no exception to this general rule. Their opposition to Queensberry was not motivated wholly by principle. They disliked the duke personally and felt an even greater distaste for the political reputation of some of his followers, yet there was an even more basic explanation for their continual opposition to him. They recognised Queensberry's appetite for influence and appreciated that it could be satisfied only at their expense. Revolution men were as deeply attached to their jobs as anyone else and quite rightly suspected Queensberry of trying to oust them, ultimately if not at once. Only a few, notably Melville and his connections, did not seem to harbour this suspicion. Even when circumstances proved their trust of Queensberry to have been naive, it did not apparently occur to them to hold him in any way responsible, which was curious. But the majority of the revolution men took up the obvious weapon to defend themselves. Queensberry's attachment to former reluctant revolutionaries and quasi-jacobites aroused uneasiness but also provided excuses. The revolution men were able to emphasise their own loyalty to William and the church establishment whilst casting suspicion on the Queensberry group's attitude to both. When Queensberry succeeded in having some of them dismissed at the beginning of Anne's reign, they did not hesitate to go into opposition. The key to alignments within the court lies in Queensberry's ambition. Such talk of revolution and presbytery as accompanied the rivalry was not mere window dressing but it was little more.

Of course this suspicion of Queensberry and his ambitions was only a particular manifestation of a general problem. Rifts within the court had not begun in 1695-6. Some of the trouble immediately after the revolution had sprung from the rivalry between Hamilton and the Dalrymples as well as from the widespread antagonism to the latters' advancement. Then the Dalrymples had split the court in opposition to Melville only to become involved, subsequently, in the notorious competition between Johnston and themselves. After the church settlement of 1690 the conflict had taken on a religious aspect — 'episcopalians' in opposition to 'presbyterians' — but on each occasion, either personally or under cover, magnates had been involved: Hamilton opposed by the rest of the higher nobility, Dalrymple supported against Melville by Atholl and the first duke of Queensberry and then, against Johnston, by all the excluded magnate interests. The outcome, the reorganisation and 'magnate coalition' of 1695-6, lasted as long as it took Queensberry and Argyll to eject Tullibardine. Now, after the victory of 1698 over Tullibardine, Queensberry was the first of the magnates since the revolution to be able not only to claim, but to seem on the way to achieving the predominance in the court they all coveted. Queensberry's rivals were doing no more than react in competition or self-defence. Suspicion and jealousy of Queensberry amongst lesser interests had grown when it became clear that the duke, however sincere his personal commitment to the revolution, was prepared on every occasion to put his family's political advantage first regardless of any wider repercussions. When poaching offices for his relatives and friends he was concerned far more with their political relationship to him than with their willingness to follow the court or even their fidelity to the revolution. Reputed jacobites, personally well-disposed to him, were preferable to revolution men not of his interest. So Queensberry's opponents tended to cluster round such of his rivals as seemed to be well placed to resist him. Likewise rival magnates were likely to do their recruiting amongst those who had reason to be mistrustful of Queensberry.

What was to be the nucleus of Queensberry's opponents within the court had gravitated towards Johnston against Dalrymple's 'episcopalian' faction and afterwards leaned, more or less overtly, to Tullibardine, especially during the squabble over Whitelaw's preferment. Tullibardine's departure into opposition left most of them still with the court but somewhat uncomfortable and disorganised. Marchmont was of this group and, as chancellor, particularly isolated. Amongst the rest, Ormiston remained in the ministry but hostile to Queensberry and Argyll; likewise Annandale whom some had been naive enough to expect to go out with Tullibardine. Both Ormiston and Annandale were bent on preserving their positions and, if possible, bettering themselves. The lord advocate was engaged in continually assessing which group mistrusted him least and shifting his ground accordingly. As Queensberry and Argyll, temporarily in alliance, showed only a single-minded devotion to the advancement of their own interests, such divisions in the ministry became progressively more serious. The two magnates resented Marchmont's position as chancellor and were united in their efforts to have him removed. They lost no opportunity of belittling his services and of emphasising his inability to muster for the court what little following he had.[5] Seafield, for the time being, was associated with Queensberry, but Seafield had already become a man apart from Scottish factions, having seen that the best prospect for his advancement lay in dedicating himself to executing the will of the crown as distinct from following one or other of the magnate interests. And, for the moment, William seemed to want him in alliance with Queensberry. Marchmont sensed his detachment and, becoming increasingly convinced that Annandale and Ormiston were after both his and Seafield's posts, he occasionally suggested to Seafield a defensive alliance. At the same time he was careful to assure Queensberry of his continued co-operation.[6]

A further complication was the increased propensity of Argyll to entertain wider visions of what was due to him. Anyone who did not instantly give him support became the target of one of his manic rages. His claims and his behaviour were both frequently unreasonable. At times he seemed to be almost permanently rampageous and empurpled. He had quarrels with Marchmont in which he was at first supported and then surreptitiously abandoned by Queensberry as the latter thought better of it.[7] Seafield failed to jump to Argyll's order in one of the latter's innumerable disputes with Teviot, and Argyll's fury against him was boundless.[8] His denunciations were freely dispensed: ' . . . none can be safe to act in conjunction with Seafield, in whom there is neither honour, honesty, friendship or courage. If I thought it were not lessening of myself to say it to a man dares not resent it, I'd send him as much signed . . . '[9] It could be only a matter of time before Argyll began to nurture resentments against Queensberry, too, though they were not yet to reach serious proportions.[10] And, it is fair to say, Argyll's disenchantment originated primarily as a reaction against Queensberry's determination to have his own way regardless of all other interests.

So these years gave rise to a situation in which almost everyone was convinced that his own position was under threat from within as well as from outside the ministry. Queensberry was suspicious of everybody beyond his personal following. Even Seafield was suspect, although Carstares attempted to reassure Queensberry on that score[11] as well as soothing him with a flow of encouraging reports about his own standing at court: ' . . . the king,' he wrote, 'is far from having it in his thoughts to compromise matters with d[uke] H[amilton] but resolves to stand by his servants . . . '[12] Not that such reports wholly reassured Queensberry, but they probably allowed him to give some attention to the discords within the ministry.

Jealousies abounded. After the adjournment of the May session of the 1700 parliament, Argyll, Annandale and Seafield went to London as a ministerial delegation to report on the situation in Scotland. Those remaining in Edinburgh showed concern over whether any of the three individually had either seen, or tried to see, the king,[13] whilst the delegates in London were in turn alarmed by reports of Queensberry's picnic to Cockenzie on which he had been accompanied by Hamilton and both the duchesses.[14] Their disquiet, though, was more than matched by that in Edinburgh, where ministers felt themselves unfairly saddled with an excessive burden on account of the rising agitation over Darien. They suspected the trio in London of opting out. Philiphaugh reported to Carstares: '... several of the king's servants here are jealous of their being at court, and the chancellor, president of the council, Carmichael and treasurer-depute have complained to his grace [the duke of Queensberry] this very day of their absence and plainly told that, if they do not come quickly and concur and join hand in hand they will be very cautious and leave it upon them to take measures above and answer for them ... I suspect if Seafield stays at court he needs expect little advice from this about the framing of any papers ... So, if he have a mind to take all upon him, he may stay, but if he desires only to take a share with the rest of the king's servants he must be present with them...'[15] Such narrow-eyed jealousy left little scope for amicable co-operation.

Some of the mistrust proved amply justified when opportunity for private advantage occurred. Annandale behaved with the utmost propriety in London until Argyll left for Scotland. He then went, significantly, to Albemarle, no doubt in the belief that his was the real power, to complain in general terms of a conspiracy on the part of his colleagues to stop his preferment in office and his elevation to marquess. His immediate demand was more modest — for a pension of £300 a year.[16] This, in the existing crisis, was blackmail and he had somehow to be placated, quickly. Seafield, at the time, felt there was no alternative to getting him the £300 but the pension was greatly resented by the rest of the ministry. Even so, Seafield intimated that Annandale was still not wholly to be trusted.[17] Melville was, as usual, dissatisfied, telling Carstares he felt under no obligation to help the administration to which he belonged.[18] Accusations of shirking, or even of being in league with the opposition, were freely bandied about.[19] In fact, after the parliamentary session of May 1700 the Scottish court's low morale rendered it quite unfit for further action. Yet ministers had to prepare for the next session which could not be too long delayed. Supply was still needed but, perhaps more important, the legality of the standing army in peacetime was about to expire and only parliament could extend it.

Both Queensberry and Seafield agreed that the problem of managing the next session was really that of bringing off from opposition those who were not fully committed resisters. It fact, under the circumstances of 1700 nothing else was ever remotely feasible. In Seafield's opinion, those who believed they were acting only for the benefit of Scotland and Scotsmen — or for their own compensation, though he forbore to say so — could be quietened: '... But there are a great many that design not to be satisfied, particularly such as are for King James or the prince of Wales, or designing places and employments...'[20] Those who had merely found themselves in collaboration with the country party as a result of the Darien failure would be the first to opt out as they realised where the opposition leaders were taking them. Seafield urged Queensberry to work on 'such of the addressers as have no by-ends'.[21] However, Queensberry found '... so many of the members are united by caballing and subscriptions to several addresses, it is to be feared that many may think themselves engaged in honour not to recede from any of their demands . . . '[22] Naturally, a public commitment made it difficult to perform a *volte face*. Bringing members back to their court allegiance was not going to be easy and, as always, it depended on whether they could be offered some way of saving face. Concessions were called for but at court there seemed no inclination to grant any. Most officers of state, in view of the meagre concessions they were to be allowed to make, concluded that the only way to manage parliament was for the king to hold it in person in the hope that his presence would moderate the opposition and reawaken the loyalties of former courtiers.[23] But, whatever hints he might have given in moments of weakness, William had no intention of going to Scotland and risking his own prestige merely to extract his officers of state from their difficulties.

Such small points of agreement existed within the administration. More prominent were the divisons: over allegations of backsliding in the king's service, over whether the court should come to terms with the opposition leaders or not and, especially, over the increasing growth of the Queensberry interest. There developed a general tendency to lay claim to being the backbone of the administration whilst denigrating the efforts of others. Queensberry complained to the king that he was receiving no support at all from most of his colleagues, a state of affairs, he was quick to stress, which was greatly encouraging the opposition.[24] The lord advocate implied that Queensberry, although showing a certain amount of vigour, was not really up to his job and that the real core of the ministry was made up of Ormiston and the advocate himself.[25] Ormiston's view of his own exertions was more modest. He was, he thought, under no obligation to show any energy in the service, not having been given his grant of £1500 and especially since the whole administration was being used for Queensberry's private ends: ' . . . let Queensberry have the use of this government to drive his designs and purposes till it ruin, some of us cannot, nor will not, follow Queensberry . . . '[26] As was to become apparent later, there was some substance in what he said. Argyll, on his return to Edinburgh, was vociferous. With few exceptions he claimed to have detected little sign that anyone but himself was doing anything at all.[27] As a result of these pronounced cracks the whole structure of the administration was visibly weakening.

The most desirable method of reducing the opposition in the next parliament became a subject of dispute. Some were persuaded that the best way was to come to terms with several of the country leaders, taking them into the ministry. Both the lord advocate and Ormiston were of this opinion, even though it could lead to substantial changes. The advocate went so far as to say that the whole foundation of the government needed reshaping.[28] Significantly, most of those who held this view were former associates of Tullibardine and not well-disposed to Queensberry. They were, in fact, men who could hope to survive such a bargain with the opposition and might even have received assurances to that effect. Those at risk in any such arrangement were against any reshuffle. Seafield opposed negotiations with the country party leaders, fearing no doubt for his job, but he also thought there was a chance of carrying a majority in parliament so that a bargain with the opposition was needless.[29] Queensberry, in his bleaker moments, allowed the thought of negotiations to cross his mind but felt that country party leaders should be called up to court only if they requested it.[30] He even reached the point of considering which opposition leaders he ought to recommend if it came to that: ' . . . I shall never advise . . . [the king's] calling up of the duke of Hamilton or his putting any trust in him because I am not persuaded of his integrity for his majesty's interest but if he thinks fit to call any person of that party the marquess of Tweeddale would be the proper person being a man that both the nation and the company gives a more entire credit to and who having sincere intentions may be better dealt with in what is really designed for the good of his country . . . '[31] If these sentiments were sincere, then they did Queensberry credit, but uncharitably it must be said that his career breeds the suspicion that his advice was carefully calculated for his own benefit. Tullibardine was not even considered, perhaps understandably. Hamilton was a rival magnate as Tweeddale was not. His public behaviour was more flamboyant than Tweeddale's and consequently he stood a greater chance of accumulating a formidable interest. Once admitted to the ministry, Hamilton could do Queensberry damage, making up in *panache* what he lacked in ability, whereas Tweeddale, a withdrawn personality and a political innocent, once he had served his purpose of confusing the opposition, could be more easily disposed of. The officers of state seemed incapable of reaching any agreement over whether to bargain or not, and it was the king who finally decided the issue by being firmly against any such accommodation with the country party leaders.[32] So the coming parliamentary session had to be managed by the existing ministry whatever its state and however formidable the task. As Seafield, at least, realised, if the court did not succeed, then the consequences would be very serious — for the ministry, for the crown, and for relations between the two kingdoms. He and a few other ministers decided to leave the capital in an attempt to see all members of parliament individually before they assembled in Edinburgh for the session. Thus Queensberry received great advice and assistance from Seafield in particular, who launched himself diligently upon this task,[33] and the benefit of Argyll's energy which, as always, showed to advantage when he was lobbying.

Although, on their return to Scotland from London, both Argyll and Seafield rendered great assistance, they received scant acknowledgement for it in Queensberry's official correspondence. The duke was taking advantage of the crisis to continue his policy of steady self-advancement to the detriment of his colleagues and even of the crown. He complained of being virtually alone in the king's service, receiving no assistance from other officers of state.[34] His henchmen supported him enthusiastically in the propagation of this lie. If the story had ever contained any grain of truth, it was during the period when Argyll and Seafield were in London. Yet Queensberry's conduct as the chief officer of the crown was not altogether exemplary even in day-to-day affairs. His inactivity on one occasion even attracted unfavourable attention at court. At the news from Darien of Campbell of Finnab's victory over the Spaniards in a minor skirmish, the Edinburgh mob ran amok and indulged in its favourite sport of breaking windows. More seriously, they burst in on the lord advocate, making him sign warrants for the release of two prisoners in detention for printing and distributing opposition literature. The riot was allowed to go on for far too long without any attempt to control it. Only the use of regular troops could have stopped the disturbance and inevitably the person who gave the order would have been very unpopular, as Seafield already was for much less cause. Queensberry failed to take any action, which greatly displeased the king. The duke was very anxious to excuse himself and subsequently disclaimed all knowledge of the event. According to the story as transmitted to court, Queensberry was asleep throughout the riot and Stewart, his secretary, failed to wake him at which the duke professed annoyance.[35] This could have been true, though unlikely. It was certainly convenient for Queensberry.[36]

But this proved to have been no more than a minor setback for the duke. He complained, as commissioner, of joint decisions having to be reached by officers of state since '... people are so slow and timorous, and so changeable in their opinion, that it is very hard to get them to fix a point ...' By way of Carstares he requested permission to take all decisions himself with the assurance, in advance, of the king's backing. Over this he had the support of those Ormiston resentfully called Queensberry's 'cabinet council'.[37] President Dalrymple wrote: '... it is long since I was satisfied joint resolutions are very slow and unsteady and that it is necessary the commissioner should take more on himself ...'[38] Both he and Philiphaugh did their best to represent Queensberry as the kingpin of the government.[39] Carstares placed all this before the king in the most favourable light and, later, was able to give Queensberry assurances. The king, he said, took decisions in Scottish affairs only with those whom Queensberry trusted and he approved of Queensberry's taking decisions himself on the spot when others had been heard.[40] On the strength of this assurance, Queensberry was able to secure, against the advice of the majority of the officers of state, Balcarres's return to Scotland from exile. It was a first step, so it proved, towards recruiting this former jacobite for his own interest.[41] Over the entire field of administration and political influence Queensberry let no point go unchallenged. He protested against Seafield's retention, as secretary, of blank commissions since he wanted them in his own hands and Argyll, out of dislike for Seafield, was persuaded to support him.[42]

By such means Queensberry was gradually gathering into his own hands a near-monopoly of influence and patronage. Under the pretext of managing parliament, as he claimed, virtually single-handed, he broached the question of his being allowed to promise places to members of the opposition and spend money on bribes. He had in mind £300 for the earl Marischal, his relative, of whose conversion to the court he claimed to have fair, though as it proved ill-founded, hopes.[43] Seafield told him: '... I am sure your grace may promise such rewards as you write of very safely and the king will perform whatever you undertake ...'[44] But Seafield had not been allowed to know exactly what was involved. The main business was being transacted not through the secretaries but through Carstares, who had promised that all Queensberry's demands would be met by the king. Money was to be remitted to Queensberry from London, secretly, no one in the ministry but Queensberry himself knowing about it.[45] The following month Queensberry reported spending £500 and was asking for another £1000. Not even Seafield was to be told about it.[46] Carstares was up to his neck in this scheme for Queensberry's aggrandisement, writing continually to emphasise the king's confidence in his commissioner and of the sizable influence he could expect to exert after the parliament.[47] Implicit in Carstares's correspondence was the assurance that Queensberry need not be inhibited by fears of a failure in parliament for which — so great was William's trust in him — he would not be blamed. Should the duke be forced to another adjournment, then the king would make a point of holding the next session in person.[48] This proved to be a rash promise which Carstares had to retract, since almost immediately afterwards William decided that he would not go to Scotland whatever the circumstances.[49] But in spite of such minor hitches the shape of these cumulative arrangements was clear. Queensberry, advised by such as Philiphaugh, had scented an opportunity to become at last the dominant interest in Scotland, whilst those who had begun to fancy him as the favourite were preparing to place their money accordingly. Only Ormiston and others as disgruntled as he, whose chances of being crowded out of the court earlier than most were substantial, took immediate alarm at the danger signals.

But, whatever the state of the ministry, the task of managing parliament had still to be faced. With the opposition leaders and their committed followers there was nothing to be done. The problem really centred on the men who found themselves in opposition only because of their Africa Company sympathies and losses over Darien which had led them to incur some obligation to the country party leaders. Fortunately for the court these were the people most vulnerable to persuasion. As courtiers unaccustomed to being out in the cold they were in a state of indecision and tension. Yet their very uneasiness made their behaviour difficult to forecast. As different pressures were brought to bear on them by one side or the other they changed almost from hour to hour, or at least gave that impression, trying perhaps to be all things to all men.[50] Seafield appreciated their difficulties: '... The heads of the party have no design to be satisfied with anything can be proposed; and though many be convinced of the dangerous consequences of bringing things to extremities yet they pretend, in point of honour, that they cannot leave or desert their party, and they are still positive that they will assert the right of Caledonia...'[51]

Queensberry received ample advice, much of it gratuitous, on tactics as well as the proposal of beneficial laws. One such recommendation was for an act of peace and war, although nothing was to come of this till 1703.[52] But it was generally realised that the pivot of the whole situation was the issue of Caledonia and how it should be handled. As a start Paterson, of all people, had been recruited by the ministry to induce within the company a more moderate disposition.[53] Like others he had his future to provide for, in which the court seemed likely to be of more assistance than the country party. Gradually some astute tactics were evolved. The general lines of the court's strategy were explained in a memorandum by Philiphaugh.[54] So great and widespread was the conviction that the Darien project had been legal and that Scotland had been wronged that some expression of the nation's dissatisfacton had to be allowed. If some 'good laws' could pass to convince the waverers of the king's concern for Scotland, it might be just possible to persuade a majority the Caledonia affair did not merit an act of parliament. This was the policy attempted. Permission was obtained from William to pass, as concessions, some 'good laws': habeas corpus, trade acts, confirmation of the company's privileges and others. To frustrate any such manoeuvre the opposition as a first priority would most probably try to push the Darien business to extremities. Queensberry, however, was able to obtain in advance, by his own cajolery and bribery and by the persuasive efforts of the other officers of state, the secret agreement of sufficient members to concede priority to the proposed 'good laws' before considering Darien. In return a solemn court undertaking had to be given that Darien would be debated before any adjournment. On that subject the members concerned made no promises concerning their conduct, but it was hoped that in due course they would approach the Darien business with moderation, withdrawing support from extreme opposition measures.[55] William was so anxious to have Scottish business out of the way that he placed very few restrictions on

Queensberry's handling of parliament and the concessions he was allowed to approve from the selected list, though Carstares privately advised the duke to concede as little as he could.[56] As always, William's main concern was with English politics, to which Scotland was necessarily subordinated. The king was afraid that any mention of the hardships Scotland had suffered at the hands of England '... may be laid hold of in this nice juncture to the obstructing of his affairs here and to the raising of such a misunderstanding between the two nations as may prove very uneasy to him ...', as the Scottish under-secretary, Robert Pringle, put it.[57]

When the new session began, Marchmont, as lord chancellor, was president of the parliament. He was not at any time a good chairman, but in this second session of 1700 he found himself struggling in an unruly house.[58] Any premature adjournment would have been politically disastrous, yet William was adamant that parliament must be adjourned before the English parliament met, and preferably as much before as possible. The king would far rather face trouble in Scotland than run any risk of jeopardising business in England, which indicates well enough his order of priorities.[59] So Marchmont's task was to try to expedite business.

Despite some early uncertainties, the court's tactics ultimately proved successful. There had at first been doubt whether the lord advocate or, for that matter, Marchmont would be present, both being inclined to plead illness.[60] Finally they brought themselves, or were brought, to attend. As much success as could have been expected was achieved but at a price, namely, the consolidation of a large country party which remained vociferous, defiant and strong enough to cause Queensberry further trouble in 1702. On a test vote over a disputed Galloway by-election at the beginning of the session the court had a majority of no more than one, and that due to the arrival in the nick of time of Sir Robert Stewart who had been unwell.[61] When the voting on committees took place, the position was seen to be slightly better. The court was able to carry its lists of nobles and burghs but was totally defeated amongst the barons. From this voting Seafield calculated that the court's strength was one hundred and eight to the opposition's ninety-five.[62]

At the outset the country party leaders repeated their earlier tactic of trying to split the court over religion, introducing again an act to abolish the king's power over general assemblies. By a majority of sixty-eight the court succeeded in postponing the topic for the current session.[63] Then the court's secretly pre-arranged order of business—the precedence of the legislative programme over Darien — was carried by thirty-one votes.[64] Consequently, by the time parliament reached the Caledonia business it was January 1701, when, instead of voting an act which would have been a gesture of defiance to the king, the court and England, a majority of one hundred and eight to eighty-four decided to confine any protest to an address.[65] Subsequently the address as drafted was approved by one hundred and one votes to sixty-one.[66]

The final controversial business was whether supply should be granted for the maintenance of troops in peacetime, and under the circumstances the outcome was highly satisfactory for the court. Three thousand men were to be kept on the establishment till 1 December 1702. For an interim period of four months, to give him time to consider how to dispose of troops surplus to establishment, the king was allowed to exceed this quota. These provisions and a whole series of 'good laws' — what the court took to be concessions — were touched by the sceptre: *habeas corpus*, prohibition on the import of foreign woollen manufactures, silks and French wines, and on the export of Scottish wool; the privileges of the Africa Company were continued, which was a token rather than a practical gesture.[67] Queensberry had, in fact, conceded the maximum William had been prepared to allow, but the avoidance of further deadlock between court and parliament was worth it.

Throughout the parliament the court vote remained fairly static whilst the opposition fell from its peak of ninety-four on the number of troops to a minimum of fifty-eight over the four months' grace.[68] Abstention or desertion rather than joining the court seems to have been the course adopted by members unable to resolve their various dilemmas. But since, before parliament met, members with some opposition sympathies over Darien could have been reckoned as being in the region of one hundred and ten, it is clear that pressures of some kind had been applied and to some purpose.

Parliament was adjourned in an uproar. Feeling had been so strong that almost every opposition defeat had resulted in a formal protest.[69] Country party leaders fully realised that adjournment deprived them of their main public platform and means of exerting pressure until the next session and were incensed at being, as they saw it, cheated of victory. The ministry for its part had survived, but only just. Its rents had been cobbled together to allow the officers of state to meet parliament decently, but after the session the schism within the court became increasingly obvious. Responsibility for this lay for the most part with Queensberry, who remained implacably determined to extend his own influence within the ministry, disregarding completely the resentment of his nominal allies. The latters' chagrin was not at all lessened by his trading on the outcome of the parliamentary session for which he claimed the credit. Parliament had not only passed off better than anyone had any right to expect, but most of his colleagues had contributed in some way to such success as had been achieved, whilst some had been indispensable. What had become clear — in fact it should have been apparent for some time—was that Portland and Carstares had badly miscalculated.

Although Queensberry's initial impetus within the court had been due at first to his representing his father's interest and then to his own status as a magnate, he owed his further rise largely to Portland and Carstares. His retention of a place in the ministry on succeeding to the title was intended as no more than a sop to the 'episcopalian' opposition to Johnston in which Queensberry had been prominent. It was far from satisfying anyone and merely irritated Queensberry. Later, in association with Argyll, he had been promoted as the secretaries, rather than William and his advisers, realised the need to satisfy the 'nobility of the first rank'. However, with little idea of what they were really about, Portland and Carstares were on the way to an achievement which could have been, and to some extent was, better than they realised. First they had attempted to reconcile what they envisaged as two religious parties, although the parties had little existence beyond contemporary jargon and their own imaginations. Then they had been brought to the point of gratifying the 'nobility of the first rank'. As it happened, the interests of two of them for the time being coincided, although one was reputedly episcopalian and the other looked upon as presbyterian, and both had been part of the 'episcopalian' opposition. So Queensberry and Argyll entered into partnership to oust from the court all vestiges of any rival magnate interest, in which aim they succeeded. Afterwards, for a brief period, there existed the basis of a possible court party. What seemed to have emerged was the almost visionary solution — a magnate alliance. It was not to last, since such alliances did not seem to be in the nature of magnate politics, but even during its brief existence neither William nor anyone in his entourage seemed to realise its significance sufficiently to try to preserve it. As soon as Queensberry began to importune the king, almost his every demand was gratified and his interest consequently extended to the great annoyance of others including Argyll. So, instead of doing all they could to maintain the alliance as long as possible, William's advisers actually undermined it and hastened the inevitable breach.

It seems that William was looking for one figure to attract the allegiance of 'presbyterians' and 'episcopalians', the reason Tullibardine was taken into the ministry in 1695. Apparently no one had learned anything from the outcome of that experiment. So in the same way Queensberry's antecedents must, for Portland and Carstares, and therefore for William, have marked him as an ideal base on which to establish a stable Scottish court party, having claims on the support of both 'presbyterians' and 'episcopalians', or so it was represented. They seem also to have swallowed much of the Queensberry group's account of the duke's indispensability. Portland and Carstares resisted almost, if not quite, to the last any acknowledgement of the reality of the magnate power groups which largely decided Scottish political alignments. They failed completely to allow for the disruptive effect of Queensberry's urge to dominate the government. In Scotland, if not England, Queensberry's aims were fully appreciated. He himself told Mar that he wanted power to serve his friends,[70] and it was in the nature of this process to spiral upwards for as long as it was permitted to do so.

This campaign, directed towards the creation of a Queensberry-Dalrymple monopoly, continued after the session to meet seemingly with success after success. The duke was allowed to remain commissioner, drawing the allowances, until he had seen the king.[71] Apart from Queensberry and the secretaries, all holders of official posts were prohibited from going to court, the prohibition being kept secret till parliament adjourned for fear of its giving rise to jealousies within the ministry.[72] Obviously by this time the collective loyalty of the officers of state, if it had any existence at all, was fragile. Yet, despite the need for this kind of precaution, Queensberry obtained permission to take with him as advisers Philiphaugh and Morton, one a dependent and the other a relative.[73] It was too much to expect that the others would be acquiescent when confronted with this, nor were they. Argyll, in particular, was greatly irritated.[74]

Queensberry intended to use his visit to court to get as much of his own way as possible without interference from competitors. One of his immediate priorities was Marchmont's dismissal. The chancellor was not only objectionable to Queensberry as a former supporter of Whitelaw, Queensberry wanted the place for one of his own nominees, lord Boyle, formerly Boyle of Kelburn.[75] His opposition to Marchmont was so strong that he resisted his appointment as commissioner to the general assembly, even preferring to see Annandale appointed instead, and there was little or no amity between Queensberry and Annandale.[76] Later he succeeded in having Sir Patrick Hume, a protégé of Marchmont, dismissed from the post of solicitor-general, having for some time past been campaigning against him and refusing to discuss business with him despite Marchmont's protests.[77] The office of solicitor was filled by a joint commission to Mr William Carmichael and yet another Dalrymple — Sir David.[78]

A further advance occurred in the Queensberry-Dalrymple interest. Before the parliament a vacancy had been created in the court of session through the death of lord Mersington. There was no shortage of candidates and the vacancy had been left for the duration of parliament to encourage aspirants to serve in hope if not full expectation. Promises were made and hints dropped, but each officer of state was concerned for his own candidate. Carstares was told, 'My lord Seafield is for all of them till the parliament sits and then for his cousin Forglen when it's over . . .'[79] Queensberry's attitude was similar but he had in mind another candidate. To strengthen the interest of president Dalrymple in the session he secured the place, in the teeth of opposition from his colleagues, for Robert Stewart of Tillicoultry, a Dalrymple man. And he still agitated for Teviot to be replaced by Ramsay as commander-in-chief in Scotland.[80] The drift of all this is plain now and was obvious enough to many at the time. Perhaps an awareness of it also began to penetrate the court, since the duke detected a certain sluggishness in carrying out his recommendations, although there could, of course, have been a number of reasons for this. William, having seen the Scottish parliament end without any actual violence, might have banished Scotland from his thoughts until the next crisis. And Albemarle's influence continued to increase, his inclinations being noticeably towards Queensberry's opponents.[81] But many people were eager to represent to William the excessive growth of the Queensberry interest and the consequent discontent within the ministry. Protests had been made at court. Carstares, at least, had become aware of the growing division in the Scottish court party, whether or not he understood the reason. As a result William might have come to see the Queensberry interest's rate of growth as unhealthy for the government of Scotland. For whatever reason the court ceased to be so immediately responsive to Queensberry's requests.

Queensberry complained of delays even in the implementation of promises he had made for managing parliament,[82] although William did say he would attend to such obligations when he returned to England from the continent.[83] Taking his cue from the top, Carstares became more cautious than hitherto in his correspondence with Queensberry.[84] It is significant that Queensberry, despite his complaints, was not by any means being completely cut off from the flow of patronage. His expectations had been so inflated by past successes that he was irked by any delay in complying with his wishes, especially when it involved disappointment to his followers. Ramsay, for instance, at Queensberry's behest, was finally given the post of commander-in-chief and had in consequence fully expected Teviot's complete eclipse. On his discovery that Teviot still retained influence at court, Ramsay became very annoyed, showing an inclination to blame Queensberry,[85] which was unfair, Teviot's influence being the last thing Queensberry wanted to preserve. For the earl Marischal, related to Queensberry but against the court in the recent parliament, the duke succeeded at last in obtaining a £500 pension and a place on the privy council.[86] But when it came to gratifying such as Mar, apprentices in the Queensberry interest, there was nothing left out of what the court would allow but small pensions which they found galling, even contemptible, and Queensberry was powerless to remedy the situation.[87] His followers expected him to deliver on the same scale as in the recent past and he was failing them, which damaged his influence. It was at this point that Queensberry became acutely aggrieved at the resistance to his demands or, as he saw it, proper pretensions, and going into a sulk he murmured of retirement from public affairs.

Queensberry felt thwarted and even deprived, but his opponents would have regarded his misgivings as unjustified. Consternation within the Scottish court at the tendencies of his policy had increased rather than otherwise. It was not merely his extravagant claims for his followers but the character of some of his attachments which caused alarm. All officers of state had an interest in the management of the next parliament and its success. Queensberry's activities did not seem to be directed with that in mind. Carmichael remarked that the duke ' . . . gives assurance of his fixedness to the present church government as the best support of that cause for which he so early appeared and ventured his all and gives me allowance to make the same known'. But, he added, 'The earl of Marischal's pension is dissatisfying to many here and some are of opinion it will be to no purpose, that it will not fix him . . . ' [88] Since Marischal was a member of the jacobite opposition, those who felt his pension was to no purpose were right. Queensberry had no more influence on his behaviour in 1701 than his offer of £300 had produced in 1700. For one who posed as leader of the revolution party it did seem a curious venture. But Queensberry's aim was not to secure Marischal's support for the ministry. It seemed more important to him that Marischal, jacobite or not, was connected with Queensberry's family and preferred the duke to his rivals — the 'old revolution men' in the court. Ormiston amongst others professed disgust at the transaction. [89]

What increasingly appeared to be at stake was a fundamental difference in policy concerning the preparations considered necessary for the next parliamentary session, due in 1702 to secure further provision for the standing forces. The opposition, since the adjournment, had remained active whilst some court supporters were becoming noticeably dissatisfied. For most there had been little reward. In due course, after the 1700-1701 parliament, Argyll had been made a duke, and Lothian and Annandale had become marquesses, but these promotions did not affect the distribution of power within the court nor make less bitter the disappointment of those who had been overlooked. If yet another harrowing session of parliament was to be avoided, with an even greater prospect of a *débâcle* than before, something had to be done, and very soon, lest the opposition should contrive a majority, or very near it, on the issue of refusing supply for the standing forces in peacetime. Little choice remained to the ministry but an attempt to take off some of the opposition by allowing them places. The length to which this was to be taken and the section of the opposition to be approached gave rise to wide differences within the court. Queensberry exhibited the attitudes characteristic of him and which became more marked as time went on. He seemed incapable of subordinating his desire to dominate the court interest to the urgent need to build up beyond the risk of challenge a court majority in parliament. Other magnates would no doubt have acted similarly. Queensberry merely happened to be in a position to try to achieve his ambition. His currently obsessive desire was to gain promotion for Philiphaugh to compensate for past disappointments. For the rest Queensberry had in mind no court strategy other than nibbling at the fringes of the 'episcopalian' interests still in opposition. His somewhat forlorn hope was that they would give him personal support inside and outside parliament. As far as the management of the next session was concerned this line of action was useless.

Queensberry's opponents in the court, on the other hand, seemed in their recommendations to be approaching the crux of the problem. Their scheme envisaged an attempt to detach from the opposition Whitelaw and his followers, Whitelaw having already indicated that he was open to suitable offers. Argyll chose to appear as the protagonist of this scheme and there is no doubt that his appraisal of the situation was more realistic than Queensberry's. But Argyll, too, was concerned with more than managing the next parliament, and his appraisal was closely connected to his own personal ambitions. The alliance between Queensberry and Argyll, which had already lasted longer than anyone had a right to expect, was coming to an end. Argyll had determined to assert his own claims, having come to resent Queensberry's grabbing policy since it forced him into a subordinate rôle. There was a further consideration. The 'presbyterian' opposition to Queensberry within the ministry favoured approaches to Whitelaw, their former ally separated from them by Queensberry's machinations. By taking up this cause, Argyll was trying to establish himself as the leader of this group in the ministry in succession to Johnston and Tullibardine.[90] If Argyll could consolidate the discontented in the court party under his own leadership, he would be in a better position to rival Queensberry's influence.

The fact of this dispute between the two court magnates was widely known. The secretary of the Africa Company, Roderick Mackenzie, wrote, ' . . . Queensberry and Argyll [are] absolutely at odds about the disposal of vacant posts to their respective friends so that some of their promises must fail . . . '[91] Since the parliament Argyll had opposed Queensberry's steady pushing and in particular had strongly objected to Stewart of Tillicoultry's becoming a lord of session. Philiphaugh had reported to Queensberry: '...a letter from the earl of Argyll to my lord president which I saw the other day which is dated the 14 of this wherein the earl does not only insist upon his former allegiance [*sic* for allegation?] of your grace's breaking engagements to him but as I remember says that if your grace continued to him as formerly this had not fallen out and one thing makes the matter harder to be adjusted is that the whole scheme has been laid without him and he meets with no yielding in any point and this he must think not equal . . . nor ought any one man to put himself in balance with all the rest . . . ' Argyll was resigned to Stewart's having the gown but could see no good coming of it.[92] There were others, including Annandale, who disapproved of Stewart's being raised to the bench as giving the president of the session too much influence in the civil court.[93] Argyll was hoping to channel such discontent into support for his opposition to Queensberry within the administration.

Queensberry in the meantime had continued to brood on his state of deprivation, and his attitude of mind and continued talk of retirement[94] became of serious concern to his followers. All the support they had invested in Queensberry might be endangered if he were to abandon himself to threats and displays of strength. Philiphaugh was particularly chastened because Queensberry had taken him to London to secure for him some promotion – a further attempt on the post of lord clerk register still held by Selkirk, the last surviving trace of Hamilton influence in the government. When Philiphaugh returned to Scotland mortified, having received nothing, he advised an equally deflated but resentful Queensberry to concentrate for the time being on holding what influence he had rather than on trying to increase it.[95] Philiphaugh and president Dalrymple offered a joint opinion that whilst Queensberry maintained any alliance with Argyll, no one who had complete dependence on Queensberry would ever be advanced to any considerable post, as had become apparent in 1698 when the duke tried to secure Philiphaugh's promotion. They turned to future prospects and in particular to the leadership of the 'presbyterian' group in the court. They doubted whether, in the long run, the presbyterians would accept domination by Argyll, of whom they had already complained so much. So they discounted Argyll's threats and advised Queensberry to push for no major promotions for the time being.[96] The implication of this advice seemed to be that Queensberry should accept the break with Argyll as permanent and even desirable rather than as a temporary aberration. It would be necessary merely for him to wait until Argyll had alienated his new supporters and was isolated, then a further Queensberry-Dalrymple campaign could begin and Queensberry could increase his interest on his own terms. Philiphaugh had earlier been even more explicit: ' . . . I am sorry your grace ever entertained or signified any fretful thought of quitting his majesty's service. Let me beg for God's sake you'll forbear that . . . for it may provoke and give your enemies advantage against you. I humbly think it was more proper to say to the king that you are so much sensible of his bounty and favour to you that you could freely trust yourself to serve in what circumstances he should appoint you but that what you proposed or desired was not for any prospect of advantage to yourself or to gratify your own friends but necessary to enable you to serve his majesty to good purpose and that when it was known what you so much urged had been rejected by his majesty it would lessen your influence in business very much, and I am confident the king's favour would not be so much slighted at this time if it were not that people here thought the king not well determined what measures to take or what persons to make use of, and this thought has a strange influence upon all in the government. All are disjointed . . . I'm sure if other measures are not taken timely and that the king do clearly point out a channel through which only he will convey his favour, it will be a foolish vain attempt for any subject to think of managing a parliament here. When your grace came down commissioner it did not contribute a little to your influence that people reckoned now when you became a man of business you would be the chief favourite of this nation. If this once misgive you'll find it hard to retrieve it. Several here takes occasion already to say that now since those in the king's service are divided and the king is balancing among them they will be able to do nothing to purpose and the king will find it his interest to discard them and take on others who will come as one man by the lump to him and do a considerable job before divisions can happen and some of the government are not free of these apprehensions . . . '[97] Philiphaugh's advice was a clear statement of the conditions which made for influence in the Scottish court in view of the attitudes prevalent in the kingdom. Signs or rumours of division demoralised ministries and encouraged others to oppose in the hope of appearing as an alternative administration. If a ministry was to remain effective, any tendency to splits had to be avoided, but this state of affairs was possible only when one interest became dominant and unchallengeable. So there was no essential difference between the aims of Queensberry and Philiphaugh, only tactics were in question. The Scottish court must be made 'of a piece', which is to say that, in the view of both, it had to be dominated by the Queensberry group. Both were out to contrive the ultimate hegemony of this interest in which Philiphaugh had invested time and patience. However, faced with opposition, Queensberry's neuroses, together with a sense of what was his due, inclined him towards sulky and even vaguely threatening postures. Philiphaugh had sufficient detachment to see that this would not do. His advice not only more befitted a courtier, it was based on an apparently realistic appraisal of the situation nicely calculated to appeal to the king. If he wanted Scotland quietly and unobtrusively managed, he would be well advised to support one interest and make it plain that that alone was the channel of favour. Enough had been granted to Queensberry to make it seem that the king had been moving in this direction. Queensberry had appeared to be within sight of his goal. Philiphaugh urged him to represent to the king that now, by denying him favours, he was both undermining the foundations that had been built on steadily since 1696 and also discounting the duke's altruistic motives, he having no aim in mind other than service to the king.

It was quite true that Scottish political attitudes indicated one theoretical solution. The ideal way of managing Scotland without overt trouble was to allow one interest to dominate the kingdom, denying any prospect of advancement to such as tried to by-pass the official managers. But the interest concerned had either to be big enough to do the job unaided or, otherwise, capable of forming stable alliances to acquire the necessary strength. Queensberry's interest, in face of opposition from Hamilton, from the Atholl interest, from Tweeddale and now from Argyll, was not strong enough to dominate parliament. Moreover, Queensberry had amply demonstrated his inability to work with anybody save on his own terms. Nor was any other magnate interest sufficiently strong to withstand a combined assault from the rest for, should any of them be given a court monopoly, that would be the outcome. In this lay one of the fundamental difficulties of Scottish government — magnates would not share power for very long if at all. In time, however impracticable such an ambition might be, each wanted a monopoly. Consequently the stability of the administration was threatened and the kingdom rendered ungovernable. Queensberry's attitude and ambitions had, by 1701, brought Scotland to this point.

There was no let up in the struggle. The post of lord clerk register, still held by Selkirk, became another subject of dispute. No one disputed that he should go. The question was that of who should succeed him. Ormiston, Philiphaugh and Whitelaw were candidates. If Ormiston were to receive it, the contest would merely be transferred to the appointment of his successor as treasurer-depute. But Queensberry supported Philiphaugh and Argyll was in favour of Whitelaw.[98] This was a trial of strength between the rival court interests, the outcome being critical for the future management of parliament. Argyll, with apparent reasonableness, set out his views for the benefit of Carstares: '... I gave both secretaries my advice at parting, particularly how to deal with lord Whitelaw and others of his squad; and, the longer I consider on it, the more I am convinced to a demonstration that if once we gain Whitelaw our work is half done, for by it we shall deprive the opposing party of their sense and get into their bowels, nor will it be in the power of the greatest of that party to prevent it and their interest will vanish. Did the D[uke] of Queensberry but rightly consider his own particular interest, as well as his majesty's, and the safety of all who acted upon the revolution, he would come frankly into the measure. But, alas! Still Philiphaugh is the burden of the song and, to speak in jockey terms, he is his dead weight as I have often told the duke in raillery formerly when he used to solicit his majesty for Carnwath, Broomhall and the rest of his family . . . '[99] The crux of Argyll's argument was that instead of wasting time with individuals who, however personally acceptable to Queensberry, were suspect to all good revolution men, it would be better to bring over to the court Whitelaw with ten or twelve of his following to support the standing army.[100]

Given the power of the magnates, such differences of opinion within the court left the crown unenviably placed. There seemed to be no immediate solution, and perhaps by this stage no practical solution existed. Within the ministry the dilemma of the crown was epitomised by the predicament of perhaps the one man on whom William could by now rely most unreservedly — Seafield, already following the policy he had evolved from at least 1696, namely that of strict obedience to the court and detachment from the magnate interests. This theme of detachment was a recurring one in Seafield's correspondence. After the 1698 parliament, for instance, he wrote: ' . . . I have been importuned these four or five days by the duke of Queensberry and earl of Argyll to make a joint representation to his majesty concerning those who have opposed him in parliament; and it is true that it is for his majesty's interest to make some examples . . . But I, being his majesty's immediate servant, am unwilling to enter into any concert without his direction . . . '[101] In 1701 the conflict between Queensberry and Argyll left him in an impossible position. The last direction he had from the crown placed him in co-operation with the Queensberry-Argyll alliance and he tried hard to hold to that. He told Carstares he was keeping himself apart from all solicitations and staying with those he was engaged to, 'for I think the most certain way to carry on the king's affairs will be by keeping unite amongst ourselves . . . '[102] But the Queensberry-Argyll alliance was now broken and Seafield, unable openly to take side with either, was in danger of isolation and inclined to despondency.[103]

Yet, although he had to avoid open involvement with either side, his own rational assessment of requirements for the next session of parliament brought him close to Argyll's position: ' . . . I find, from all that I meet with that, if we continue firm to one another, there will be no great difficulty in managing his majesty's affairs in the next session of parliament. I have seen my lord Whitelaw and he is indeed very ready to be engaged in his majesty's service and, if what my lord duke of Argyll proposed were done, he would use his utmost endeavours to promote his majesty's interest, but you know the difficulty remains. My lord duke of Queensberry continues positive and division would be of very fatal consequence to our party . . . '[104] What he was really asking for was a firm order from the king to impose unity on terms which would make parliamentary management possible. But whether Seafield realised it or not, continuing 'firm to one another' was no longer a possibility. The time for royal commands was over. In 1698, had terms of employment been made clear to both Queensberry and Argyll, their alliance might conceivably have been longer lived. As it was, the court had helped Queensberry to destroy the alliance. Now, if Argyll had his way the court would very likely lose Queensberry. Should Argyll be overruled, then his co-operation would be restricted or even withdrawn. There were limits to the humiliation magnates would accept. Even Seafield's inclination to an accommodation with Whitelaw did not endear him to Queensberry's camp.

And Seafield's views, arrived at through considerations of sheer practicality, were already putting him in some strange company. When, as secretary Ogilvy, he had opposed Whitelaw's candidature for the presidency of the session, coolness had developed between the two. Now he was in favour of making Whitelaw an officer of state. In the past, Argyll, too, had attacked Seafield in manic terms, and even in 1701, when they favoured the same course of action, he could not resist a sly dig at him: ' . . . to be free, v[iscount] Seafield has the misfortune not to be trusted by some, though I presume they wrong him . . . '[105] In fact they did wrong him. His detached attitude was never really understood in Scotland where, unlike England, there was no tradition of men who were virtually permanent civil servants. To the magnates Seafield, unwilling as he was to be swayed by Scottish partisan politics and continually waiting his cue from outside Scotland, was dangerous.

Seafield appreciated in 1701 that Scotland's problems were beyond internal solution. Some decision from William was necessary, although whatever he ordered was just as likely to lead to disruption as to produce anything constructive. But William was slow, as usual, to make any sign. Indeed, it seems likely that William had already decided that the Scottish problem was insoluble — at least by further adjustments in the court. That he had correctly analysed the problem is open to question. At one point he was reported as having said that 'he had not the good fortune to know what would satisfy a Scotchman'.[106] And there, of course, was the mistake. The king, Portland and Carstares had been trying to produce a compromise between largely imaginary interests whose demands, being looked upon as mainly religious, were thought capable up to a point of being satisfied, whereas they were dealing with nobles of insatiable appetite to whom compromise was an alien concept. But whatever William's appraisal of Scottish politics, it led him to the right conclusion. His providing no indication of how he intended the 1702 parliament to be managed was almost certainly due to his inability to envisage any immediate course of action. There was little to be done. He was to die without having made any move affecting the Scottish court's internal dispute. At his death Queensberry and Argyll were still in confrontation, their conflict unresolved. Selkirk held on as lord clerk register, not to be dismissed until the next reign, and Whitelaw remained in opposition.

After William's death the parliament of 1702 showed clearly the continuing split within the court. The opposition seceded in a body and boycotted the session as illegal. Those who remained to continue the parliament were courtiers, but divided into two groups however categorised: 'presbyterian' and 'episcopalian', revolution men and those whose fidelity to the 1689 settlement was not so firm or, simply, Queensberry against Argyll. Those who disliked Queensberry and feared for their jobs in the face of his aggressive place-hunting clustered round Argyll, to whom men such as Marchmont now found themselves allied. On straightforward issues such as ratifying the queen's title to the throne, voting the cess and the act allowing negotiations for a union, the court managed to maintain unanimity. But Marchmont's introduction of the abjuration oath, which disrupted proceedings and led to a premature adjournment, was a deliberate blow by Queensberry's opponents against the duke and his followers, and nothing was better calculated to embarrass the Queensberry faction in the ministry. Marchmont, Ormiston and their sympathisers were far from convinced that Queensberry deserved to be looked on as the leader of the 'revolution party', and the abjuration issue was intended to place on him the burden of proof and perhaps, in the process, discredit him. Both principle and tactics were involved and the two cannot be disentangled. Whatever the motivation, circumstances enabled Queensberry to wriggle out of the trap with a great show of concern for court unity, although he was made to suffer for it in 1703. In that year his opponents in the court helped to disrupt the parliament and ruined Queensberry's chances of success as commissioner for that session.[107]

But by that time William was dead and Anne was on the throne. Had William lived long enough, it is not easy to see how the parliament of 1702 could have been handled. Conceivably, though it is improbable, he could have acted in accordance with advice said to have been given to Anne in 1704, by Stair, namely to manage without parliament, making up Scotland's deficit out of English funds. With no parliament at all, political obstruction might well have been prevented, and the long-term consequences would have been a disaster for both kingdoms. As things stood in 1701, those closely involved with the hazards of managing Scotland found themselves driven to one conclusion, whatever they saw as the root cause of the trouble. Whether they imagined the kingdom to be crippled by the intransigence of two religious groups in rivalry or whether they realised that the complexity of the Scottish problem was created by a combination of three elements — the strength of the magnates in relation to the political scale of the kingdom; their ability and willingness to obstruct business in a small, underdeveloped but sovereign parliament; and the English connection, which meant that Scottish developments had a far wider significance than they would otherwise have possessed — there was only one solution. To make them manageable, Scottish problems had to be placed in a different context — a united kingdom. If Scotland's own institutions did not serve to resolve her internal tensions, then she had to be brought within the scope of some more effective constitutional apparatus. After years of moving from one blind alley to another, William had been driven to this realisation.

Despite his willingness in 1689 to placate the Scottish convention by his favourable reference to union, William was, in practice, for most of his reign, quite opposed to the possibility on the ground that the project would be a nuisance. According to Dartmouth, the king spoke to the earl of Jersey on the subject of union and said that 'in his opinion it would be an advantage, for it could not be done without admitting a good number of Scotch members into both houses who must depend upon the crown for their subsistence, but said he was not desirous the experiment should be made in his reign . . . '[108] The foreseeable complications must have seemed awesome, and the king was not one to invite difficulties. Yet towards the end of the reign union proposals emanated on two occasions from William and his English ministry. Scotland had become an urgent problem just at a time when the acquisition of Scottish support at Westminster began, to the English ministry, to seem a desirable objective. A court initiative for union in 1700 was stifled by the opposition. In 1701 a second attempt was made when William took advantage of an opportunity in the lords for broaching the topic again. He recommended union to the consideration of both houses. As a result the project was taken to the full length of acts of parliament in both kingdoms to permit the appointment of commissioners and the opening of negotiations. English and Scottish commissioners held meetings over the winter of 1702-3 though, for a variety of reasons, without a successful outcome.

Whether this initiative would have resulted in union had William lived is impossible to say, but his message to parliament on the subject was his last. Anne's accession in 1702 created a different situation. Not only did it produce in Scotland the illusion of an increased freedom of manoeuvre, but Scottish problems were themselves temporarily overshadowed by the outbreak of war. But Scotland's political condition was fundamentally unchanged, and although it took some time for them to realise its urgency, Anne and her ministers inherited the problem and its solution, the latter eventually being put into effect by the union of 1707. Probably the most important short-term effect of the Scottish parliament's abolition was the speedy fulfilment of the court's main intention — a dramatic reduction in the power of the Scottish factions. Save on the part of one or two of the more percipient, there seemed to be no general realisation at the union of what was happening to the power structure of the northern kingdom. Without a sovereign, but quite irresponsible, parliament to legitimise their disruptive tactics, the Scottish magnates found their stature greatly reduced as they entered a wider political field. Their tactical style was ineffective in the United Kingdom parliament and they soon realised that they stood to gain more by co-operation than by obstruction. The ambition of monopolising the Scottish administration ceased to be a realisable one. In a comparatively short time Scotland was politically transformed. Instead of being a major source of distraction to the English court, the admission into both houses of the Westminster parliament of Scottish members who had to 'depend on the crown for their subsistance',[109] their patronage prospects, or both, led to a substantial access of strength for successive administrations of the United Kingdom.

In the event, William's quite unusual readiness at the end of his reign to embark on the complications, and even hazards, of a union project was fully justified. The fact that his appraisal of the causes of Scotland's instability was quite wrong hardly seems, by 1701, to have mattered. Scotland was unmanageable and the condition had to be dealt with, its causation being immaterial. The only practicable solution to the kingdom's real problems just as to her supposed problems, had they existed, was union. But the origins of Scotland's political dislocation are relevant to any judgement of the effectiveness or otherwise of William's reign. What emerges from any examination of Scottish policy after the revolution, even when all allowances have been made, is a realisation of how inept it was. Ultimately the responsibility for this lay with William. Even if the advice he received was almost uniformly bad, it reflects on his choice of advisers and on his own judgement. Portland had been given special oversight of Scotland but could not have been expected to know much about its problems. For the most part both he and William were guided by Carstares, who ought to have known a great deal. Offerings were made by others, but everything was filtered through this central process of assessment and decision of which William himself formed a part. The effect was to produce in London and Holland a distortion of the reality of Scottish politics into a presbyterian *versus* episcopalian model through the efforts of those whose interests were served by perpetuating this view. Scottish nobles would represent to the court anything which seemed likely to provide them with extra leverage in their importunity. At some stage in the process of decision it should have been possible to penetrate smokescreens of this kind, but William continued to be imposed upon. If the king were ever 'ill-served in Scotland', it was by his advisers whose record for faulty appraisal and uncomprehending intrigue was remarkably consistent, whether it was the Dalrymples who had helped to produce the fiasco of the revolution settlement as well as later misfortunes, or 'Cardinal' Carstares who, aside from his steady though misguided support of Melville for old times' sake or whatever reason, detected the key to Scottish management in one misconceived arrangement after another. Interest groups were taken up and in turn represented as either possessing the capacity to incline the presbyterians to moderation or as being the ideal instrument for reconciling both religions. So the court teetered from one mistake to the next until the *impasse* of 1701. It seems that William and his advisers neither understood fully what it was they were trying to do in Scotland nor appreciated the consequences of what they actually did.

Not religious rivalry but sheer faction on the part of rival families was the most serious of Scotland's problems. Had the Scottish parliament after 1689 been engaged in any kind of consistent struggle which transcended personal ambition, whether against royal prerogative, English influence or for the promotion of Scottish interests, it would be possible to lament its passing. As it was, the parliament was no more than an instrument of magnate rivalries and the kingdom was well rid of it.

NOTES

1. *Carstares S.P.*, 377, Blantyre to Carstares, 10 Jun. 1698; *ib.*, 508, same to same, 18 Nov. 1699.
2. See above, p. 129.
3. See below, p. 155ff.
4. *Carstares S.P.*, 460, Buchan to Carstares, 19 Feb. 1699.
5. *Ib.*, 389, 393, 400, 411 and above, p. 126.
6. *Carstares S.P.*, 454, Stewart to Carstares, 12 Oct. 1698; *ib.*, 512, Ormiston to same, 30 Nov. 1699; *ib.*, 588, Argyll to same, 1 Aug. 1700; *ib.*, 620, Stewart to same, 17 Aug. 1700; *ib.*, 624, same to same, 22 Aug. 1700; Buccleuch (Drum.), Queensberry Letters, xiv, [Seafield] to [Queensberry], 27 Oct. 1698; *Marchmont Papers*, iii, 195, Marchmont to Seafield, 19 Dec. 1699; *ib.*, 200, same to same, 28 Dec. 1699; *ib.*, 202, same to Queensberry, 2 Jan. 1700.
7. *Carstares S.P.*, 457, Argyll to Carstares, 31 Jan. 1699; *ib.*, 464, same to same, 5 Mar. 1699; *ib.*, 471, Queensberry to same, 18 Mar. 1699.
8. *Ib.*, 464, 465, 472.
9. *Ib.*, 494, Argyll to Carstares, 9 Sep. 1699.
10. Buccleuch (Drum.), Union, i, [president Dalrymple] to [Queensberry], 25 May [1699].
11. *Ib.*, Queensberry Letters, xiv, [Carstares] to [Queensberry], 14 Feb. 1699.
12. *Ib.*, xvi, [same] to [same], 10 Jun. 1700.
13. *Ib*; *ib.*, Seafield, Seafield to [Queensberry], 15 Jun. 1700.
14. HMCR *Johnstone MSS*, 116-17, Anstruther to Annandale, 13 Jun. 1700; *ib.*, 118, Queensberry to Annandale, 27 Jun. 1700.
15. *Carstares S.P.*, 529, Philiphaugh to Carstares, 19 Jun. 1700; *ib.*, 525, Ormiston to same, 13 Jun. 1700.
16. Buccleuch (Drum.), Seafield, [Seafield] to [Queensberry], 3 Jul. 1700.
17. *Ib.*, [same] to [same], [Jul. 1700]; *Carstares S.P.*, 561, Queensberry to Carstares, 13 Jul. 1700; *ib.*, 571, same to same, 19 Jul. 1700; SRO, GD248, Box 5/2, Miscellaneous Letters . . . (copies of letters to the king and Carstares, [1700]).
18. *Carstares S.P.*, 514, Melville to Carstares, 4 Jun. 1700; *ib.*, 578, same to same, 26 Jul. 1700.
19. *Ib.*, 535, 571, 574, 665.
20. *Ib.*, 590, Seafield to Carstares, 2 Aug. 1700.
21. *Ib.*, 595, same to same, 6 Aug. 1700; Buccleuch (Drum.), Seafield, Seafield to [Queensberry], 13 Jun. 1700.
22. *Carstares S.P.*, 602, [Queensberry] to [Carstares], 9 Aug. 1700.
23. *Ib.*, 518, 559, 616, 628. Rochester seems to have been deeply involved in consultations with the Scots and agreed that the king should go to Edinburgh: SRO, GD248, Box 5/2, Miscellaneous Letters . . ., copy of letter to [Carstares, 1700].

24. Buccleuch (Drum.), Union, i, [Queensberry] to [the king], copy, [1700].
25. *Carstares S.P.*, 547, Stewart to Carstares, 30 Jun. 1700; *ib.*, 554, same to same, 12 Jul. 1700.
26. *Ib.*, 592, Ormiston to same, 3 Aug. 1700; *ib.*, 608, same to same, 10 Aug. 1700.
27. *Ib.*, 565, Argyll to same, 13 Jul. 1700; *ib.*, 598, same to same, 8 Aug. 1700.
28. *Ib.*, 551, Ormiston to same, 3 Jul. 1700; *ib.*, 553, Stewart to same, 3 Jul. 1700; *ib.*, 574, same to same, 20 Jul. 1700; *ib.*, 607, same to same, 10 Aug. 1700.
29. Buccleuch (Drum.), Seafield, [Seafield] to [Queensberry], 24 Jul. 1700; *Carstares S.P.*, 628, same to Carstares, 30 Aug. 1700.
30. *Ib.*, 571, Queensberry to same, 19 Jul. 1700.
31. Buccleuch (Drum.), Union, i, [same] to [Seafield], copy, [1700].
32. *Ib.*, Carstares, [Carstares] to [Queensberry], 19 Jul. 1700.
33. *Ib.*, Stair, Seafield to [Queensberry], 17 Sep. 1700; *ib.*, same to [same], 30 Sep. 1700; *Carstares S.P.*, 632, 636, 650.
34. *Ib.*, 535, Queensberry to Carstares, 20 Jun. 1700; *ib.*, 556, Philiphaugh to same, 11 Jul. 1700.
35. *Ib.*, 548, W. Stewart to same, 30 Jun. [1700].
36. Fraser, *Melvilles*, ii, 181, Carstares to Melville, 26 Jun. 1700; Buccleuch (Drum.), Stair, [Seafield] to [Queensberry], 26 Jun. 1700; *ib.*, Queensberry Letters, xvi, [Carstares] to [Queensberry], 26 Jun. 1700; *ib.*, Seafield, [Seafield] to [same], 4 Jul. 1700.
37. *Carstares S.P.*, 630, Queensberry to Carstares, 31 Aug. 1700; *ib.*, 637, same to same, 9 Sep. 1700; *ib.*, 657, Ormiston to same, 24 Sep. 1700.
38. *Ib.*, 652, to Carstares, 17 Sep. 1700.
39. *Ib.*, 659, 660.
40. Buccleuch (Drum.), Queensberry Letters, xvi, [Carstares] to [Queensberry], 26 Sep. 1700; *ib.*, [same] to [same], 7 Oct. 1700. Cf. NUL, Portland, PwA 373, Queensberry to Portland, 8 Oct. 1700.
41. Buccleuch (Drum.), Queensberry Letters, xvi, [Carstares] to [Queensberry], 26 Sep. 1700; *Carstares S.P.*, 616, 630.
42. *Ib.*, 665, Argyll to Carstares, 18 Oct. 1700; Buccleuch (Drum.), Queensberry Letters, xvi, [Carstares] to [Queensberry], 1[8?] Dec. 1700.
43. *Carstares S.P.*, 583, Queensberry to Carstares, 31 Jul. 1700.
44. Buccleuch (Drum.), Seafield, 6 Aug. 1700.
45. *Ib.*, Queensberry Letters, xvi, [Carstares] to [Queensberry], 16 Aug. 1700; *ib.*, [same] to [same], 22 Aug. 1700.
46. *Carstares S.P.*, 637, Queensberry to Carstares, 9 Sep. 1700.
47. Buccleuch (Drum.), Queensberry Letters, xvi, [Carstares] to [Queensberry], 25 Jul. 1700; *ib.*, [same] to [same], 29 Jul. 1700; *ib.*, [same] to [same], 3 Dec. 1700.
48. *Ib.*, [same] to [same], 25 Oct. 1700; *ib.*, [same] to [same], 2 Nov. 1700.
49. Japikse, i, 351-2, the king to Portland, 7 Nov. 1700.
50. Buccleuch (Drum.), Union, i, [Queensberry] to [the king], draft, [1700]; *Carstares S.P.*, 556, Philiphaugh to Carstares, 11 Jul. 1700.
51. *Ib.*, 669, Seafield to Carstares, 19 Oct. 1700.
52. See the series of memoranda in Buccluech (Drum.), Col., bundle i, especially 'Some reasons for the passing of the said act', [1700].
53. *Carstares S.P.*, 583, Queensberry to Carstares, 31 Jul. 1700.
54. Buccleuch (Drum.), Col., bundle i, 'Memorial', [1700].
55. *Ib.*, [Queensberry's memorial, 1700]; *Carstares S.P.*, 671, 637, 683; BL, Add. MSS 6420, 32, 4 Oct. 1700.
56. Buccleuch (Drum.), Queensberry Letters, xvi, 16 Nov. 1700; *ib.*, Col., bundle i, additional instructions, [1700].
57. *Ib.*, Union, i, Pringle to [Queensberry], 18 Dec. 1700.
58. *Marchmont Papers*, iii, 215, 216, 217.
59. Buccleuch (Drum.), Union, i, Pringle to [Queensberry], 27 Dec. 1700.
60. *Ib.*, Queensberry Letters, xvi, [Carstares] to [Queensberry], 25 Oct. 1700, *Carstares S.P.*, 667, Queensberry to Carstares, 19 Oct. 1700.
61. Hume, *Diary*, 9; *Marchmont Papers*, iii, 213, Marchmont to Pringle, 19 Nov. 1700.
62. *Carstares S.P.*, 671, Seafield to Carstares, 7 Nov. 1700; Hume, *Diary*, 11-12.
63. *Ib.*
64. *Ib.*, 13; *APS*, x, 208; Buccleuch (Drum.), Col., bundle i, [Philiphaugh's] 'Memorial', [Nov. 1700].
65. *APS*, x, 245-6; Hume, *Diary*, 50-52; *Carstares S.P.*, 684, Philiphaugh to Carstares, 15 Jan. 1701; *ib.*, 690, same to same, 16 Jun. [sic for Jan] 1701.

66. *APS*, x, 248-50.
67. *Ib.*, 272-341.
68. A division took place on each point: 108-94, 107-78, 111-58 (*ib.*, 258, 269, 293-4: Hume, *Diary*, 64, 67-8, 70-71).
69. *Marchmont Papers*, iii, Marchmont to Pringle, 6 Feb. 1701.
70. SRO, GD124, Box 16, MM849/4, 25 Oct. 1701.
71. Buccleuch (Drum.), Pringle, Pringle to [Queensberry], 6 Feb. 1701.
72. *Ib.*, same to [same], 11 and 25 Jan. 1701.
73. *Ib.*, Carstares, [Carstares] to [Queensberry], 20 Feb. 1701.
74. *HMCR Mar and Kellie MSS*, i, 223, Annandale to Mar, 26 Mar. 1701.
75. Buccleuch (Drum.), Carstares, [Carstares] to [Queensberry], 4, 7 and 20 Feb. 1701; *ib.*, Pringle, Pringle to [same], 8 Feb. 1701.
76. *Ib.*, Seven Letters, [Philiphaugh] to [same], 7 Aug. 1701.
77. *Marchmont Papers*, iii, 220, Marchmont to the king, 19 Apr. 1701.
78. Buccleuch (Drum.), Queensberry Letters, xvi, Sir D. Dalrymple to [Queensberry], 1 May 1701.
79. *Carstares S.P.*, 611, J. Stewart to Carstares, [1700].
80. Buccleuch (Drum.), Seven Letters, [Philiphaugh] to [Queensberry], 22 Jul. 1701.
81. *Ib.*, Stair, Rochester to [Queensberry], 28 Feb. [*sic* for Jan.] 1700/01.
82. *Carstares S.P.*, 706, Queensberry to Carstares, 12 Aug. 1701.
83. Buccleuch (Drum.), Queensberry Letters, xvi, [Carstares] to [Queensberry], 26 Aug. 1701.
84. *Ib.*, [same] to [same], 8 and 19 Aug. 1701.
85. *Ib.*, Seven Letters, [Philiphaugh] to [Queensberry], 5 Jul. 1701.
86. *Carstares S.P.*, 704, Ormiston to Carstares, 29 Jul. 1701.
87. SRO, GD124, Box 16, MM849/2, Mar to Queensberry, draft, 31 Jul. 1701; *ib.*, MM849/3, Queensberry to Mar, 12 Aug. 1701.
88. *Carstares S.P.*, 701, to Carstares, 29 Jul. 1701.
89. *Ib.*, 704, Ormiston to same, 29 Jul. 1701.
90. Buccleuch (Drum.), Seven Letters, [Philiphaugh] to [Queensberry], 7 Aug. 1701.
91. SRO, GD205, Letters from Individuals, R. Mackenzie to W. Bennet, 11 Jun. 1701.
92. Buccleuch (Drum.), Seven Letters, [Philiphaugh] to [Queensberry], 21 Jun. 1701.
93. *Carstares S.P.*, 699, Seafield to Carstares, 22 Jul. 1701.
94. Buccleuch (Drum.), Queensberry Letters, xvi, Annandale to [Queensberry], 1 Oct. [1701].
95. *Ib.*, Seven Letters, to [Queensberry], 8 Jul. 1701.
96. *Ib.*, [Philiphaugh] to [same], 7 Aug. 1701.
97. *Ib.*, [same] to [same], 22 Jul. 1701.
98. *Ib.*, Stair, [   ] to [same], 10 Jun. 1701.
99. *Carstares S.P.*, 697, 17 Jul. 1701.
100. Buccleuch (Drum.), Stair, Sir D. Dalrymple to [Queensberry], 8 Sep. 1701.
101. *Carstares S.P.*, 441, Seafield to Carstares, 10 Sep. 1698.
102. *Ib.*, 699, to same, 22 Jul. 1701.
103. Buccleuch (Drum.), Seven Letters, [Philiphaugh] to [Queensberry], 22 Jul. 1701.
104. *Carstares S.P.*, 708, to Carstares, 16 Aug. 1701.
105. *Ib.*, 697, to same, 17 Jul. 1701.
106. Burnet, i, 512, Dartmouth's note (h).
107. Riley, 'The Scottish parliament of 1703', *SHR*, xlvii (1968).
108. Burnet, i, 512, Dartmouth's note (h).
109. *Ib.*

Appendix A:
Members of the Convention Parliament, 1689-1702[1]

Key to lists:
Column

1. The session of 1689:
    O = Club[2]
    C = Court when a positive attitude can be identified.

2. The first session of 1690:
    O = Recruits to the club.
    C = Converts to the court where identified.

3. The second session of 1690:
    p = Present. With few exceptions these were courtiers and supporters of Melville.

4. Group alignments, 1692-6, where known:
    J = Johnston
    D = Dalrymple
    J/D = Change of allegiance over the period.

5. The session of 1698:
    O = Opposition
    C = Court
    O/C = Ambivalent

6. The opposition's petition of 1700 asking that parliament should meet at the time to which it had been adjourned:
    O = Those who subscribed.[3]

7. The session of 29 October 1700–1 February 1701:
    O = Opposition over Darien.[4]
    O* = Opposition extended to standing army.[5]
    C = Court[6]

8. Members of the 'rump' parliament of 1702:
    C = Present – all courtiers unless otherwise indicated.

Note:

Inclusion in the list is for the most part confined to those who took their seats in any of the sessions. Absence due to failure to take the oaths or for any other reason is denoted by 'abs' in the relevant column. Ineligibility, e.g. as in the case of a peer's minority or an elected member having been expelled, is denoted by a dash. Blanks in columns 1, 4, 5 and 7 indicate a lack of information. A blank in column 2 indicates that the member continued to attend parliament with no change of allegiance from the previous session.

PEERS.	1	2	3	4	5	6	7	8	
Aboyne	abs	abs	abs				C	abs	Took the oaths 1698
Annandale	O		abs	J	O/C		C	C	
Arbuthnot, 3rd viscount (d. 1694)	O	abs	abs	–	–		–	–	4th viscount did not attend
Argyll	O		p	D	C		C	C	
Atholl	abs	O	abs		abs		O	abs	
Balcarres	abs	O	abs		abs		abs	abs	
Bargany	O		abs	J	O	O	O*	abs	
Belhaven	C		abs	J/D	O	O	O*	abs	
Bellenden	abs	abs	abs		C		C	C	Took the oaths 1698
Blantyre			abs	J/D		O	O*	abs	
Boyle (as David Boyle of Kelburn)			abs	D	C		C	C	
Breadalbane	abs	O	abs	D	abs		C	abs	
Buchan (Cardross until 1695)	C		abs	J	C		C	C	
Burleigh, Balfour of, 3rd baron (d. 1696-7)			abs	D	–		–	–	
Burleigh, Balfour of, 4th baron	–	C	p		O	O		C	Sat 1690 as Master of Burleigh, lord clerk register
Callendar, 3rd earl (d. 1692)	abs	O	abs	–	–		–	–	Heir a minor
Carmichael (Hyndford from 1701)	C		p	J	C		C	C	
Carnwath	abs		p	D	C		C	abs	
Cassillis (d. 1701)	C		abs	D		O	C	–	Heir a minor
Colvill	abs	abs	abs		–	O	O*	abs	Took the oaths 1700 after being fined and expelled 1693
Crawford, 18th earl (d. 1698)	C		p	J	–		–	–	
Crawford, 19th earl	–	–	–		O/C		C	C	
Dalhousie (suceeded 1696)	–	–	–				C	C	Predecesser in exile
Douglas (d. 1700)	C		p	D	C		–	–	
Duffus	abs	O	abs	D	abs	O	O*	abs	
Dundonald (d. 1690)	abs		–	–	–		–	–	Heir a minor
Dupplin (as Thomas Hay of Balhousie)	–	–	–	J	O		C	abs	Created a peer 1697
Eglinton	C		p	J	C		C	C	

Appendices

PEERS.	1	2	3	4	5	6	7	8	
Elibank (Minor. Took seat in 1698)	—	—	—				O*	abs	
Elphinston	C		abs	D			C	C	
Erroll (d. 1704)	C	abs	abs	D	C		abs	abs	
Findlater	abs	abs	abs	J	C		C	C	Took the oaths 1695
Forbes, 13th baron (succeeded 1697)	—	—	—		C		C	C	
Forfar	C		p	J	C		C	abs	
Forrester	O		abs	D	C		O*	abs	
Frazer	abs	abs	abs			O	C	C	Took the oaths 1695
Galloway, 5th earl (Took seat 1695)	—	—	—		C		C	C	3rd and 4th earls both died 1690
Glencairn	O Commissioner								
Hamilton, 3rd duke (d. 1694)		O	p p	D	—		C	C	
Hamilton, 4th duke						O		abs	
Jedburgh, 4th baron (d.1692)	abs	abs	abs		—		O*	—	
Jedburgh, 5th baron	—	—	—		—		—	C	
Kellie (Minor. Took seat 1700)	—	—	—	D	C		C	C	
Kenmure (d. 1698)	C	—	abs	D	—		—	—	
Kincardine (d. 1705)	abs	—	abs		—		—	—	Withdrew 1690. Fined and expelled 1693
Kinnaird, 2nd baron (d. 1701)	abs	O	abs		abs	O	abs	—	1st baron d. 1689
Kintore	C		abs	D	C		C	C	
Lauderdale (Sir John Lauder of Hatton became 5th earl 1695)	—	—	—		O/C		C	C	
Leven	C		p	D	C		C	C	
Lindores	abs	abs	abs		abs	O	O	abs	
Linlithgow, 3rd earl (d. 1690)	abs	—	—		—		—	—	Took the oaths 1700
Linlithgow, 4th earl (d, 1695)	—	O	abs	D	—		—	—	Heir a minor
Lothian	C		p	D	C		C	C	
Loudoun (Took seat 1696)	—	—	—	D	C		C	C	

PEERS.	1	2	3	4	5	6	7	8	
Lovat, 9th baron (Failed to qualify 1693; d. 1696)	abs	O	abs	J	—		—	—	Succession disputed after his death
Mar, 22nd earl (d. 1689)	—	—	—	—	—		C	C	
Mar, 23rd earl (Took seat 1696)	—	—	—	—	C		C	C	
March (created peer 1697)	—	—	—	—	C		C	C	
Marchmont (as Sir Patrick Hume of Polwarth; then lord Polwarth)	O	C	p	J	Commis-sioner		O*	abs	
Marischal (Took seat 1698)	—	Commis-sioner	—		C	O	C	C	
Melville	abs	abs	Commis-sioner	D	C				
Menteith (d. 1694 and title lapsed)	abs	abs	abs		—		—	—	
Morton	O	—	p	J/D	C		C	C	
Nairne (Failed to qualify 1693)	abs	O	p		—		—	—	
Newark (Failed to qualify 1693; d. 1694)	—	O	p		—		—	—	Peerage extinct on his death
Northesk (Took seat 1698)	—	—	—		C		C	C	
Pitsligo (Forbes of), 3rd baron (d. 1690)	abs	—	—		—		—	—	
Pitsligo (Forbes of), 4th baron (Took seat 1700)	—	—	—		—		O*	abs	
Portmore (Abstentee. Ordered to attend 1700)	abs	abs	abs	D	abs		C	abs	
Queensberry, 1st duke (d. 1695)	abs	O	abs	D	C		—	—	
Queensberry, 2nd duke	—	—	—				Commis-sioner	Commis-sioner	Lord High Treasurer 1693 as Drumlanrig
Reay (Took seat 1700)	—	—	—		—		C	C	
Rollo	O	—	abs	J/D	—		—	abs	
Rosebery (as Archibald Primrose of Dalmeny)	—	—	—		C		C	C	
Ross	O	—	abs	J	O/C	O	O*	abs	
Rothes (Took seat 1700)	—	—	—		—		O*	abs	
Ruglen (created peer 1697)	—	—	—		O	O	O*	abs	

PEERS.	1	2	3	4	5	6	7	8	
Rutherfurd	abs[7]	O	—				abs	abs	
Ruthven	C	C	p	J	O		—	abs	
Saltoun, 11th baron (d. 1693)	abs	abs	abs		—		O*	—	
Saltoun, 12th baron	—	—	—	D	O	O	C	abs	
Seafield (as Sir James Ogilvy)	O		abs	J	C		C	C	
Selkirk (absent in attendance on the king)		abs	abs		abs		abs	abs	
Southesk (Failed to qualify 1693; d. 1699)	abs	O	abs		—		—	—	Heir a minor
Stair, 1st viscount (d. 1695)	—	C	p	D	—		—	—	
Stair, 1st earl (as Sir John Dalrymple)	C		p	D	abs		C	C	
Strathallan (Absentee as lord Maderty. Took seat as Strathallen 1700)	abs	abs	abs		abs	O	O*	abs	
Strathmore	abs	O	abs	D	C		O*	abs	
Sutherland	C[8]		p	J	O	O		abs	
Tarbat	—	O	abs	D	C		C	C[12]	
Tarras (d. 1693 and title extinct)			abs		—		—	—	
Teviot (created peer 1697)	—	—	—	J	C		abs	abs	
Torphichen, 6th baron (d. 1696)	O	—	p	D	—		—	—	
Tullibardine (created peer 1696)	—	—	—		O	O	O*	abs	
Tweeddale, 1st marquess (d. 1697)	abs	abs	abs	J	—		—	—	
Tweeddale, 2nd marquess	—	—	—	J	O	O	O*	abs	lord high treasurer 1695 as Yester
OFFICERS OF STATE (not otherwise listed):	1	2	3	4	5	6	7	8	
Montgomerie, lord high treasurer	—	—	—		—		C	—	
Raith, treasurer-depute	—	C	p	D	—		—	—	
Campbell, Sir George, of Cessnock, lord justice clerk	—	C	p		—		—	—	
Johnston, James, lord secretary	—	—	—	J	—		—	—	
Stewart, Sir James, lord advocate	—	—	—	J/D	C		C	C	

BARONS.	1	2	3	4	5	6	7	8	
Abercrombie, Sir James, of Birkenbog	—	—	—		C	O	C	C	
Agnew, Sir Andrew, of Lochnaw	O	—	abs				abs	abs	
Anstruther, Sir William, ygr., of Anstruther	C		p	D	O	O	O*	abs	
Arbuthnot, Alexander, of Knocks	C	O	abs			O	C	C	Took the oaths 1700
Arnot, Sir David, of Arnot[10]	abs[7]	—	abs		—		O*	abs	
Baillie, George, of Jerviswood	—	—	—	J	abs	O	O*	abs	
Baillie, William, of Lamington	O	—	p	J	—	O	O*	abs	
Bennet, William, of Grubbet	—	—	—	J		O	O*	abs	
Blair, William, of Blair	abs	—	—		—				
Boyle, David, of Kelburn (see peers under Boyle)									
Brodie, George, of Moyness	—	—	—		O	O	O	abs	
Brodie, James, of Brodie	O	—	abs	J	—	O	O	C	
Bruce, David, of Clackmannan[10]	abs	—	abs		—		—	—	
Buntine, Maj. Hugh, of Kilbride	—	—	p	J	C		C	abs	
Burnet, Sir Thomas, of Leys			p	J	O	O	O*	abs	
Caldwell, John, of Caldwell	—	—	p		—		—	—	(d. 1700)
Campbell, Alexander, ygr., of Calder	—	—	—		—		—	C	
Campbell, Sir Colin, of Aberuchill	—	—	p	D	O/C		C	C	
Campbell, Sir Colin, of Ardkinglas	—	—	—		C		C	C	
Campbell, Sir Duncan, of Auchinbreck[13]	abs	—	p		—		—	—	
Campbell, Sir Hugh, of Calder[10]	O	—	abs		C		C	C	
Campbell, Capt. John, of Carrick	O	—	abs		—		C	C	
Campbell, John, of Mamore	—	—	—		—		C	C	
Campbell, John, of Schankistone	—	—	—		—		C	C	
Carmichael, Sir Daniel, of Mauldslie	O	abs	abs		—	O	—	—	(d. 1693)
Carnegie, James, of Finavon	—	—	—		—		O*	abs	
Clerk, Sir John, of Penicuik	—	—	p	D	C		C	C	
Cockburn, Adam, of Ormiston	O	—	p	J	C		C	C	
Cockburn, Archibald, of Langton	O	—	p		—		—	—	

Appendices 171

BARONS.	1	2	3	4	5	6	7	8	
Colquhoun, William, of Craigston[11]	O	–	abs	J	abs	O	O*	abs	
Craig, Robert, of Riccarton	–	–	–	J	abs	O	O*	abs	
Craigie, James, ygr., of Dumbarnie	–	–	–			O	O*	abs	
Craigie, William, of Gairsay	abs	–	abs		abs	O	O*	C	
Craufurd, John, of Kilbirnie	–	–	–				C	–	(d. 1701-2)
Creichton, William, of Crawfordton	–	–	–				–	–	
Cunningham, William, ygr., of Craigends[11]	C	–	p				–	C	
Dalzell, Sir John, of Glenae	abs	–	–				–	C	(d. 1689)
Dempster, John, of Pitliver	O	C	p	J	C		C	C	
Denholm, William, of Westshiels	–	–	p	J	C		C	C	
Douglas, Archibald, of Cavers	–	–	–	D	–		C	–	(d. 1698)
Douglas, Sir William, of Cavers	–	–	p	J	C		–	C	
Drummond, Adam, of Megginch	–	C	p	J	–		C	–	(d. 1699)
Drummond, Thomas, of Riccarton	O	–	p	J	–		–	abs	
Duff, Alexander, of Braco	O	–	abs		C	O	O*	abs	
Dunbar, Alexander, of Westfield	–	–	–		C		C	abs	
Dunbar, Patrick, of Machriemore	–	–	–		C		C	C	
Dunbar, Thomas, of Grange[10]	O	C	abs		–		–	–	
Dundas, Robert, of Arniston	–	–	–		–		O*	abs	
Eliot, Sir Gilbert, of Stobs[10]	abs	abs	abs		C		C	–	
Elphinstone, James, of Logie	–	–	–	D	–		C	C	(d.1689-90)
Erskine, Sir Charles, of Alva	–	–	–		–		–	–	(d. 1695-6)
Erskine, David, of Dun	C	–	p	J	–		–	abs	
Erskine, Sir John, of Alva	–	–	–		–	O	O*	C	
Forbes, Duncan, of Culloden	O	C	p	J	O/C	O	–	abs	
Forbes, Sir John, of Craigievar	–	–	abs		C		C	abs	
Forbes, Samuel, of Foveran	–	–	–		C		O*	abs	
Foulis, Sir James, of Colinton[10]	abs	abs	abs		–		–	–	
Fullerton, John, of Kinnaber	–	–	–	J	–		–	abs	
Gilmour, Sir Alexander, of Craigmillar	–	–	p	J	–	O	O*	abs	
Gordon, Adam, of Dalpholly	O	–	abs		C	O	–	–	(d. 1700)

BARONS.	1	2	3	4	5	6	7	8	
Gordon, Alexander, of Gaithy	—	—	—		—	O	O*	abs	
Gordon, John, ygr., of Carroll	—	—	—		—		O	abs	
Gordon, John, ygr., of Embo[10]	abs[7]	O	abs		—		—	—	(d. before 1693)
Gordon, William, of Craig	—	—	p		—		—	—	
Grant, Ludovic, of Grant	abs[9]	O	abs	J	O	O	O*	abs	
Haldane, John, of Gleneagles[10]	abs	—	abs		—		O*	abs	
Hamilton, Claud, of Barns	O	—	abs		C		O*	C	
Hamilton, James, of Aikenhead	—	—	p		C	O	C	abs	
Hay, John, of Lochloy	—	—	p		—		O*	—	
Hay, Robert, of Strowie	—	—	—	D	O	abs	O*	abs	(d. before 1693)
Hay, Thomas, of Balhousie (see peers under Dupplin)									
Hepburn, William, of Beinston	—	—	—	J	C	O	O*	abs	
Home, Sir John, of Blackadder	—	—	p	J	—	O	O*	abs	
Horseburgh, Alexander, of Horseburgh	—	—	—				C	C	
Houston, John, ygr., of Houston	O	—	p				O*	abs	
Hume, Sir Patrick, of Polwarth (see peers under Marchmont)									
Johnstone, Alexander, of Elschieshields	abs	—	—		—	O	O	abs	
Johnstone, James, of Corhead	O	—	—		abs		—	—	(d. 1690)
Johnstone, Sir James, of Westerhall	—	—	p		—		C	C	(d. 1700)
Johnstone, Sir John, of Westerhall	—	—	—		abs		O*	abs	
Kilpatrick, Sir Thomas, of Closeburn	—	—	—		abs	O	O*	abs	
Lauder, Sir John, of Fountainhall	—	—	p	D	O	O			
Lauder, Sir John, of Hatton (see peers under Lauderdale)									
Livingston, William, of Kilsyth	—	—	—		—		—	abs	
Lockhart, Sir John, of Castlehill	—	—	—		—		—	—	(d. before 1695)
Lockhart, Richard, of Lee	O	—	—		—	O	—	—	(d. 1695-6)
McDowall, William, of Garthland	O	—	abs				—	—	(d. 1700)
MacGuffock, Hugh, of Rusco	C	—	abs				—	abs	

Appendices

BARONS.	1	2	3	4	5	6	7	8	
Mackenzie, Sir Alexander, of Coul	–	–	–		abs		O	abs	
Mackenzie, Sir George, of Newtyle	abs	–	–		–		–	–	(d. 1690)
Mackenzie, Kenneth, of Cromarty	–	–	–		–		C	C	
Mackenzie, Roderick, of Prestonhall	–	–	–	D	–		O	abs	
Maitland, Sir John, of Ravelrig	C	–	p		–		–	–	
Manson, Alexander, of Brigend	–	–	–		–		–	–	(In the parliament of 1693 only)
Maxwell, Sir John, of Pollock	C	–	p	J	C		C	C	
Melville, James, of Halhill	–	–	p	D	O		C	C	
Menzies, Sir Alexander, of Menzies	–	–	–		–		–	–	(d. before 1695)
Milne [Mill?], James, of Balwyllo[11]	–	–	–		–		–	–	
Mitchell, Charles[14]	–	–	–		–		–	–	
Moir, James, of Stoneywood	–	–	abs	D	C	O	O*	abs	
Moncrieff, George, of Reidie	–[9]	C	p	D	O		C	C	
Monro, Alexander, of Bearscrofts	–	–	p	J	O	O	O*	abs	
Monro, Sir George, of Culcairn	–	–	abs		–		–	–	(d. 1693)
Munro, Sir John, of Foulis	O	–	p		–		–	–	(d. 1697)
Munro, Sir Robert, of Foulis	–	–	–		–		abs	abs	
Montgomerie, Francis, of Giffen	–	C	p	J	C		C	C	
Montgomerie, Sir James, of Skelmorlie	O	–	–		–		–	–	
Morison, William, of Prestongrange	–	–	p	D	C	O	C	C	
Mure, William, of Rowallan	–	–	p	J	–		–	–	(d. 1700)
Murray, Sir Alexander, of Blackbarony	–	–	–		–	O	O*	abs	
Murray, Alexander, of Halmyre	–	–	–		–		–	–	(d. 1700)
Murray, Sir Archibald, of Blackbarony	C	–	–	J	C		C	–	(d. 1700)
Murray, David, of Stanhope[10]	abs	abs	abs		–		–	–	
Murray, Patrick, of Livingstone	O	–	p	J	O	O	O*	abs	
Murray, Patrick, of Pennyland	–	–	–		–	O	O*	abs	
Napier, Alexander, of Culcreuch[11]	–	–	p		–		–	–	
Ogilvy, Sir Patrick, of Boyne[10]	abs	–	abs		–	O	–	–	
Pollock, Robert, of Pollock	–	–	–		–		O*	C	
Porterfield, Alexander, of Porterfield	–	–	–		–		C	C	

BARONS.	1	2	3	4	5	6	7	8	
Primrose, Archibald, of Dalmeny (see Rosebery)									
Pringle, George, of Torwoodlee	—	—	—		—		—	—	(d. 1689)
Pringle, James, of Torwoodlee	—	—	abs	J	O	O	O*	abs	
Ramsay, James, ygr., of Banff[10]	—	—	—		—		—	—	
Reid, Robert, of Baldovie	—	—	—		C		C	C	(d. 1700)
Riddell, Sir John, of Riddell	—	—	p		—		—	abs	
Rose, Hugh, of Kilravock	—	—	—	J	O	O	O*	abs	
Scott, Sir Francis, of Thirlestane	—	—	—		—	O	O*	abs	
Scott, James, of Gala	—	—	—		—	O	—	C	
Scott, James, of Logie	—	—	—		C	O	C	C	
Scott, James, ygr., of Logie	—	—	—		—	O	C	C	
Scott, John, of Wooll	—	—	—		—		—	—	
Scott, Sir Patrick, of Ancrum[10]	O	—	abs		—		—	C	
Scott, Sir William, ygr., of Harden[10]	O	—	abs		—		—	abs	
Sharp, John, of Hoddam	—	—	—		—	O	—	abs	(d. 1693)
Sharp, Thomas, of Houston	—	—	—		—		O*	—	
Shaw, Sir John, of Greenock	—	—	—		—		O*	—	
Sinclair, James, of Freswick	abs	abs	abs		—		—	C	
Sinclair, Sir Robert, of Stevenson	C	—	p	D	C		C		
Stewart, Sir Archibald, of Burray	—	—	—		—		—	—	
Stewart, Sir James, of Bute[10]	abs	abs	abs		—		O*	abs	
Stewart, John, ygr., of Blackhall	—	—	—		—		—	C	
Stewart, John, of Sorbie	—	—	—	D	—		C	C	
Stewart, William, of Ambrismore	—	—	—		C		C	C	
Stewart, Sir William, of Castlemilk	—	—	—		C		C	C	
Stewart, William, of Castlestewart	—	—	—		—		C	C	
Swinton, Sir John, of Swinton	—	—	p	J	C	O	C	C	
Urquhart, John, of Craighouse[11]	—	—	—		—		—	—	

Appendices

BURGHS.	1	2	3	4	5	6	7	8	
Aikenhead, Sir Patrick, (Dunfermline)	—	—	—		—		—	—	(d. 1699)
Ainsley, Adam (Jedburgh)	O	—	abs		—	O	—	—	(d. 1700)
Alves, William (Sanquhar)	—	—	—		—		C	C	
Anderson, John (Dornoch)	—	—	—		—		C	C	
Anderson, John (Inverurie)[10]	O	abs	abs		—		C	—	
Anderson, John (Glasgow)	C	—	abs	J	C	O	C	C	
Beattie, William (Inverbervie)	—	—	abs		—		—	abs	
Bethune, George (Kilrenny)[10]	abs	abs	abs		—		—	—	(d. 1698)
Blair, Bryce (Annan)	O	—	abs		—		—	C	
Boswall, John (Kirkcaldy)	O	—	abs	J	C		O*	—	
Boswall, John (Sanquhar)	C	—	abs		—	O	—	C	(d. 1692)
Brodie, William (Forres)	—	—	—		C		C	C	
Brown, Hugh (Inverary)	O	—	abs	D	C		C	C	
Bruce, Sir Alexander (Sanquhar)	—	—	—	D	—		C	C[15]	
Campbell, Charles (Campbeltown)	—	—	—		—		C	C	
Campbell, James (Renfrew)	—	—	—		—		C	C	
Carnegie, John (Forfar)	—	—	abs		—		—	—	(d. 1698)
Chieslie, Sir Robert (Edinburgh)	—	—	—		C	O	—	abs	
Christie, David (Dysart)	—	—	abs		—		—	—	
Cleland, Robert (Anstruther-Wester)	O	—	p	J	—	O	O*	abs	
Cochrane, Walter (Aberdeen)	—	—	—		—		—	—	(d. 1694)
Cochrane, William (Renfrew)	O	—	abs	D	—	O	—	—	
Cruikshank, Robert (Aberdeen)	—	—	—	J	—		—	C	
Cultrane, William (Wigtown)	—	—	abs		—		C	C	
Cunningham, Alexander (Irvine)	O	—	p	J	C	O	C	C	
Cuthbert, John (Inverness)	—	—	abs		—		O*	abs	
Dalrymple, David (Culross)	—	—	—		C		C	C	
Dalrymple, Hugh (New Galloway)	—	—	p	D	C		C	C	
Dalrymple, Sir John (Stranraer. See Stair, 1st earl)									
Dick, John (Stirling)[16]	—	—	—		—		—	—	

176   *King William and the Scottish Politicians*

BURGHS.	1	2	3	4	5	6	7	8	
Edgar, Alexander (Haddington)	—	—	—			O	O*	abs	(d. 1697)
Erskine, William (Culross)	O	—	p	J	abs				(d. 1700 but infirm from 1696)
Ewart, John (Kirkcudbright)	—	—	abs			O	O*	abs	
Fall, Robert (Dunbar)	—	—	—	J	C		C	abs	
Fletcher, James (Dundee)	—	—	abs	J	C		C	C	
Forbes, Robert (Inverurie)	O	—	—			O	O*	abs	
Gedd, Alexander (Burntisland)	C[8]	—	abs	J	—		—	—	(d. 1693)
Gordon, Alexander (Aberdeen)	O	—	abs		—		—	—	(d. 1692)
Gordon, George (Dornoch)	abs	—	abs		—		—	—	(d. 1690)
Gordon, James (New Galloway)[7]		O	—		—		—	—	(d. 1697)
Halkett, Sir Charles (Dunfermline)	O	—	abs	J	—		—	—	(d. 1696)
Hall, Sir John (Edinburgh)	—	—	p	J	—		—	—	
Hamilton, James (Dunfermline)	—	—	—		—	O	O*	abs	
Hamilton, Sir John (Cullen)	O	—	abs		C		C	C	
Hamilton, Thomas (Lanark)	O	—	—	J	C	O	O	C	
Hamilton, Sir William (Queensferry)	O	—	p	J	O			abs	
Heggins, William (Linlithgow)		—	abs		—		—	—	Vacated seat to become presbyterian minister
Houston, Patrick (Renfrew)	—	—	—		—		—	—	(d. 1699)
Hume, Sir Alexander (Kirkwall)	—	—	—		C			C	
Hume, Sir Andrew (Kirkcudbright)	—	—	—		—		C	C	
Innes, Robert (Fortrose)	abs	abs	abs		—		—	—	
Johnston, Robert (Dumfries)	—	—	—	J	C		C	C	
Johnston, William (Annan)	—	—	—		C		C	C	
Kennan, James (Dumfries)	O	—	abs		—		—	—	(d. 1695)
Kennedy, Hugh (Stirling)		—	p		—		—	—	(d. 1693)
Kennedy, Thomas (Lochmaben)	O[9]	—	abs		—		—	—	(d. 1695)
Lauder, James (Haddington)	—	—	abs	D	—		—	—	(d. 1696)
Lyon, John (Forfar)	—	—	—		—	O	O	abs	
Mackenzie, Kenneth (Dingwall)[11]	abs	abs	abs		—		—	—	
Maitland, David (Lauder)	abs	abs	abs		abs		C	C	

Appendices

BURGHS.	1	2	3	4	5	6	7	8	
Maule, Henry (Brechin)[10]	abs	abs	abs						
Melville, Robert (Cupar)	O		abs						(d. 1693)
Menzies, William (Lochmaben)				J	C		C	C	
Molison, Francis (Brechin)				J	C	O	O*	abs	
Moncrieff, George (Crail)			abs	J			O	abs	
Mudie, James (Montrose)	O		abs				C	C	
Muir, Sir Archibald (Cupar)				J	C		C	C	
Muir, John (Ayr)	O		abs	D	C	O	C	C	
Muir, John (Peebles)	O		p	J			C	C	
Murdoch, Patrick (Whithorn)			abs		abs		C	C	
Murray, John (Selkirk)	O		p	D	C		C	abs	
Murray, Patrick (Anstruther-easter)						O	O*	abs	
Murray, Sir Patrick (Stranraer)			p	J/D		O	O	C	
Napier, Francis (Stirling)								C	
Ogilvy, Sir Alexander (Banff)									
Ogilvy, Sir James (Cullen. See Seafield)									
Ross, John (Nairn)									
Ross, William (Tain)			p				C	C	
Scott, John (Rutherglen)			p				C	C	
Scott, Walter (Jedburgh)	O		abs			O	O	abs	
Scougall, James (Kintore)							C	C	
Scrymgeour, John (Dundee)				J	C		C	C	Appointed lord of session 1696
Simpson, Daniel (Fortrose)				D		O	—	C	
Sinclair, Archibald (Wick)			p	J			O*	abs	
Sleigh, John (Haddington)	abs						C	abs	
Smith, George (Pittenweem)	O		abs	J		O	—	—	(d. 1690)
Smith, James (Dunbar)[10]			abs				O*	abs	
Smith, James (St. Andrews)	O		abs	J		O	—	C	
Smith, Robert (Perth)	O		p			O	C	abs	
Smollett, James (Dumbarton)		C	abs	D	C		O*	C	
Spence, David (Anstruther-easter)[10]	O	abs	abs				—	—	

BURGHS.	1	2	3	4	5	6	7	8	
Spittal, Alexander (Inverkeithing)	O	–	p	J	–		–	–	(d. 1696)
Spittal, James (Inverkeithing)	–	–	–				O	abs	
Stevenson, Alexander (Kilrenny)	–	–	abs	J		O	O	abs	
Stevine, Patrick (Arbroath)			abs			O	O	abs	
Stewart, James (Elgin)	O	–	–			O		abs	
Stewart, Robert (Rothesay)	–	–	abs			O	O*	abs	
Stewart, Robert (Rothesay and Dingwall)[10]	abs	abs	abs	D	C	O	C	C	Took oaths 1698 as M.P. for Dingwall
Stewart, Sir Robert (North Berwick)	–	–	–		–		C	C	
Stewart, Thomas (North Berwick)	O	–	abs	J			–	–	(d. 1698)
Stewart, Walter (Banff)	O	–	abs			O	C	abs	
Stewart, Walter (Linlithgow)	–	–			–		–	C	
Stirling, George (Edinburgh)	O	C	p		–		–	–	(d. 1695)
Swinton, Alexander (Dysart)	–	–	–				C	C	
Thomson, Alexander (Edinburgh)	–	–	–					C	
Thomson, Patrick (Stirling)	–	–	–		–		–	–	(d. 1697. Sat in parliament of 1696 only.)
Traill, George (Kirkwall)[10]	abs	abs	abs		–		–	–	
Tulloch, Thomas (Forres)[10]	abs	abs	abs		–		–	–	
Wallace, Hugh (Kintore)[10]	abs		abs		–		–	–	
Wallace, Patrick (Kinghorn)	O	–	p				O	C	

Appendix B: The Opposition of 1700-1702

	PRESENT IN THE SESSION 1700-1701	SIGNING THE ADDRESS	SHOWING OPPOSITION SYMPATHIES 1700-1702	STAYING WITH THE COUNTRY PARTY	REVERTING TO THE COURT	DIED	BEHAVIOUR OPEN TO DOUBT
NOBLES[17]	67	20	24	21(31.3%)	1	1	1
BARONS	85	43	55[18]	42(49.4%)	8	2	—
BURGHS	67	28	32	23(34.3%)	5	1	—
TOTALS	219	91	111[19]	86	14[20]	4[21]	1[22]

Analysis of the Opposition of 1700-1702 according to constituencies. (Peers excluded)

It is impossible to say with certainty how many members had their political allegiance modified by the Darien episode. Opposition in the 1698 parliament had been confined to a committed thirty with some support from a further hesitant twenty. In the following two years there had clearly been a swing to the country party of between sixty and eighty, for whatever reason. Some of the increase and its consolidation had doubtless resulted from Queensberry's attack on the Hamilton family and its connections after the 1698 parliament. The entry of the fourth duke of Hamilton into parliament in 1700 at a time when Darien feeling was high must have provided both a focus and leadership for opposition. But, since members joined the opposition for various reasons, all that can be said with certainty is that at least nineteen identifiable former courtiers were found as opposition sympathisers in 1700. There were undoubtedly more.

A particularly strong country party representation came from some areas. 'Particularly strong' is a vague description, but if one takes an opposition return of 50% or more to be significant — a useful though arbitrary device — then country sympathies were especially strong amongst members from:
1. The south-east border to the Firth of Forth (Berwick, Edinburgh, Haddington, Lanark, Linlithgow, Peebles, Roxburgh, Selkirk);
2. The east coast (Fife, Forfar, Kincardine);
3. The north (Elgin, Inverness, Ross, Sutherland).

The reasons for this must be conjectural. Conceivably support for the Darien project was strong in these areas, though in economic as distinct from political terms this seems unlikely. More obvious is the probable influence exerted by local noble interests. Country nobles were particularly strong in the south-east border shires, the south-east coast and Fife. Forfar and Kincardine were dominated by the jacobite interests of Panmure and

Marischal. In comparison the country vote was low or non-existent from areas controlled by the court nobility: Argyll, Ayr, Dumfries, Dumbarton, Kirkcudbright and Wigtown. This is quite striking if one bears in mind the relative distribution of club membership in 1689-90 when, with Argyll, Annandale and Queensberry with the club, opposition members predominated from territory under their influence.[23]

It is arguable that court members in areas with a strong opposition return found themselves lobbied or otherwise brought under pressure to such an extent that they wavered or departed from their usual allegiance. This could explain why Seafield had more trouble than most in his north-eastern territory. Significantly, too, those members whose opposition was subsequently moderated, or who returned to the court, were frequently men either in close connection with court nobility, as Sir James Abercrombie, Forbes of Culloden, Morison of Prestongrange, Brodie of Brodie and Robert Stewart (Dingwall) — that same Stewart of Tillicoultry whose later promotion to the court of session caused dissension between Argyll and Queensberry — or men of a strongly independent cast of mind which they were quite prepared to assert when they saw fit, **Robert Pollock of Pollock, for example** or, more notably, Walter Stewart of Pardovan (Lithlithgow).

To such motivations could have been added an anti-Queensberry movement, seizing the opportunity to attack the duke with a good excuse. Forbes of Culloden had earlier shown himself unsympathetic to Queensberry and not necessarily tied to Marchmont when the latter chose to remain in alliance with him. Grant of Grant was his associate and he had gone firmly into opposition by 1698. A strong antipathy towards the court appeared amongst the Gordons from Sutherland, though the attitude of the earl of Sutherland himself was more cautious. These, with Brodie of Brodie and others, were the men Stair labelled as 'north country presbyterians' whom he hoped would see the danger of upsetting the existing court interest.[24]

Even so, perhaps the slide from the court was too great to be accounted for in such personal terms, leaving a certain amount still to be explained, though conceivably not much. One thing seems certain: the self-aggrandising policy followed by Queensberry from 1696, and even more from 1698, had created a magazine of irritation ready to explode over Darien or anything else which developed.

Appendices

SHIRE	BURGHS	NUMBER OF MEMBERS PRESENT 1700-1701	OPPOSITION SYMPATHISERS	FULL OPPOSITION IN PARLIAMENT, 1700-1701	REVERSION TO COURT
Aberdeen		4	2	2	
	Aberdeen	1	1		1
	Inverurie	1			
	Kintore	1			
		7	3	2	1
Argyll		3			
	Campbeltown	1			
	Inverary	1			
		5	—	—	—
Ayr		4	1	1[25]	
	Ayr	1			
	Irvine	1			
		6	1	1	—
Banff		2	2	1	1
	Banff	1			
	Cullen	1			
		4	2	1	1
Berwick		4	3	2	1
	Lauder	1			
		5	3	2	1
Bute		1			
	Rothesay	1	1	1	
		2	1	1	—
Caithness		1	1	1	
	Wick	1			
		2	1	1	—
Clackmannan		1	1	1	
		1	1	1	—
Cromarty		2	1	1	
		2	1	1	—
Dumfries		4	2	2	
	Annan	1			
	Dumfries	1			
	Lochmaben	1			
	Sanquhar	1			
		8	2	2	—
Dumbarton		2	1	1	
	Dumbarton	1			
		3	1	1	—
Edinburgh		4	3	3	
	Edinburgh	2	1[31]		
		6	4	3	—

SHIRE	BURGHS	NUMBER OF MEMBERS PRESENT 1700-1701	OPPOSITION SYMPATHISERS	FULL OPPOSITION IN PARLIAMENT, 1700-1701	REVERSION TO COURT
Elgin and Forres		2	1	1[27]	
	Elgin	1	1[31]		
	Forres	1	1		1
		4	3	1	1
Fife		4	1	1	
	Anstruther-Easter	1	1	1	
	Anstruther-Wester	1	1	1	
	Burntisland	1	1	1	
	Crail	1	1	1	
	Cupar	1			
	Dunfermline	1	1	1	
	Dysart	1			
	Inverkeithing	1	1	1	
	Kilrenny	1	1	1	
	Kinghorn	1	1	1[28]	
	Kirkcaldy	1	1	1[28]	
	Pittenweem	1	1	1	
	St. Andrews	1	1		1
		17	12	11	1
Forfar		4	3	1	2
	Arbroath	1	1	1	
	Brechin	1	1	1	
	Dundee	1			
	Forfar	1	1	1	
	Montrose	1			
		9	6	4	2
Haddington		4	3	2	1
	Dunbar	1	1	1	
	Haddington	1	1	1	
	North Berwick	1			
		7	5	4	1
Inverness		2	2	1	1
	Inverness	1	1	1	
		3	3	2	1
Kincardine		2	2	1	1
	Inverbervie	1	1[31]		
		3	3	1	1
Kinross		1	1	1	
		1	1	1	—

Appendices

SHIRE	BURGHS	NUMBER OF MEMBERS PRESENT 1700-1701	OPPOSITION SYMPATHISERS	FULL OPPOSITION IN PARLIAMENT, 1700-1701	REVERSION TO COURT
Kirkcudbright		2			
	Kirkcudbright	1			
	New Galloway	1			
		4	—	—	—
Lanark		4	2	2	
	Glasgow	1			
	Lanark	1			
	Rutherglen	1	1	1	
		7	3	3	—
Linlithgow		2	2	2	
	Linlithgow	1	1[29,31]		
	Queensferry	1	1	1	
		4	4	3	—
Nairn		2	2[31]	1	
	Nairn	1			
		3	2	1	—
Orkney and Zetland		1	1	1	
	Kirkwall	1			
		2	1	1	—
Peebles		2	1	1	
	Peebles	1	1		1
		3	2	1	1
Perth		4	2	2	
	Culross	1			
	Perth	1	1	1	
		6	3	3	—
Renfrew		3	2	2[26]	
	Renfrew	1			
		4	2	2	—
Ross		1	1	1	
	Dingwall	1	1		1
	Fortrose	1	1	1	
	Tain	1			
		4	3	2	1
Roxburgh		4	3	2	1
	Jedburgh	1	1[30]		
		5	4	2	1
Selkirk		2	2	2	
	Selkirk	1			
		3	2	2	—

SHIRE	BURGHS	NUMBER OF MEMBERS PRESENT 1700-1701	OPPOSITION SYMPATHISERS	FULL OPPOSITION IN PARLIAMENT, 1700-1701	REVERSION TO COURT
Stirling		3	3	3	
	Stirling	1			
		4	3	3	—
Sutherland		2	2[30]	2	
	Dornoch	1			
		3	2	2	—
Wigtown		2	1[30]		
	Stranraer	1	1	1	
	Whithorn	1			
	Wigtown	1			
		5	2	1	—

Appendices 185

NOTES TO APPENDICES.

1. Some of the information tabulated here, e.g., columns 1, 2, 4 and 5, is based on documentation too unwieldy to be cited. Where information concerning attitude or allegiance is lacking, a blank has been left in the appropriate space. But even where some evidence exists, absolute precision seems impossible to attain (see above p. 43, n. 8). It is probable that whereas court managers sought, and historians still seek, accurate categorisation, many members of parliament thought their interests best served by remaining elusive and unclassifiable.
2. Those subscribing the club address of 1689 are listed in Fraser, *Melvilles*, iii, 209-12.
3. Those subscribing the country party address of 1700 asking that parliament be summoned are listed at Buccleuch (Drum.), Col., [1700].
4. Lists of members preferring an act of parliament asserting Scotland's right to Darien and of those protesting against the address as drafted can be found in *APS*, x, 246, 251.
5. Those dissenting from votes in favour of the standing forces are listed in *ib.*, 269, 293-4.
6. Members voting for an address over Darien rather than an act: *ib.*, 247.
7. Signed club address though seemingly absent from the 1689 session.
8. Claimed to have signed the club address in error.
9. Club supporter who did not sign the address.
10. Seat declared vacant 1693 on failure to take the oaths.
11. Vacated seat through failure to sign the association.
12. Claimed to have left parliament as an individual protest against an act confirming church government, 1702.
13. Seat declared vacant on petition from freeholders accusing him of being unsound in mind and principles: *APS*, x, 209-10.
14. Elected 1700 but the return was questioned and finally he did not take his seat.
15. Expelled 1702 for saying that presbyterianism was inconsistent with monarchy.
16. Expelled for threatening another member, 1695.
17. Including the commissioner and two officers of state sitting *ex officio*.
18. Includes two members for the same Sutherland seat: Adam Gordon of Dalpholly, deceased, and his successor, John Gordon of Carroll.
19. At least nineteen of these can be identified as former courtiers. There were certainly others who had changed sides; in all forty according to Marchmont (*Marchmont Papers*, iii, 207, to the king, 20 Jun. 1700).
20. Viz., Burleigh, Sir James Abercrombie of Birkenbog, Alexander Arbuthnot of Knocks, Duncan Forbes of Culloden, William Morison of Prestongrange, James Scott of Logie, James Scott, ygr., of Logie, James Scott of Wooll, Sir John Swinton of Swinton, William Brodie (Forres), Robert Cruikshank (Aberdeen), John Muir (Peebles), James Smith (St Andrews), Robert Stewart (Dingwall). In addition to these there were others who had sufficiently recovered to stay behind with the rump of 1702: John Craufurd of Kilbirnie (raised to the peerage in 1703 at Queensberry's

request), James Brodie of Brodie, Robert Pollock of Pollock, John Boswall (Kirkcaldy), Walter Stewart (Linlithgow), Patrick Wallace (Kinghorn).
21. Viz., Kinnaird, Adam Gordon of Dalpholly, William McDowall of Garthland, Adam Ainslie (Jedburgh).
22. Viz., Cassillis.
23. See above, p. 33, n. 68.
24. Buccleuch (Drum.), Stair, Stair to Queensberry, 9 Oct. 1700.
25. Craufurd of Kilbirnie was fully with the opposition, 1700-1701, but was court by 1702 and raised to the peerage as Garnock by 1703.
26. Pollock of Pollock had reverted to the court by 1702.
27. Dunbar of Westfield seems to have avoided commitment to either side, 1700-1701, but was absent in 1702.
28. Opposition 1700-1701 but did not sign the address and had reverted to the court by 1702.
29. Reverted to the court by 1702.
30. Sitting members died 1700:
    McDowall of Garthland (Wigtownshire) was not replaced by Stewart of Sorbie till 1702;
    Gordon of Dalpholly (Sutherland) was replaced by Gordon of Gaithy in 1700.
31. Signed address but not fully associated with the opposition in 1700-1701.

BIBLIOGRAPHICAL NOTE

FROM the wide range of secondary material demanding to be read, comparatively little proved to be of immediate relevance. Such items appear in the list of abbreviations or, if cited less frequently, are referred to in the notes.

For those embarking on a study of the reign of William II and III in Scotland the best starting point is W. Ferguson, *Scotland: 1689 to the Present*. The first chapter deals with William's reign, and an excellent bibliography for the period is provided on pp. 422-5. His more recent survey of the reign in *Scotland's Relations with England: a Survey to 1707* (Edinburgh, 1977), chapter 9, is both terse and trenchant and can be recommended to anyone wishing to savour, in a short space, the sordid character of Anglo-Scottish politics in the late seventeenth century. To supplement Dr Ferguson's contribution it is difficult to recommend anything better than W.L. Mathieson's two books: *Politics and Religion in Scotland, 1550-1695* (Glasgow, 1902) and *Scotland and the Union, 1695-1747* (Glasgow, 1905). Obviously the works have dated but the author's robust cynicism provides compensation. Those who still doubt whether such a bilious view of the seventeenth-century Scottish nobility and gentry is justified should devote time to reading the correspondence in the *Leven and Melville Papers* and the letters printed by Macpherson in his *Original Papers* . . .

A somewhat different outlook appears in James Halliday's important article, 'The Club and the Revolution in Scotland, 1689-90', *SHR*, xlv, which should be read. Mr Halliday has few or no illusions concerning Scottish politicians at that time but his evaluation of the significance of the parliaments of 1689 and 1690 differs somewhat from that to be found in this book. His reconstruction of the club parliaments demands serious consideration as an alternative view of what Scottish politicians achieved, in spite of themselves, when in opposition.

Index

Persons and places appearing in the appendices have not been included in this index.

Aberdeen, 29
abjuration oath, proposed, 1702, 159-60
Achallader, 69
Africa Company, Scottish, *see* Company of Scotland
Albemarle, Arnout Joost van Keppel, first earl of, 130-1, 145, 153
Annandale, William Johnston, fourth earl and first marquess of, 29, 31, 33 n. 68, 48, 89, 108, 111-2, 113, 114, 118, 121, 122, 128-9, 132, 141, 144, 145, 152, 154, 155; and 'Montgomerie's plot', 40-1 and n. 121; ally of Johnston, 83, 90, 91; stayed with the court, 1698, 126
Anne, queen of England and Scotland, 7, 142, 160, 161
Anstruther, William, younger, of Anstruther, 31 n. 57
'Antediluvians', the, 56
Argyll, 33 n. 68
Argyll, Archibald Campbell, tenth earl and first duke of, 3, 9, 14-5, 17, 18, 19, 23, 24, 26-7, 30, 31, 33 n. 68, 100, 107, 108, 110, 117, 141, 142, 154, 157; commissioner of the great seal, 1689, 28; and highland settlement, 66, 67, 69; and the changes of 1695-6, 110-14 *passim*; rivalry with Tullibardine, 1696-8, 119-23, 125; in alliance with Queensberry, 126, 127, 128-30; and court divisions, 1700-02, 144-60 *passim*
Argyll, family interest of, 3, 66
armed forces, Scottish, 33, 58, 67, 69, 71, 118, 125, 127, 150-1
Arran, James Douglas, earl of, *see* Hamilton, fourth duke of
'articles', committee of the, 4, 9, 22, 23-4, 26, 27, 38, 42
association, the, of 1696, 111-2, 118 and n. 9, 141
Atholl, family interest of, 3, 38, 93, 108, 157
Atholl, John Murray, first marquess of, 3, 14, 17, 28, 29, 51, 55, 59, 107, 108, 117, 134; and the revolution, 11-3, 49; joins the 'club', 35 and n. 89; and 'Montgomerie's plot', 40-1; in opposition to Melville, 58, 143; and highland settlement, 67, 69
Ayrshire, 33 n. 68

Baillie, George, of Jerviswood, 7, 90, 142
Baillie, Robert, of Jerviswood, 16 n. 41
Baird, James, 113

Balcarres, Colin Lindsay, third earl of, 22, 31, 40, 41 n. 118, 52, 148; in opposition to Melville, 59
Banffshire, 33 n. 68
Bargany, John Hamilton, second baron, 31 n. 57
baron courts, 32
barons, estate of, 9, 32 and n. 64, 33 n. 68, 52, 118, 127, 137, 150
Bass Rock, 49
Bath, 12, 93
Bennet, William, of Grubbet, 142
Berwickshire, 33 n. 68
bishops, English, 95
bishops, Scottish, and government, 3-4, 42; and the revolution, 4, 8-9
Blantyre, Alexander Stewart, fifth baron, 142
Boyle, David Boyle of Kelburn, first baron, 123, 128, 152
Breadalbane, John Campbell, first earl of, 40, 90, 100, 107, 109; and highland scheme, 67-71, 84; on treasury commission, 1692, 74, 86, 89, 92-3, 94-5, 97
Bruce, Sir Alexander, of Broomhall, 41, 59, 64, 158; as muster-master, 61-2
Buchan, David Erskine, fourth baron Cardross and ninth earl of, 142
burghs, estate of, 9, 23, 32, 33 n. 68, 98, 100 and n. 132, 118, 127, 137, 150
Burnet, Gilbert, bishop of Salisbury, 2, 4, 25, 48, 50, 54, 72, 109
Burnet, Sir Thomas, of Leys, 142

Caithness, 33 n. 68
Cameron, Sir Ewen, of Lochiel, 71
Cameronians, 28
Camerons, 66
Campbell, captain Alexander, of Finnab, 132, 147
Campbell, Sir George, of Cessnock, 83
Campbells of Argyll, 66, 84
Cardross, Henry Erskine, third baron, 57
Carmarthen, Thomas Osborne, first marquess of, *see* Leeds, duke of
Carmichael, John Carmichael, second baron (cr. earl of Hyndford, 1701), 90, 111, 112, 136, 145, 154; commissioner to the general assembly, 1690, 55-6, 62; declined office of secretary, 73-4; appointed secretary, 129
Carmichael, William (joint solicitor-general), 152

Index

Carstares, William, 2, 5, 36 n. 94, 37, 39, 61, 64, 69, 89, 97, 100, 101, 110, 120, 122, 123, 125, 127, 129, 134, 136, 145, 157, 158; his support of Melville, 57-8, 60, 70, 73, 75, 93, 94; and the ministerial changes of 1695-6, 107-9, 114, 117, 126; and Scottish government, 129-31, 151; as Queensberry's agent at court, 144-53 *passim*

Cassillis, John Kennedy, seventh earl of, 13, 69, 92

Charles II, king of England and Scotland, 3, 13

Church of England, 52, 55, 121

Church of Scotland, 25, 59, 121, 143; settlement of, 3-4, 9, 26, 32, 35-9, 42, 51, 54, 55-6, 143; abolition of lay patronages in, 9, 38, 39; ministers of, 25, 37, 87-8, 134; general assembly of, 55-6, 62-3, 73, 74-5, 85-6, 87-8, 95, 135, 137-8, 150, 152; commission of general assembly of, 63-4; policy of, 61, 62-5; commissions of visitation of, 63-4, 74, 93; further settlement of, 82-4, 95-6, 118-9

Clackmannan, 33 n. 68

claim of right, 1689, 9, 24

clergy, 'conforming' Scottish, 9, 25, 36 and n. 94, 47, 54, 55, 62-5, 74-5, 82

'club', the, 9, 54, 56, 112; in 1689, 22-8 and n. 8, 29, 39; composition of, 29-33 and n. 68, 34-5; in 1690, 35, 37-9; and the 'plot', 39-41

Cockburn, Adam, of Ormiston (lord justice clerk and treasurer-depute), 7, 31 n. 57, 83, 90, 108, 111, 114, 118, 122, 129, 141, 143-4, 145, 146, 148, 149, 154, 157, 159-60

Company of Scotland trading to Africa and the Indies, 98, 123, 127-8, 131-8, 149, 151, 155

Convention (1689), *see* parliament of Scotland

convocation of Canterbury, 37, 54

country party, Scottish, its composition and rise, 125-37 *passim*, 142; and the court, 1700-02, 145-59; analysis of, 179-84

court, English, 5, 12, 36, 62, 99, 101, 117, 131, 135, 146

court, Scottish, 9, 30, 32, 42, 57, 90, 100 n. 132, 101, 112, 113, 131, 133, 135; party, 5, 123; its reconstruction, 1689, 15-9, 25, 29, 33; in 1689 parliament, 23, 26, 27, 32; its reconstruction, 1696, 110-14 *passim*, 125; and the parliament of 1698, 126-8; and the Darien crisis, 131-8 *passim*, 144-51 *passim*; divisions in, 1700-02, 141-60

Crawford, William Lindsay, eighteenth earl of, 32, 58 n. 62, 83, 90; president of parliament, 15-6, 17, 19, 23 and n. 8, 30, 31, 41-2; and the Scottish Church, 35-7 and n. 94, 54, 63

Cromarty, 33 n. 68

crown, English, 49, 142

crown, Scottish, 5, 24, 26, 47, 53, 59, 82, 98, 129, 144, 147, 158

customs, Scottish, 135; tack of, 127

Dalkeith, Henrietta, lady (wife of James Scott, styled earl of Dalkeith), 127

Dalrymples, the, 34, 43, 47, 50, 51, 55, 57, 86, 120, 123, 126, 142, 143, 152, 156, 162; their campaign of self-advancement, 16-8; general antipathy towards, 23-4, 29-31; their struggle with Melville, 45-75 *passim*; *see* Dalrymple, Sir David, Sir Hugh; Stair, first viscount and first earl of

Dalrymple, Sir David (joint solicitor-general), 152

Dalrymple, Sir Hugh (president of session), 71, 120, 122-3, 125, 126, 131, 132, 134, 148, 153, 155, 156

Dalrymple, Sir James, of Stair, *see* Stair, first viscount of

Dalrymple, Sir John, master of Stair, *see* Stair, first earl of

Danby, Thomas Osborne, first earl of, *see* Leeds, duke of

Darien project, 1, 32, 97, 128, 131-8, 145, 149, 150

Dempster, John, of Pitliver, 29-30

Devonshire, William Cavendish, fourth earl and first duke of, 50

Douglas, James Douglas, second marquess of, 112

Douglas, lieutenant-general James, 58, 59

Douglas, [   ], of Gogar, 58

Drumlanrig, James Douglas, earl of, *see* Queensberry, second duke of

Drummonds, the, *see* Melfort; Perth, fourth earl of

Dumfriesshire, 33 n. 68, 128-9

Dunbartonshire, 33 n. 68

Dunblane, 33

Dundee, John Graham of Claverhouse, viscount of, 8, 12-3, 53, 65

Dunfermline, 56 and n. 47

Dunlop, William, minister, 93

East India Company, English, 98-9

East Lothian, 8, 49, 51, 52, 56

Edinburgh, 8, 12, 13, 15, 16, 18, 28, 34, 41, 50, 68, 73, 134, 137, 144, 145, 147; castle, 8, 13, 33, 95; tolbooth, 56; lord provost of, 33, 61; and the £3000 bond, 72, 96, 113, 126

Elginshire, 33 n. 68

England, 1, 4, 6, 8, 9, 11, 30, 37, 38, 53, 89, 150; party structure in, 141-2

English, the, 35, 54, 55, 99; opinion of, 22, 42, 107, 118, 125; episcopalian sympathies of, 84 and *see* Leeds, Nottingham; and Darien, 131-7 *passim*

episcopacy, voted a 'grievance', 9, 12, 25, 26, 53

episcopalians (and 'episcopalians'), 3-4, 6-7, 12, 17, 25, 32 n. 62, 35, 36-7 and n. 94, 38, 39, 42, 47 and n. 1, 51 and n. 15, 53, 54, 55-6, 58 and n. 66, 59, 60, 61, 62-5 and n. 112, 68, 70, 74-5, 81, 82-4, 112, 118, 121, 143, 151, 152, 159, 161; political opposition of to Johnston, 1692-5, 85-102, 107; and parliament, 85-8, 95-6 and n. 110; and the changes of 1695-6, 108, 114, 117

Erroll, John Hay, twelfth earl of, 112

estates, Scottish, proposal to hold illegal meeting of, 1700, 135; and *see* parliament of Scotland
exchequer, Scottish, 111, 123
excise, roup of, 72 and n. 156

Fauconberg, Thomas Belasyse, second viscount and first earl of, 50, 52
Ferguson, Robert (the 'Plotter'), 2
Fife, 33 n. 68, 56, 92
'Fifteen rising, 13, 65
Findlater, James Ogilvy, third earl of, 31, 99-100, 113
Fletcher, Andrew, of Saltoun, 81 n. 1
Forbes, Duncan, of Culloden, 29, 57, 118
Forsyth, James, minister, 63
Fort William, 66, 67, 69, 96
Fox, Sir Stephen, 50

Galloway, 150
Galloway, James Stewart, fifth earl of, 96
Glencairn, John Cunningham, eleventh earl of, 31 n. 57
Glencoe, massacre of, 1, 19, 84, 86; enquiry of 1695 into, 94, 96-7, 99
Glenorchy, John Campbell, styled lord, 100
Gordon, Alexander, provost of Aberdeen, 29
Gordon, George Gordon, first duke of, 8, 53
Grant, Ludovic, of Grant, 23, 118
great seal, keeper of (1689), 19; commission for (1689), 28; and *see* lord chancellor
'grievances', the, 9, 22, 23-4, 26

Haddington, Thomas Hamilton, sixth earl of, 92, 96
Halifax, George Savile, first marquess of, 50, 52, 54
Hall, Sir John, lord provost of Edinburgh, 33
Hamilton, Anne, duchess of, 14, 128 n. 30
Hamilton, lord Basil, 134
Hamilton, family interest of, 3, 123, 127, 128, 129, 133
Hamilton, lieutenant-colonel James, deputy governor of Fort William, 96
Hamilton, James Douglas, fourth duke of (formerly earl of Arran), 14, 15, 108, 128 and n. 30, 131, 133, 142, 144, 146-7, 157; and 'Montgomerie's plot', 40-1; and the Darien crisis, 134, 137, 138
Hamilton, William, third duke of, 3, 12, 13, 29, 49, 53, 55, 58 n. 59, 63, 69, 82, 91, 107, 108, 127, 128 n. 30, 143; and Scottish 'council' (1689), 8; as lord high commissioner, 1689, 9, 17-20, 22-8 and n. 8, 33, 34; and the revolution, 14, 15; and the 'club', 1690, 35 and n. 89, 37-8; and changes of 1692, 71, 74, 81; as lord high commissioner, 1693, 83, 85, 88, 89; his further ambitions, 89; his death, 90
Hamilton, Sir William, of Whitelaw, 23, 29, 31 and n. 57, 40, 41, 58, 82, 86, 90, 98, 118, 125, 126, 127, 133, 142, 152, 155; and the post of president of session, 119-22, 159; as candidate for post of lord clerk register, 157-8

Hay, Alexander, of Spott, styled lord, 49
Hay, David, of Belton, styled lord, 49-50, 56
Hay, Sir James, 50, 52
Hay, William, of Drumelzier, 132
hearth tax, 71, 92
highlands, Scottish, settlement of, 61, 67-71, 84; problem of, 65-6
Hill, colonel John, governor of Fort William, 66-7, 69
Holyrood palace, 89, 97
Home, Sir John, of Blackadder, 129, 142
Hume, Sir Patrick, solicitor-general, 152
Hume, Sir Patrick, of Polwarth, *see* Marchmont

Inglis, Alexander, keeper of the great seal, 1689, 19
Inverlochy, 66, 69
Interregnum, 32
Inverness-shire, 33 n. 68

jacobites, 9, 12, 13, 14, 38, 47 and n. 1, 58, 65 n. 112, 74, 93, 133, 134-5, 142, 143, 148, 154
jacobitism, 53, 65, 66, 69, 123
James II and VII, king of England and Scotland, 2, 3, 5, 8-9, 11, 13, 16, 24, 40, 41, 49, 50, 52, 66, 69, 141, 145
Johnston, Alexander, 72, 107
Johnston, Archibald, of Wariston, 2
Johnston, James, 'Secretary' (secretary of state), 2, 25, 50, 57, 60, 72, 107, 108, 109, 110, 111, 112, 117, 118 n. 7, 119, 120, 121, 122, 126, 130, 151, 155; as secretary, 74, 75, 81-102 *passim*, and nn. 33, 132; rivalry with Dalrymple, 81-102 *passim*, 143; and the religious settlement, 82-6, 118, 119; his dismissal, 108; and the country party, 125, 134, 135

Kellie, Alexander Erskine, fourth earl of, 96
Kelso, 57
Kennedy, Hugh, 33
Killiecrankie, battle of, 1, 13, 65
Kincardine, Alexander Bruce, second earl of, 49
Kinross, 33 n. 68
Kintore, John Keith, first earl of, 13, 70, 73
Kirkcudbright, stewartry of, 33 n. 68
Kirkliston, parish of, 63

Lanarkshire, 33 n. 68
Lauderdale, John Lauder, fifth earl of, 118
Lauderdale, John Maitland, first duke of, 48, 49
Leeds, Thomas Osborne, first earl of Danby, first marquess of Carmarthen and first duke of, 54, 59, 60, 62, 63, 64; and the ministerial change of 1692, 68, 70 and n. 147, 71; with opposition to Johnston, 91, 99
Lennox, Charles Lennox, seventh duke of (and sixth duke of Richmond), 136
Leslie, John Leslie, styled lord, *see* Rothes
Leven, David Leslie, fifth earl of, 56, 57, 61, 72, 126, 141

Index

Lindores, John Leslie, fourth baron, 142
Linlithgow, George Livingston, fourth earl of, 40, 41, 90, 94, 107, 108, 109; in opposition to Melville, 59, 70, 73; in treasury commission, 1692, 74, 75, 86, 88, 89, 92-3
Linlithgowshire, 33 n. 68
Livingston, Sir Thomas, C-in-C Scotland, *see* Teviot
Lockhart, Sir George, of Carnwath, president of session, 16, 49
Lockhart, Sir William, solicitor-general, 19, 27, 30, 64, 68, 69, 83
London, 2, 11, 12, 14, 15, 16, 18, 23, 25, 27, 31, 37, 39, 48, 49, 57, 59, 62, 68, 70, 83, 93, 100, 107, 129, 144, 145
Londonderry, 50
lord advocate, *see* Stair; Stewart, Sir James, of Goodtrees
lord chancellor, 12, 13, 14, 19, 27, 33, 90; and *see* great seal; Marchmont; Tweeddale
lord clerk register, 33, 74, 88, 109, 155, 157; and *see* Selkirk; Tarbat
lord high admiral, 136
lord justice clerk, 28 n. 52, 30, 83, 128; and *see* Cockburn; Maxwell
lord privy seal, 33, 73, 113; and *see* Melville; Queensberry
Lothian, Robert Kerr, fourth earl and first marquess of, 73-5, 90, 96, 112, 154

Macdonald, Alasdair, of Glengarry, 69
Macdonald, Alasdair (MacIain), of Glencoe, 84
Macdonalds, of Glencoe, 71, 84
Mackay, major-general Hugh, C-in-C Scotland, 27, 57, 66, 67
Mackenzie, Sir George, of Rosehaugh, 11, 30
Mackenzie, John, minister, 63
Mackenzie, Roderick, Africa Company secretary, 155
Mackenzie, Roderick, of Prestonhall, 67
Macleans, 66
magnates, Scottish, 3, 42, 47, 51, 70; and the revolution, 11-20; and opposition to Johnston, 107; and the changes of 1695-6, 108-14 *passim*; and the court split, 1700-02, 143-60 *passim*; and Scottish politics, 161-2; and *see* nobility; Argyll; Atholl; Hamilton; Queensberry
Mar, John Erskine, twenty-third earl of, 123, 135, 152, 153
March, lord William Douglas, seventh earl of, 123
Marchmont, Sir Patrick Hume, first baron Polwarth, and first earl of, 2, 7, 29, 50, 54, 89, 119, 141; left 'club', 1690, 34, 38; with Melville group, 57; with Johnston, 89; as lord chancellor, 112, 114, 117, 118, 122, 125, 129, 132, 133, 143, 144, 145, 150, 152, 159-60; as commissioner to 1698 parliament, 126, 127, 128
Marischal, George Keith, seventh earl, 13
Marischal, William Keith, eighth earl, 142, 148, 153, 154

Mary, queen of England and Scotland, 7, 9, 15, 18, 24, 30, 36 n. 94, 39, 68
master of works, 33
Maule, Henry, 133
Maxwell, Sir John, of Pollock, lord justice clerk, 29 n. 52, 108-9, 114
Meldrum, Robert, minister, 74
Melfort, John Drummond, first earl of, 11
Melville, family of, 27, 30, 47, 57, 82, 87, 88, 90, 92, 109, 126, 129
Melville, George Melville, fourth baron and first earl of, 2, 18, 19, 23, 25, 43, 49, 54, 55, 56, 64, 65, 81, 83, 96, 100 n. 132, 101, 126, 136-7, 141, 143, 145, 162; as lord high commissioner, 1690, 9, 22, 28-9, 31, 33-42 and n. 94; appointed secretary, 15 and n. 35, 16, 17, 30; in rivalry with Dalrymple as secretary, 47-75 *passim*; and Scottish administration, 58 and n. 63, 72-3; and highlands, 67-9; and ministerial changes, 1692, 70, 73 and n. 168, 101; appointed lord privy seal, 73; with opposition to Johnston, 86, 87, 90, 92-3, 94; and the ministerial changes of 1695-6, 107, 112, 113-4 and n. 44, 117; appointed lord president, 113-4
Melville, James, of Cassingray, collector of the hearth tax, 92
Melville, James, of Halhill, 127 and n. 11
Midlothian, 33 n. 68, 56
mint, Scottish, 49, 114, 128
Moncrieff, George, of Reidie, 31
Montgomerie, Sir James, of Skelmorlie, 9, 18, 19, 23, 26-7, 29; his motives for opposition, 30-1 and n. 57; and 'Montgomerie's plot', 39-41 and n. 118, 56, 68, 83
Montrose, James Graham, fourth marquess of, 92
Morton, James Douglas, eleventh earl of, 112, 129, 152
Munro, Alexander, of Bearscrofts, 30, 118
Murray, Sir Archibald, of Blackbarony, 51, 90, 91
Murray, Sir James, of Philiphaugh, 7, 16 and n. 41, 34, 123, 128, 131, 134, 137, 142, 145, 149, 152, 154, 155-7
Murray, lord John, *see* Tullibardine
Murray, Sir Patrick, 83
Murray, Patrick, of Livingston, 31 n. 57, 90
muster-master, 58, 61-2

Nairne, William Murray, second baron, 134
Namur, capture of, 95 n. 110
New Caledonia, *see* Darien
nobility, Scottish, 32, 52
Nottingham, Daniel Finch, second earl of, 54, 62, 69, 74; and the ministerial change of 1692, 68, 70, 71

Ogilvy, Sir Alexander, of Forglen, 153
Ogilvy, Sir James, *see* Seafield
Orkney, George Hamilton, first earl of, 114

Panmure, James Maule, fourth earl of, 133
parliament of England, 35, 62, 98-9, 118, 160
parliament of Scotland, 162;
  acts of, 9 n. 23:
    incapacitating act (1689), 9, 24, 27
    turning the convention into a parliament (1689), 22
    abolishing the crown's ecclesiastical supremacy (1689 and 1690), 26, 37
    restoration of ministers deprived in 1661 (1690), 37
    abolishing the articles (1690), 38
    abolishing lay patronages (1690), 39
    abolishing the 'yule vacance' (1690), 39
    supply (1690), 39, 42
    rescinding forfeitures (1690), 42
    settling the peace and quiet of the church (1693), 87-8, 95, 100
    trade act (1693), 88, 97, 98
    church act (1695), 95-6, 100
    for a company trading to Africa and the Indies (1695), 97, 98-9, 100
    supply (1698), 127-8
    habeas corpus (1701), 149, 150
    prohibiting imports (1701), 150-1
    prohibiting export of wool (1701), 151
    continuing privileges of the Africa Company (1701), 151
    ratifying Anne's title (1702), 159
    for union negotiations (1702), 159
    supply (1702), 159
  convention, 1689, 4, 8-9, 16, 18, 49, 51, 52-3, 101; analysis of membership, 165-78
  1689 session, 9, 10, 15, 22-8, 29, 33, 38 n. 106, 53, 55, 83; committee of estates of, 18; 'club' opposition in, 29-33, 34-5
  1690, first session, 9, 37-42 and n. 106, 47, 55, 96; court preparations for, 33-4; opposition alliance in, 34-5
  1690, second session, 58 and n. 59
  1693 session, 82, 83, 84-8; parties in, 100 n. 132
  1695 session, 93-8, 99, 100, 110, 111; parties in, 100 n. 132
  1696 session, 117-9, 125
  1698 session, 126-8, 133, 134, 158
  1700 session, 135, 137, 141, 145
  1700-01 session, 135, 137, 145, 148-51, 153, 154
  1702 session, 154, 159-60
  1703 session, 160
Paterson, William, 132, 149
patronages, lay, 9, 25
Peeblesshire, 33 n. 68
peers, estate of, 9, 32, 33 n. 68, 118, 127, 137, 150
Penstoun's tavern, 33
Perth, 135
Perth, James Drummond, fourth earl of, 11, 13
Perthshire, 33 n. 68, 135
Polwarth, Sir Patrick Hume, first baron, *see* Marchmont

Portland, William Bentinck, first earl of, 2, 5, 16, 18, 35, 54, 69, 71, 91, 95, 101, 112, 122, 123; his support of Melville, 57-8, 59, 60, 70, 73, 75, 94; and the ministerial changes of 1695-6, 107-9, 114, 117; and Scottish government, 129-31, 151, 152, 159-62
presbyterianism, 31, 35 n. 89, 38, 51 n. 15, 58, 83
presbyterians (and 'presbyterians'), 3-4, 6-7, 8, 9, 12, 13, 16, 17, 25, 31-2 and n. 62, 34, 35-7 and n. 94, 38-9, 42, 47, 51, 52-3, 54, 55, 58 n. 66, 59, 62-5, 69, 70, 71, 74-5, 82-3, 118, 121, 133, 134, 135-6, 137-8, 142, 143, 151, 152, 156, 159, 161; and church policy, 1692-5, 85-8, 93, 95-6; and the ministerial changes of 1695-6, 108, 112, 114, 117
Preston, Sir Richard Graham, first viscount of, 50
Primrose, Archibald, of Dalmeny, 128
Pringle, Robert, undersecretary, 150
privy council, Scottish, 2, 11, 17, 19, 20, 23, 25, 28, 29, 31, 33, 35, 36, 48, 50, 56, 57, 63-4, 69, 74, 83 and n. 11, 90, 92, 95, 110, 123, 127, 153

Queensberry, family interest of, 38
Queensberry, James Douglas, second duke of, 16, 35, 58 n. 60, 70, 90, 117, 132; and the revolution, 13; in treasury commission, 1692, 74, 93; and the ministerial changes of 1695-6, 108, 109, 110-14 *passim*; appointed lord privy seal, 113; rivalry of with Tullibardine, 1696-8, 119-23, 125; growth of his interest, 123, 128-30; in court alliance with Argyll, 126, 127, 128-30; lord high commissioner, 1700, 137-8; and the court split, 1700-02, 141-60
Queensberry, William Douglas, first duke of, 3, 17, 28, 29, 30, 33 n. 68, 49, 51, 55, 60, 73, 89, 90, 93, 99, 100, 107, 108, 141; and the revolution, 11, 13-4, 53; joins 'club', 1690, 34-5 and n. 89; and 'Montgomerie's plot', 40-1; in opposition to Melville, 58, 59, 68, 70, 143; in opposition to Johnston, 90, 91

Raith, Alexander Melville, styled lord, 126; and the treasury, 61, 71-3, 74, 92, 108-9, 111
Ramsay, general George, C-in-C Scotland, 128, 153
revolution of 1688-90 in Scotland, 1-2, 6, 141; commencement of, 11ff; settlement, 4-5, 8-10; magnates and, 11-20
Ridpath, George, 135
Rochester, Laurence Hyde, first earl of, 146 n. 23
Ross, William Ross, twelfth baron, 29, 31 and n. 57, 90, 133; and 'Montgomerie's plot', 40-1
Rothes, John Leslie, styled lord Leslie and then ninth earl of, 56, 92
Rothes, Margaret, countess of, 92
Roxburghe, John Ker, fifth earl of, 56, 96, 99
Roxburghe, Margaret, dowager countess of, 56, 96
Roxburghshire, 33 n. 68
Ruglen, John Hamilton, first earl of, 122, 128; appointed general of the mint, 114; in opposition, 127

Rutherfurd, Robert Rutherfurd, fourth baron, 38 n. 106
Ruthven, David Ruthven, second baron, 57, 118
Ryswick, treaty of (1697), 125

St Ninians, parish of, 63
Schomberg, Frederick Herman, count and first duke of, 50
Scotland, 23, 25, 32, 37; poor state of in 1698, 125-6; nature of politics in, 3-8, 10; problems of government in, 1-8 *passim*, 10, 47-8; religious divisions in, 3-4, 6-7, 10; consequences of religious settlement of, 47, 62-5; and *see* episcopalians; presbyterians
Scott, Sir Francis, of Thirlestane, 8, 51, 132, 133
Seafield, Sir James Ogilvy, first viscount and first earl of, 7, 24, 29, 31, 40, 41, 58, 82, 90, 96-7, 100, 111, 129, 134, 145, 147, 148, 153; appointed secretary of state, 1695, 108; and the changes of 1695-6, 112-4, 117; and the ministerial rivalry, 1696-8, 121-2; and the 1698 parliament, 126, 128; and Portland's eclipse, 130-1; and the Darien project, 132, 133, 135; detached political stance of, 144, 158-9
'secret service' money, 33
secretary of state, Scottish, 54, 73, 97, 112, 129-30, 131, 134, 151; and *see* Carmichael; Johnston; Melville; Seafield; Stair; Tullibardine
Selkirk, Charles Douglas, second earl of, 53; as lord clerk register, 109, 114, 129, 133, 155, 157, 159
Selkirkshire, 33 n. 68
session, court of, 9, 23, 24, 27, 28 n. 52, 29, 86, 96, 97, 101; lords of, 67, 86; extraordinary lords of, 83, 94, 113; significance of the presidency of, 119-20, 122
Shrewsbury, Charles Talbot, twelfth earl and first duke of, 50, 54, 94, 98, 101, 136
signet office, 29
solicitor-general, *see* Carmichael; Dalrymple; Hume; Lockhart; Seafield
Spittall, Alexander, of Leuchat, 31 n. 57
Stair, Sir James Dalrymple, first viscount of, 2, 23, 24, 29, 30, 35, 49, 50-1 and n. 15, 62, 81, 86, 96, 100, 101, 109, 119, 120; influence of at the revolution, 16-9 and n. 42
Stair, Sir John Dalrymple, master of Stair, second viscount and first earl of, 30, 57, 61, 70, 117, 118, 129, 143, 160; and the revolution, 5, 7, 9, 11, 12; appointed lord advocate, 15, 19; and the new court interest, 16-9, 30-1; and the 1689 parliament, 22-8; and the 1690 parliament, 28, 33, 41; struggle of with Melville, 47-75 *passim*; appointed joint secretary, 59-61, 67; and religious policy, 63-4, 85-9, 93-4, 95-6; and the highland scheme, 66, 67-71, 84; and the treasury, 71-3; rivalry of with Johnston, 81-102 *passim*, 107; dismissal, 108
Steel's tavern, 135
Stewart, Duncan, of Appin, 69

Stewart, Sir James, of Goodtrees, 15, 57, 82, 83, 98-9, 109, 114, 117, 120, 122, 132, 137, 144, 146, 147, 150
Stewart, James, sheriff of Bute, 134, 142
Stewart, Sir Robert, 150
Stewart, Robert, of Tillicoultry, 153, 155
Stirling, George, 11, 31 n. 57
Stirling, presbytery of, 63
Strathmore, Patrick Lyon, first earl of, 73
Stuart, James Edward, prince of Wales, 145
Sutherland, 33 n. 68
Sutherland, George Gordon, fifteenth earl of, 29 and n. 50, 112
Swinton, Alexander, of Mersington, lord of session, 153
Sydney, Henry (later viscount Sydney and first earl of Romney), 50, 81 n. 1

Tarbat, George Mackenzie, first viscount of, 7, 30, 38, 54, 83, 88, 109; and the revolution, 11, 12, 53; his highland scheme, 67-8, 69 and n. 137; appointed lord clerk register, 74, 75
Tarras, Walter Scott, first earl of, 31 n. 57
Tenison, Thomas, archbishop of Canterbury, 81 n. 1, 82, 88
test oath (1681), 2, 16
Teviot, Sir Thomas Livingston, first viscount of, C-in-C Scotland, 84 n. 15, 110, 111-2, 113, 121, 123, 128, 131, 144, 153
Teviotdale, 57
tories, English, 4, 65, 92, 130, 135, 141-2
treasurer-depute, *see* Cockburn; Raith
treasury, Scottish, 48, 50, 55, 57, 58 and nn. 60, 62, 61, 67, 71-3, 74, 92-3, 97, 108, 111
Tullibardine, John Murray, earl of, 12, 13, 93, 108, 109, 134, 141, 142, 143, 146, 155; and 'Montgomerie's plot', 41; appointed secretary, 108; and the changes of 1695-6, 109-14 *passim*, 117; lord high commissioner, 1696, 117-8, 130; his rivalry with Queensberry, 119-23, 125; and the country party, 125, 126, 127, 129, 132, 133, 135, 147
Tweeddale, John Hay, second earl and first marquess of, 8, 14, 57, 64, 68, 70, 107, 108, 109, 110, 118, 119, 125, 126, 130; his character and early career, 48-9; and the revolution, 49-51; and the union project of 1689-90, 51-3; his lobbying in England, 53-5; his rivalry with Melville, 56 and n. 47, 57-61, 63-4; and the ministerial changes of 1692, 72-3, 75; as lord chancellor, 54, 73, 81-102 *passim*, 110, 111, 112
Tweeddale, John Hay, second marquess of (formerly lord Yester), 16, 55, 57, 83 and n. 11, 91, 92, 112, 118, 157; and the revolution, 49-54 and nn. 10, 13, 56 and n. 51; as country party leader, 125, 127, 132, 133, 134, 137, 147

union of England and Scotland, 27, 32, 52; need for perceived, 7-8, 160-2; Cromwellian, 49; scheme of 1689-90, 49-53, 160; proposals for 1700-01, 160-2; negotiations of 1702-3, 160; of 1707, 161

United Kingdom, 32, 161

Vernon, James, 137

whigs, English, 4, 130, 141-2

William III and II, king of England and Scotland, 7, 11, 12, 13, 23, 29, 30, 33, 34, 35, 36 and n. 94, 38, 40, 48, 49, 59, 72, 81, 84 n. 15, 87, 91, 93, 111, 112, 120, 122, 125, 126, 129, 141, 142, 143, 144, 145, 148, 149, 156-7, 158; his attitude to Scotland, 1-2, 5-6, 57-8; plot to assassinate, 1696, 2, 110, 111, 141; ignorance of Scottish affairs, 2-3; advice received by, 2-3, 5; his errors in Scottish policy, 7-8, 10; accepts throne jointly, 9, 15, 30; and the reconstruction of the court interest, 1689, 15-9; and the revolution settlement, 22, 23-4, 38-9, 55; and the union project, 1689-90, 51-2; appointed Dalrymple as secretary, 59-61; and Scottish religious policy, 62-5, 74-5, 82, 95 n. 105; and highland settlement, 66-8, 69; and the ministerial changes of 1692, 73-5; and ministerial rivalries, 1692-6, 88-9, 93-4, 97, 100-2; and the trade act of 1695, 97-8; and the ministerial changes of 1695-6, 107-10, 113-4, 117; relationship with Portland, 129-31; and the Darien crisis, 132-7 *passim*; and the parliament of 1700-01, 146 and n. 23, 149-51; and Scottish government, 151-2, 159-62

Yester, John Hay, styled lord, *see* Tweeddale, second marquess of